PREPARATION FOR THE PRAXIS SERIES™

PRAXIS II EXAM

Joan U. Levy
Norman Levy

15th Edition

THOMSON

ARCO™

Australia • Canada • Mexico • Singapore • Spain • United Kingdom • United States

An ARCO Book

ARCO is a registered trademark of Thomson Learning, Inc., and is used herein under license by Peterson's.

About The Thomson Corporation and Peterson's

With revenues of US$7.2 billion, The Thomson Corporation (www.thomson.com) is a leading global provider of integrated information solutions for business, education, and professional customers. Its Learning businesses and brands (www.thomsonlearning.com) serve the needs of individuals, learning institutions, and corporations with products and services for both traditional and distributed learning.

Peterson's, part of The Thomson Corporation, is one of the nation's most respected providers of lifelong learning online resources, software, reference guides, and books. The Education Supersite[SM] at www.petersons.com—the internet's most heavily traveled education resources—has searchable databases and interactive tools for contacting U.S.-accredited institutions and programs. In addition, Peterson's serves more that 105 million education consumers annually.

For more information, contact Peterson's, 2000 Lenox Drive, Lawrenceville, NJ 08648;
800-338-3282; or find us on the World Wide Web at: www.petersons.com/about

ISBN 0-7689-1100-1 (book only)
      0-7689-0878-7 (with CD)

Printed in the United States of America

10 9 8 7 6 5 4 3 2 1   04 03 02

Contents

About the Authors

Joan U. Levy, Ph.D.

B.A., City College of New York; M.S. in Guidance and Counseling, Fordham University; Ph.D. in Behavioral Science. Director of NJL College Preparation and Learning Center. Guidance Counselor and Educational Evaluator for the New York City Board of Education with over twenty years of teaching and guidance experience.

Norman Levy, Ph.D.

B.E., City College of New York; M.S. in Operations Research, New York University; Ph.D. in Educational Administration. Executive Director of NJL College Preparation and Learning Center, a private tutoring, test preparation, and college guidance service.

Other ARCO Books by Joan U. Levy and Norman Levy

- *Master AP U.S. Government and Politics*
- *Essential Math for College-Bound Students*
- *Mechanical Aptitude and Spatial Relations Tests*

Acknowledgments

A book of this magnitude is not merely the work of the authors. Writers rely heavily on the support and encouragement of colleagues and the input of other professionals and students.

The authors would like to thank the following people: Marshall Reiss for his musical contributions to the manuscript; Arthur Getsel, Alfred Ellis, William Schuck, and the staff of NJL College Preparation for their contributions; and Linda Bernbach and the ARCO editorial staff for their unfailing assistance.

Introduction

The Praxis Series: Professional Assessments For Beginning Teachers

The Praxis Series consists of standardized examinations designed to measure the academic proficiencies of students entering or completing teacher preparation programs and individuals seeking professional certification. Developed and administered by the Educational Testing Service, the Praxis Series assesses knowledge and skills at three levels of proficiency.

- Praxis I: Academic Skills Assessments measures basic proficiency in reading, mathematics, and writing.
- Praxis II: Subject Assessments measures content area knowledge.
- Praxis III: Classroom Performance Assessment provides a training and evaluation framework for classroom performance.

Praxis I: Academic Skills Assessments

Praxis I: Academic Skills Assessments measures basic proficiency in reading, mathematics, and writing by means of the Academic Skills Assessments or the Computer-Based Academic Skills Assessments (CBT). It may be used as an entrance exam for teacher-training programs or as a preliminary licensing exam.

The Academic Skills Assessments

The Academic Skills Assessments is a traditional paper-and-pencil test containing standard multiple-choice questions and an essay question on a designated topic. It consists of three tests, as follows:

Test 1: Reading. A 60-minute test consisting of 40 multiple-choice questions based on 100- to 200-word passages and shorter statements of a sentence or two. Questions fall into the following topic areas:

Literal Comprehension (approximately 55% of test questions)

- main idea questions
- supporting idea questions
- organization questions
- vocabulary questions

Critical and Inferential Comprehension (approximately 45% of test questions)

- argument evaluation questions
- inferential reasoning questions
- generalization questions

Test 2: Mathematics. A 60-minute test consisting of 40 multiple-choice questions divided among the following topic areas:

Conceptual Knowledge (approximately 15% of test questions)

- number sense
- operation sense

Procedural Knowledge (approximately 30% of test questions)

- computation
- estimation
- solving ratio, proportion, and percent problems
- solving equations and inequalities
- probability
- algorithmic thinking

Representations of Quantitative Information (approximately 30% of test questions)

- interpretation of graphs, charts, and tables
- identifying and recognizing patterns in data
- predicting trends and making inferences from data
- understanding relationships between values in a table or graph

Measurement and Informal Geometry (approximately 15% of test questions)

- U.S. and metric systems
- using geometric concepts to solve linear, area, and volume problems
- recognizing and using geometric properties and relationships

Formal Mathematical Reasoning (approximately 10% of test questions)

- interpreting logical connectives and quantifiers
- determining validity of arguments
- identifying generalizations

Test 3: Writing. A 60-minute test divided into two 30-minute sections. One section consists of 45 multiple-choice questions, and the other section consists of a single essay question on an assigned topic. The multiple-choice questions are divided among the following topic areas:

Usage (approximately 55% of multiple-choice questions)

- identifying errors in grammar
- identifying errors in word choice or idiom
- identifying errors in punctuation and capitalization
- identifying sentences that have no errors

Sentence Correction (approximately 45% of multiple-choice questions)

- selecting the correct and most effective rephrasing of a sentence
- correcting errors of grammar, usage, and word choice

The Computer-Based Academic Skills Assessments (CBT)

The CBT is a computer-delivered test. The questions appear on the computer screen, and examinees indicate their answers using the computer keyboard or a mouse. Questions may require examinees to select single or multiple responses, to highlight or reorder information, or to provide their own answers.

The CBT is a computer-adaptive test. This means the test questions are selected by the computer based on an examinee's answers to previous questions. In a computer-adaptive test, the computer calculates a score after each question and uses this score to choose the next question.

Like the Academic Skills Assessments, the CBT consists of three tests. Candidates may take one, two, or all three tests at one time. Following is a brief description of each computer-based test. For the computer-based test, the writing test must be completed on a word processor. Handwritten essays are no longer permitted.

READING	75 minutes
	46 multiple-choice questions
MATHEMATICS	75 minutes
	46 multiple-choice questions
WRITING	45 minutes
	51 multiple-choice questions
	30 minutes – 1 essay question

Test 1: Reading. A 75-minute test consisting of 46 computer-generated test questions based on 200- to 400-word passages—some accompanied by graphs, charts, or diagrams—from the areas of social science, science and nature, humanities, and education. Questions may require test takers to highlight information, move information from one place to another, choose one or more answers, or check boxes in a table. Questions fall into the following topic areas:

Comprehension (approximately 60% of test questions)

- main idea and summary questions
- supporting idea and detail questions
- organization questions

Analysis and Application (approximately 40% of test questions)

- applying ideas presented to other situations
- recognizing arguments and their logic
- determining inferences and assumptions
- defining words in context
- distinguishing facts from opinions

Test 2: Mathematics. A 75-minute test consisting of 46 computer-delivered questions that may require test takers to highlight an answer choice, arrange numbers in order, complete a graph or table, mark a point on a scale, or enter a numerical response. Questions are divided among the following topic areas:

Number Sense and Operation Sense (approximately 25% of test questions)

- understanding the order of numbers
- recognizing equivalent forms of a number
- performing computations in problem solving
- selecting a sequence of operations
- recognizing alternative ways to solve problems

Mathematical Relationships (approximately 20% of test questions)

- interpreting and applying ratios, proportions, and percents
- determining probabilities
- formulating equations
- solving equations and inequalities

Data Interpretation (approximately 25% of test questions)

- reading and understanding data presented in various formats
- recognizing relationships in data
- constructing and completing tables, charts, and graphs
- determining average, range, median, or mode of a set of data

Geometry and Measurement (approximately 20% of test questions)

- determining length, perimeter, area, and volume of two- and three-dimensional figures
- using various systems of measurement and converting from one to another

Reasoning (approximately 10% of test questions)

- interpreting sentences containing logical connectives and quantifiers
- drawing conclusions from given statements
- determining validity of conclusions

Test 3: Writing. A 75-minute test presented in two sections: a 45-minute computer-adaptive section containing 30 multiple-choice questions and a 30-minute essay section consisting of a single essay. The writing test is divided among the following topic areas:

Error Recognition (50% of test score)

- recognizing errors in structure
- recognizing errors in word choice
- recognizing errors in punctuation and capitalization

Essay Writing (50% of test score)

- ability to formulate a thesis or state a position clearly
- ability to organize ideas logically and support ideas with appropriate examples or details
- ability to vary sentence structure and write clearly, correctly, and effectively

Praxis II

Praxis II includes the new Listening Skills Test, the Praxis Specialty Area tests, the Multiple Subjects Assessment for Teachers (MSAT), and the Subject Assessments, including the Content Area Performance Assessment test. The Core Battery, the Social Studies, and the Middle School Mathematics tests: Content Knowledge tests have been discontinued.

Listening Skills Test

As its name implies, the new Listening Skills Test measures proficient listening skills. The questions measure the teacher's ability to recall and understand spoken messages, especially those with educational content. The Listening Skills Test, Code 0740, is a 60-minute test with 60 multiple-choice questions. It is similar to the Core Battery Communication Skills test listening section that was given previously. The Listening Skills Test is divided into three parts:

PART A	25 QUESTIONS	Students listen to short statements or questions and either answer a question or choose a statement that is supported by the statement.
PART B	20 QUESTIONS	Students hear dialogues between two people. They are then asked multiple-choice questions about the dialogue.
PART C	15 QUESTIONS	Students hear short talks by speakers. Each talk is followed by multiple-choice questions.

Multiple Subjects Assessment for Teachers (MSAT)

The Multiple Subjects Assessment for Teachers (MSAT) is used to test the knowledge and critical-thinking skills of prospective elementary school teachers. The MSAT consists of a multiple-choice test called the Content Knowledge Test and a short-answer test called Content Area Exercises. The MSAT is currently offered six times a year: in September, November, January, March, April, and June. The use of calculators without a QWERTY keypad *is* permitted on the MSAT exams.

The Content Knowlege Test is a 2-hour test consisting of 120 multiple-choice questions divided among the following subject areas:

- Literature and Language Studies   24 questions
- Mathematics   24 questions
- Visual and Performing Arts   12 questions
- Physical Education   8 questions
- Human Development   8 questions
- History/Social Sciences   22 questions
- Science   22 questions

· Content Area Exercises is a three-hour test consisting of 18 short essay questions divided among the following subject areas:

• Literature and Language Studies	3 questions
• Mathematics	3 questions
• Visual and Performing Arts	2 questions
• Physical Education	2 questions
• Human Development	2 questions
• History/Social Sciences	3 questions
• Science	3 questions

Note: Nonprogrammable calculators are allowed for the MSAT tests

Specialty Area Tests and New Subject Assessments

The chart on the following pages indicates test times and the number of multiple-choice or essay questions for the other specialty area tests and subject assessments that are part of Praxis II.

Praxis III

Praxis III, Classroom Performance Assessment, is the final level in the Praxis Series. Praxis III involves assessment of individual performance of beginning teachers by trained observers using standardized criteria. Praxis III is beyond the scope of this book.

For Additional Information About the Praxis Series

Additional information about test dates and registration procedures can be found in the *Registration Bulletin* that is available at most college education offices or from Educational Testing Service at the following address:

The Praxis Series
Educational Testing Service
P.O. Box 6051
Princeton, NJ 08541-6052
Phone: 609-771-7395

Specialty Area Tests and New Subject Assessments

TEST CODE	TEST FEE	SUBJECT AREA	TEST TIME	NUMBER OF MULTIPLE-CHOICE QUESTIONS	NUMBER OF ESSAY QUESTIONS
		Arts			
20131	$70	Art Making	1 hr	-	2 + 2 exercises
20132	$70	Art: Content, Traditions, Criticism, and Aesthetics	1 hr	-	3
10133	$70	Art: Content Knowledge	2 hrs	120	-
10110	$70	Music Education	2 hrs	150	-
30111	$70	Music: Concepts and Processes	1 hr	-	2
20112	$70	Music: Analysis	1 hr	-	1 + 2 exercises
10113	$70	Music: Content Knowledge	2 hrs	135	-
10640	$70	Theatre	2 hrs	108	-
		Biology and General Science			
10230	$70	Biology	2 hrs	150	-
20231	$55	Biology: Content Knowledge, Part 1	1 hr	75	-
20232	$55	Biology: Content Knowledge, Part 2	1 hr	75	-
30233	$70	Biology: Content Essays	1 hr	-	3
30234	$70	Life Science: Pedagogy	1 hr	-	1
20030	$70	Biology and General Science	2 hrs	160	-
10430	$70	General Science	2 hrs	120	-
10431	$55	General Science: Content Knowledge, Part 1	1 hr	60	-
10432	$55	General Science: Content Knowledge, Part 2	1 hr	60	-
30433	$70	General Science: Content Essays	1 hr	-	3
		Business and Technology			
10700	$70	Agriculture	2 hrs	140	-
10900	$70	Agriculture CA	2 hrs	148	-
10780	$70	Agriculture PA	2 hrs	140	-
10100	$70	Business Education	2 hrs	160	-
10650	$70	Computer Literacy/Data Processing	2 hrs	120	-
10810	$70	Cooperative Education	2 hrs	157	-
10120	$70	Family and Consumer Sciences	2 hrs	150	-
10560	$70	Marketing Education	2 hrs	120	-
10050	$70	Technology Education	2 hrs	150	-
10890	$70	Vocational General Knowledge	2 hrs	110	-
10791	$55	Business PA: Accounting	1 hr	80	-

TEST CODE	TEST FEE	SUBJECT AREA	TEST TIME	NUMBER OF MULTIPLE-CHOICE QUESTIONS	NUMBER OF ESSAY QUESTIONS
10792	$55	Business PA: Data Processing	1 hr	87	-
20793	$55	Business PA: Marketing	1 hr	80	-
20794	$55	Business PA: Office Technology	1 hr	86	-
30795	$55	Business PA: Secretarial	1 hr	83	-
10050	$70	Technology Education	2 hrs	-	-
		Education			
10020	$70	Early Childhoold Education	2 hrs	150	-
20010	$70	Education in the Elementary School	2 hrs	150	-
10011	$70	Elementary Education: Curriculum, Instruction, and Assessment	2 hrs	110	-
20012	$85	Elementary Education: Content Area Exercises	2 hrs	-	4
20550	$70	Health Education	2 hrs	120	-
10850	$70	Health and Physical Education	2 hrs	145	-
10090	$70	Physical Education	2 hrs	150	-
10091	$70	Physical Education: Content Knowledge	2 hrs	120	-
30092	$70	Physical Education: Movement Forms—Analysis and Design	1 hr	-	2
20093	$70	Physical Education: Movement Forms—Video Evaluation	1 hr	-	2
20530	$70	Pre-Kindergarten Education	2 hrs	103	-
10860	$70	Safety/Driver Education	2 hrs	125	-
		Education of Students with Disabilities			
10320	$70	Education of Students with Mental Retardation	2 hrs	150	-
10350	$70	Special Education	2 hrs	150	-
10352	$55	Special Education: Application of Core Principles Across Categories of Disability	1 hr	50	-
20351	$55	Special Education: Knowledge-Based Core Principles	1 hr	60	-
20371	$55	Special Education: Teaching Students with Behavioral Disorders/Emotional Disturbance	1 hr	50	-
20381	$55	Special Education: Teaching Students with Learning Disabilities	1 hr	50	-
20321	$55	Special Education: Teaching Students with Mental Retardation	1 hr	50	-
10690	$70	Special Education: Preschool/Early Childhood	2 hrs	110	-
10880	$70	Teaching Speech to Students with Language Impairments	2 hrs	120	-
10370	$70	Teaching Students with Emotional Disturbance	2 hrs	120	-
10380	$70	Teaching Students with Learning Disabilities	2 hrs	120	-
10290	$70	Teaching Students with Orthopedic Impairments	2 hrs	130	-
10280	$70	Teaching Students with Visual Impairments	2 hrs	120	-

TEST CODE	TEST FEE	SUBJECT AREA	TEST TIME	NUMBER OF MULTIPLE-CHOICE QUESTIONS	NUMBER OF ESSAY QUESTIONS
		English, Reading, and Communication			
20800	$70	Communication (PA)	2 hrs	150	-
10041	$70	English Language, Literature, and Composition: Content Knowledge	2 hrs	150	2
20042	$85	English Language, Literature, and Composition: Essays	2 hrs	-	2
30043	$70	English Language, Literature, and Composition: Pedagogy	1 hr	-	2
10640	$70	Theater	2 hrs	-	-
10300	$70	Reading Specialist	2 hrs	145	-
10220	$70	Speech Communication	2 hrs	150	-
20360	$70	Teaching English as a Second Language	2 hrs	120	-
		Guidance, Administration, and School Services			
10340	$70	Audiology	2 hrs	150	-
10410	$70	Educational Leadership: Administration and Supervision	2 hrs	145	-
10310	$70	Library Media Specialist	2 hrs	145	-
20420	$70	School Guidance and Counseling	2 hrs	140	-
10400	$70	School Psychologist	2 hrs	135	-
20330	$70	Speech-Language Pathology	2 hrs	150	-
		Languages			
10840	$55	Foreign Language Pedagogy PA	1 hr	55	-
10170	$70	French (contains listening)	2 hrs	155–160	-
10171	$70	French: Productive Language Skills (contains speaking)	1 hr	-	9 exercises
30172	$70	French: Linguistic, Literary, and Cultural Analysis	1 hr	-	3 exercises
20173	$70	French: Content Knowledge (contains listening)	2 hrs	140	-
20180	$70	German (contains listening)	2 hrs	160	-
20181	$70	German: Content Knowledge (contains listening)	2 hrs	140	-
10620	$70	Italian (contains listening)	2 hrs	130	-
10600	$70	Latin	2 hrs	130	-
10190	$70	Spanish (contains listening)	2 hrs	160	-
10191	$70	Spanish: Content Knowledge (contains listening)	2 hrs	140	-
20192	$70	Spanish: Productive Language Skills (contains speaking)	1 hr	-	9 exercises
30193	$70	Spanish: Linguistic, Literary, and Cultural Analysis	1 hr	-	3 exercises
30194	$70	Spanish: Pedagogy	1 hr	-	3 exercises

TEST CODE	TEST FEE	SUBJECT AREA	TEST TIME	NUMBER OF MULTIPLE-CHOICE QUESTIONS	NUMBER OF ESSAY QUESTIONS
		Mathematics			
10060	$70	Mathematics	2 hrs	110	-
10061	$70	Mathematics: Content Knowledge	2 hrs	50	-
20063	$70	Mathematics: Proofs, Models, and Problems, Part 1	1 hr	-	4 exercises
30064	$70	Mathematics: Proofs, Models, and Problems, Part 2	1 hr	-	3 exercises
20065	$70	Mathematics: Pedagogy	1 hr	-	3
		Physical Science			
20240	$70	Chemistry	2 hrs	120	-
20241	$55	Chemistry: Content Knowledge	1 hr	50	-
30242	$70	Chemistry: Content Essays	1 hr	-	3
10070	$70	Chemistry, Physics, and General Science	2 hrs	140	-
20570	$70	Earth/Space Science	2 hrs	120	-
20571	$70	Earth Science: Content Knowledge	(2 hrs)	(100)	-
20481	$55	Physical Science: Content Knowledge	1 hr	60	-
20482	$55	Physical Science: Content Essays	1 hr	-	3
30483	$70	Physical Science: Pedagogy	1 hr	-	1
30260	$70	Physics	2 hrs	100	-
10261	$55	Physics: Content Knowledge	1 hr	50	-
30262	$70	Physics: Content Essays	1 hr	-	3
		Social Sciences			
10910	$70	Economics	2 hrs	105	-
10830	$70	Environmental Education	2 hrs	140	-
30920	$70	Geography	2 hrs	135	-
10930	$70	Government/Political Science	2 hrs	125	-
20390	$70	Psychology	2 hrs	120	-
20950	$70	Sociology	2 hrs	115	-
10940	$70	World and U.S. History	2 hrs	130	-

Taking Praxis II Assessments

Registering for Praxis II

Test dates and registration procedures are listed in the free Registration Bulletin, which is available at most college education offices or from Educational Testing Service at the following address:

The Praxis Series
Educational Testing Service
P.O. Box 6051
Princeton, NJ 08541-6051
Phone: 800-772-9476 (toll-free)

Information is also available at the ETS Web site: www.ets.org. In general, registration materials are due four to six weeks before the test date, and score reports are mailed four to six weeks after the test date.

What to Bring to the Test Center

On the day of the test, each candidate should bring the following items:

- Appropriate photo identification. A driver's license, a student ID card, a passport, or military identification will do.
- Admission ticket or letter of authorization
- Three sharpened No. 2 pencils with erasers
- A blue or black pen for the essay or constructed-response tests
- A watch. The tests are timed and you may not be able to see the clock in the examination room.

Test-Taking Tips

1. Answer every question! Specialty Area test scores are based on the number of questions you answer correctly. You are not penalized for incorrect answers, so it pays to guess! In fact, you should answer every question since a good guess can add to your score and a bad one has no ill effect.

2. Watch your timing! Each Praxis test is timed. Use the tests in this book to practice under timed conditions. Wear a watch or use a stopwatch and become comfortable with the time allowances given to you. Each question is worth the same number of points, so don't waste time on very difficult questions; instead, select your best educated guess for a hard question and continue with the rest of the test. Work as quickly as you can without getting careless. If you have time at the end of a subtest, check your work. You may not go on to the next test or go back to a previous test.

3. Mark your answer sheet carefully! Use only No. 2 pencils. Make sure you mark the answers in the correct row. Fill the answer bubbles completely, and if you change your mind about an answer, be sure to erase your first answer completely before you enter your new choice.

Special Testing Arrangements

Candidates with a physical, emotional, learning, visual, or hearing disability who cannot take a Praxis test under standard conditions may request special test-taking arrangements. Candidates whose religious beliefs do not allow testing on Saturdays or members of the U.S. armed forces whose military duties preclude Saturday testing can request a Monday administration on the Monday immediately following the Saturday test.

Candidates requesting special arrangements can do so by contacting:

The Praxis Series
Test Administration Services
Educational Testing Service
P.O. Box 6054
Princeton, NJ 08541-6054

How Praxis II Is Scored

Specialty Area test scores range from 250 to 990 with intervals of 10 points. Scores are reported with two- or three-letter codes preceding the score to identify the examination. For example, Music Education would be ME and Physical Education would be PE. A candidate may receive scores as follows:

ME 560 (Music Education 560)

PE 780 (Physical Education 780)

The report for each Specialty Area test also gives the number and percent of questions answered correctly in each of the content categories measured by the test.

Each score report also compares the candidate to others who took the same edition of the test. About 25 percent of the candidates are in the low category, 25 percent are in the high category, and 50 percent fall in the average category.

For each test date, candidates receive one copy of their scores, and they can ask for up to three copies of their scores to be sent out. These requests must be made on the answer sheet. Only that particular test date scoring will be sent approximately four to six weeks after the test date. Scores are retained for five years only. After that time, they cannot be reported or sent.

Candidates who want scores reported to places that were not listed on the answer sheet must send a letter to ETS or complete an Additional Score Report request form. The request together with the appropriate fee should be mailed to:

The Praxis Series
Educational Testing Service
P.O. Box 6052
Princeton, NJ 08541-6052

Canceling Your Score

Candidates cannot cancel previous scores from their permanent score record; however, they can cancel scores from a specific test if the request is received by ETS within seven days of that particular administration. Candidates who wish to cancel a score should fill out a Request for Score Cancellation form and send it immediately to ETS. Once scores have been canceled, they will not be reported to the candidate or to anyone else, and they cannot be reinstated on the record. There is no test refund for canceled scores.

Answer Grid

1. Ⓐ Ⓑ Ⓒ Ⓓ   17. Ⓐ Ⓑ Ⓒ Ⓓ   33. Ⓐ Ⓑ Ⓒ Ⓓ   49. Ⓐ Ⓑ Ⓒ Ⓓ   65. Ⓐ Ⓑ Ⓒ Ⓓ

2. Ⓐ Ⓑ Ⓒ Ⓓ   18. Ⓐ Ⓑ Ⓒ Ⓓ   34. Ⓐ Ⓑ Ⓒ Ⓓ   50. Ⓐ Ⓑ Ⓒ Ⓓ   66. Ⓐ Ⓑ Ⓒ Ⓓ

3. Ⓐ Ⓑ Ⓒ Ⓓ   19. Ⓐ Ⓑ Ⓒ Ⓓ   35. Ⓐ Ⓑ Ⓒ Ⓓ   51. Ⓐ Ⓑ Ⓒ Ⓓ   67. Ⓐ Ⓑ Ⓒ Ⓓ

4. Ⓐ Ⓑ Ⓒ Ⓓ   20. Ⓐ Ⓑ Ⓒ Ⓓ   36. Ⓐ Ⓑ Ⓒ Ⓓ   52. Ⓐ Ⓑ Ⓒ Ⓓ   68. Ⓐ Ⓑ Ⓒ Ⓓ

5. Ⓐ Ⓑ Ⓒ Ⓓ   21. Ⓐ Ⓑ Ⓒ Ⓓ   37. Ⓐ Ⓑ Ⓒ Ⓓ   53. Ⓐ Ⓑ Ⓒ Ⓓ   69. Ⓐ Ⓑ Ⓒ Ⓓ

6. Ⓐ Ⓑ Ⓒ Ⓓ   22. Ⓐ Ⓑ Ⓒ Ⓓ   38. Ⓐ Ⓑ Ⓒ Ⓓ   54. Ⓐ Ⓑ Ⓒ Ⓓ   70. Ⓐ Ⓑ Ⓒ Ⓓ

7. Ⓐ Ⓑ Ⓒ Ⓓ   23. Ⓐ Ⓑ Ⓒ Ⓓ   39. Ⓐ Ⓑ Ⓒ Ⓓ   55. Ⓐ Ⓑ Ⓒ Ⓓ   71. Ⓐ Ⓑ Ⓒ Ⓓ

8. Ⓐ Ⓑ Ⓒ Ⓓ   24. Ⓐ Ⓑ Ⓒ Ⓓ   40. Ⓐ Ⓑ Ⓒ Ⓓ   56. Ⓐ Ⓑ Ⓒ Ⓓ   72. Ⓐ Ⓑ Ⓒ Ⓓ

9. Ⓐ Ⓑ Ⓒ Ⓓ   25. Ⓐ Ⓑ Ⓒ Ⓓ   41. Ⓐ Ⓑ Ⓒ Ⓓ   57. Ⓐ Ⓑ Ⓒ Ⓓ   73. Ⓐ Ⓑ Ⓒ Ⓓ

10. Ⓐ Ⓑ Ⓒ Ⓓ   26. Ⓐ Ⓑ Ⓒ Ⓓ   42. Ⓐ Ⓑ Ⓒ Ⓓ   58. Ⓐ Ⓑ Ⓒ Ⓓ   74. Ⓐ Ⓑ Ⓒ Ⓓ

11. Ⓐ Ⓑ Ⓒ Ⓓ   27. Ⓐ Ⓑ Ⓒ Ⓓ   43. Ⓐ Ⓑ Ⓒ Ⓓ   59. Ⓐ Ⓑ Ⓒ Ⓓ   75. Ⓐ Ⓑ Ⓒ Ⓓ

12. Ⓐ Ⓑ Ⓒ Ⓓ   28. Ⓐ Ⓑ Ⓒ Ⓓ   44. Ⓐ Ⓑ Ⓒ Ⓓ   60. Ⓐ Ⓑ Ⓒ Ⓓ   76. Ⓐ Ⓑ Ⓒ Ⓓ

13. Ⓐ Ⓑ Ⓒ Ⓓ   29. Ⓐ Ⓑ Ⓒ Ⓓ   45. Ⓐ Ⓑ Ⓒ Ⓓ   61. Ⓐ Ⓑ Ⓒ Ⓓ   77. Ⓐ Ⓑ Ⓒ Ⓓ

14. Ⓐ Ⓑ Ⓒ Ⓓ   30. Ⓐ Ⓑ Ⓒ Ⓓ   46. Ⓐ Ⓑ Ⓒ Ⓓ   62. Ⓐ Ⓑ Ⓒ Ⓓ   78. Ⓐ Ⓑ Ⓒ Ⓓ

15. Ⓐ Ⓑ Ⓒ Ⓓ   31. Ⓐ Ⓑ Ⓒ Ⓓ   47. Ⓐ Ⓑ Ⓒ Ⓓ   63. Ⓐ Ⓑ Ⓒ Ⓓ   79. Ⓐ Ⓑ Ⓒ Ⓓ

16. Ⓐ Ⓑ Ⓒ Ⓓ   32. Ⓐ Ⓑ Ⓒ Ⓓ   48. Ⓐ Ⓑ Ⓒ Ⓓ   64. Ⓐ Ⓑ Ⓒ Ⓓ   80. Ⓐ Ⓑ Ⓒ Ⓓ

Listening Skills Test 1

60 minutes — 60 questions

The Listening Section is divided into three parts, each with different directions. For each part, the questions and information on which they are based are to be read aloud to you. You will hear each question only once, so listen carefully. (A listening script for this text appears on page 25.)

Part A

Directions: There are two kinds of questions in Part A. In one you will be asked to answer a short question. In the other, you will be asked to demonstrate your understanding of a short statement. When you hear a question, read the four answer choices printed in the book, select the one you believe to be correct, and blacken the letter of your choice on the answer sheet. When you hear a statement, read the four answer choices and select the one that is closest in meaning to or best supported by the statement you heard. Blacken the letter of your answer choice on the answer sheet.

1. (A) I agree that every dictionary should have a pronunciation guide.
   (B) The table of contents and the index are valuable reference guides.
   (C) It is in the introduction to the dictionary and at the bottom of each page.
   (D) Yes, a pronunciation guide is quite helpful.

2. (A) In fact, the report card is issued on a regular basis.
   (B) Correct, all report cards are pretty much the same.
   (C) Yes, it indicates the average achievement level of the two classes.
   (D) It effectively measures the teacher's assessment of each student as an individual.

3. (A) All students have similar levels of ability.
   (B) It is agreed that restriction of the workshop to gifted and talented students can be questioned.
   (C) Workshops of average complexity should be offered to average students.
   (D) Right, it appears that average students should remain in a heterogeneous grouping.

4. (A) Only teachers with provisional certification received an invitation to attend the training session.
   (B) Teachers with permanent certification have no need of further training.
   (C) We had not even considered training teachers with provisional certification until recently.
   (D) Each category of teachers has its own needs and deficiencies.

5. (A) The guidance department admitted it was totally responsible for the unnecessary delay.
   (B) It appears that the guidance department needs a complete reorganization.
   (C) The guidance department's efficient processing of the applications was slowed down by unforeseen circumstances.
   (D) These unavoidable delays would have been completely avoidable if the guidance department had started sooner.

6. (A) I usually find reference books to be very useful.

   (B) The large volume on the extreme left is exactly what I need.

   (C) That librarian is not in charge of reference books.

   (D) In reality, I've had a lot of difficulty learning how to use reference books.

7. (A) Special education has detrimental effects on students' lives.

   (B) Mainstreaming students has never worked well.

   (C) Peers and special education students should be isolated from one another for as long as possible.

   (D) Mainstreaming special education students into regular academic classes is the natural consequence of its originally stated purpose for existence.

8. (A) Homework inhibits a student's learning style.

   (B) Student completion of homework assignments is an actual reinforcement of the teacher's lesson.

   (C) Giving homework proves that the teacher did not do his job properly.

   (D) It's certainly true that students should be allowed to make their own decisions about homework.

9. (A) Skillful use of computers will enhance all students' overall educational progress.

   (B) It's about time that serious education is being stressed over computer video games.

   (C) I certainly agree that reading and writing proficiency takes priority over computer usage.

   (D) Computers have no important place in contemporary education.

10. (A) Supervisors should just let teachers do their jobs in the classroom.

    (B) You're right, supervisors who never teach tend to be more objective when observing teachers.

    (C) Supervisors who also teach would be more well balanced in performing their duties.

    (D) Yes, as a rule, supervisors seem to be out of touch with reality.

11. (A) Multiple-choice tests serve little purpose in today's schools.

    (B) Achievement tests measure and chart a student's past and current mastery of basic skills.

    (C) Essay tests would be a much more creative approach.

    (D) In our multi-diverse culture, tests are quite subjective and ineffective.

12. (A) Every student should have a dictionary in the home for ready reference.

    (B) In truth, textbooks need constant improvement.

    (C) Study aids in a textbook actually accelerate the learning process via helpful explanations.

    (D) If you don't read the textbook, you can't pass the course.

13. (A) It would be a much better idea for parents to hire private tutors for their children.

    (B) On the contrary, students are too busy with other after-school activities.

    (C) Participation by students in extracurricular organizations looks good on college applications.

    (D) A special learning center for students is being provided to enhance their skills and remediate problems.

14. (A) It's a terrific idea to have teachers work as volunteers in the school library.

    (B) Finally, the teachers have given permission to students to go to the school library during the school day.

    (C) The teachers approve of having the school library provide extended hours for the students.

    (D) I'm glad that the teachers and the school administration are actually talking to each other.

15. (A) Generally, school board meetings are not very interesting to students.

    (B) I think that students would find a school board meeting to be a public forum of community interest.

    (C) Civics teachers should really keep their opinions to themselves.

    (D) I agree that school board meetings should be open to the public.

16. (A) Educational instruction time is of greater importance than school announcements.

    (B) This would be the right time to allow students to participate in the decision-making process.

    (C) That's correct; only the school principal can allow an exception to school policy.

    (D) Yes, the number of school announcements should be increased whenever necessary.

17. (A) No, each subject is unique in its own way.

    (B) Since writing skills are essentially thinking skills, every school subject would benefit from reinforcement of them.

    (C) In a visual society addicted to television, writing skills are of little value.

    (D) Short-answer tests are most appropriate in science and mathematics courses.

18. (A) Report cards make parental involvement in the learning process quite unnecessary.

    (B) There are too many working parents to make regular communication time efficient.

    (C) It's very true that teacher-parent contact can damage a student's self-respect.

    (D) Teachers should inform parents of student progress, positive or negative, whenever necessary.

19. (A) Right, the bottom line is that grades are not very important.

    (B) What a student says is not as important as what a student does.

    (C) After-school detention should solve the problem.

    (D) There should be a clear-cut separation between a student's social conduct evaluation and his academic performance.

20. (A) Yes, parents should mind their own business when it comes to evaluating a teacher's instruction techniques.

    (B) It is quite beneficial for teachers to have the opportunity to meet with parents to discuss mutual concerns.

    (C) No, teachers should not let their objectivity be compromised by outside influences.

    (D) Students do have a right to be heard about the necessity to attend summer school.

21. (A) I prefer movies.

    (B) About once a month.

    (C) The theater is too far.

    (D) I go with my sister.

22. (A) I got it a few days ago.

    (B) My daughter did very well this semester.

    (C) Report cards have been sent already.

    (D) I don't know what to do about my son's grades.

23. (A) We're going to Spain for a month.

    (B) We haven't had a vacation in two years.

    (C) Our return is not definite.

    (D) We're planning to go in two weeks.

24. (A) Lasers have been used in surgery for about two years.

    (B) Lasers destroy both healthy and infected tissue.

    (C) Laser surgery usually heals promptly.

    (D) Lasers are the best tools to use in surgery.

25. (A) It is three blocks north of here on the left.

    (B) There are two pharmacies nearby.

    (C) The pharmacy I use is ten blocks away.

    (D) I plan to go the pharmacy after school.

26. (A) The party starts at 8 p.m. tonight.

    (B) I will drive to the party.

    (C) I hope you can get a lift to the party.

    (D) All of our friends will be there.

27. (A) I have three more classes today.

    (B) I don't know when I'll have time to do the work.

    (C) My other class let out late today.

    (D) I hope to be on time from now on.

28. (A) You put them in your desk drawer.

    (B) I didn't know you wore glasses.

    (C) To which pair of glasses are you referring?

    (D) When did you lose them?

Part B

Directions: Part B consists of several short conversations between two speakers. Each conversation is followed by one or more questions about what was said. As you hear each question, read the four answer choices printed in the book and decide which one is best. Blacken the letter of your answer choice on the answer sheet.

29. (A) Eric is not mature enough yet to discuss the problem.

    (B) The guidance counselor does not think it is beneficial to involve a student in such a sensitive issue.

    (C) School policy indicates that the parents should always be contacted first.

    (D) Discussing the problem with Eric's parents first would prepare him for schedule changes suggested by the school authorities.

30. (A) It stalled.

    (B) It had a bad muffler.

    (C) The carburetor needed replacement.

    (D) The mechanic could not tell yet.

31. (A) The price range the man wanted to spend

    (B) The community he wished to live in

    (C) The number of children he has

    (D) The type of house he wanted

32. (A) The PTA has had many complaints from the school board.

    (B) Students don't dress as well today as they did twenty years ago.

    (C) The principal believes that it will promote the general student welfare and improve the learning environment.

    (D) The principal has always made unilateral decisions without consulting any other parties.

33. (A) She had not been able to contact Dawn.

    (B) She resented Dawn's new job.

    (C) She did not know Dawn was working.

    (D) She thought Dawn did not like her.

34. (A) The president outrightly refused to support the proposal.

    (B) The president will support the proposal fully.

    (C) The whole matter should be tabled until the entire PTA board can study it.

    (D) The president complained to the school board about the principal.

35. (A) The teacher won't let the student ask any questions in class.

    (B) The student is being picked on by other students in the class.

    (C) The student is having difficulty with homework assignments.

    (D) The student feels embarrassed by the teacher's comments.

36. (A) The teacher professed to look all of the students in the eye, not just the student who had complained.

    (B) The teacher said that if the student had done the homework, there wouldn't be any problem.

    (C) The teacher gave detention to the unruly students.

    (D) The teacher wrote up the student for insolence and turned the matter over to the dean.

37. (A) School is boring and unchallenging.

    (B) No one understands how the child feels.

    (C) The child's lunch was stolen by an unknown person.

    (D) The child is so much more mature than the other students.

38. (A) The parent helps the child to identify the real problems and suggests solutions.

    (B) The parent expresses dismay at the child's extremist words.

    (C) The parent concludes that the classroom teacher is at fault.

    (D) The parent loses self-control and scolds the child.

39. (A) Detailed and circumstantial

    (B) Exact and specific

    (C) Inflated and unspecific

    (D) General and philosophical

40. (A) By e-mail
    (B) By letter
    (C) By telephone
    (D) In person

41. (A) The following Friday
    (B) The next day
    (C) The following Tuesday
    (D) We cannot tell from the dialogue.

42. (A) In person
    (B) By telephone
    (C) By e-mail
    (D) By fax

43. (A) Agrees with the woman on the problem of new cars
    (B) Belittles the importance of safety in new cars
    (C) Answers the woman's question
    (D) Disagrees on what needs to be changed

44. (A) Teacher
    (B) Doctor
    (C) Car salesman
    (D) Baker

45. (A) The publication of a city directory is a commercial enterprise.
    (B) The size of a city directory limits the space devoted to advertisements.
    (C) Many city directories are published by dictionary and encyclopedia concerns.
    (D) City directories are published by nonprofit organizations.

46. (A) The premise that children who have watched too much television have short attention spans
    (B) That television may have harmful effects
    (C) What constitutes excessive television watching
    (D) Who the young children are

47. (A) Where children should be raised
    (B) How much money is needed to raise a family
    (C) Their religious values
    (D) What constitutes a culturally empty environment

48. (A) Suburban living
    (B) Homogeneous grouping in classrooms
    (C) Socializing only within one's social class
    (D) Multicultural education

Part C

Directions: Part C consists of several short talks. You will hear each talk only once, so be sure to listen carefully in order to remember what the speaker says. Each talk is followed by several questions. When you hear a question, read the four answer choices and decide which one is best. Then blacken the letter of your answer choice on the answer sheet.

49. (A) Addiction to television is the major reason for the breakup of the American family unit.

    (B) Students, on the average, were smarter thirty years ago.

    (C) A proper balance between reading and television viewing will bring families together and prevent divorce.

    (D) Greater involvement in reading by children and parents would probably result in higher scores on college-entrance examinations.

50. (A) Television has virtually displaced reading as a source of information.

    (B) The verbal section of the Scholastic Aptitude Test thirty years ago placed greater emphasis on reading.

    (C) Children do not watch television as much as their parents.

    (D) Gaining information and knowledge from television is much easier and faster than going to school.

51. (A) Parent-child bonding is not important in the age of the nuclear family.

    (B) Competition between parents and children is a healthy experience.

    (C) It's not a good idea to watch television as a family unit.

    (D) Parents who read with and to their children positively stimulate their educational development.

52. (A) Viewing television rather than reading

    (B) Reading rather than watching television

    (C) Competing with adults rather than with their peers

    (D) Worrying about the Scholastic Aptitude Test

53. (A) To show how urgent it is to stop the use of the great books in our modern schools

    (B) To prove that the study of sociology is more important than the study of the liberal arts

    (C) To make a case for keeping the classics as an integral part of our school curricula

    (D) To dramatize the benefits of a multi-diverse culture

54. (A) Eliminate grammar textbooks from English courses

    (B) Put an end to the study of literary masterpieces of the past

    (C) Restrict the study of literature to the classics

    (D) Abolish all areas of study not relevant to the needs of society

55. (A) An anthropology textbook

    (B) A *Babysitter's Club* novel

    (C) A sports almanac

    (D) Shakespeare's *Romeo and Juliet*

56. (A) The sooner the older teachers leave, the better.

    (B) In our democratic society, the students should have a say in running the schools.

    (C) Younger and older teachers should work together as a team.

    (D) Critics and observers of our schools should mind their own business.

57. (A) Their dedication outweighs their desire for a good salary.

    (B) Students are demanding personnel with whom they can identify.

    (C) School boards prefer youth over experience.

    (D) Senior teachers are quickly arriving at retirement age.

58. (A) They can achieve the maximum salary level.

    (B) They can share their subject mastery and teaching experience with the new, younger teachers.

    (C) The school boards and the communities get their money's worth.

    (D) The school districts have a slower rate of employee turnover.

59. (A) Hopes of fame and fortune

    (B) A desire for better living conditions

    (C) A belief that the monarchy was always right

    (D) A search for spices to preserve meats

60. (A) Dutch East India Company trading with the Native Americans for fur

    (B) Sieur de la Salle setting up trading posts

    (C) James Oglethorpe settling in Savannah, Georgia

    (D) Francisco Coronado searching for the Seven Cities of Cibola in Arizona and New Mexico

Listening Script 1

Part A

1. Where in the dictionary would you find the pronunciation guide?

2. Is this report card an accurate measurement of student progress?

3. Even though this is a workshop for gifted and talented students, why aren't students of average ability eligible?

4. Since the training session was specifically provided for teachers with provisional certification, all teachers with permanent certification were not invited.

5. Even though the guidance department was processing the college applications as quickly as possible, there was still an unavoidable delay.

6. Which reference book on the librarian's desk would be most helpful to you?

7. The ultimate goal of special education classes is adequately to prepare the students to be mainstreamed into academic courses with their peers.

8. Why should a homework assignment be an extension of and an appropriate conclusion to the teacher's daily lesson?

9. Computer literacy should be an integral part of any student's general education skills.

10. Why would it be helpful for supervisors of teachers to actually teach a class of their own on a regular basis?

11. How are student achievement tests used as an evaluation of academic progress?

12. A glossary is a specialized dictionary of terms used in a textbook and is needed in most textbooks to facilitate learning.

13. Why is the school constructing and equipping a tutoring laboratory for the students?

14. It is the teachers' unanimous recommendation that the school library be open both before and after school.

15. Why is the civics teacher suggesting that her students attend school board meetings?

16. General school announcements should never be made during regular classroom instruction time.

17. The writing process should be emphasized in every subject.

18. When would be an appropriate time for a teacher to contact parents of students?

19. It is not educationally sound to include a student's behavior in the grading process.

20. Parent-teacher nights are designed to increase communication about a student's overall academic achievement.

21. How frequently do you go to the theater?

22. When did you receive your child's report card?

23. When are you leaving for vacation?

24. Which statement is based on opinion rather than fact?

25. Where is the closest pharmacy to our school?

26. How will you be coming to the party?

27. Why were you late to class today?

28. Have you seen my glasses?

Part B

Question 29 is based on the following conversation:

Guidance Counselor: As Eric's teacher, how do you suggest we handle this problem?

Teacher: Eric is very sensitive. I suggest we talk to his parents first before we meet with him.

Guidance Counselor: Down-tracking a student to a remedial level is not an easy subject to address. Perhaps Eric's parents should discuss the situation with him prior to our participation.

Teacher: That is a good idea. His parents' involvement is likely to place a more positive character on the class change for Eric.

29. Why does Eric's teacher believe that talking to Eric's parents will be helpful?

Question 30 is based on the following conversation:

Mechanic: Your car will be ready in about an hour. The muffler had to be replaced.

Customer: I appreciate your prompt attention to the car. I'll be back to pick it up at 4:30.

30. What was wrong with the car?

Question 31 is based on the following conversation:

Male Customer: Can you help me? I'm interested in buying a house in this town.

Salesperson: There are lots of houses on the market now. What style house are you looking for?

Male Customer: I'm not sure. Tell me what's available.

31. What did the salesperson need to know?

Question 32 is based on the following conversation:

Principal: As principal of this school, I'm convinced that prohibiting students from wearing coats, hats, beepers, and portable radios while in the school building would contribute to the good order of the school.

Parent: But wouldn't you be impeding the students' personal freedoms and sense of self-responsibility?

Principal: I don't think so. Students need adult guidance on these matters so as to promote the overall well-being of every student.

32. Why does the principal want to ban outer clothing, beepers, and radios in school?

Question 33 is based on the following conversation:

Woman: Have you heard from Dawn? I've been trying to reach her for days, but no one answers the telephone.

Man: I saw her last week. She had just gotten a teaching job in a new district, and she seemed very happy.

33. Why was the woman concerned?

Question 34 is based on the following conversation:

Principal: I would like to institute a peer review board to have students help make decisions about other students' unruly behavior. You're the President of the PTA. What do you think?

PTA President: I wholeheartedly agree with your proposal. I think it will give students more say in running the school and more power over their own lives.

34. What does the PTA President feel about the peer review board proposal?

Question 35 is based on the following conversation:

Student: Why are you always picking on me in class? I'm so embarrassed.

Teacher: Actually, I'm not picking on you at all. Perhaps you're taking my comments too personally.

35. Why does the student complain to the teacher?

Question 36 is based on the following conversation:

Student: There you go again. You always seem to be looking at *me* when you ask questions.

Teacher: The truth is, I look at all of my students during class time. I believe that eye contact between students and teacher helps the learning process. I'm sorry that you're so upset.

36. How did the teacher respond to the student's accusation?

Question 37 is based on the following conversation:

Child: I hate school and I'm never going back.

Parent: But you've always liked school before. What happened?

Child: Somebody stole my sandwich from my lunch box, and I don't know who it was.

Parent: Now I understand why you're so angry. I'll help you solve that problem, but maybe you should give school another chance.

37. Why does the child say he hates school and will never go back?

Question 38 is based on the following conversation:

Female Child: Mom, why did we have to move? I don't like my new school. I want to go back to the old school!

Parent: I know it's hard to begin a new school in a new community. Perhaps we should invite some children from your class to come to our house to play.

38. How does the parent respond to the child's statement?

Question 39 is based on the following conversation:

Car Salesman: This little car is the best, the greatest, the most fantastic economy car on the market. Everyone who has bought it loves it.

Woman: Try more information and less pitch next time, fella.

39. How would the woman describe the Salesman's remarks?

Questions 40–42 are based on the following conversation:

Girl: May I please speak to Dawn?

Mom: She's not available. She is visiting her grandparents. Can she call you back?

40. How was the girl trying to reach her best friend, Dawn?

41. When did the conversation take place?

42. How does this conversation take place?

Questions 43–44 are based on the following conversation:

Woman: Do you believe that auto manufacturers should stop making such shoddy products and start showing concern for public safety?

Man: I think auto manufacturers should work on lower car prices.

43. What is true about the man's response?

44. The woman is least likely to be which of the following?

Question 45 is based on the following conversation:

Man: Aren't city directories prepared and published by the cities concerned?

Woman: Not at all. The directory business is as much a private business as is the publishing of dictionaries and encyclopedias. The companies which finance publication make their profits through the sales of the directories and through advertising.

45. What point does the woman make?

Question 46 is based on the following conversation:

Speaker 1: It has been shown that young children who have been exposed to too much television suffer from unusually short attention spans.

Speaker 2: What is defined as "too much"—an hour a day, two hours a day, five hours a day?

46. What do both speakers disagree on?

Questions 47–48 are based on the following conversation:

Speaker 1: City life is dangerous, expensive, and noisy. It is no place to raise a family.

Speaker 2: That may be so, but suburban life is dull, culturally empty, and narrow.

47. What do both speakers disagree on?

48. What would speaker 2 probably favor?

Part C

Questions 49–52 are based on the following passage:

It seems obvious that the major reason that students' scores in the verbal section of the Scholastic Aptitude Test have declined over the past thirty years is that reading has become a "lost art." The average student today spends far more time watching television than reading a book. If an elementary school student were to develop the habit of reading newspapers, magazines, stories, and books for 20 hours per week instead of viewing television programs, that same student would earn an above-average score on his college-bound examinations. If parents were also to withdraw from their television viewing, they would set a stimulating example for their children by reading together as a family. In essence, the family that reads together achieves together.

49. What is the major theme of this talk?

50. Why does the speaker call reading a "lost art"?

51. What does the final sentence mean: "The family that reads together achieves together"?

52. According to the passage, today's students spend far more time doing which of the following?

Questions 53–55 are based on the following passage:

Though some educational reformers claim that classic novels have little relevance in our culturally diverse society, it is obvious that the classics have immense literary value in our schools. Such magnificent masterpieces as *A Tale of Two Cities, Huckleberry Finn,* and *Les Misérables* are the very foundation of our liberal arts culture and provide a civilizing influence upon our society. Integrating these great works into our academic programs in the schools will make students truly literate and worldly wise. On the contrary, abandoning the classics in favor of "more socially relevant" works in our multiethnic social structure would be a distinct disservice to all.

53. What is the purpose of this passage?

54. What do some reformers of our educational systems want to do?

55. Which of the following is an example of a great literary classic?

Questions 56–58 are based on the following passage:

Now is the time when many older "senior" teachers will soon be retiring. A whole generation of well-educated teachers with many years of educational experience will eventually be part of our historical past. Some critics of the schools say that it's about time to let younger teachers with new ideas take the reins of our academic institutions. Other observers claim that the solid, leavening influence of the more experienced teachers is both necessary and helpful for our schools to meet the many needs of our students. Time will soon tell, for it might be the best thing for all concerned to encourage the senior teachers to stay on for a while and share their wealth of experience with the new, eager, but nevertheless inexperienced teachers.

56. What is the theme of this passage?

57. What is the major reason for the current increase in the number of young teachers entering education?

58. Why should incentives be provided for older teachers to remain after retirement age?

Questions 59–60 are based on the following passage:

Nations sent early explorers for three reasons: gold, glory, and God. Later explorers were sent out for new materials, trading posts, and places to colonize.

59. According to this passage, what motivated early explorers?

60. Which of the following could be considered an early explorer?

Answer Key

Listening Skills 1 – Part A

1. C	15. B
2. D	16. A
3. B	17. B
4. A	18. D
5. C	19. D
6. B	20. B
7. D	21. B
8. B	22. A
9. A	23. D
10. C	24. D
11. B	25. A
12. C	26. B
13. D	27. C
14. C	28. A

Listening Skills 1 – Part B

29. D	39. C
30. B	40. C
31. D	41. C
32. C	42. A
33. A	43. D
34. B	44. A
35. D	45. B
36. A	46. C
37. C	47. A
38. A	48. D

Listening Skills 1 – Part C

49. D	55. D
50. A	56. C
51. D	57. D
52. A	58. B
53. C	59. A
54. B	60. A

Answer Grid

1. Ⓐ Ⓑ Ⓒ Ⓓ   17. Ⓐ Ⓑ Ⓒ Ⓓ   33. Ⓐ Ⓑ Ⓒ Ⓓ   49. Ⓐ Ⓑ Ⓒ Ⓓ   65. Ⓐ Ⓑ Ⓒ Ⓓ

2. Ⓐ Ⓑ Ⓒ Ⓓ   18. Ⓐ Ⓑ Ⓒ Ⓓ   34. Ⓐ Ⓑ Ⓒ Ⓓ   50. Ⓐ Ⓑ Ⓒ Ⓓ   66. Ⓐ Ⓑ Ⓒ Ⓓ

3. Ⓐ Ⓑ Ⓒ Ⓓ   19. Ⓐ Ⓑ Ⓒ Ⓓ   35. Ⓐ Ⓑ Ⓒ Ⓓ   51. Ⓐ Ⓑ Ⓒ Ⓓ   67. Ⓐ Ⓑ Ⓒ Ⓓ

4. Ⓐ Ⓑ Ⓒ Ⓓ   20. Ⓐ Ⓑ Ⓒ Ⓓ   36. Ⓐ Ⓑ Ⓒ Ⓓ   52. Ⓐ Ⓑ Ⓒ Ⓓ   68. Ⓐ Ⓑ Ⓒ Ⓓ

5. Ⓐ Ⓑ Ⓒ Ⓓ   21. Ⓐ Ⓑ Ⓒ Ⓓ   37. Ⓐ Ⓑ Ⓒ Ⓓ   53. Ⓐ Ⓑ Ⓒ Ⓓ   69. Ⓐ Ⓑ Ⓒ Ⓓ

6. Ⓐ Ⓑ Ⓒ Ⓓ   22. Ⓐ Ⓑ Ⓒ Ⓓ   38. Ⓐ Ⓑ Ⓒ Ⓓ   54. Ⓐ Ⓑ Ⓒ Ⓓ   70. Ⓐ Ⓑ Ⓒ Ⓓ

7. Ⓐ Ⓑ Ⓒ Ⓓ   23. Ⓐ Ⓑ Ⓒ Ⓓ   39. Ⓐ Ⓑ Ⓒ Ⓓ   55. Ⓐ Ⓑ Ⓒ Ⓓ   71. Ⓐ Ⓑ Ⓒ Ⓓ

8. Ⓐ Ⓑ Ⓒ Ⓓ   24. Ⓐ Ⓑ Ⓒ Ⓓ   40. Ⓐ Ⓑ Ⓒ Ⓓ   56. Ⓐ Ⓑ Ⓒ Ⓓ   72. Ⓐ Ⓑ Ⓒ Ⓓ

9. Ⓐ Ⓑ Ⓒ Ⓓ   25. Ⓐ Ⓑ Ⓒ Ⓓ   41. Ⓐ Ⓑ Ⓒ Ⓓ   57. Ⓐ Ⓑ Ⓒ Ⓓ   73. Ⓐ Ⓑ Ⓒ Ⓓ

10. Ⓐ Ⓑ Ⓒ Ⓓ   26. Ⓐ Ⓑ Ⓒ Ⓓ   42. Ⓐ Ⓑ Ⓒ Ⓓ   58. Ⓐ Ⓑ Ⓒ Ⓓ   74. Ⓐ Ⓑ Ⓒ Ⓓ

11. Ⓐ Ⓑ Ⓒ Ⓓ   27. Ⓐ Ⓑ Ⓒ Ⓓ   43. Ⓐ Ⓑ Ⓒ Ⓓ   59. Ⓐ Ⓑ Ⓒ Ⓓ   75. Ⓐ Ⓑ Ⓒ Ⓓ

12. Ⓐ Ⓑ Ⓒ Ⓓ   28. Ⓐ Ⓑ Ⓒ Ⓓ   44. Ⓐ Ⓑ Ⓒ Ⓓ   60. Ⓐ Ⓑ Ⓒ Ⓓ   76. Ⓐ Ⓑ Ⓒ Ⓓ

13. Ⓐ Ⓑ Ⓒ Ⓓ   29. Ⓐ Ⓑ Ⓒ Ⓓ   45. Ⓐ Ⓑ Ⓒ Ⓓ   61. Ⓐ Ⓑ Ⓒ Ⓓ   77. Ⓐ Ⓑ Ⓒ Ⓓ

14. Ⓐ Ⓑ Ⓒ Ⓓ   30. Ⓐ Ⓑ Ⓒ Ⓓ   46. Ⓐ Ⓑ Ⓒ Ⓓ   62. Ⓐ Ⓑ Ⓒ Ⓓ   78. Ⓐ Ⓑ Ⓒ Ⓓ

15. Ⓐ Ⓑ Ⓒ Ⓓ   31. Ⓐ Ⓑ Ⓒ Ⓓ   47. Ⓐ Ⓑ Ⓒ Ⓓ   63. Ⓐ Ⓑ Ⓒ Ⓓ   79. Ⓐ Ⓑ Ⓒ Ⓓ

16. Ⓐ Ⓑ Ⓒ Ⓓ   32. Ⓐ Ⓑ Ⓒ Ⓓ   48. Ⓐ Ⓑ Ⓒ Ⓓ   64. Ⓐ Ⓑ Ⓒ Ⓓ   80. Ⓐ Ⓑ Ⓒ Ⓓ

Listening Skills Test 2

60 minutes—60 questions

The Listening Section is divided into three parts, each with different directions. For each part, the questions and information on which they are based are to be read aloud to you and do not appear in the test book. Only the directions and answer choices are printed. You will hear each question only once, so listen carefully. (A listening script for this test appears on page 41.)

Part A

Directions: There are two kinds of questions in Part A. In one you will be asked to answer a short question. In the other, you will be asked to demonstrate your understanding of a short statement. When you hear a question, read the four answer choices printed in the book, select the one you believe to be correct, and blacken the letter of your choice on the answer sheet. When you hear a statement, read the four answer choices and select the one that is closest in meaning to or best supported by the statement you heard. Blacken the letter of your answer choice on the answer sheet.

1. (A) The child did not go to school.
   (B) The child was sad.
   (C) The child was consistent.
   (D) The child had a bad cough.

2. (A) I came on the school bus.
   (B) I was absent yesterday.
   (C) I am late because of an accident.
   (D) I am going home on foot.

3. (A) It was not on the shelf.
   (B) It provided me with a lot of information.
   (C) It was in the library stacks.
   (D) It is a biology textbook.

4. (A) The course was required for college graduation.
   (B) The course was not mandatory.
   (C) A course's reputation is unimportant.
   (D) The professor was hard to reach.

5. (A) The Navy continued the search.
   (B) The search was ineffective in finding the item.
   (C) The Navy needed additional help.
   (D) The painstaking search was fruitful.

6. (A) She was working on the problem for a long time.
   (B) She works in a state-of-the-art laboratory.
   (C) She is investigating sleep patterns.
   (D) She used many experiments that all pointed in that direction.

7. (A) The food was elegantly served.
   (B) The prices were too high for her.
   (C) She enjoys French food.
   (D) The restaurant was located on the waterfront.

8. (A) He did not look good.
   (B) Appearances may deceive.
   (C) He appeared humble but was not.
   (D) He was imposing, not humble.

9. (A) I've never been to Long Island.
   (B) I hope to visit you next week.
   (C) I've lived here for five years.
   (D) I moved here from Atlanta.

10. (A) Some people did well on the Spanish test.
    (B) I failed that Spanish exam.
    (C) Spanish is not an easy subject.
    (D) He is in my Spanish class.

11. (A) Soldiers have difficult jobs.

    (B) The soldiers were not members of that division.

    (C) The 82nd Airborne Division was tough.

    (D) The soldiers of the 82nd Airborne Division went to battle.

12. (A) We divided the work for her sake.

    (B) Finishing the work was impossible.

    (C) Dividing the work helped us to complete it.

    (D) Three people worked hard on the assignment.

13. (A) The customer did not buy the suit.

    (B) You helped the customer select a suit.

    (C) There were many customers in the store.

    (D) The customer did not bring cash.

14. (A) I am going to the movies.

    (B) I will be home at 11 p.m.

    (C) I am going out with two friends.

    (D) I will leave at approximately 7 p.m.

15. (A) I am worried about my grades.

    (B) I cannot speak to you now.

    (C) I am not afraid of her.

    (D) I cannot come today.

16. (A) The child should be in special education.

    (B) The child needs to improve her reading.

    (C) The child was in third grade twice.

    (D) The child is retarded.

17. (A) A system of education is apolitical.

    (B) Education should be judged by the caliber of its students.

    (C) A system of education must change to meet the needs of its students.

    (D) Teachers should never be given tenure.

18. (A) The child was upset because he had fallen in the playground.

    (B) The child did not come to school because he was ill.

    (C) The child was absent today.

    (D) The child and his sister are under the age of six.

19. (A) He was optimistic about its success.

    (B) He is very hard working.

    (C) He was the leader of the project.

    (D) He was involved in many things.

20. (A) Dawn had three choices.

    (B) Applying to college is the best choice.

    (C) Dawn was deciding between two options.

    (D) Decision making is a learned skill.

21. (A) She was eating cherries.

    (B) She was saving the Swiss for later.

    (C) She was eating Muenster.

    (D) Cheese is a dairy product.

22. (A) Biofeedback is used mainly in hospitals.

    (B) All people should learn biofeedback techniques.

    (C) Biofeedback allows people to monitor their own responses.

    (D) Improving your health is not possible without biofeedback.

23. (A) A person is born with his habits.

    (B) Habits cannot be changed.

    (C) Habits do not need repetition.

    (D) Habits are learned behaviors.

24. (A) The sun is strongest and most harmful between 10 a.m. and 2 p.m.

    (B) If you sun yourself between 2 a.m. and 2 p.m., you will get heat stroke.

    (C) No one knows the effects of sunbathing between 10 a.m. and 2 p.m.

    (D) The best time to get a tan is before 10 a.m.

25. (A) Dawn was expecting the news.

    (B) The news was very good.

    (C) Dawn was alone when she heard the news.

    (D) The news was disappointing.

Part B

Directions: Part B consists of several short conversations between two speakers. Each conversation is followed by one or more questions about what was said. As you hear each question, read the four answer choices printed in the book and decide which one is best. Blacken the letter of your answer choice on the answer sheet.

26. (A) Displeased
    (B) Dispassionate
    (C) Dissociated
    (D) Disconcerted

27. (A) By telegram
    (B) By telephone
    (C) In person
    (D) By proxy

28. (A) Eager and interested
    (B) Distraught and livid
    (C) Mildly annoyed
    (D) Cheerful and optimistic

29. (A) In the faculty conference room
    (B) In the classroom
    (C) In the principal's office
    (D) Outside the school

30. (A) To appease the principal
    (B) By the teacher's request
    (C) The speaker wished to come
    (D) To discuss a relevant topic with the staff

31. (A) He is genuinely concerned.
    (B) He is apathetic.
    (C) He is sanguine.
    (D) He is callous and unfeeling.

32. (A) She does not want to go out.
    (B) She is bored.
    (C) She is feeling ill.
    (D) She does not have money.

33. (A) young adolescents
    (B) in primary grades
    (C) engaged
    (D) of different religions

34. (A) She is uninterested in the man's dilemma.
    (B) She helps the man clarify his options.
    (C) She is badgering the man with irrelevant questions.
    (D) She is curious about the man's trip.

35. (A) He answered the woman's question.
    (B) He gave information about a different station.
    (C) He was helpful to the woman.
    (D) He gave misinformation.

36. (A) With whom he is planning to see the movie
    (B) If she has seen *Anastasia* previously
    (C) The time she asked the question
    (D) What the price of the movie was

37. (A) 2 p.m.
    (B) 4 p.m.
    (C) 6 p.m.
    (D) 8 p.m.

38. (A) Mr. Levy is unavailable to come to the door.
    (B) Mr. Levy does not want the package.
    (C) the package came to the wrong house.
    (D) the package is very important to Mr. Levy.

39. (A) In person
    (B) By letter
    (C) By fax
    (D) By e-mail

40. (A) A person the child does not want to see
    (B) A place the child does not want to go
    (C) An activity the child does not want to do
    (D) A time that is inconvenient

41. (A) A friend who died
    (B) An acquaintance who hasn't been seen
    (C) Someone who is undergoing hard times
    (D) A rival who won

42. (A) Only the Navajos live on reservations.
    (B) All Native Americans live on reservations.
    (C) The largest reservation is in the southwest.
    (D) The Navajo reservation is in New England.

43. (A) Instinctive
    (B) Comparative
    (C) Ethnocentric
    (D) Unilateral

44. (A) He agrees with the woman.
    (B) He disagrees with the woman.
    (C) He is undecided.
    (D) He has no opinion.

45. (A) The legality of media coverage
    (B) Where crack is available
    (C) How to combat the crack problem
    (D) Whether or not crack poses a significant problem

Part C

Directions: Part C consists of several short talks. You will hear each talk only once, so be sure to listen carefully in order to remember what the speaker says. Each talk is followed by several questions. When you hear a question, read the four answer choices and decide which one is best. Then blacken the letter of your answer choice on the answer sheet.

46. (A) To send some of their children to college
    (B) To increase their land
    (C) To leave their homeland and study in college
    (D) To negotiate a treaty

47. (A) In the twentieth century
    (B) In the nineteenth century
    (C) In the eighteenth century
    (D) In the seventeenth century

48. (A) Commissioners of Maryland and Virginia and Indians of the Six Nations
    (B) Pennsylvanians and Americans
    (C) Southerners and Northerners
    (D) Leaders of William and Mary and Indians of the Six Nations

49. (A) Scientists do not understand the ear.
    (B) The ear is a remarkable mechanism.
    (C) The ear is very sensitive.
    (D) The ear is so complicated that it is not well understood.

50. (A) The power requirement of the ear is tiny.
    (B) The power requirement of the ear is 20 decibels.
    (C) The power requirement of the ear is generated by a single mosquito.
    (D) The power requirement of the ear is extremely sensitive.

51. (A) A simpler and happier time
    (B) An older doll
    (C) A new type of doll
    (D) An adventure doll

52. (A) Adventure hero
    (B) Lasting figure
    (C) Venerable standby
    (D) Teddy bear

53. (A) Early childhood education
    (B) A simpler and happier time
    (C) Types of dolls that smile
    (D) Dolls that break easily

54. (A) Athens and the United States
    (B) Justice in Ancient Athens
    (C) Testifying Under Oath
    (D) The Duties of Juries

55. (A) They liked to serve on juries.
    (B) A juryman agreed to listen to both sides.
    (C) Any person might accuse another of a crime.
    (D) The slaves were troublesome.

56. (A) The jury might condemn the accuser instead of the accused.
    (B) The jury might be very large.
    (C) Cases were judged by men over 30 years old.
    (D) There was a limit on the time a trial could take.

57. (A) Create more rehabilitation centers
    (B) Do away with rehabilitation centers
    (C) Put drug addicts in jail
    (D) Eliminate the source of the drugs

58. (A) Wise
    (B) Misguided
    (C) Adequate
    (D) Undetermined

59. (A) No great art was ever created without tears.
    (B) Every man can be an artist.
    (C) Because we cannot see it, music is not art.
    (D) The artist must simplify and then complicate.

60. (A) The artist did not fulfill his role.
    (B) A portion of the community is wrong in its opinions.
    (C) This is not a work of art.
    (D) The community should not display the work.

Listening Script 2

Part A

1. Although he adopted a pleasant demeanor, the child was really depressed.

2. How did you come to school?

3. Where did you find that text?

4. Since the course was not only optional but also extremely difficult, few students registered for it.

5. The Navy scoured the area for over a month, but the painstaking search turned up no clues.

6. How did the scientist come to that conclusion?

7. Why did she leave the restaurant?

8. He looked very imposing but was in reality very humble.

9. Have you lived in New York for long?

10. Did anyone pass the difficult Spanish test?

11. Were the soldiers members of the 82nd Airborne Division?

12. For the sake of expediency, we divided the work among the four of us.

13. If you had been more helpful, the customer might have purchased the suit.

14. When are you going out tonight?

15. What concerns you?

16. Because the child's reading scores were low, she was not able to advance to the next level.

17. How should a system of education be judged?

18. Why was the child distraught?

19. What was his attitude toward the project?

20. Dawn had trouble making up her mind between applying to college and looking for a job.

21. What kind of cheese was she eating?

22. Biofeedback is a treatment technique in which people are trained to improve their health by using signals from their own bodies.

23. A habit is an action that is repeated so often that it can be done without a second thought.

24. Anyone wishing to minimize the effects of the sun or to avoid heatstroke should confine her sunning to before 10 a.m. or after 2 p.m.

25. Dawn tensed her shoulders after hearing the report.

Part B

Question 26 is based on the following conversation between a mother and a child:

Mother: I am not pleased with your attitude. I wish you would try to be more cooperative.

Child: I don't know what you mean!

Mother: When I ask you to clean up, I expect you to clean up, not sulk.

Child: I'm not sulking.

26. How does the mother feel?

Question 27 is based on the following conversation:

Woman: Is this Built Right Appliances? I'd like to know when someone can come to check my washing machine. It is not draining water.

Man: You must have the wrong number. This is not Built Right Appliances.

27. How is the woman trying to contact the appliance repair shop?

Question 28 is based on the following conversation:

Man: Today's faculty meeting will deal with the issue of discipline in our school. I've brought Dr. Levy, an expert in child psychology, to speak to all of us.

Woman: Why do all of us need to listen to the lecture? Why isn't it optional for those who are interested?

Man: The lecture is part of our professional development of educators. It can open us up to new thoughts and ideas.

28. How does the woman feel about the lecture?

Question 29 is based on the following conversation:

Teacher: I thought the faculty conference was called for 4:00. It's 4:15 now, so why don't we get started?

Assistant Principal: I'm sorry for the delay. The Principal is meeting with the Superintendent, and we can't begin until she arrives.

29. Where does this conversation take place?

Question 30 is based on the following conversation:

Teacher 1: Have you met Dr. Kim? He's the featured speaker at today's faculty meeting.

Teacher 2: No, we've never met. But I've heard Dr. Kim speak, and I know he's an expert on a subject of great concern to our staff.

30. Why was Dr. Kim brought into the school?

Question 31 is based on the following conversation:

Girl: I cannot go to the dance tonight. I haven't finished my homework, and my parents won't allow me to go out.

Boy: That's ridiculous. It's Friday night. Everyone goes out on Friday night. You can do your homework on Saturday or Sunday.

Girl: My parents are adamant. They won't let me go until I've done my work.

Boy: Well then, I may just go with someone else.

Girl: Suit yourself!

31. How does the boy feel about the girl's problem?

Question 32 is based on the following conversation:

Child: Mom, I am not feeling well. I don't know what the matter is.

Mother: Why don't you rest for a while? I will take your temperature and see if you have a fever.

32. What is the girl's problem?

Question 33 is based on the following conversation:

Boy: I'd like to see you Saturday night. Are you free to come to the eighth grade sock hop?

Girl: I'd love to go. What time will you pick me up?

33. What is probably true about the boy and girl?

Question 34 is based on the following conversation:

Man: I cannot decide upon which trip to take. Should I visit Florida or California?

Woman: What is your budget for the trip? How long can you be away? Do you prefer sightseeing or resting on your vacation?

34. What is true about the woman?

Question 35 is based on the following conversation:

Woman: Which train goes to Albertson, New York?

Man: The next train will leave from Pennsylvania Station to Roslyn, New York, at 5:43 p.m. on Track 18. All aboard.

35. What is true about the man?

Questions 36–37 are based on the following telephone call:

Man: What time is the next showing of the featured movie today?

Recorded Announcement: This is a recording. *Anastasia* is playing today at 2, 4, 6, and 8 p.m. Tickets are available for all performances.

36. In order to know the answer to the man's question, what would one have to know?

37. If the man planned to have dinner at 5:30 p.m., which showing would he probably want to catch?

Question 38 is based on the following conversation:

    Doorbell rings.

Female 1:   There's a package for Mr. Levy to be delivered.

Female 2:   Please leave it outside the front door.

38. What can be inferred from this conversation?

Questions 39–40 are based on the following conversation:

Female Child: I won't do it! You can't make me! I hate her!

Adult: Calm down. Take a deep breath. Think about what you are saying.

39. How does this conversation take place?

40. Which of the following might not be involved in this conversation?

Question 41 is based on the following conversation:

Man: Have you seen her lately? She looks just awful!

Woman: The break up was very hard on her. It was completely unexpected.

41. What is the conversation about?

Question 42 is based on the following conversation:

Man: Did you know that today there are more than 200 reservations in the United States, established for various tribes of Native Americans through special treaties with the federal government?

Woman: I know. The largest is the Navajo reservation in Arizona, New Mexico, and Utah. Its 15 million acres make it about the size of New England.

42. Which of the following is true about reservations?

Questions 43–44 are based on the following conversation:

Woman: Your legislative system would be much better if it were English like ours.

Man: I don't think so. The English system may be good for England, but our system is good for Sudan.

43. How could the woman's point of view be described?

44. What is true about the man?

Question 45 is based on the following conversation:

Speaker 1:   I believe the media has shown us that the nation has a serious drug problem, especially the threat posed by crack. Crack has dominated media attention during the recent surge in drug coverage.

Speaker 2:   The Federal Drug Enforcement Administration disagrees. They claim the drug is generally not available in some major cities and not widely available in others. They consider crack a secondary, not a primary, problem in most areas.

45. On what point do both speakers disagree?

Part C

Questions 46–48 refer to the following passage:

On June 17, 1744, the commissioners from Maryland and Virginia negotiated a treaty with the Indians of the Six Nations at Lancaster, Pennsylvania. The Indians were invited to send boys to William and Mary College. In a letter the next day, they declined the offer.

46. What was offered to the Indians?

47. When was this treaty negotiated?

48. Who negotiated the treaty?

Questions 49–50 refer to the following passage:

The ear is indeed a remarkable mechanism, as it is so complicated that its operation is not well understood. Certainly it is extremely sensitive. At the threshold of audibility, the power requirement is inconceivably tiny. If all the people in the United States were listening simultaneously to a whisper (20 decibels), the power received by all their collective eardrums would total only a few millionths of a watt—far less than the power generated by a single flying mosquito.

49. Why is the ear misunderstood?

50. What is the power requirement of the ear?

Questions 51–53 refer to the following passage:

Once upon a time, little girls treasured Raggedy Ann dolls and boys their teddy bears throughout childhood. The playthings were symbols of a simpler and perhaps happier time, an era in which dolls and toys had special, lasting meaning. The last decade has brought about a startling revolution in the dollhouse. Parents still can buy Raggedy Ann and charming baby dolls, which just sit and smile. But these venerable standbys are being nudged aside by the "action" dolls, fashion figurines such as Barbie and adventure heroes of the G.I. Joe genre.

51. According to the passage, what example does Barbie represent?

52. G.I. Joe belongs to which of these categories?

53. What does the author use Raggedy Ann and teddy bears to symbolize?

Questions 54–56 refer to the following passage:

Like the United States today, Athens had courts where a wrong might be righted. Since any citizen might accuse another of a crime, the Athenian courts of law were very busy. In fact, unless a citizen was unusually peaceful or very unimportant, he would be sure to find himself in the courts at least once every few years. At the trial, both the accuser and the person accused were allowed a certain time to speak. Free men testified under oath as they do today, but the oath of a slave was counted as worthless. To keep citizens from being too careless in accusing each other, there was a rule that if the person accused did not receive a certain number of negative votes, the accuser was condemned instead.

54. Which title best expresses the main idea of this selection?

55. Why were people in Athens frequently on trial in a court of law?

56. Why was an Athenian likely to avoid accusing another without a good reason?

Questions 57–58 refer to the following passage:

According to Congressman X, too much of our taxpayers' money is spent on rehabilitation of drug addicts. Most of those in rehabilitation centers go back to taking narcotics. Instead of wasting money on rehabilitation, we should use the money to get rid of drug peddlers.

57. How does Congressman X believe the drug addiction problem should be solved?

58. According to Congressman X, what is true about the current use of taxpayers' money?

Questions 59–60 refer to the following passage:

The artist's role is to find that which is similar in all of us and draw upon that to produce a work that both unites us and separates us. Each of us should see something different in the work, although the underlying thing we grasp in it is the same.

59. The author would agree with which of the following?

60. A piece of artistic work has aroused great conflict in the community. The author would believe which of the following?

Answer Key

Listening Skills 2 – Part A

1.	B	14.	D
2.	A	15.	A
3.	C	16.	B
4.	B	17.	B
5.	B	18.	A
6.	D	19.	A
7.	B	20.	C
8.	B	21.	C
9.	C	22.	C
10.	A	23.	D
11.	B	24.	A
12.	C	25.	D
13.	A		

Listening Skills 2 – Part B

26.	A	37.	D
27.	B	38.	A
28.	C	39.	A
29.	A	40.	D
30.	D	41.	C
31.	D	42.	C
32.	C	43.	C
33.	A	44.	B
34.	B	45.	D
35.	B		
36.	C		

Listening Skills 2 – Part C

46.	A	54.	B
47.	C	55.	C
48.	A	56.	A
49.	D	57.	D
50.	A	58.	B
51.	C	59.	D
52.	A	60.	A
53.	B		

Principles of Learning and Teaching

This assessment is divided into three discrete grade level clusters:

Grades K–6

Grades 5–9

Grades 7–12

The tests use short answer essays and multiple-choice items. The assessment is designed to evaluate a beginning teacher's knowledge of a number of job-related information. The test includes three case histories, each providing a specific teaching situation. The examinee must answer two short-answer questions which will be scored on a scale of 0–3. The examinee will also answer seven multiple-choice questions on the case. In addition, the test contains thirty more multiple-choice questions of an educational nature.

TEST:	PRINCIPLES OF LEARNING AND TEACHINGS
	Grades K–6 (0522)
	Grades 5–9 (0523)
	Grades 7–12 (0524)
ALLOTTED TIME:	Two hours
QUESTIONS:	3 Case Histories — 7 multiple-choice questions
	2 constructed-response questions
	30 Multiple-Choice questions

The Case History

Each case history presents a detailed teaching situation appropriate for Grades K-6, Grades 5-9 or Grades 7-12. After the case history is presented, approximately six multiple-choice questions are given to test the prospective teacher's knowledge of the pedagogy presented in the history. Following the multiple-choice questions are two short essays related to the case history. Essays are scored from 1 (lowest score) to 3 (highest score). Then twenty-four discrete multiple-choice questions are presented on a variety of educational issues. Each multiple-choice question in the Principles of Learning and Teaching (PLT) examination is followed by four possible choices.

The following is an illustration of a case history. Case histories presented in the PLT test are typically at least 1,000 words long and are followed by seven multiple-choice questions, two constructed-response (essay) questions, and additional discrete (stand-alone) multiple-choice questions.

Case History: K-6

Directions: The case history below is followed by three multiple-choice questions. Choose the best answer for each question.

Case History #1

Anthony White is in Mr. Garner's fifth-grade class at Community Elementary School. Anthony is new to the district, having recently moved from California, where his mother was stationed in the (5) Army. Anthony is an outgoing boy who enjoys playing video games with his older brothers. His teacher, Mr. Garner, is both new to the district and to the teaching profession.

On Friday morning, Mr. Garner was prepar-(10) ing a reading lesson while most of the students were gone from the classroom. When they returned from music, he watched them and talked to them to see how the music class had gone. Mr. Garner realizes that at this age, moving from one (15) class to another can sometimes be problematic for them, so he likes to find out early on which students are having problems. All of a sudden Anthony storms into the classroom and approaches Chad. Mr. Garner asks the two boys what the (20) problem is. Anthony pushes Mr. Garner aside and punches Chad on the back. At this point, Mr. Garner restrains Anthony and tells him to calm down. In fact, he tells Anthony that he will release him as soon as he calms down. A few sec-(25) onds later, Anthony calms himself and Mr. Garner takes Anthony into the hall. Mr. Garner says to Anthony, "I'd like us to try to figure out how to solve this problem together." Anthony is silent, but Mr. Garner knows that he is listening. "What (30) just happened back there in the classroom? Do you know that you did something that's against the school's rules?" asks Mr. Garner. Anthony says that he knows that he shouldn't have punched Chad, but Chad had made him angry. "He called (35) me a name, and I couldn't let him get away with that," Anthony tells him. Meanwhile, Chad denies calling Anthony anything. Mr. Garner tells Chad that he will get his turn to tell his side of the story, but right now, Anthony is talking. Mr. (40) Garner asks Anthony if he believes that hitting Chad has solved his problem. Anthony says no, he feels sorry that he might have hurt Chad. Mr. Garner asks Anthony, "And hitting is against one of our rules, right?" Anthony agrees. Mr. Gar-(45) ner asks Anthony if he can think of another way to solve this particular problem. "I could tell somebody," he replies. Mr. Garner tells him that this is an excellent idea and asks him to think of someone he could talk to. Immediately Anthony men-(50) tions Mr. Garner. He tells him that he really likes him and feels that they have something in common: they are both new to the school. "I'm glad to hear that, Anthony," Mr. Garner says. He then asks Anthony if there is something that he could (55) do to help him with this problem. Anthony asks him to talk to Chad, too. Mr. Garner says that he will, and then he will bring them both together to talk.

Mr. Garner lets Anthony go back into the class-(60) room and has a conversation with Chad. He agrees that he was also wrong and wants to apologize to Anthony and to the class. During lunch, Mr. Garner brings the two boys together and they talk about what had happened, how they both felt about (65) it, and their individual plans for preventing problems in the future. Mr. Garner tells them how proud he is of them and makes plans for the three of them to talk again in a couple of days.

One week later, after noticing that Anthony and (70) Chad seem to be getting along, he decides that additional intervention is unnecessary and does not follow up with the boys.

Two days later, both Anthony and Chad are suspended from the bus for two days for fight- (75) ing.

Directions: Each multiple-choice question is followed by four answer choices. Choose the one that is best in each case.

1. Which of the following concepts for effectively implementing a systems approach to managing student behavior did Mr. Garner clearly use?

   (A) School personnel will better serve students with behavioral problems when procedures exist for coordinating with the surrounding community.

   (B) Outside consultation should be implemented when a student continues to display behavioral difficulties.

   (C) The teacher has a responsibility to use behavioral change methods that are geared toward altering the student's behavior.

   (D) Teachers need to receive assistance from their peers while they continue to examine their efforts to help students who continue to display behavioral difficulties.

Answer: The correct answer is **(C)**. Mr. Garner realized that both students would need to develop appropriate strategies and skills for solving their problems.

2. When Mr. Garner asked Anthony if he knew that he had done something that was against the school's rules, Anthony's response indicated that he

   (A) does not relate his own actions to the school's rules.

   (B) is still angry.

   (C) has no intentions of following the school's rules.

   (D) understands the school's rules.

Answer: The correct answer is **(A)**. There is no indication from Anthony's response that Anthony is aware of the school's rules for acceptable behavior.

3. Which of the following would have been the most appropriate way for Mr. Garner to follow up with Anthony and Chad?

   (A) Recording the dialogue that took place as he attempted to help Anthony solve the problem.

   (B) Referring them to the principal for punitive action.

   (C) Rewarding Chad for not punching Anthony.

   (D) Bringing them together to discuss how they intended to prevent any future problems and to offer assistance when necessary.

Answer: The correct answer is **(D)**.

Practice Constructed-Response Question

Directions: Question 4 requires that you write a short response. Your answer should indicate your knowledge of the principles of learning and teaching. You will write your answers in an answer book that will be provided at the testing center.

4. What are three effective proactive strategies to handle minor discipline problems in the classroom before they become major disturbances? Be sure to include examples to support your strategies.

Practice Discrete Multiple-Choice Questions

Directions: Each question is followed by four answer choices. Choose the best answer to each question.

5. A teacher gives her first-grade class a page that has a story in which pictures take the place of some words. The teacher is using which approach or method?

   (A) A whole-language approach

   (B) A language experience approach

   (C) The Spaulding method

   (D) The rebus method

Answer: The correct answer is (**D**). A rebus is a puzzle in which pictures replace words in a story.

6. A theory of socialization viewed by Carl Rogers and Abraham Maslow emphasizes that

   (A) people grow toward the goal of self-actualization.

   (B) conflicts during different stages of development have to be resolved.

   (C) modeling plays a part in determining social skills.

   (D) conditioning plays a part in creating social skills.

Answer: The correct answer is (**A**). Rogers and Maslow believed that people progress through various stages until they reach a point of total emotional fulfillment.

7. In setting up a behavior modification program, a teacher observes Briana for three 1-hour sessions. The teacher randomly chooses another student in the class as a control. During this time, the teacher tallies the number of times Briana and the control student leave their seats per each one-hour period. The teacher is recording baseline data using a

   (A) time interval.

   (B) variable interval.

   (C) frequency count.

   (D) fixed interval.

Answer: The correct answer is (**C**). This passage describes the procedure in developing a frequency count to record baseline data before implementing a behavior modification program.

8. The principal of a middle school wishes to improve discipline. She sets up a committee of teachers, parents, and administrators to study this problem. After a series of meetings, they make ten recommendations. The principal then meets with the committee and tells them that although their recommendations have some merit, she has come up with her own strategy to deal with discipline and that she hopes the committee will help in its implementation. This principal could be described as being

   (A) egocentric.

   (B) democratic.

   (C) collegial.

   (D) discriminating.

Answer: The correct answer is (**A**). This administrative behavior describes an egocentric principal. This is someone who acts democratically, but is really unwilling to give up any power.

Sample Multiple-Choice Questions

Directions: Each question or incomplete statement is followed by four answer choices. For each question, select the answer or completion that is best and blacken the corresponding space on the answer sheet.

1. A seventh-grade student receives a score of 93 on the verbal part and 91 on the performance part of the WISC III. On the Woodcock Johnson Psychoeducational Battery—Revised, the same student received a standard score of 91 on the word-identification subtest and a standard score of 97 on the passage-comprehension subtest. Based on this information, we can assume that

(A) the student probably needs to be placed in a remedial reading program.

(B) no decision can be made unless we find out grade-equivalent values.

(C) the student does not need any services.

(D) the student is probably functioning in the low-average range.

2. It is important that a teacher adequately assess the cause of a behavior problem. If a student is constantly fighting during a group reading lesson, this behavior may be the result of all of the following *except*

(A) the reading material may be too difficult.

(B) the reading material may be too easy.

(C) the child may dislike reading because of a history of constant failure in this area.

(D) the need for the child to be involved in psychotherapy.

3. Many educators feel that standardized reading scores are not a valid measure for determining the progress of a local school district. It is felt that other factors contribute to an increase or a decline in a school's reading scores. All of the following are variables affecting reading *except*

(A) recent foreign immigration to the immediate area.

(B) the special education population of a school.

(C) whether school-based management has been successfully implemented.

(D) the socioeconomic status of an area.

4. Research shows that tests that best predict how much a person will profit from further education are usually achievement tests that measure how much a person has learned already. This illustrates that

(A) there is no validity to achievement tests.

(B) the distinction between aptitude and achievement tests tends to break down.

(C) college performance can best be measured by criterion-referenced tests.

(D) there is no statistical difference between an achievement test and an aptitude test.

5. Tests are often used and abused by people who have little psychometric training. Tests are meaningless unless interpreted accurately. Which of the items below is *not* an example of a testing abuse?

(A) The invidious comparison of one group to another

(B) Overinterpretation by the public

(C) Focus study on test performance rather than toward direct and meaningful learning goals

(D) Screening out applicants to special programs

6. Children with Attention Deficit Disorders are likely to exhibit which of the following characteristics?

   I. Hyperactivity

   II. Impulsivity

   III. Distractibility

   IV. Depression

(A) II and III only

(B) I only

(C) III and IV only

(D) I, II, and III only

7. Comparing performance on different versions of the same test is a measure of

    (A) alternate-form reliability.

    (B) split-half reliability.

    (C) test-retest reliability.

    (D) correlational reliability.

8. All of the following are examples of gross-motor skills *except*

    (A) posture.

    (B) throwing.

    (C) balance.

    (D) fastening.

9. When tests are used for program evaluation, they can be misinterpreted. Which of the following difficulties can arise when tests are used to assess the efficacy of various instructional techniques?

    I. Schools may not be similar.

    II. Teachers can have different styles.

    III. There is no valid test measuring this concept.

    IV. The children being taught may be different.

    (A) I and III only

    (B) II and IV only

    (C) I only

    (D) I, II, and IV only

10. As a result of an accident, a fifth-grade teacher now has an orthopedic condition that prevents him from climbing stairs. His classroom was originally on the fourth floor of the school. The teacher requests that his class now be stationed on the first floor. The building administrator denies this request, saying that no classrooms are available. What resource does this teacher have?

    (A) The teacher should inform his union representative and file a grievance.

    (B) The teacher has to accept the judgment of his principal.

    (C) The teacher should retire on disability.

    (D) The teacher should inform the superintendent of his school district that the administrator's action is in violation of the ADA.

11. Computers have been primarily used in labs or as technological tools outside of the classroom. All of the following probably would result if computers were effectively used as an integral part of the classroom environment *except*

    (A) whole class to small group instruction would be facilitated.

    (B) test-based assessment to assessment based on products, progress, and effect.

    (C) competitive to cooperative social structure.

    (D) more emphasis on drill and practice.

12. According to Harold W. Stevenson and James W. Stigner in their book *The Learning Gap: Why Our Schools Are Failing and What We Can Learn from Japanese and Chinese Education*, which of the following is the main reason Asian teachers are more effective in instructing large heterogeneous classes than American teachers?

    (A) Asian teachers are better trained in dealing with large group environments.

    (B) Asian culture values education more highly than does Western culture.

    (C) Asian teachers are more likely to teach lessons rather than just lecture; they try to get students to explain their reasoning and evaluate their answers.

    (D) Asian educators are more likely to use mastery learning techniques; Japanese and Chinese teachers do not go forward until they are sure each student understands a specific concept.

13. Which of the following is a valid criticism of public school choice?

    (A) It is less effective than private school choice.

    (B) Parents prefer to send their children to neighborhood schools.

    (C) Too many choices tend to confuse parents who may know little about different types of methodologies.

    (D) Public school choice is not supported by federal mandates.

14. Most research demonstrates that the auditory function most related to reading is

    (A) memory.

    (B) sequencing.

    (C) discriminating.

    (D) closure.

15. All of the following are characteristics of good spellers *except*

    (A) they may substitute other words for those they cannot spell.

    (B) good knowledge of sequential probability.

    (C) good immediate memory for visual material.

    (D) high interest in reading.

16. You arbitrarily divide a single test into two halves. However, if the performance of a norming sample is significantly different on each part, the test

    (A) is probably measuring different skills.

    (B) parts probably supplement each other.

    (C) needs a more homogeneous norming sample.

    (D) has a high standard deviation.

17. A student who has difficulty following directions, playing board games, and beginning homework promptly most likely has a problem in

    (A) organization.

    (B) visual-motor skills.

    (C) study skills.

    (D) social development.

18. Which of the following are some problems in trying to measure test-retest reliability?

    I. The practice effect may increase a student's score.

    II. A student may have acquired additional knowledge in the intervening time period.

    III. Test questions may become outdated.

    IV. Two parts of the same test may measure different attributes.

    (A) I and III only

    (B) I and II only

    (C) III and IV only

    (D) I, II, and IV only

19. Students can better remember how to spell a word when

    (A) they have a good listening and reading vocabulary.

    (B) they can memorize all forty-five phonemes of the English language.

    (C) sequencing skills are developed.

    (D) they are given short lists to memorize.

20. Which of the following is *not* a factor in errors in measurement?

    (A) Illness during a test session

    (B) A test containing items a student was never taught

    (C) Test anxiety inhibiting a score

    (D) Usage of less than three correlating coefficients in measuring reliability

21. The best approach to use in teaching a student how to spell words such as *led*, *lead*, and *washed* would be to

    (A) develop the student's morphological skills.

    (B) teach the student to sound out the word.

    (C) teach phonological units.

    (D) develop visual-memory skills.

22. A social studies teacher administers an objective test after a unit on the Civil War. The exam contains many questions comparing the Civil War to the Vietnam War. Which of the following is a possible technical flaw this exam may have?

    (A) It may have poor content validity.

    (B) The correlation coefficient for criterion validity may be too high.

    (C) The teacher should use a split-half reliability measure.

    (D) The distribution of scores may skew the bell-shaped curve.

23. Which of the following best describes the spelling errors of a sixth-grader who spells *manufacture* as *manfacture* and *happiness* as *happness*?

    (A) Substitutions of one sound for another

    (B) Omissions of a sound or syllable from a word

    (C) Adding a sound or syllable to the original

    (D) Putting sounds in the wrong order

24. Which of the following are the primary goals of classroom tests?

    I. To rank students in the class

    II. To practice what has been learned

    III. To find out what has been learned to guide further instruction

    IV. To determine eligibility for special pull-out programs

    (A) I only

    (B) III only

    (C) II and III only

    (D) III and IV only

25. A fourth-grade student has difficulty in motor planning. He does not know which way to form round manuscript letters and which way to form loops on small letters. He applies too much pressure, often breaking a pencil. The best strategy to deal with this problem is to

    (A) use a multisensory approach.

    (B) teach the child cursive to keep him in one direction.

    (C) use tracing and copying exercises.

    (D) teach the student how to use a spell checker on a word processor.

26. In terms of instructional planning, which of the following does research tell us about the use of tests in the classroom?

    (A) Several large tests given per term facilitate learning and retention.

    (B) Many tests taken at short intervals are superior in terms of learning and retention to one long exam.

    (C) Essay tests have higher reliability than objective examinations.

    (D) Instead of using objective exams to facilitate learning, it is best to give groups of students cooperative learning projects.

27. Susan will learn this year to form declarative and interrogative sentences that will convey her thoughts, ideas, and feelings. She will begin to use capitals and end her sentences with either a question mark, exclamation point, or period. Susan also will begin to use quotation marks. She will continue to learn how to spell those words most frequently used in her writing and reading. This student is probably in

    (A) second grade.

    (B) kindergarten.

    (C) sixth grade.

    (D) eighth grade.

28. Which of the following are examples of projective tests?

    I. Thematic Apperception Test

    II. Minnesota Multiphasic Personality Inventory

    III. Rorshach

    IV. Kuder Preference Record

    (A) I, II, and III only

    (B) II and IV only

    (C) I and III only

    (D) II and III only

29. Why do people consider essay examinations to be more valid than objective tests?

    (A) Essay questions are easier to make up.

    (B) Essay tests lend themselves to split-half reliability studies.

    (C) Students need to study less intensively to answer an essay question.

    (D) Students draw together knowledge and demonstrate understanding rather than simply remember isolated facts.

30. According to the latest research, one of the *least* effective ways to teach reading is to

    (A) read Endicott Award-winning stories to a kindergarten class.

    (B) develop a sight vocabulary using the organic method.

    (C) sound out letters one at a time.

    (D) teach antonyms, synonyms, and roots.

Answer Key and Explanations

1. C	6. D	11. D	16. A	21. A	26. B
2. D	7. A	12. C	17. A	22. A	27. A
3. C	8. D	13. C	18. B	23. B	28. C
4. B	9. D	14. A	19. A	24. C	29. D
5. D	10. D	15. A	20. D	25. B	30. C

1. **The correct answer is (C).** The student's academic achievement and intelligence are both in the average range. Therefore, the student is working to his potential and thus needs no services. Standard scores of 80 to 89 are considered low average. Therefore, (D) is incorrect because scores in the 90s are definitely in the average range. The student probably has no significant deficits; thus choice (A) is wrong. One does not need to know choice (B) when a student has average standard scores.

2. **The correct answer is (D).** In order to change a child's behavior, a teacher may have to change environmental factors in the classroom. The correct answer is (D) because such a variable would not immediately change a student's classroom behavior. Choices (A), (B), and (C) are all antecedents that can be altered to modify inappropriate classroom behavior.

3. **The correct answer is (C).** If most students in a school are recent immigrants, the reading score of a school would be lowered (A). If a school had many special education classes containing students with severe academic delays, scores again would be lowered, choice (B). Research shows that if a school is located in an area containing pockets of poverty, again the school would have many students scoring below grade level, choice (D). The only choice that would possibly not be a major factor in determining reading scores is choice (C). It does not matter who manages a school. What matters more is whether effective instructional techniques are being utilized in conjunction with the other factors mentioned above.

4. **The correct answer is (B).** Aptitude tests are supposed to measure potential, while achievement tests measure skills already learned. However, in this case, we are using an achievement test to determine aptitude. A good example of this type of examination is the SAT. The other three choices do not make sense.

5. **The correct answer is (D).** Tests are supposed to be used to screen out applicants. The other three choices are examples of test abuses.

6. **The correct answer is (D).** Children who have ADD are often hyperactive, impulsive, disinhibited, and distractible. Therefore, the only correct answer is choice (D).

7. **The correct answer is (A).** Comparing performance on different versions of the same test is called alternate-form reliability. Choice (B) is measured by dividing a test in half by taking all even- and all odd-numbered choices. Choice (C) is measured by giving the same test over a few days later. Choice (D) does not exist.

8. **The correct answer is (D).** Choices (A), (B), and (C) are all gross-motor skills. Fastening buttons or snaps, choice (D), is an example of a fine-motor skill.

9. **The correct answer is (D).** Any valid achievement test could be used to measure the effectiveness of an academic program. There are no tests per se to measure a particular instructional program or procedure (III). The other three choices are all factors that can lead to misinterpretation of tests used to measure instructional effectiveness.

10. **The correct answer is (D).** Under the Americans with Disabilities Act (1991), an employee who is physically challenged has to have reasonable accommodations made, i.e., accessibility. Therefore, the correct answer is choice (D). Choice (A) is wrong because this is not a union issue. A federal law overrides any collective bargaining agreement. Choices (B) and (C) make no sense in light of the 1991 ADA Act as well as Section 504 of the 1973 Vocational Rehabilitation Act.

11. **The correct answer is (D).** The key word in this question is "effectively." Computers have primarily

been used for drill and practice. This is no better than having a workbook on a video screen. If computers were truly integrated into instruction, choices (A), (B), and (C) would result.

12. **The correct answer is (C).** In this recent study, these two authors have observed hundreds of Asian classrooms. They discovered that Asian classes are not really much larger than American classes. This rules out choice (A). More importantly, the authors saw that Asian teachers truly use effective instructional techniques, choice (C). American teachers are more interested in the correct answer than in developing cognitive skills. Although Asians value education highly, choice (B), the authors did not view this as the primary reason their students do better than ours. Choice (D) is incorrect because mastery learning does not develop thinking skills.

13. **The correct answer is (C).** When lay parents are given a catalog listing various magnet-type schools, they have no way of knowing which instructional program is most effective for their child or if a school's methodology has any validity in terms of instructional effectiveness. Choices (A) and (B) are opinions not based on any empirical research. Choice (D) is wrong because the concept is supported by the Federal Department of Education.

14. **The correct answer is (A).** Though the other three factors are important in developing reading skills, if students are unable to remember phonetic and structural sounds, they will not be able to learn to decode. Furthermore, poor auditory memory tends also to inhibit comprehension skills. Choices (B), (C), and (D) are all components of phonic analysis, and students deficient in these areas can learn compensatory techniques.

15. **The correct answer is (A).** Research shows that good spellers are competent readers, choice (D). Good spellers also have well-developed visual memory and sequencing skills, choices (C) and (B). Therefore the correct choice is (A). Poor spellers usually substitute similar-sounding or similar-looking words for words they cannot spell.

16. **The correct answer is (A).** In terms of split-half reliability, the two parts must contain questions measuring the same skills. You probably would get different reliability scores if all the odd questions on a math test measured fractional concepts while all the even questions measured whole number computations.

17. **The correct answer is (A).** This student has a problem in organization. He/she probably has a visual/auditory sequencing problem. Choice (B) is wrong because problems in visual-motor development usually show up primarily in spelling and written expression. Choice (C) is incorrect because the problem is not in the student's inability to do the homework but in his/her inability to begin the task in an orderly and sequential manner. Choice (D) makes no sense.

18. **The correct answer is (B).** Students tend to do better when a test is administered a second time. In addition, if the intervening time period is significant, the student could be taught some of the items on the test. Item III makes no sense since the intervening period between test administrations is relatively small. Item IV would be a significant factor when measuring split-half reliability.

19. **The correct answer is (A).** Good spelling ability correlates with good reading and listening skills. Choices (B) and (D) are incorrect because these skills are specific strategies that are usually taught to poor spellers. Choice (C) is wrong because it is only one of many strategies used by good spellers.

20. **The correct answer is (D).** Choices (A), (B), and (C) are all factors that can cause errors in measurement. The final choice does not mean anything and is thus the correct answer.

21. **The correct answer is (A).** Good spellers have developed morphological skills. Such spellers understand words and word parts as units of meaning. In this case, it would be the understanding of homonyms and past tense. Teaching students to sound out these irregular words using phonic analysis would not be an effective approach, choices (B) and (C). These words also deviate from regular linguistic patterns, i.e., *ed* sounding like /t/. Choice (D) is wrong because not all students can effectively utilize this strategy.

22. **The correct answer is (A).** The students may not have been taught any content material about the Vietnam War and may not be able to answer such

comparative questions. Therefore, the test may not be testing what it is supposed to be testing. The test may be evaluating higher-level comparative skills instead of whether a student understands the period between 1861 and 1865. Choice (C) is wrong because the technical flaw has nothing to do with reliability. Choice (D) is incorrect because the problem tells us nothing about the distribution of scores.

23. **The correct answer is (B).** This student is omitting a syllable. The student is neither changing a sound, choice (A), nor adding a syllable, choice (C). Nor does he have a problem in sequence, choice (D).

24. **The correct answer is (C).** Tests should be used to practice and to guide further instruction. Though teachers often use tests to rank students (item I), research shows that exams should not be used in a way that fosters competition or stigmatization. Item IV is wrong because it is usually standardized tests that determine eligibility for special pull-out programs, such as Chapter 1 reading.

25. **The correct answer is (B).** This student has a directionality problem, and the best strategy to use to remediate this difficulty is to teach cursive writing. Choice (A) would best be used in letter recognition and not in writing. Choice (D) would be a strategy used with high school students who have severe problems in spelling and fine-motor control. Choice (C) is not the most effective strategy to use with students with directionality problems.

26. **The correct answer is (B).** Research shows that by giving many tests, retention is enhanced. Choice (A) is incorrect because by giving few tests, the student does not have much chance to practice what he has learned. Choice (C) is wrong because objective tests usually have higher reliability than subjective tests. Choice (D) makes no sense.

27. **The correct answer is (A).** This student is probably in second grade, where the mechanics of writing and spelling are emphasized. Choice (B) is wrong because students do not learn skills in written expression in these grades. Choices (C) and (D) are incorrect because creative writing and not mechanics are usually emphasized in these grades.

28. **The correct answer is (C).** These two exams are examples of projective tests that are used by psychologists to interpret a subject's feelings. Item II is obviously a personality test, and IV is a vocational inventory.

29. **The correct answer is (D).** Essay exams can tap higher-level cognitive skills, i.e., application, synthesis, and evaluation. Choice (A) is wrong because essays are usually more difficult to make up. Choice (B) is incorrect because the reliability of essay tests is usually poor. Choice (C) makes no sense because such a statement cannot be empirically proven.

30. **The correct answer is (C).** The least effective strategy to teach reading is choice (C). You cannot teach reading by sounding out individual letters because English has many irregular phonic patterns. The other three choices are adequate strategies to use in the teaching of various reading skills.

Specialty Area Tests

About the NTE
Specialty Area Tests

Praxis II Subject Assessments offers 120 separate NTE Programs Specialty Area Tests measuring mastery of content and teaching techniques in a wide range of school subjects and specialties and subspecialties within those subjects. Many of these Specialty Area Tests have limited use because their subject matter is specific to a particular state, such as Accounting in Pennsylvania, or because the subject itself is not widely taught, such as Japanese, or simply because not many states require beginning teachers to prove their proficiency in those subjects.

For more detailed information about all the Specialty Area Tests as well as about other tests in the Praxis Series, contact:

> The Praxis Series
> Educational Testing Service
> P.O. Box 6051
> Princeton, NJ 08541-6052

This final section of the book provides sample questions similar to those used on the 18 most popular NTE Specialty Area tests given nationwide. You will find an answer key for all these specialty area test questions on page 179.

Test: Biology and General Science (0030)

Time: 2 hours
Number of Questions: 160
Format: Multiple-choice questions

Purpose of the Test

Designed to measure the preparation of prospective secondary school biology and/or physical science teachers

Content Categories

- History, Philosophy, and Methodology of Science; Science, Technology, and Society—(10 percent)
- Molecular and Cellular Biology of Prokaryotes and Eukaryotes—(15 percent)
- Biology of Plants, Animals, Fungi, and Protists—(20 percent)
- Evolution—(12 percent)
- Ecology—(13 percent)
- Chemistry—(10 percent)
- Physics—(10 percent)
- Earth and Space Science—(10 percent)

Category Descriptions

History, Philosophy, and Methodology of Science; Science, Technology, and Society

1. Relevant history, philosophy, and methodology of science
2. Issues related to the intersection of science, technology, and society (including environmental issues

Molecular and Cellular Biology of Prokaryotes and Eukaryotes

1. Structure and function of cells and biologically important macromolecules
2. Molecular biology of genes and gene function, including viruses
3. Cellular bioenergetics, including photosynthesis and respiration

Biology of Plants, Animals, Fungi, and Protists

1. Principles of Mendelian and classical genetics
2. Characteristics, structure and function, reproduction and development, regulation and control, and behavior

Evolution

Mechanisms, population genetics, origin of life, systematics, and phylogeny

Ecology

1. Dynamics, intraspecific competition, and life-history patterns of populations
2. Energetics, interspecific relationships, and characteristics of communities
3. Aquatic and terrestrial systems, interrelationships, and biogeochemistry of ecosystems
4. Environmental issues

Chemistry

1. Structures, states, and properties of matter
2. Reactions and kinetic theory including acids/bases, oxidation/reduction, and catalysts

Physics

1. Mechanics, energy and heat, electricity and magnetism, wave phenomena, atomic and nuclear physics
2. Environmental issues related to physics

Earth and Space Science

1. Astronomy, geology, oceanography, meteorology
2. Environmental issues related to Earth and space science

Biology and General Science

Directions: Each question or incomplete statement is followed by five answer choices. For each question, circle the answer or completion that is best.

1. If the apparatus shown below is placed in a moderately warm location, within a few hours the

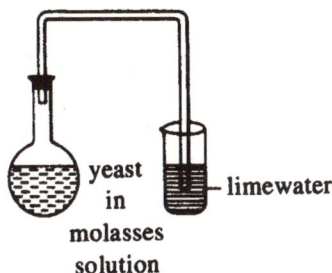

yeast in molasses solution — limewater

(A) molasses solution will flow into the beaker.
(B) molasses solution will turn brown.
(C) limewater will turn milky.
(D) limewater will flow into the flask.
(E) None of these.

Base your answers to questions 2, 3, and 4 on the pedigree chart below, where individual B is a hemophiliac male who is heterozygous for brown eyes. Individual A is his blue-eyed wife, who does not carry any genes for hemophilia.

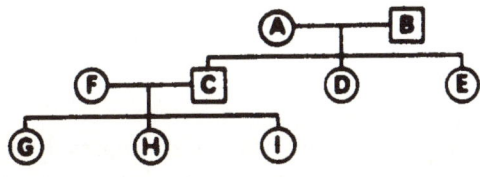

2. What is the probability that individual D is a hemophiliac?

(A) 0

(B) $\frac{1}{1}$

(C) $\frac{1}{2}$

(D) $\frac{1}{3}$

(E) $\frac{1}{4}$

3. Which best represents the genetic makeup for eye color of individual H?

(A) Homozygous brown
(B) Homozygous blue
(C) Heterozygous brown
(D) Heterozygous blue
(E) It cannot be determined from the information given.

4. If individual E marries a male who is a hemophiliac, which statement is true?

(A) All of her sons must be hemophiliacs.
(B) All of her daughters must carry at least one gene for hemophilia.
(C) All of her daughters must be hemophiliacs.
(D) 50 percent of her sons can be hemophiliacs, but none of her daughters can be hemophiliacs.
(E) 50 percent of her daughters can be hemophiliacs, but none of her sons can be hemophiliacs.

5. The image formed by a convex mirror compared to the object is usually

(A) inverted and imaginary.
(B) erect and smaller.
(C) real and inverted.
(D) erect and imaginary.
(E) inverted and larger.

6. Unicellular organisms ingest large molecules into their cytoplasm from the external environment without previously digesting them. This process is called

(A) pinocytosis.
(B) peristalsis.
(C) plasmolysis.
(D) osmosis.
(E) transpiration.

7. Which one of the following compounds stores energy that is immediately available for active muscle cells?

(A) Creatine phosphate

(B) Glycogen

(C) Glucose

(D) Glycine

(E) Messenger RNA

8. The ciliary muscle is used for the process of

(A) locomotion.

(B) food transportation.

(C) blinking.

(D) accommodation.

(E) respiration.

9. An atom of chlorine, atomic number 17 and atomic weight 35, contains in its nucleus

(A) 35 protons.

(B) 17 neutrons.

(C) 35 neutrons.

(D) 18 neutrons.

(E) 18 electrons.

10. The structure that does not include nucleic acid is the

(A) gene.

(B) chromosome.

(C) centriole.

(D) ribosome.

(E) chromatin.

Questions 11 and 12 refer to the figure below.

Diagram *X* represents the nucleus of a somatic cell of a mature spermatocyte. The following questions relate to the six *numbered* diagrams immediately below Diagram *X*.

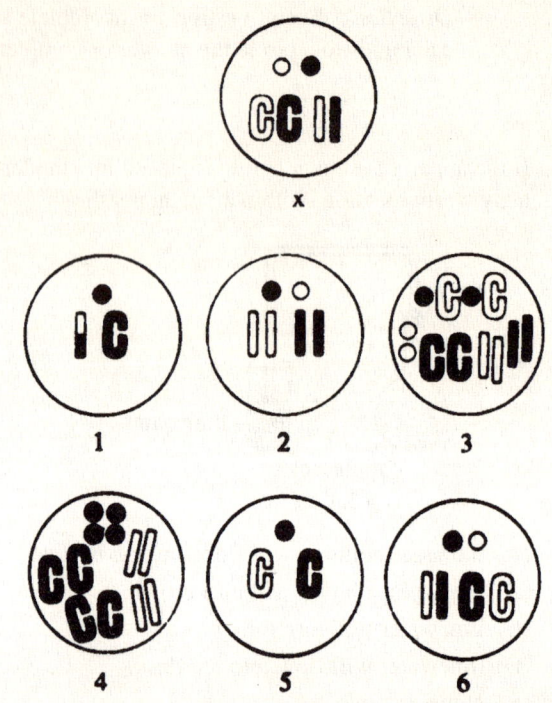

11. A functional sperm nucleus from a pollen grain produced by this plant could resemble

(A) 1

(B) 2

(C) 5

(D) 4

(E) 6

12. If meiotic division had *not* accompanied the formation of both gametes, a nucleus of the zygote formed would most likely have resembled

(A) 1

(B) 2

(C) 3

(D) 4

(E) 5

13. An organism having characteristics of both plants and animals is the
    (A) amoeba.
    (B) paramecium.
    (C) sponge.
    (D) euglena.
    (E) planaria.

14. Under the Linnaean system of classification, each kingdom is divided into related
    (A) phyla.
    (B) classes.
    (C) families.
    (D) genera.
    (E) species.

15. The major portion of ultraviolet radiation that reaches the Earth is absorbed in the
    (A) troposphere.
    (B) stratosphere.
    (C) mesosphere.
    (D) thermosphere.
    (E) hydrosphere.

16. Cirrus, dew point, fronts, and isotherm are terms commonly associated with the field of
    (A) meteorology.
    (B) archeology.
    (C) oceanography.
    (D) mineralogy.
    (E) seismology.

17. Which one of the following pairs is composed of the two *least* related members?
    (A) Sea cucumber—sea lily
    (B) Horseshoe crab—octopus
    (C) Nautilus—garden slug
    (D) Scallop—squid
    (E) Hydra—sea anemone

18. In organic chemistry, the prefix is an important indication of the structure of the compound. For example:

Prefix	Number of carbons
meth-	1
eth-	2
pro-	3
but-	4
pent-	5

    Given the compounds $CH_3CH_2CH_2CH_3$ and

    $$CH_3 \quad CH \quad CH_3$$
    $$|$$
    $$CH_3$$

    These compounds are both
    (A) alkynes.
    (B) alkenes.
    (C) isomers of butane.
    (D) isomers of propane.
    (E) isomers of pentane.

19. How does the heat from the sun reach the Earth?
    (A) Conduction
    (B) Convection
    (C) Condensation
    (D) Sublimation
    (E) Radiation

Questions 20–23 are based on the following schematic diagram.

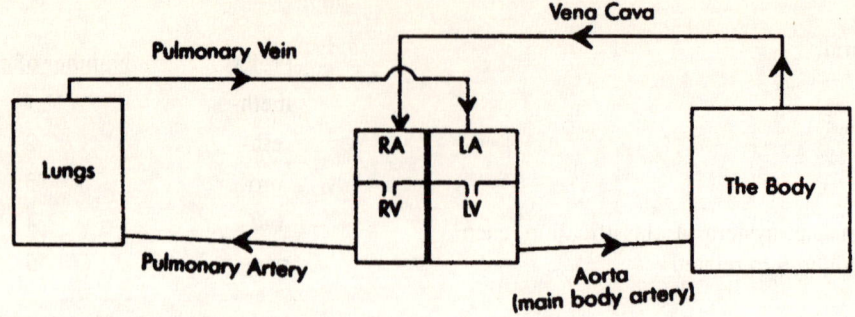

RA = Right Atrium   LA = Left Atrium
RV = Right Ventricle   LV = Left Ventricle

**The above diagram indicates how blood circulates
in the human body.**

20. According to the diagram, in which direction do
arteries carry blood?

(A) To the heart

(B) Away from the heart

(C) Both to and from the heart

(D) Only to the body

(E) Between the body and lungs

21. To which of the following does the left ventricle
pump blood?

(A) The pulmonary artery

(B) The vena cava

(C) The pulmonary vein

(D) The left atrium

(E) All parts of the body

22. The blood found in the pulmonary vein has just
left the lungs. Which of the following statements is
true about this blood?

(A) It is rich in iron.

(B) It is poor in oxygen.

(C) It is rich in oxygen.

(D) It has no blood cells.

(E) It lacks the ability to fight germs.

23. Which of the following sequences shows the actual flow of blood?

(A) Lungs, the heart, right atrium, right ventricle

(B) The body, the lungs, vena cava, aorta

(C) Vena cava, right atrium, left ventricle, aorta

(D) Right ventricle, pulmonary artery, lungs, pulmonary vein

(E) Right ventricle, right atrium, vena cava, the
lungs

24. It is *least* likely to rain when the clouds in our sky
are

(A) nimbostratus.

(B) nimbus.

(C) cirrus.

(D) altocumulus.

(E) cumulonimbus.

25. A form of binary fission in which one of the two
offspring is smaller than the other is

(A) spermatogenesis.

(B) budding.

(C) mitosis.

(D) parthenogenesis.

(E) cogenesis.

Test: Business Education (0100)

Time: 2 Hours
Number of Questions: 120
Format

Multiple-choice questions. Calculators without QWERTY keyboards are allowed.

Purpose of the Test

Designed to measure the preparation of those planning to teach in business education programs at the high school level

Content Categories

- United States Economic Systems—(10 percent)
- Money Management—(14 percent)
- Business and Its Environment—(11 percent)
- Professional Business Education—(20 percent)
- Processing Information—(17 percent)
- Office Procedures and Management, Communications, and Employability Skills—(14 percent)
- Accounting and Marketing—(14 percent)

Category Descriptions
United States Economic Systems

1. Free enterprise, entrepreneurship, and business organization/management: principles of management, business plans, and forms of business organizations

2. Government and banking: fiscal and monetary policies, GDP, taxation, and regulations

3. Economic principles: inflation, deflation, supply and demand, price systems, international trade, labor-management relations

Money Management

1. Business mathematics: Calculations related to interest rates, financial management, budgets, loans, and extensions

2. Consumer education: budgeting, marketplace decisions, information resources, and consumer rights

3. Finance: banking, investing, credit, current value theory

Business and Its Environment

1. Business and consumer law: contracts, agent and principal, insurance, consignment, negotiable instruments, tort law, bankruptcy, consumer legislation, discrimination, negotiation, and global economy

2. Job standards, work standards, business ethics, and policies: peer relationships, employee evaluations, productivity measures

Professional Business Education

1. Current trends and issues: equipment, curriculum, instructional materials, interpretation and use of research

2. Student organizations: PBL, DECA, FBLA, Junior Achievement, Business Professionals of America

3. Professionalism: work ethics, human relations, professional organizations and literature, public relations

4. Methodology/teaching strategies: cooperative, simulation, competency-based, skill areas, group and individual, working with special-needs students, interactive computer software, selecting and/or determining standards for skilled and non-skilled subjects

5. Community relations: advisory committees, partnerships/alliances, visits

6. Federal vocational legislation: Carl D. Perkins Vocational Education Act of 1963 and subsequent amendments

7. Mission/objectives of business education: occupational preparation, responsibility to the business community, responsibility to society, personal-use skills, economic, literacy, training and retraining

8. Curriculum planning and program development: technological concerns, needs assessments, prescription of program outcomes, determination of content and materials, teaching strategies, activities, and evaluation

9. Department management: organization of a department, program evaluation, staffing, budgets, and equipment

10. Classroom management: record keeping, equipment safety, organizing and using classroom resources, managing classroom time and space

11. Counseling in business education: orientation, career awareness, career exploration, preparation, employment information and trends

Processing Information

1. Keyboarding, production, word processing, proofreading, editing, formatting, and entering and verifying data

2. Specialized types of information: statistical, legal, medical

3. Graphics, reprographics

4. Records management, database applications, spreadsheets, data security

5. Processing mail, shorthand and transcription systems, equipment use

6. Simulation productivity

7. Computer literacy, Internet technology

Office Procedures and Management, Communications, and Employability Skills

1. Business communications: written communications, oral communications, telecommunications, listening skills, communication barriers

2. Employability skills: self-assessment techniques, applications, references, job-search techniques, termination, advancement

3. Office procedures and management: workflow topics, assessing references, records management, record keeping, managing travel and meetings, handling mail

Accounting and Marketing

1. Accounting: accounting concepts; terminology and applications; accounting systems; basic accounting cycle of source documents, verifications, analyzing, recording, posting, trial balance, and statement

2. Marketing: sales techniques, advertising, display, buying, wholesale/retail, distribution, service occupations, market analysis, warehousing, inventory control

Business Education

Directions: Each question or incomplete statement is followed by five answer choices. For each question, circle the answer or completion that is best.

1. The accounting equation is correctly stated as
   (A) Owner's Equity = Assets + Liabilities
   (B) Owner's Equity - Assets = Liabilities
   (C) Owner's Equity = Liabilities - Assets
   (D) Assets = Liabilities + Owner's Equity
   (E) Assets + Liabilities + Owner's Equity = 1

2. The purpose of a petty cash fund is to
   (A) take the place of the cash account.
   (B) provide a common drawing fund for the owners of the business.
   (C) provide a fund for making currency expenditures.
   (D) provide a valuation account for cash.
   (E) create a voucher file.

3. The bookkeeper should prepare a bank reconciliation mainly to determine
   (A) which checks are outstanding.
   (B) whether the checkbook balance and the bank statement balance are in agreement.
   (C) the total number of checks written during the month.
   (D) the total amount of cash deposited during the month.
   (E) the monthly net cash flow.

4. Which is the correct procedure for calculating the rate of merchandise turnover?
   (A) Gross Sales divided by Net Sales
   (B) Cost of Goods Sold divided by Average Inventory
   (C) Net Purchases divided by Average Inventory
   (D) Gross Purchases divided by Net Purchases
   (E) Closing Inventory minus Starting Inventory

5. What does the abbreviation CPA represent?
   (A) Certified Professional Accountant
   (B) Certified Public Accountant
   (C) Certified Professional Auditor
   (D) Certified Public Auditor
   (E) Certified Private Auditor

6. A set of instructions that guides the processing of data by an electronic computer is called a
   (A) file.
   (B) diagram.
   (C) program.
   (D) record.
   (E) flowchart.

7. The selling price of a share of stock as published in a daily newspaper is called the
   (A) book value.
   (B) face value.
   (C) par value.
   (D) market value.
   (E) maturity value.

8. Which type of endorsement is shown below?

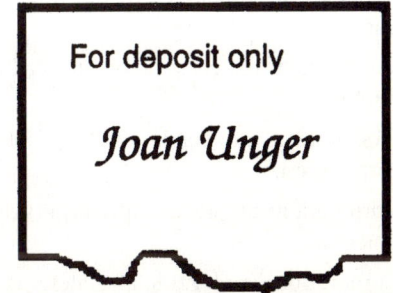

   (A) Restrictive
   (B) Blank
   (C) Full
   (D) Qualified
   (E) Contingent

9. Which phase of the data processing cycle is the same as calculating net pay in a manual system?

   (A) Input

   (B) Processing

   (C) Storing

   (D) Output

   (E) Printing

10. A business check guaranteed for payment by the bank is called a

    (A) bank draft.

    (B) certified check.

    (C) cashier's check.

    (D) personal check.

    (E) money order.

11. Which of the following *cannot* be used as input into a computer?

    (A) Punched card

    (B) Magnetic tape

    (C) Optical scanner

    (D) Printer

    (E) Keyboard

12. Which item on the bank reconciliation statement would require the business to record a journal entry?

    (A) A deposit in transit

    (B) An outstanding check

    (C) A canceled check

    (D) A bank service charge

    (E) A deposit made after the reconciliation closing date

13. Which statement is *not* true of the American corporation?

    (A) Securities of the corporation are readily transferable.

    (B) Stockholders are liable for the debts of the corporation.

    (C) Corporation employees perform specialized functions.

    (D) Corporations are legal in all states.

    (E) Corporations can raise capital easily because of free transferability of securities.

14. Of the following, which one corresponds to a fixed cost?

    (A) Payments for raw materials

    (B) Labor costs

    (C) Transportation charges

    (D) Insurance premiums

    (E) Manager's salary

15. The statement "Today, the dollar is worth about forty-five cents" describes

    (A) inflation.

    (B) prices.

    (C) supply and demand.

    (D) taxation.

    (E) deflation.

16. The consumer price index, an economic measure published by the United States government, may rise in response to certain domestic or foreign events. Which of the following headlines would be *least* likely to cause an increase in the consumer price index?

    (A) "Bumper Harvest Expected in California"

    (B) "Thousands of Chickens Slaughtered in Southeastern Drought"

    (C) "Frost Hits Orange Groves in Coldest Florida Winter"

    (D) "U.S. Imposes Tariffs on Imported Autos"

    (E) "U.S. Embargo on Asian Microchips"

17. Personal income minus personal income taxes is called

    (A) real income.

    (B) gross income.

    (C) elastic income.

    (D) disposable income.

    (E) wages or salary.

18. The Taft-Hartley Act of 1947 provided for all of the following *except*

    (A) permitting employers to sue unions.

    (B) requiring a sixty-day cooling-off period before strikes.

    (C) permitting union contributions to political campaigns.

    (D) requiring union leaders to take oaths that they were not Communist party members.

    (E) requiring unions to make public financial statements.

19. Which of the following is responsible for investigating fraudulent advertising and the sale of harmful products?

    (A) Federal Trade Commission

    (B) Securities and Exchange Commission

    (C) Department of Labor

    (D) Interstate Commerce Commission

    (E) Department of Human Services

20. In order to compute the income taxes you owe the federal government this year, your employer is required to give you a ____ that lists your earnings and withholding for the past year.

    (A) 1040A form

    (B) W2 form

    (C) Social Security form

    (D) exemption statement

    (E) W4 form

21. The basic components of total demand are

    (A) human resources, natural resources, and capital resources.

    (B) consumption, investment, and government spending.

    (C) inflation, deflation, and taxes.

    (D) imports and exports.

    (E) food, clothing, and housing.

22. Americans pay many different types of taxes to federal, state, and local governments. Choose the best example of a tax that we do *not* pay in the United States.

    (A) Payroll tax

    (B) Excise tax

    (C) Value-added tax

    (D) Sales tax

    (E) Income tax

23. Susan Johnson earned $15,000 last year. Sam Milner earned $63,000 last year. Each person was required to pay a special tax of $350. Which of the following terms best describes this tax?

    (A) Proportional

    (B) Regressive

    (C) Inexpensive

    (D) Progressive

    (E) Unearned

24. Payments to a worker, his dependents, and/or survivors in the event of retirement, disability, or death are generally covered by the system of insurance known as

    (A) unemployment compensation.

    (B) Social Security.

    (C) workers' compensation.

    (D) pension fund.

    (E) profit sharing.

25. A short period of somewhat decreased business activity is known as a

    (A) boom.

    (B) depression.

    (C) recession.

    (D) crash.

    (E) demand.

Test: Chemistry (0240)

Time: 2 hours
Number of Questions: 120
Format: Multiple-choice questions

Purpose of the Test

Designed to measure the preparation of those planning to teach secondary school chemistry

Content Categories

- Structure of Matter—(17 percent)
- States of Matter—(17 percent)
- Reactions of Matter—(48 percent)
- Particulate Samples of Matter—(8 percent)
- Laboratory Handling of Matter; Environmental Issues Related to Chemistry—(10 percent)

Category Descriptions

Structure of Matter

1. Atomic and nuclear structure
2. Bonding
3. Intermolecular forces

States of Matter

1. Phase changes
2. Gases, liquids, and solids
3. Solutions: noncolligative and colligative properties, concentrations

Reactions of Matter

1. Acids and Bases
2. Kinetics
3. Thermodynamics
4. Equilibrium
5. Electrochemistry and oxidation-reaction
6. Stoichiometry

Particulate Samples of Matter

1. Periodic properties and trends
2. Types of organic compounds and their principal reactions and important inorganic compounds
3. Familiar metals and nonmetals
4. Names and formulas

Laboratory Handling of Matter; Environmental Issues Related to Chemistry

1. Safety precautions
2. Data handling
3. Important techniques and experiments
4. Environmental issues related to chemistry

Chemistry

Directions: Each question or incomplete statement is followed by five answer choices. For each question, circle the answer or completion that is best.

1. If redox reactions are forced to occur by use of an externally applied electric current, the procedure is called
   (A) neutralization.
   (B) esterification.
   (C) electrolysis.
   (D) hydrolysis.
   (E) saponification.

2. Given the equation:

   $$C_6H_{12}O_6 \xrightarrow[\text{zymase (from yeast)}]{} 2C_2H_5OH + 2CO_2$$

   The reaction represented by the equation is called
   (A) polymerization.
   (B) fermentation.
   (C) esterification.
   (D) saponification.
   (E) neutralization.

3. The structure ⬡ represents a molecule of

   (A) cyclopentane.
   (B) cyclopropane.
   (C) toluene.
   (D) benzene.
   (E) cyclohexane.

4. Which particle has a negative charge and a mass that is approximately $\frac{1}{1836}$ the mass of a proton?
   (A) A neutron
   (B) An alpha particle
   (C) An electron
   (D) A positron
   (E) A photon

5. In 6.20 hours, a 100-gram sample of $^{112}_{47}Ag$ decays to 25.0 grams. What is the half-life of $^{112}_{47}Ag$?
   (A) 1.60 hours
   (B) 3.10 hours
   (C) 6.20 hours
   (D) 12.4 hours
   (E) 18.6 hours

6. Which ion is the conjugate base of H_2SO_4?
   (A) SO_3^{2-}
   (B) S^{2-}
   (C) HSO_3^-
   (D) HSO_4^-
   (E) $H_3SO_4^+$

7. What is the name of the process that begins with the joining of monomer molecules?
   (A) Fermentation
   (B) Polymerization
   (C) Esterification
   (D) Hydrogenation
   (E) Isomerization

8. A 9.90-gram sample of a hydrated salt is heated to a constant mass of 6.60 grams. What was the percent by mass of water contained in the sample?
   (A) 66.7
   (B) 50.0
   (C) 33.3
   (D) 16.5
   (E) 133.3

9. Which process occurs when dry ice, $CO_2(s)$, is changed into $CO_2(g)$?
   (A) Crystallization
   (B) Condensation
   (C) Sublimation
   (D) Solidification
   (E) Decomposition

10. How many moles of water are contained in 0.250 mole of $CuSO_4 \cdot 5H_2O$?

    (A) 62.5

    (B) 40.0

    (C) 4.62

    (D) 4.50

    (E) 1.25

11. Which is the formula for magnesium sulfide?

    (A) MgS

    (B) $MgSO_3$

    (C) MnS

    (D) $MnSO_3$

    (E) $MgSO_4$

12. Which formula represents a polar molecule?

    (A) CH_4

    (B) Cl_2

    (C) NH_3

    (D) N_2

    (E) CO_2

13. Which of the following gases is monatomic at STP?

    (A) Hydrogen

    (B) Chlorine

    (C) Oxygen

    (D) Helium

    (E) Nitrogen

14. The type of reaction represented by the equation $C_2H_4 + H_2 \rightarrow C_2H_6$ is called

    (A) substitution.

    (B) polymerization.

    (C) addition.

    (D) esterification.

    (E) dehydration.

15. The four single bonds of a carbon atom are spatially directed toward the corners of a regular

    (A) triangle.

    (B) rectangle.

    (C) square.

    (D) tetrahedron.

    (E) cube.

16. Which equilibrium expression best represents the ionization constant (K_a) for the weak-acid equilibrium below?

$$HX(aq) \rightleftharpoons H^+(aq) + X^-(aq)$$

(A) $K_a = \dfrac{\left[H^+\right] + \left[X^-\right]}{\left[HX\right]}$

(B) $K_a = \dfrac{\left[HX\right]}{\left[H^+\right] + \left[X^-\right]}$

(C) $K_a = \dfrac{\left[H^+\right]\left[X^-\right]}{\left[HX\right]}$

(D) $K_a = \dfrac{\left[HX\right]}{\left[H^+\right]\left[X^-\right]}$

(E) $K_a = \dfrac{\left[H^+\right] - \left[X^-\right]}{\left[HX\right]}$

17. Which hydrocarbon is a member of the alkane series?

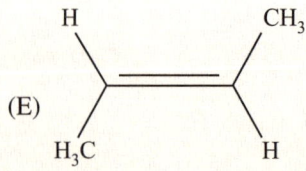

18. The graph below illustrates the change in the volume of a gas sample as its temperature rises at constant pressure.

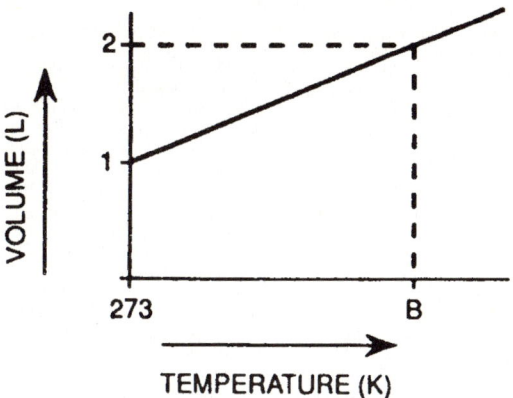

What temperature is represented by point B?

(A) 546 K

(B) 298 K

(C) 273 K

(D) 0 K

(E) 400 K

19. What is the heat of vaporization of water in calories per gram?

(A) 79.7

(B) 273

(C) 373

(D) 539

(E) 100

20. Which electron configuration represents an atom in the excited state?

(A) $1s^2 2s^1$

(B) $1s^2 2s^2 2p^6$

(C) $1s^2 2s^2 2p^6 4s^1$

(D) $1s^2 2s^2 2p^6 3s^2 3p^3$

(E) $1s^2 2s^2 2p^6 3s^1$

21. Which sublevel configuration correctly represents a completely filled third principal energy level?

(A) $3s^2 3p^6 3d^8$

(B) $3s^2 3p^2 3d^{10}$

(C) $3s^2 3p^6 3d^{10}$

(D) $3s^2 3p^6 3d^5$

(E) $3s^2 3p^5 3d^9$

22. One of the products of a fermentation reaction is

(A) an alcohol.

(B) an alkane.

(C) a salt.

(D) an ester.

(E) a ketone.

23. Which salt forms a colored aqueous solution?

(A) $Mg(NO_3)_2$

(B) $NaNO_3$

(C) $Ca(NO_3)_2$

(D) $Ni(NO_3)_2$

(E) $BaCl_2$

24. The graph below represents a solid being heated at a uniform rate, starting at a temperature below its melting point.

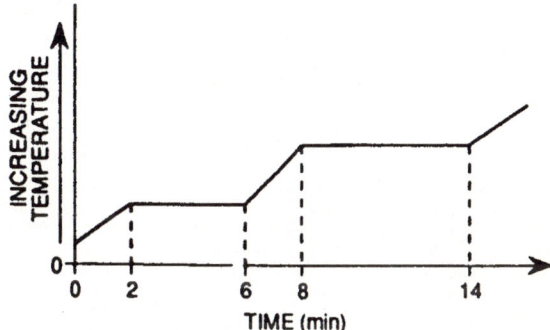

Once the solid reaches its melting point, how many minutes are required to completely melt the solid?

(A) 6

(B) 2

(C) 8

(D) 4

(E) 5

25. Given the reaction:

$$2SO_2(g) + O_2(g) \rightarrow 2SO_3(g)$$

What is the total number of liters of $O_2(g)$, measured at STP, that will react completely with 4.00 moles of SO_2?

(A) 1.00 L

(B) 0.500 L

(C) 22.4 L

(D) 44.8 L

(E) 67.2 L

Test: Early Childhood Education (0020)

Time: 2 hours
Number of Questions: 120
Format: Multiple-choice questions

Purpose of the Test

Designed to measure the preparation of prospective teachers of preschool through primary-grade students

Content Categories

- Understanding the Nature of the Growth, Development, and Learning of Young Children—(31 percent)
- Recognizing Factors That Influence Individual Growth and Development—(10 percent)
- Recognizing Appropriate and Inappropriate Applications of Developmental and Curriculum Theory—(12 percent)
- Planning and Implementing Curriculum—(29 percent)
- Evaluating and Reporting Student Progress and the Effectiveness of Instruction—(12 percent)
- Understanding Professional and Legal Responsibilities—(6 percent)

Category Descriptions

Understanding the Nature of the Growth, Development, and Learning of Young Children

1. Language Development: oral language development, including speaking (bilingual skills, storytelling), listening comprehension, developing vocabulary and understanding language systems; written language development, such as invented spelling, print awareness, and ideas in writing

2. Cognitive development: concepts of the physical world and of causal relationships and signing in all communication systems, such as art, mathematics, and music; skill development in areas such as manipulative skills, symbol recognition, and logical reasoning

3. Person/social development: self-concept, locus of control, learning style, temperament, sex, gender role, stages of social behavior, effect of discrimination, stereotypes, and aggression

4. Physical development: typical and atypical growth and development; symptoms of illness; fine and gross motor development; safety; and health

Recognizing Factors That Influence Individual Growth and Development

1. Familial Factors: family relationships, parental attitudes, birth order, and siblings
2. Physiological factors: effects of genetic and congenital maturational factors
3. Nutritional/hygienic factors: diet, sleep, exercise, and environmental conditions
4. Cultural factors: effects of the interaction of cultural values; roles of the primary transmitters of the culture (schools, community, family, and the mass media); and effects of political, economic, and cultural influences, including ethnic, regional, and religious influences

Recognizing Appropriate and Inappropriate Applications
of Developmental and Curriculum Theory

1. Understanding major early childhood curriculum models and approaches, such as Montessori, Froebel, Bank Street, Bereiter/Engelmann, Kamii, Weikert, Head Start, Emergent Literacy, developmentally appropriate practice, play-based and integrated curriculums.

2. Understanding the contributions of major streams of developmental and learning theory to early childhood education practices, such as psychoanalytic, social-learning, behaviorist, and cognitive theories.

Planning and Implementing Curriculum

1. Organizing and managing the physical learning environment: use of materials, indoor space, outdoor space, and equipment

2. Managing interpersonal interactions in the classroom: recognizing how teacher's behavior and attitudes effect children's learning and development, helping children learn to manage their behavior

3. Utilizing outside resources in curriculum planning and implementation: family and community

4. Planning, selecting, and implementing appropriate curriculum experiences and instructional strategies: whole language, language experience, and basal approaches; mathematics manipulatives; inquiry and discovery in science; physical/motor experiences; aesthetic and affective experiences, social experiences

Evaluating and Reporting Student Progress and the Effectiveness of Instruction

1. Maintaining useful records of a child's development and progress in learning

2. Using formal and informal assessment results in planning for a class and for individuals

3. Selection and use of formal and informal assessment instruments for evaluating developmental progress and effectiveness of curriculum experiences

4. Communicating effectively with parents about a child's total development progress

Understanding Professional and Legal Responsibilities

1. Being cognizant of legal responsibilities and regulations that affect teaching in the early childhood setting

2. Maintaining effective interactions with other adults who function within the learning setting

Early Childhood Education

Directions: Each question or incomplete statement is followed by five answer choices. For each question, circle the answer or completion that is best.

1. In establishing early childhood management, a teacher asks a child to assume responsibility for her actions, discusses the effect of the action, and has the child make a plan of how she will handle the situation the next time. These factors are all components of
   (A) life space interview.
   (B) time out.
   (C) reality therapy.
   (D) managing surface behavior.
   (E) behavior modification.

2. In organizing the curriculum of an early childhood class, one should
   I. provide a variety of learning centers.
   II. use a thematic approach in the teaching of various concepts.
   III. use a developmental approach to provide for differences in learning style.
   IV. provide the students with a lot of factual material, such as photographs and books to increase cognitive ability.

   (A) II, III, and IV only
   (B) I and II only
   (C) I, II, and III only
   (D) I only
   (E) III and IV only

3. All of the following statements would describe the cognitive development of a preschool youngster *except*
   (A) has little concept of clock time.
   (B) can tell sex differences.
   (C) sees many divergent objects as equivalent.
   (D) cannot recognize pictures depicting various emotional responses.
   (E) does not understand irony and metaphor.

4. Which educational theorist does *not* subscribe to the open educational approach to early childhood education?
   (A) Pestalozzi
   (B) Froebel
   (C) Montessori
   (D) Dewey
   (E) Hewlett

5. Which skills are often neglected in a first- and second-grade language arts curriculum?
   I. How to use and enjoy reading
   II. Thinking skills
   III. How to interpret the symbols of reading
   IV. Answering of *wh* questions

   (A) III and IV only
   (B) I and III only
   (C) II and IV only
   (D) I and II only
   (E) all of the above

6. Which would be an appropriate social studies question to ask of a first-grade student?
   (A) Where would you go to get a prescription?
   (B) Why did the Pony Express end?
   (C) Why do more people live in the United States than in Canada?
   (D) Which animal quacks?
   (E) How does a government get money to pay for goods and services?

7. All of the following are good ways to manage a preschool classroom *except*

   (A) have the day planned in advance for the students.

   (B) use specific social-behavioral procedures to minimize classroom discipline problems.

   (C) use color codes for identifying materials and classifying books.

   (D) organize furniture to make the room as easily accessible as possible.

   (E) teach rules as they need to learn them during the course of the year.

8. How would you describe the social-emotional behavior of a typical six-year-old child from a middle-class background?

   (A) Socially interacts with members of the opposite sex

   (B) Sparing in affection

   (C) A member of a gang

   (D) Well on the way to developing an independent identity

   (E) Scorns all things childish

9. This educator stresses the use of multiage groupings and self-correcting material in creating a prepared environment to meet a child's need to organize the world. The theory being described is that of

   (A) Piaget.

   (B) Bruner.

   (C) Rousseau.

   (D) Montessori.

   (E) Pestalozzi.

10. Part of an early childhood music curriculum is teaching children to identify, play, and explain the purpose of various types of instruments. Which of the instruments below is considered a rhythm instrument?

    (A) Wrist bells

    (B) Xylophone

    (C) Marimba

    (D) Guitar

    (E) Ukulele

11. Which does *not* describe four- to six-year-old children in the preoperational stage of development?

    (A) Rapidly acquiring language and learning new words

    (B) Constantly exploring, manipulating, and experimenting with the environment

    (C) Beginning to see the viewpoints of people other than themselves

    (D) Concrete in understanding the physical environment

    (E) Good understanding of concepts that reflect physical and tactile alternatives reflecting a common characteristic

12. All of the following are ways parents can play a part in a child's learning progress *except*

    (A) observing their child read, give reports, and write essays.

    (B) following through on classroom assignments.

    (C) extending their own education to better educate their child.

    (D) inquiring to make sure the curriculum fits with their moral standards.

    (E) being a classroom volunteer.

13. Using a basal reading approach, a first-grader will learn all the following decoding and/or comprehension skills *except*

    (A) CVC words.

    (B) consonant blends and diagraphs.

    (C) recalling facts of a story.

    (D) syllabication of multisyllable words.

    (E) sequencing.

14. Which does *not* illustrate the social behavior of a nursery school child?

    (A) Preschool children develop a vocabulary of scatology.

    (B) A preschooler's social life revolves around the world of play.

    (C) Boys and girls settle property disputes by snatching and fleeing.

    (D) Whereas boys engage in physical combat, girls use their tongues as weapons.

    (E) Boys and girls rarely resort to crying if they are hurt or angry.

15. All of the following are examples of reading readiness skills *except*

    (A) auditory discrimination.

    (B) sequencing.

    (C) visual discrimination.

    (D) identification of initial blends.

    (E) recognition of uppercase and lowercase letters.

16. In teaching multiplication to a third-grade student, which method should lead to the greatest understanding of the concept?

    (A) Drilling of basic facts

    (B) Teaching that multiplication is a faster way of adding

    (C) Weaning children away from the multiplication table

    (D) First teaching the concept of partial products

    (E) Prohibiting the use of calculators

17. Which concepts are developed by using blocks in a preschool setting?

    I. Measurement, area, spatial relations, and seriation

    II. Balance, gravity, and stability

    III. Oral language usage

    IV. Prereading skills such as visual discrimination and matching

    (A) I, II, and III only

    (B) I and II only

    (C) I, II, III, and IV

    (D) II, III, and IV only

    (E) II only

18. An effective management technique used in kindergarten to let children know how many students can play at a learning center at one time is to

    (A) assign which children can use each center at the beginning of the week.

    (B) let the students choose who can be at each learning center.

    (C) set up colored clothespins at each center and let each child using the center take one and return it after play.

    (D) set up a check chart for the students to fill in.

    (E) color code the objects at each center.

19. Which type of play is most characteristic of a four- to six-year-old child?

    I. Solitary play

    II. Onlooker play

    III. Associative play

    IV. Cooperative play

    (A) I, II, and III only

    (B) II only

    (C) IV only

    (D) II and IV only

    (E) III and IV only

20. Pouring a set amount of water from a tall, thin glass to a thick, fat one illustrates

    (A) transduction.

    (B) conservation.

    (C) cross-classification.

    (D) volume.

    (E) cause and effect.

21. All of the following are disadvantages of a basal reading approach *except*

    (A) vocabulary unrelated to a child's experiences.

    (B) little child input.

    (C) little student-student interaction.

    (D) little room for individualization.

    (E) highly structured.

22. Which factors describe the role of play in the preschool and early childhood years?

    I. A child makes a game of everything he does.

    II. A child can separate reality from fantasy.

    III. Play is a way of trying on different roles.

    IV. Imagination tends to increase due to expanding knowledge and emotional range.

    (A) I, III, and IV only

    (B) II, III, and IV only

    (C) III and IV only

    (D) I and II only

    (E) I, II, and III only

23. Which is a good game to improve spelling skills informally?

    (A) Hangman

    (B) Mystery sheet

    (C) Create poem booklets

    (D) Secret code for letters

    (E) Play "find the bell"

24. Which reading approach for lower-grade students encourages the instructor to write down exactly what is said so that the child can get the idea that print is talk written down and that he or she can read it?

    (A) Organic reading

    (B) Directed reading-thinking approach

    (C) Individualized reading

    (D) Language experience

    (E) Cloze

25. Many early childhood theorists believe that an effective learning environment should be one that meets the social, emotional, motor, and cognitive needs of a child. Such an environment would be based on all of the following beliefs *except*

    (A) children grow and learn at different rates unrelated to chronological age.

    (B) children need to be motivated to learn, and they learn best when they follow an organized structure directed by the teacher.

    (C) learning is something a child does rather than something done to him.

    (D) play is a child's way of working and learning.

    (E) children learn from each other.

Test: Education in the Elementary School (0010)

Time: 2 hours

Number of Questions: 150

Format: Multiple-choice questions

Purpose of the Test

Designed to measure the preparation of prospective teachers of primary grades (K-3) through upper-elementary/middle-school grades (4-8)

Content Categories

- Reading/Language Arts—(34 percent)
- Mathematics—(17 percent)
- Science—(14 percent)
- Social Studies—(14 percent)
- Fine Arts—(14 percent)
- Physical Education—(7 percent)

Category Descriptions

Reading/Language Arts

1. Strategies for word recognition
2. Comprehension
3. Major approaches to and effective strategies for the teaching and assessment of listening, speaking, reading, and writing skills
4. Strategies for locating and using information
5. Readiness factors in reading and writing
6. Integration of reading and language arts
7. Children's literature

Mathematics

1. Number theory
2. Problem solving
3. Estimation and approximation
4. Prenumber concepts, decimal numeration, operations on sets of numbers
5. Geometry: nonmetric, metric, and coordinate
6. Handheld calculators and computers
7. Probability and statistics
8. Measurement
9. Selection and use of manipulatives
10. Content-specific pedagogy

Science

1. Describing objects and events in unambiguous language
2. Observing similarities and differences in objects and events in the environment
3. Model building and forecasting
4. Basic principles of health education
5. Forming hypotheses, planning and conducting experiments, and organizing data
6. Content-specific pedagogy

Social Studies

1. Governments
2. Human behavior in society
3. Social organizations
4. Social structures: communication, industrialization, technology, economics, and transportation
5. Skills: organizing data, comparing and contrasting, model building, problem solving, planning, and forecasting, as they relate to social studies content
6. Content-specific pedagogy

Fine Arts

1. Music and art of other cultures
2. Teaching strategies to encourage creativity and appreciation of music and art
3. Instrumental music
4. Art therapy
5. Basic concepts in music and art: rhythm, melody, harmony, and timbre in music; design in art
6. Knowledge about and appropriate activities for music and art education for various grade levels

Physical Education

1. Classroom and playground safety procedures
2. Design of appropriate activities for various grade levels
3. High- and low-organization games
4. Value of games and sports
5. Movement exploration
6. Body coordination and movement coordination activities

Education in the Elementary School

Directions: Each question or incomplete statement is followed by five answer choices. For each question, circle the answer or completion that is best.

1. To maintain good student behavior, teachers must constantly monitor compliance with class procedures and student involvement in learning. All are effective monitoring techniques *except*

   (A) scan the whole class and move about the room.

   (B) focus entirely on the students you are teaching when instructing small groups.

   (C) check the progress of each student when students are working on individual assignments and give verbal and nonverbal feedback.

   (D) avoid letting groups of students congregate around your desk to obstruct your view of the class.

   (E) begin all work as whole group activities before individual seatwork is assigned.

2. Which author was *not* involved in the Progressive movement, which swept through elementary education in the early part of the twentieth century?

   (A) William White

   (B) Francis Parker

   (C) John Dewey

   (D) Edward L. Thorndike

   (E) William Wirt

3. A major problem in elementary schools today is teacher burnout. Instructors have to learn to stay relaxed and to enjoy their jobs. All are good techniques to avoid burnout *except*

   (A) learn to separate yourself from your students' problems at the end of the day.

   (B) take acting lessons to improve your stage presence.

   (C) do lesson plans and mark homework during lunch periods to avoid doing work at home.

   (D) focus on even small positive events.

   (E) learn to tolerate some things and ignore others.

4. Which of the following are effective techniques an elementary instructor can use to teach about ecology and conservation?

   I. Classify different trees, animals, and insects.

   II. Study a garden and chart the food chains between one species and another.

   III. Discuss interesting and motivating facts about different animals and plants.

   IV. Place different chemicals on plants and observe; then describe the effects in a journal.

   (A) II and IV only

   (B) I, III, and IV only

   (C) II and III only

   (D) I, II, and IV only

   (E) I only

5. A good way to avoid sexual stereotypes in the classroom is by encouraging children to try activities associated with the other sex. The most effective way to go about this is to

   (A) refuse to take no for an answer, even when a student does not wish to participate in an activity.

   (B) encourage parents to tell the students they must participate in activities usually done by the opposite sex.

   (C) have boys participate in cooking but in the safety of like-sex groups.

   (D) teach social studies lessons about sexual stereotypes.

   (E) put several girls in a boys' activity, such as building a model airplane.

6. Which of the following are good examples of high-level pivotal questions that give history a human dimension that ten- or eleven-year-olds can grasp?

    I. What was Martin Luther King's feeling when he spent a night in jail for going into a white restaurant?

    II. How did Cortés feel about taking the belongings of the Aztecs and keeping them?

    III. How did the Native Americans feel when the skills they always lived by could no longer be applied to the living conditions imposed upon them by their European conquerors?

    IV. How did the tools of a medieval manor influence the living conditions of people at that time?

    (A) II, III, and IV only

    (B) I, II, and IV only

    (C) I, II, and III only

    (D) III and IV only

    (E) IV only

7. It has been concluded that children whose parents read to them show improved academic achievement. Recent research has shown that

    (A) most parents stop reading to their children after age nine

    (B) children do not need constant reinforcement to become lifelong readers

    (C) there is little correlation between being a good reader and watching television

    (D) reading skill only slightly correlates with socioeconomic status

    (E) American children in the middle grades are statistically the best readers as compared to other Western countries

8. Which is *not* an effective method to improve reading comprehension?

    (A) Activate background knowledge

    (B) Have students predict what will happen next in a story

    (C) Teach the meaning of Greek and Latin prefixes to improve vocabulary comprehension

    (D) Visualize events within a story

    (E) Analyze information about a story aloud

9. All of the following describe the development of children age eight to eleven *except*

    (A) they shift from impulsivity to the ability to grasp the meaning of social organization and adaptation

    (B) sex differences in IQ scores become more evident

    (C) there is an increased objectivity in thinking

    (D) they understand the law of conservation

    (E) abstract thinking and judgment come into play

10. Examining the history of elementary education in the United States, one can conclude that

    (A) public support for education has existed since colonial times in the United States

    (B) religion has played little role in shaping education in the United States

    (C) school funding was adequate in the late eighteenth and early nineteenth century

    (D) education is a right under the United States Constitution

    (E) state-supported public education did not come into general existence until the middle of the nineteenth century

11. Why should a middle-grade student study the Eskimos, Aztecs, and Native Americans in preference to the Greeks and Romans?

    (A) Roman and Greek society is more complexly structured, requiring abstract conceptualization of many broad social science concepts.

    (B) Eskimo, Aztec, and Native American cultures are better known to elementary school students and demonstrate complex social structures in a simpler fashion.

    (C) Roman and Greek cultures are too simplistic for this age level.

    (D) The teaching of Roman and Greek civilization is mandated by the state to be taught in secondary school only.

    (E) Students of this age have to be taught one civilization at a time to facilitate comprehension.

12. All are effective methods to handle students who chronically avoid work *except*

    (A) give assistance or modify the assignment for students who cannot complete their work

    (B) break the assignment into smaller parts

    (C) call the parent in to create a plan of action

    (D) keep the student a few minutes after school to help complete assignments

    (E) safeguard the student's self-image by not lowering his or her grade

13. During the middle school years, reading should
    (A) be taught as a separate subject
    (B) focus on the development of phonic analysis
    (C) be used as a way to gain information from various subject areas
    (D) concentrate on basal stories to develop specific skills
    (E) be taught in the afternoon before the end of the day

14. A ten-year-old boy in fourth grade comes from a dysfunctional family and has been abused and neglected. He has been in six foster homes and has attended nine different elementary schools. The student is presently decoding on the second-grade level, but he can comprehend material orally at the fourth- or fifth-grade level. The most probable cause(s) of this student's reading problem is (are)

    I. neurological factors
    II. emotional factors
    III. poor teaching
    IV. immaturity

    (A) I and III only
    (B) I only
    (C) III only
    (D) I and IV only
    (E) II only

15. Which is *not* an effective lesson reinforcing the application of geographic concepts?
    (A) Using a physical map to figure out which sites are practical as settlements in terms of food, shelter, and transportation
    (B) Learning the capitals and topographical features of politically significant countries
    (C) Charting the spread of a nineteenth-century typhoid epidemic using a London street map
    (D) Comparing and contrasting ethnic and political maps to figure out the causes of both World Wars
    (E) Having students inflate or deflate the size of countries based on their Gross Domestic Product

16. Progressing from the factual, to comprehension, to application, to analysis, to synthesis, and finally to evaluation was developed by
    (A) Hertzberg.
    (B) Maslow.
    (C) Bloom.
    (D) Bruner.
    (E) Piaget.

17. The *best* way to develop math concepts is by
    (A) learning key words to decide operations.
    (B) solving problems by looking for correct answers.
    (C) learning math as applied to actual situations, such as its being a tool of science.
    (D) using a concrete approach to solving problems.
    (E) showing students multiple approaches to solving math examples and problems.

18. A science teacher would conduct experiments using images and lenses to give students an understanding of
    (A) laser beams.
    (B) turbines.
    (C) barometers.
    (D) natural law.
    (E) mirrors.

19. All are problems in meeting the needs of medically fragile students *except*
    (A) they are mandated to be in classes that contain only other health-impaired children.
    (B) teachers have to perform medical duties without the benefit of medical supervision or assistance.
    (C) such children have the right to attend public school and be provided with medical assistance.
    (D) paraprofessionals are asked to perform procedures that are not part of their job description.
    (E) dealing with a child's medical needs takes time away from academics.

20. Critics of multicultural education as it is presently being taught at the elementary level state that

    (A) too few ethnic groups are being discussed.

    (B) such a curriculum does not foster a national identity.

    (C) there should no longer be any emphasis on Western Civilization.

    (D) such a curriculum must have a bilingual component.

    (E) sexual orientation should be an important aspect of such a curriculum.

21. Which is an inappropriate way to manage off-task behavior?

    (A) Redirect a student's attention to task and check his progress to make sure he is continuing to work.

    (B) Make eye contact or move closer to the student.

    (C) Remind the student of the correct procedure to use, and ask him if he remembers it.

    (D) Directly tell the student to stop any inappropriate response.

    (E) Stop an activity to correct a child who is no longer on task.

22. A child who is in the resource room is placed in your class. He sometimes has difficulty understanding you or following directions. Effective methods to deal with such a youngster are described by all of the following *except*

    (A) seat him as close to you as possible.

    (B) work individually with the student when the rest of the class is busy.

    (C) talk with the resource room teacher to find out what he can do.

    (D) ask the child's previous year's teacher for suggestions.

    (E) give the child less demanding work than the rest of the class.

23. On the first day of school, a student comes in 45 minutes late. Which of the following statements describes the best way to handle this situation?

    (A) Do not allow the student in the room until you discuss with her the rules of punctuality.

    (B) Treat her as warmly as the other students, and tell her you will talk to her about what she missed as soon as you can.

    (C) Give the class some seatwork activity while you bring this student to your desk so as to write a note to her parent.

    (D) Send her to an administrator to let her know your firm stand about punctuality.

    (E) Tell her she must come tomorrow with her parents.

24. The *least* effective procedure in the teaching of historical concepts would be to

    (A) look at pictures of buildings that existed fifty to 100 years earlier on a particular neighborhood street.

    (B) study old maps of a city and compare the differences to a modern street map.

    (C) have students interview old people for recollections of how they got around before cars were plentiful.

    (D) examine commonplace appliances used 100 years ago.

    (E) read about important political leaders and heroes of their community.

25. Which are effective methods in teaching students critical reading skills?

    I. Interpret editorials about a particular subject from different newspapers.

    II. Read and interpret three different reviews on a movie.

    III. Identify and categorize different propaganda techniques.

    IV. Distinguish fiction from nonfiction materials.

    (A) I and II only

    (B) III and IV only

    (C) III only

    (D) I, II, and III only

    (E) I, III, and IV only

Test: Education of Students with Mental Retardation (0320)

Time: 2 hours
Number of Questions: 150
Format: Multiple-choice questions

Purpose of the Test

Designed to measure the preparation of those who have completed teacher training programs in mental retardation

Content Categories

- Educational Principles and Professional Considerations—(14 percent)
- Understanding Students with Mental Retardation—(25 percent)
- Knowledge of Assessment Principles and Practices—(10 percent)
- Delivery of Services—(21 percent)
- Design and Implementation of Instruction—(30 percent)

Category Descriptions

Educational Principles and Professional Considerations

1. Child-development issues in learning, social, motor, cultural, and linguistic skills areas
2. Professional advocacy in relation to families, colleagues, and community
3. Legal aspects in relation to students, parents, confidentiality, and schools

Understanding Students with Mental Retardation

1. Characteristics of children with mental retardation, such as adaptive and affective behaviors; learning and motivation; and physical, personality, and motor development
2. Definition and degrees of severity of mental retardation
3. Causation and prevention, including genetic and environmental factors
4. Public attitudes, post-school adjustment, family adjustment, early intervention, community-based training
5. History, trends, and contemporary issues (including special education philosophies)
6. Characteristics of students with mental retardation with secondary disabilities such as speech impediments, physical disabilities, and behavior disorders

Knowledge of Assessment Principles and Practices

1. Basic measurement concepts such as validity, reliability, standard deviation, nondiscriminatory evaluation, and norm-referenced and criteron-referenced techniques
2. Ability to select, administer, and interpret teacher-administered assessments
3. Knowledge, interpretation, and application of specialized evaluations

Delivery of Services

1. Teacher's role as a multidisciplinary team member

2. Knowledge of Individuals with Disabilities Education Act

3. Knowledge of placement options within the school and district, including appropriate least restrictive environment

4. Collaboration with other school personnel

Design and Implementation of Instruction

1. Basic curriculum models and related materials, including social learning, life-centered, daily living, community-based, and functional academics

2. Appropriate use and adaptation of instructional methods, materials, and approaches, such as task analysis, diagnostic-prescriptive, direct and adapted instruction, computers, adaptive devices, and augmentative communication

3. Classroom management, including social environment, student behavior, behavior modification, and non-aversive methods

Education of Students with Mental Retardation

Directions: Each question or incomplete statement is followed by five answer choices. For each question, circle the answer or completion that is best.

1. Using task analysis, a teacher has to write short-term goals to improve the fine-motor development of a moderately retarded student. Which of the following objectives will facilitate the development of this skill?

   I. The student will push a button that is halfway through a loop using his forefinger and thumb four out of five times.

   II. The student will button his coat two out of three times.

   III. The student will use snaps on his jacket, with 80 percent accuracy.

   IV. The student will pick up small buttons from a table and push them through $\frac{1}{8}$-inch slots eight out of ten times.

   (A) I and IV only
   (B) II and III only
   (C) I and III only
   (D) II and IV only
   (E) IV only

2. Why has it been difficult to define mental retardation?

   (A) Researchers cannot define the nature of intelligence.
   (B) Different disciplines view mental retardation from their own perspectives.
   (C) It cannot be determined which abilities to include in the definition.
   (D) Intellectual and emotional factors are not independent of each other.
   (E) All of the above.

3. All these statements describe trainable mentally retarded students *except*

   (A) IQ between 25 and 50 on most standardized intelligence tests.
   (B) can hold an independent job if it is structured.
   (C) need to learn self-care skills and common safety rules.
   (D) need supervision, protection, and care.
   (E) can learn to walk, feed themselves, and speak single phrases but at a very slow pace.

4. Cognitive growth is seen as a continuous interaction between the individual and the environment. The more a child is stimulated, the greater his intellectual development. Accordingly, a mentally retarded child proceeds through the same intellectual stages as a normal-functioning child but at a slower pace. These ideas are best associated with

   (A) Bruner.
   (B) Bijou.
   (C) Terman.
   (D) Piaget.
   (E) Gagne.

5. Which skill would be *least* emphasized in the education of severely retarded students?

   (A) Self-care
   (B) Total communication
   (C) Occupational skills
   (D) Socialization
   (E) Prevocational skills

6. Why are methods and procedures used to instruct mentally retarded students also used for autistic children?

(A) Methods to teach autistic children are not yet well developed.

(B) Autistic children need a less structured approach to learning.

(C) Many autistic children are functionally retarded although their intellectual development may really be higher.

(D) Such instruction rapidly increases the intellectual and social ability of autistic children.

(E) Both autistic and retarded children benefit from small class environments.

7. Which of these people worked with the "Wild Boy of Aveyron," thus proving that intelligence was fluid and not fixed?

(A) Binet

(B) Itard

(C) Sequin

(D) Montessori

(E) Rousseau

8. Which can best describe the development of rehabilitative practices for the mentally retarded in the 1960s and 1970s?

(A) Judicial and legislative responsibility for the mentally retarded became widely recognized.

(B) There was an increase in the institutionalization of the mentally retarded in this era.

(C) There was a widespread formation of parent organizations for the mentally retarded during this time.

(D) Theories disproving fixed intelligence came into existence during this period.

(E) The teaching of retarded children included individualized instruction, working with the whole child as well as motor and sensory education.

9. A moderately retarded student who is fourteen years old is still not independent enough to use public transportation. He is in a program that should primarily focus on

(A) the development of any vocational aptitudes.

(B) the use of repetitive tasks to develop physical, social, emotional, and intellectual skills.

(C) being in a part school/part work type of program.

(D) enhancing his sensory and motor skills.

(E) developing self-care skills for independent living.

10. The teaching of mildly retarded students today involves all of the following concepts *except*

(A) maximization of potential skills.

(B) normalization.

(C) use of behavioral objectives.

(D) development of recreational and family-living skills.

(E) attainment of statewide minimum standards for the acquisition of a high school diploma.

11. Which of these items describe(s) the mildly retarded child?

I. Should not focus on academic development

II. First four years of life are important in stimulating such a child

III. Some forms of mild retardation are reversible

IV. Can be taught social skills

(A) I, II, and III only

(B) I only

(C) III and IV only

(D) II, III, and IV only

(E) I, III, and IV only

12. America is about fifteenth among modern industrialized nations in the prevention of mental retardation. All of the following should be found in the establishment of effective preventive programs *except*

(A) the development of an extensive network of prenatal programs.

(B) redesigning institutional programs to prevent problems caused by maternal deprivation or lack of stimulation.

(C) complete maternal care for high-risk mothers.

(D) genetic counseling and comprehensive diagnostic centers for each community.

(E) an extensive child welfare network to prevent the abuse and neglect of such children.

13. All of the following are valid techniques in the education of the mentally retarded student *except*
    (A) programmed instruction.
    (B) computer-assisted instruction.
    (C) task analysis.
    (D) behavior modification.
    (E) multisensory approaches.

14. Which of the following are arguments in favor of special classes for the retarded?
    I. Significant improvement in the academic achievement of such youngsters
    II. Greater opportunity for individualized instruction
    III. Protects against academic failure and social rejection
    IV. Results in the development of higher self-concepts

    (A) I and III only
    (B) I, III, and IV only
    (C) I and III only
    (D) I and IV only
    (E) III and IV only

15. As an example of an independent living skill, you might choose
    (A) banking and keeping a budget.
    (B) functional literacy.
    (C) maintaining a home.
    (D) working.
    (E) any of the above.

16. Which of the following *least* describes the learning characteristics of a moderately retarded student?
    (A) The student needs to be given one-step directions.
    (B) The child needs concrete, repetitive experiences in a structured environment.
    (C) The student must actively manipulate different materials.
    (D) The pupil has a short attention span resulting in restlessness and physical activity.
    (E) The student needs to develop reading comprehension skills and problem solving at a slower academic pace.

17. All are contributing to a general decline in the ranks of those labeled mentally retarded *except*
    (A) mental retardation is relative to a student's cultural situation.
    (B) more borderline cases are being labeled learning disabled.
    (C) learning disability is perceived as a safer label than mental retardation.
    (D) the criteria for the label have changed during the last few years.
    (E) most diseases and environmental factors causing mental retardation have been cured or drastically reduced.

18. Which of the following are valid reasons why mental retardation is *not* evenly distributed among the different segments of the population?
    I. Incidence increases as students age out of educational programs.
    II. Racial differences exist.
    III. There is higher incidence in lower socioeconomic groups.
    IV. More males than females are retarded.

    (A) II, III, and IV only
    (B) I only
    (C) I and II only
    (D) III and IV only
    (E) I, II, and III only

19. Which would *not* be an appropriate economic skill to teach a mildly retarded student?
    (A) Keeping a household budget
    (B) Keeping accurate records so as to fill out income tax forms
    (C) Shopping wisely
    (D) Handling money and making change
    (E) Reading a sales receipt

20. Which of the following are achievable goals in the education of moderately retarded students?

    I. Development of positive self-concept

    II. Economic independence

    III. Ability to interact favorably with others

    IV. Participate in community and recreational activities

    (A) II, III, and IV only

    (B) I, III, and IV only

    (C) I, II, and III only

    (D) II only

    (E) II and III only

21. According to federal and state law, a child with an IQ below 25 on a standardized intelligence test would be labeled

    (A) profoundly retarded.

    (B) mentally retarded.

    (C) severely retarded.

    (D) moderately retarded.

    (E) mildly retarded.

22. Which author feels that mental retardation is the result of genetic inheritance?

    (A) Jensen

    (B) Piaget

    (C) Guiford

    (D) Terman

    (E) Bruner

23. According to such intelligence tests as the WISC III or the Stanford Binet, a child who is considered moderately retarded would have a flat IQ score of about

    (A) 75

    (B) 42

    (C) 20

    (D) 84

    (E) 79

24. Which is key in labeling a child as mentally retarded?

    (A) Having intellectual ability in the deficient range according to a standardized IQ test

    (B) Being adaptively retarded as determined by observation and an adaptive rating scale given to a caregiver

    (C) Determining that a deficient IQ will not increase at some future time

    (D) Making sure the retardation is cognitively based and not caused by any other childhood disorder

    (E) Determining that the student is at least three years below his present grade level according to academic testing

25. The illusion of retardation may be created by the fact that a person considered competent in one environment may be considered incompetent in another. Which of the following are valid examples of this concept?

    I. Computer literacy movement in education

    II. Moving from a rural to an urban area

    III. Using phonics as opposed to a whole-language approach

    IV. Moving from a halfway house to a group home

    (A) I and III only

    (B) II and IV only

    (C) III and IV only

    (D) I and II only

    (E) II only

Test: Educational Leadership: Administration and Supervision (0410)

Time: 2 hours
Number of Questions: 120
Format: Multiple-choice questions

Purpose of the Test

Designed to assess a candidate's knowledge of the functions of an administrator or supervisor

Content Categories

- Determining Educational Needs—(8 percent)
- Curriculum Design and Instructional Improvement—(13 percent)
- Development of Staff and Program Evaluation—(16 percent)
- School Management—(33 percent)
- Individual and Group Leadership Skills—(30 percent)

Category Descriptions

Determining Educational Needs

1. Expectations concerning students at various developmental and instructional levels
2. Assessments of community needs, expectations, and population projects
3. Recognition of specific needs of diverse populations and mobile populations
4. Awareness of national perspective on education
5. Interpretation of research and assessment data for decision making

Curriculum Design and Instructional Improvement

1. Curriculum goals, decision processes in design, strategies for implementation, and determination of instructional objectives
2. Instructional methods and techniques, such as team teaching, direct teaching, group instruction, contract method, individualized instruction, and interdisciplinary instruction
3. Instructional resources and research data related to curriculum needs, such as personnel, materials, technology, finance, business and industry, advisory groups, community agencies, and institutions
4. Learning theories and learning processes

Development of Staff and Program Evaluation

1. Assessment of staff abilities and determination of their needs
2. Establishment and implementation of staff development
3. Strategies for behavioral change
4. Indicators of achievement relating to goals and objectives
5. Knowledge of types, methods, and procedures of evaluation and instructional staff assessment
6. Applications of evaluation and research findings in goal setting and change

School Management

1. Organizational and operational features of school management, including structures, programs and services, and personnel selection and evaluation procedures

2. Governing and control features of school management, including educational functions of local, state, and federal agencies; formal and informal agencies; and the process of participatory government involving students and faculty and community members

3. Business and fiscal features of school management, including financial resources, support services, and budgeting

4. Legal features, including negotiations and bargaining, due process for staff members and students, and judicial and legislative provisions

Individual and Group Leadership Skills

1. Understanding individual behavior and divergent behavior of students and staff and community members

2. Understanding and affecting group dynamics

3. School-community relations, including diverse values and use of community resources

4. Communication skills

5. Creating and maintaining a positive affective environment, such as existing school cultures communication flow and informal leadership

Educational Leadership: Administration and Supervision

Directions: Each question or incomplete statement is followed by five answer choices. For each question, circle the answer or completion that is best.

1. Frederick Taylor, Henri Fayol, Luther Gulick, and Lyndall Urwick are all associated with

   (A) Leadership Theory.

   (B) Scientific Management Theory.

   (C) Humanistic Theory.

   (D) Social Systems Theory.

   (E) Bureaucratic Theory.

2. A social studies teacher tries to get her students to relate abstract concepts to a particular situation. According to Bloom, she would ask questions focusing on which developmental level?

   (A) Comprehension

   (B) Evaluation

   (C) Analysis

   (D) Application

   (E) Synthesis

3. All are associated with the application of social systems theory to organizational and administrative structures *except*

   (A) Parsons.

   (B) Barnard.

   (C) Getzels.

   (D) Etzioni.

   (E) Weber.

4. Teacher education programs at the college level during the 1970s and 1980s focused on the development of

   (A) techniques to pass standardized national examinations in the area of education.

   (B) competency-based objectives that had to be met by each candidate.

   (C) the application of liberal arts to teaching in the schools.

   (D) a more laissez-faire attitude due to a decrease in state testing of new teachers.

   (E) criteria to increase the ability level of those students entering the education field.

5. The dichotomy between the monocratic, bureaucratic type of organization and the pluralistic, collegial type of organization has been defined by Theory X and Theory Y according to which author?

   (A) Maslow

   (B) McGregor

   (C) Argyris

   (D) Herzberg

   (E) Weber

6. All are major teacher personnel problems today in the field of education *except*

   (A) states' refusing to give money to retool teachers.

   (B) less able students entering teaching.

   (C) the women's movement making education a more attractive field to enter.

   (D) salaries of urban teachers not keeping pace with those of the suburbs.

   (E) teacher education programs' not training teachers to deal with an urban environment.

7. Which of the following are some reasons why an unannounced observation is an effective supervisory technique?

   I. The supervisor sees what is really going on in the classroom.

   II. The personality characteristics of a supervisor do not impinge when observing in this manner.

   III. A teacher's lesson will be more spontaneous.

   IV. This technique reduces teacher anxiety.

   (A) IV only

   (B) I, II, and III only

   (C) I only

   (D) I, III, and IV only

   (E) II only

8. In terms of organizational structure, "span of control" means

   (A) that every person knows to whom and for what he is responsible.

   (B) the development of standardized procedures for routinizing administrative operations.

   (C) the assigning to each administrator no greater a number of persons than the administrator can supervise directly.

   (D) the delegation of authority from superordinates to subordinates.

   (E) having a single executive head responsible for all decisions.

9. Which is *not* an aspect of clinical supervision?

   (A) The teacher selects the area he or she wishes to improve.

   (B) A supervisor directly informs the teacher of his or her strengths and weaknesses without any teacher input.

   (C) Its purpose is to develop and improve instructional competencies.

   (D) The teacher determines the faults of his or her lesson.

   (E) Follow-up observation activities are developed jointly by the instructor and supervisor.

10. Public education is not a right according to the United States Constitution. Nonetheless, a part of the Constitution has been interpreted by the courts as prohibiting a state from denying to a child an equal education because he or she is handicapped or emotionally disturbed. This interpretation is based on (the)

    (A) Fourteenth Amendment.

    (B) Tenth Amendment.

    (C) Sections eight and ten of Article One.

    (D) Fifth Amendment.

    (E) First Amendment.

11. Ned Flanders is associated with a model relating to

    (A) clinical supervision.

    (B) micro-teaching.

    (C) interaction analysis.

    (D) needs assessments.

    (E) teacher effectiveness.

12. A tenured teacher is having difficulty in the classroom. He cannot manage the class, and students often leave and roam the halls. His pacing is so slow that he tends to lose the students that do stay in his class. The noise level in his room is deafening. How should a building principal deal with this situation?

    I. Give him the minimal number of students legally possible.

    II. Remove him from teaching duties because he is doing great damage to the students.

    III. Allow him to teach in another area if he is competent to do so.

    IV. Have the teacher immediately dismissed for incompetence.

    (A) III and IV only

    (B) I and III only

    (C) II and IV only

    (D) III only

    (E) I and II only

13. Edmund, Rosenshine, and Berliner are best known for their research in

    (A) clinical supervision.

    (B) developing performance objectives for teachers.

    (C) effective teaching techniques.

    (D) cooperative learning.

    (E) shared decision making.

14. A quality classroom teacher would exhibit all of the following behaviors *except*

    (A) helping pupils to explore, discuss, check, or test questions or ideas.

    (B) responding to pupils' answers by reflecting them back to the class to provide further questioning, thought, and discussion.

    (C) smiling or appearing relaxed and cheerful.

    (D) responding to pupils' questions or ideas with scorn.

    (E) acknowledging his own errors.

15. It is easiest to charge and dismiss a tenured teacher for

    (A) inefficiency.

    (B) incompetency.

    (C) failure to maintain license.

    (D) conduct unbecoming a teacher.

    (E) insubordination.

16. The concept that leadership effectiveness is "dependent upon the appropriate matching of the individual's leadership style of interacting and the influence which the group situation provides" was postulated by

    (A) Lipham.

    (B) Stogdill.

    (C) Fiedler.

    (D) Getzels.

    (E) Berelson.

17. A new principal is appointed to a public school. His goal is to improve the school's academic achievement. What is the first thing he should do as an administrative leader?

    (A) Give a needs assessment to the teachers and then form a representative committee to prioritize the information

    (B) Form a committee to carry out the changes he recommends for the school

    (C) Abandon the policies of the previous principal and start from scratch

    (D) Create a new reading curriculum based upon the latest research

    (E) At the first faculty conference, outline approximately twelve important changes to be made in the school

18. Effective schools have all of the following characteristics *except*

    (A) high expectations.

    (B) an emphasis on academic achievement and quality instruction.

    (C) a school climate or atmosphere emphasizing discipline.

    (D) an emphasis on crisis management.

    (E) constant pupil evaluation.

19. According to most research, a principal's time is mostly taken up with

    (A) discipline problems.

    (B) paperwork.

    (C) instructional leadership.

    (D) supervision.

    (E) scheduling.

20. The author most closely associated with the theory of clinical supervision is

    (A) Fiedler.

    (B) Cogan.

    (C) Flanders.

    (D) Berliner.

    (E) Getzels.

21. Direct instruction is the teaching of large groups by focusing on factual or literal questions and using controlled practice techniques. According to research, direct instruction

    (A) benefits low-functioning students.

    (B) benefits average students.

    (C) develops abstract thinking skills.

    (D) shows the need to individualize instruction with weaker students.

    (E) should be modified by using more open approaches.

22. A trend that will probably affect public education is that

    (A) parents will place a greater emphasis on literacy due to multinational competition.

    (B) a larger percentage of the school-age population will be made up of minority groups.

    (C) education is becoming a federal responsibility.

    (D) there will be greater choice between public and private schools.

    (E) economic restructuring will force more women back into education.

23. Upward mobiles, indifferents, and ambivalents are three personality types that impact upon the social structure of an organization. This social systems approach was developed by

    (A) Barnard.

    (B) Etzioni.

    (C) Presthus.

    (D) Carlson.

    (E) Griffiths.

24. Before the 1950s, studies in leadership focused on

    I. great men.

    II. an interactional or group approach.

    III. studies of traits.

    IV. a social systems approach.

    (A) I, II, and III only

    (B) III and IV only

    (C) II, III, and IV only

    (D) I and III only

    (E) I only

25. In terms of dismissing tenured teachers for incompetence, most state laws

    (A) put the onus on the school district to help the teacher improve his or her skills.

    (B) allow an informal hearing for dismissal.

    (C) allow the district to determine who will be on any arbitration panel.

    (D) put the burden on the teacher as to why little effort was made to improve his or her skills.

    (E) allow for immediate contract termination if the instructor is employed for less than a minimal period of time.

Test: Family and Consumer Sciences (0120)

Time: 2 hours
Number of Questions: 120
Format: Multiple-choice questions

Purpose of the Test

Designed to measure the preparation of prospective family and consumer sciences teachers in middle through senior high schools

Content Categories

- The Family —(14 percent)
- Human Development —(11 percent)
- Management—(12 percent)
- Consumer Economics—(12 percent)
- Nutrition and Food—(15 percent)
- Clothing and Textiles—(9 percent)
- Housing—(8 percent)
- Family and Consumer Sciences Education—(19 percent)

Category Descriptions

The Family

1. Family structures and stages
2. Family functions, including education and development of family members, and the physical and psychological support of family members
3. Factors affecting family relationships

Human Development

1. Theories of development: Gesell and Ilg, Havinghurst, Erikson, Piaget, and Maslow
2. Development tasks and processes: physical, social, psychological/emotional, and intellectual and moral development
3. Development requiring special resources, including special needs, gifted conditions, drug and alcohol abuse, teenage pregnancies, and teen suicide

Management

1. Management theory: work simplification, time management, and organization of activities
2. Management processes and techniques: goal setting; decision making; assessing and using resources; strategies for change; and identification and clarification of family values, goals, and standards in decisions

Consumer Economics

1. Consumer rights and responsibilities: legal and ethical considerations
2. Social influences on consumer decisions
3. Consumer resources: private and government
4. Selection of services and products
5. Financial planning and management
6. Consumer protection

Nutrition and Food

1. Factors influencing nutritional needs
2. Functions and sources of nutrition
3. Nutritional guidelines
4. Related health problems as well as prevention and treatment strategies
5. Sociocultural aspects of food
6. Meal/food management
7. Food selection and purchase topics
8. Food preparation, storage, and preservation

Clothing and Textiles

1. Wardrobe management
2. Types and characteristics of fibers, production of properties of fabrics

Housing

1. Functions and types of housing
2. Factors that affect consumer decisions

Family and Consumer Sciences Education

1. Philosophical and professional concerns: quality of life; sex-role stereotypes; dual home/work role preparation; integration of the cognitive, affective, and psychomotor skills; and role of professional organizations
2. Characteristics of family/consumer education and of occupational family and consumer sciences education
3. Planning, implementation, and evaluation of community advisory committees, laboratory settings, demonstrations, youth organizations, special needs, and assessments

Family and Consumer Sciences

Directions: Each question or incomplete statement is followed by five answer choices. For each question, circle the answer or completion that is best.

1. Which of the following is *not* a myth?

   (A) Vitamins give you "pep" and "energy."

   (B) Timing of vitamin intake is crucial.

   (C) Vitamin C "protects" against the common cold.

   (D) Synthetic vitamins, manufactured in the laboratory, are identical to natural vitamins in their effect on the body.

   (E) The more vitamins the better.

2. The unit of electrical *energy* most commonly associated with the use of electrical appliances is the

   (A) horsepower.

   (B) watt.

   (C) kilowatt-hour.

   (D) amp.

   (E) volt.

3. Which of the following is a high-fiber food?

   (A) Grapefruit

   (B) White rice

   (C) Lettuce

   (D) Peeled potatoes

   (E) Brown rice

4. The introduction of solid food to a baby's diet is normally recommended at the age of

   (A) 1–3 months.

   (B) 2–4 months.

   (C) 4–6 months.

   (D) 6–8 months.

   (E) 8–10 months.

5. Which of the following has the greatest number of calories?

   (A) Four celery sticks

   (B) A small apple

   (C) A large green pepper

   (D) Ten mushrooms

   (E) A small tomato

6. If 3 teaspoons = 1 tablespoon
   16 tablespoons = 1 cup
   2 cups = 1 pint

   then $\frac{1}{2}$ pint is equivalent to how many teaspoons?

   (A) $10\frac{1}{2}$

   (B) 12

   (C) 21

   (D) 24

   (E) 48

7. All the following are faucet components *except*

   (A) stem.

   (B) O ring.

   (C) escutcheon.

   (D) washer.

   (E) float ball.

Questions 8 and 9 are based on the following bill.

SW **Valley Water Company** INCORPORATED
360 West End Road • Redwood, New York 10994

BILLING DATE	SERVICE ADDRESS	
JUN 03	15 Jones AVE	45-110-13

METER NUMBER	FOR THE PERIOD		NO OF DAYS IN PERIOD	RATE CODE	METER READINGS		CONSUMPTION IN 100 CU. FT.	BILLING CODE	AMOUNT
	FROM	TO			PREVIOUS	PRESENT			
05445074	0221	0331	38		1355	1364	9		31.19
30669421	0331	0522	52		0000	0022	22		62.71
					SUMMER RATE				
					WINTER RATE				

BUDGET PAYMENT PLAN	
COST FOR WATER	BALANCE IN PLAN
CONSUMED THIS PERIOD	AFTER PAYMENT OF AMOUNT DUE

ONE HUNDRED CUBIC FEET EQUALS 748 GALLONS. YOUR CONSUMPTION FOR THE CURRENT BILLING PERIOD WAS **23,188** GALLONS.

AMOUNT DUE
$93.90

PAYABLE ON OR BEFORE
JUN 20 86

8. Based on this bill, how many gallons of water were used from February 21 to March 31?
   (A) 1,364
   (B) 6,732
   (C) 16,456
   (D) 28,424
   (E) Cannot be determined from the information given

9. How much does 100 cubic feet of water cost in the winter, given the fact that the winter rate ends on March 31?
   (A) $1.42
   (B) $1.46
   (C) $3.02
   (D) $3.47
   (E) $6.97

10. Do not use lightweight plastic containers such as margarine tubs in a microwave because they
    (A) reflect the microwaves causing sparks.
    (B) inhibit the cooking process.
    (C) melt.
    (D) burn the corners of the heated item.
    (E) cause pitting on the oven walls.

11. Local authorities are most likely to receive the greatest part of their revenues from
    (A) sales taxes.
    (B) property taxes.
    (C) payroll taxes.
    (D) personal income taxes.
    (E) corporate income taxes.

12. How many square yards of carpet are required to completely cover the floor of a room 9 ft ∞ 12 ft?
    (A) 6
    (B) 12
    (C) 27
    (D) 54
    (E) 108

13. It is recommended that each of the following not be frozen *except*
    (A) cream cheese.
    (B) hard-cooked eggs.
    (C) mayonnaise.
    (D) mashed potatoes.
    (E) carbonated drinks.

14. The sentence that is *not* true with respect to preventing or retarding mildew growth is:

    (A) Avoid putting away any clothing or material items when wet.

    (B) Poorly lighted areas help prevent growth and can even kill the mildew.

    (C) Disinfectant can slow or stop growth.

    (D) Silica gel is effective against mildew growth.

    (E) Proper air flow helps prevent growth.

15. The tool used to locate a point directly below a ceiling hook is a

    (A) plumb bob.

    (B) line level.

    (C) transit.

    (D) drop gauge.

    (E) vertical shaft.

16. A recession may be best described as

    (A) a limited period when unemployment rises and business activity slows down.

    (B) a limited period of rising prices, increased industrial output, and falling wages.

    (C) the extended aftermath of a long depression.

    (D) a sudden and acute rise in unemployment, business activity, and industrial output.

    (E) an extended period in which wages, prices, employment, and industrial output rise and fall rapidly and inexplicably.

17. In a sample survey, questions are asked of a group of people who

    (A) volunteer to participate in the sample.

    (B) are able to understand the goals of the researcher.

    (C) are carefully selected to be representative of a larger group.

    (D) are familiar with statistical techniques.

    (E) are chosen at random from the population at large.

18. The short form of the 1980 census asked questions on all of the following *except*

    (A) whether a person was of Spanish/Hispanic origin or descent.

    (B) whether a person was married.

    (C) whether a home had complete indoor plumbing.

    (D) whether a person was black.

    (E) whether a person was heterosexual.

19. In a well-known experiment, psychologists frustrated young children by placing a wire fence between the children and a pile of toys. When finally allowed to play with the toys, the children smashed and destroyed them. This reaction is an example of

    (A) displaced aggression.

    (B) absence of aggression.

    (C) dormant aggression.

    (D) rational aggression.

    (E) sustained aggression.

20. A convertible mortgage is which of the following?

    (A) An adjustable-rate mortgage that, at the buyer's option, can be converted to a fixed-rate loan

    (B) A fixed-rate mortgage that, at the buyer's option, can be converted to an adjustable-rate loan

    (C) A fixed-rate mortgage that, at the lender's option, can be converted to an adjustable-rate loan

    (D) An adjustable-rate mortgage that, at the lender's option, can be converted to a fixed-rate loan

    (E) A balloon mortgage that, at the buyer's option, can be converted to a fixed-rate loan

21. The federal agency that insures deposits in savings and loan associations and savings banks is the

    (A) FNMA

    (B) FHA

    (C) FSB

    (D) FSLIC

    (E) FHLMC

22. Which instrument is specially designed for fixed-income and retiree homeowners who have little or no mortgage debt, offering them the ability to receive monthly payments to supplement income while still retaining home ownership?

    (A) Reverse-annuity mortgage

    (B) Conventional mortgage

    (C) Balloon mortgage

    (D) Variable-rate mortgage

    (E) Second mortgage

23. All of the following draw funds from a deposit account *except*

    (A) ATM card.

    (B) asset card.

    (C) credit card.

    (D) debit card.

    (E) check writing.

24. Insurance that extends the liability coverage beyond the underlying limits for auto and home, usually up to $1 million dollars, is called

    (A) whole-life coverage.

    (B) umbrella coverage.

    (C) overinsured coverage.

    (D) accidental coverage.

    (E) extended-benefit coverage.

25. This type of insurance has no savings or investment component, is relatively inexpensive pure insurance for young people, and is coverage for a defined number of years and must then be renewed; its premiums increase with age. It is called

    (A) whole life.

    (B) straight life.

    (C) limited payment life.

    (D) term.

    (E) endowment.

Test: Introduction to the Teaching of Reading (0200)

Time: 2 hours
Number of Questions: 100
Format: Multiple-choice Questions

Purpose of the Test

Designed to measure the preparation of prospective elementary or secondary school teachers in the area of reading

Content Categories

- Reading as a Language-Thought Process—(13–17 percent)
- Text Structure—(8–12 percent)
- Instructional Process in the Teaching of Reading—(38–42 percent)
- Affective Aspects—(13–17 percent)
- Environmental/Sociocultural Factors—(18–22 percent)

Category Descriptions

Reading as a Language-thought Process

1. Theoretical approaches to the reading process, acquisition and understanding of language, metacognition
2. Relationships between listening, speaking, and writing, especially reading/writing connection

Text Structure

1. Structure for narrative and expository text, syntactic complexity, organization, vocabulary, and story grammars
2. Clues in semantics, syntax, graphemes, and experience

Instructional Processes in the Teaching of Reading

1. Use of strategies, such as reciprocal teaching, critical questioning, monitoring, scaffolding, schema, language expansion, story grammars, scripts, organizational patterns, and guided oral and silent reading
2. Age-appropriate strategies
3. Classroom management, including cooperative groups, use of paraprofessionals, centers, peer grouping, and computers
4. Content area reading
5. Study skills
6. Use of criterion-based tests, achievement tests, and individual and group assessment strategies

Affective Aspects

Use of art expression, drama, and media to motivate reading and writing

Environmental/Sociocultural Factors

1. Understand factors that influence literacy and biliteracy development, including parental support, home/school congruence, approaches, and teacher expectations

2. Recognize influence of family and peers and of the differences between socioeconomics, regional, and cultural linguistics

3. Select appropriate instructional strategies to address above factors

Introduction to the Teaching of Reading

Directions: Each question or incomplete statement is followed by five answer choices. For each question, circle the answer or completion that is best.

1. Using an Informal Reading Inventory, the instructional level measuring inferential comprehension would be approximately

   (A) 70 percent.

   (B) 90 percent.

   (C) below 60 percent.

   (D) 99–100 percent.

   (E) 90–95 percent.

2. Which is *not* a major contribution to poor reading scores in school?

   (A) Emotional factors causing academic blockage

   (B) Limited and fragmented instructional programs

   (C) Inadequately prepared teachers

   (D) Dependency on workbooks and ditto sheets

   (E) Improper use of reading materials

3. A sixth-grade student of average potential has comprehension skills on grade level. He is asked to find several factual details about the Lewis and Clark Expedition from his textbook. The most probable reason the student may be unable to do this activity is because

   (A) he may have difficulty reading the material.

   (B) he does not know how to use the table of contents or index.

   (C) he has poor inference skills.

   (D) the student cannot organize the information.

   (E) the pupil is reading material above his grade level.

4. According to research, which is *not* an effective way of teaching vocabulary and improving concept development in children?

   (A) Teach cloze to develop context clues

   (B) Teach words children have an immediate need for

   (C) Develop work-study skills in the context of need

   (D) Teach prefixes and roots

   (E) Teach multiple meanings and figurative language

5. Which is an example of teaching phonics synthetically?

   (A) Introducing letters and then related sounds

   (B) Teaching sounds using a multisensory approach

   (C) Using computer-assisted instruction to develop sound relationships

   (D) Using phonograms rather than individual sounds to develop word analysis skills

   (E) Teaching letter-sound relationships from sight words already known

6. Which is a good definition of reading according to psycholinguistic theory?

   (A) Reading is the ability to discriminate letters and sounds.

   (B) Reading is the act of identifying the symbol and obtaining meaning from the identified symbol.

   (C) Reading is the translation of symbols into sounds.

   (D) Reading reconstructs a message encoded by a writer in graphic language.

   (E) Reading is thinking and the reconstructing of ideas of others.

7. There are a variety of reading programs and strategies available in the teaching of reading to students of average intellectual ability. According to research, which of the programs below is the *most* effective?

   (A) A basal approach

   (B) Initial teaching alphabet

   (C) A rebus approach

   (D) A basal approach using strong word-attack applications

   (E) A language experience approach

8. Some effective approaches in developing reading readiness in preschool are

   I. labeling objects in a classroom.

   II. teaching sound-symbol relationships using specialized workbooks.

   III. reading picture books about a variety of subjects.

   IV. formal teaching of auditory discrimination skills.

   (A) I, II, and III only

   (B) I and III only

   (C) II and IV only

   (D) I only

   (E) II only

9. Who attributed reading difficulty to neurological immaturity and failure to establish cerebral dominance?

   (A) Chall

   (B) Chomsky

   (C) Fernald

   (D) Orton

   (E) Delacato

10. The use of the cloze technique comes from which reading theory?

    (A) Linguistics

    (B) Psycholinguistics

    (C) Process theory

    (D) Organic model

    (E) Compensatory comprehension model

11. Results of standardized tests

    I. show how well children are reading compared to other children.

    II. help determine in which reading group a child should be placed.

    III. determine which skills students are deficient in.

    IV. are expressed in grade and age scores.

    (A) I and II only

    (B) II and III only

    (C) I, II, and III only

    (D) I, II, and IV only

    (E) II and IV only

12. The primary focus of reading in the middle grades is

    (A) reading to gather information from various materials.

    (B) analyzing different points of views.

    (C) synthesizing information from various sources.

    (D) drawing conclusions from open-ended stories.

    (E) teaching affixes and nonphonetic words to improve decoding ability.

13. Recent research has shown that the use of colored lenses with some learning disabled students

    (A) does not reduce extraneous stimuli when reading.

    (B) decreases reversals and transpositions while reading.

    (C) helps them improve their ability to comprehend material.

    (D) does not significantly improve reading problems in such students.

    (E) tends to increase word blindness.

14. Teaching reading readiness in kindergarten should emphasize
    I. the teaching of initial-letter sounds.
    II. the teaching of sight vocabulary.
    III. the use of a variety of informal language activities.
    IV. playing recordings and showing filmstrips containing a variety of stories.

    (A) III only
    (B) I and II only
    (C) III and IV only
    (D) IV only
    (E) II and III only

15. Research has shown that when students learn to read at three years of age,
    (A) these students are more intelligent than those pupils who do not learn how to read until seven years of age.
    (B) by the time these students are in third and fourth grade, there is no significant difference in reading ability between them and the late readers.
    (C) such students are more likely to go on to higher education than those who first read at seven or eight years.
    (D) comprehension skills develop before perceptual skills.
    (E) academically oriented preschool programs will improve their achievement along with that of all children.

16. Sylvia Ashton Warner is most associated with the
    (A) basal approach.
    (B) multisensory approach.
    (C) organic approach.
    (D) phonics approach.
    (E) linguistic approach.

17. Examples of reading diagnostic tests are the
    I. Metropolitan Achievement Test
    II. Durrell Analysis of Reading Difficulty
    III. California Reading Test
    IV. Roswell-Chall Auditory Blending Test

    (A) I, III, and IV only
    (B) I and III only
    (C) III and IV only
    (D) II, III, and IV only
    (E) II and IV only

18. Recognition of figurative language is an example of a
    (A) word-recognition skill.
    (B) word-meaning skill.
    (C) comprehension skill.
    (D) study skill.
    (E) appreciation skill.

19. A reading system using a 44-character core alphabet to avoid inconsistencies in sound-letter relationships describes
    (A) i/t/a.
    (B) linguistic readers.
    (C) simplified spelling.
    (D) DMS.
    (E) Unifon.

20. If a student constantly repeats words and phrases while reading passages, it can be concluded that he or she may have
    (A) visual perceptual problems.
    (B) tracking problems.
    (C) visual discrimination problems.
    (D) memory problems.
    (E) language-processing problems.

21. A child is given a passage slightly above his ability so as to analyze his miscues. He constantly omits the final *s* in almost all verbs and plural nouns. It can be concluded that the errors made may possibly be due to
    (A) problems in grammar development.
    (B) inability to see obvious mistakes.
    (C) variations in dialect.
    (D) graphic similarity between the miscue and the actual word.
    (E) auditory similarity between the miscue and the actual word.

22. A teacher writes on the board:

    Rearrange these items so that each subgroup is placed under its proper heading.

    The instructor is

    (A) developing study and organization skills.

    (B) planning to teach the concept of developing main ideas.

    (C) developing a skill in word meaning.

    (D) developing word-recognition skills.

    (E) teaching students to separate important from unimportant details.

23. Having first-grade students supply missing letters sequentially in groups teaches

    (A) letter-recognition skills.

    (B) dictionary skills.

    (C) organizational skills.

    (D) sound-symbol skills.

    (E) discrimination skills.

24. This program develops reading skills by stimulating discussion, creating a story, and developing word skills. Which approach is being described?

    (A) The whole-language approach

    (B) Individualized reading

    (C) The language-experience approach

    (D) The organic approach

    (E) The basal approach

25. Words such as *few*, *oil*, *out*, *should*, *toy*, and *buy* contain

    (A) vowel diagraphs.

    (B) silent vowels.

    (C) vowel diphthongs.

    (D) phonically irregular words.

    (E) short vowels.

Test: Mathematics (0060)

Time: 2 hours
Number of Questions: 110
Format: Multiple-choice questions. Graphing, scientific, or four-function calculators are allowed.

Purpose of the Test

Designed to measure the preparation of prospective secondary school mathematics teachers

Content Categories

- Basic (Precollege) Mathematics—(38 percent)
- Precalculus Mathematics—(27 percent)
- Advanced College-Level Mathematics—(25 percent)
- Professional Understanding and Pedagogy—(10 percent)

Category Descriptions

Basic Mathematics

1. Number concepts and elementary number theory topics
2. Elementary and intermediate algebra topics
3. High school geometry topics including visualization in 2-space and 3-space

Precalculus Mathematics

1. College algebra, trigonometry, and analytic geometry
2. Algebraic, trigonometric, logarithmic, exponential, and absolute value functions
   Also related to functions: domain, range, composite, inverse, one-to-one mappings, graphical properties, and recursive

Advanced College-level Mathematics

1. Calculus: real numbers, maxima and minima, least upper bound, points of inflection, asymptotes, polar coordinates, derivatives and integrals, continuity, mappings into or onto a set, convergence of series. Single variables only.
2. Linear and abstract algebra, including the properties of groups, rings, fields, matrices, determinants, vectors, vector spaces, and linear transformations
3. Computer science and discrete mathematics
4. Probability and statistics, including permutations, and combinations; mean, median, and mode as measures of central tendency; range; standard deviation; simple distribution, especially normal distribution

Professional Understanding and Pedagogy

1. Important trends in mathematics education
2. Important developments in the history of mathematics
3. Knowledge of professional journals and resources
4. Pedagogy such as teaching methods, curriculum, and analysis of student error

Mathematics

Directions: Each question or incomplete statement is followed by five answer choices. For each question, circle the answer or completion that is best.

1. The expression $\log r + \log r^2$ is equal to
   (A) $\log (r + r^2)$
   (B) $3 \log r$
   (C) $\log r$
   (D) r^3
   (E) r

2. The expression $x^{-1} + y^{-1}$ is equal to
   (A) $(x + y)^{-1}$

   (B) $\dfrac{1}{x + y}$

   (C) $x + y$

   (D) $\dfrac{x + y}{xy}$

   (E) $\dfrac{xy}{x + y}$

3. Find the sum of the infinite geometric series
   $$2, \frac{4}{3}, \frac{8}{9}, \ldots$$
   (A) $8\frac{3}{4}$

   (B) $7\frac{1}{3}$

   (C) 6

   (D) $5\frac{3}{8}$

   (E) $5\frac{1}{4}$

4. What is the negation of $\sim p \lor \sim q$?
   (A) $p \land q$
   (B) $\sim p \land \sim q$
   (C) $p \lor q$
   (D) $p \land \sim q$
   (E) $p \lor \sim q$

5. $\left[\frac{1}{2} (\cos 10° + i \sin 10°)\right]^3 =$
   (A) $\frac{1}{2} (\cos 1000° + i \sin 1000°)$
   (B) $\frac{1}{8} (\cos 10° + i \sin 10°)$
   (C) $\frac{1}{8} (\cos 30° + i \sin 30°)$
   (D) $\frac{1}{2} (\cos 30° + i \sin 30°)$
   (E) $\frac{1}{6} (\cos 13° + i \sin 13°)$

6. $y = (2x^2 + 3)^5$. Find $\frac{dy}{dx}$
   (A) $\frac{1}{6} (2x^2 + 3)^6$
   (B) $20x(2x^2 + 3)^4$
   (C) $5(2x^2 + 3)^4$
   (D) $5(4x)^4$
   (E) $2x^3 + 13$

7. If x varies inversely as t and if $x = 6$ when $t = 2$, find x when $t = 4$.
   (A) $1\frac{1}{2}$
   (B) 3
   (C) 1
   (D) 12
   (E) 36

8. The equation $\dfrac{x}{3} + \dfrac{y}{2} = 1$ represents a(n)
   (A) line.
   (B) parabola.
   (C) circle.
   (D) ellipse.
   (E) hyperbola.

9. Perform the indicated matrix operation.

$$\begin{pmatrix} 1 & 2 \\ 3 & 4 \end{pmatrix}\begin{pmatrix} 1 & 0 \\ 1 & 1 \end{pmatrix} =$$

(A) $\begin{pmatrix} 2 & 2 \\ 4 & 5 \end{pmatrix}$

(B) $\begin{pmatrix} 1 & 0 \\ 3 & 4 \end{pmatrix}$

(C) $\begin{pmatrix} 1 & 2 \\ 3 & 4 \end{pmatrix}$

(D) $\begin{pmatrix} 2 & 4 \\ 6 & 8 \end{pmatrix}$

(E) $\begin{pmatrix} 3 & 2 \\ 7 & 4 \end{pmatrix}$

10. A committee of 4 is to be chosen from 3 boys and 4 girls. How many different ways are there to choose committees that will contain exactly 2 boys and 2 girls?

(A) 18

(B) 35

(C) 12

(D) 7

(E) 6

11. Which graph does not represent a function?

(A)

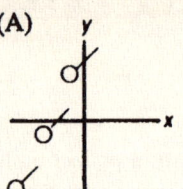

(B)

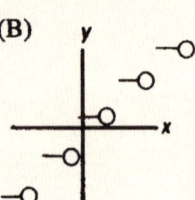

(C)

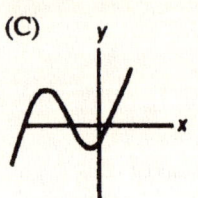

(D)

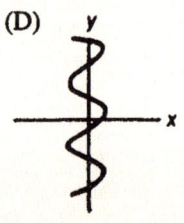

(E)

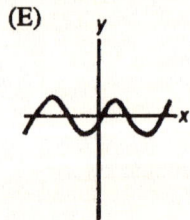

12. How many liters of water must be evaporated from 84 liters of a 20% salt solution to raise it to a 35% salt solution?

(A) 14

(B) 16

(C) 24

(D) 36

(E) 34

13. Find the third term of the expansion $(2x - y)^4$.
    (A) $12x^2y^2$
    (B) $24x^2y^2$
    (C) $4xy^3$
    (D) $-12x^2y^2$
    (E) $4x^3y$

14. Evaluate $\displaystyle\sum_{k=3}^{5}\left(k^2 - 1\right)$.
    (A) 24
    (B) 12
    (C) 48
    (D) 49
    (E) 47

15. In a group of 40 students, 25 applied to NJL College and 30 applied to Joshua University. If 3 students applied to neither NJL nor Joshua, how many applied to both schools?
    (A) 6
    (B) 12
    (C) 18
    (D) 19
    (E) 11

16. What is the remainder when $x^5 - 1$ is divided by $x - 1$?
    (A) 0
    (B) -2
    (C) 2
    (D) -1
    (E) 1

17. $y = \dfrac{(x+2)(x-3)(x-1)}{(x-7)(x+5)}$ has a vertical asymptote at
    (A) $x = -2$
    (B) $x = 3$
    (C) $x = 1$
    (D) $x = 7$
    (E) $x = 5$

18. What statement will this miniprogram print?

1	LET A = 3
2	LET B = 4
3	LET C = $(B - A)^2$
4	IF C > 0 GO TO INSTRUCTION 7
5	IF C = 0 GO TO INSTRUCTION 9
6	IF C < 0 GO TO INSTRUCTION 11
7	PRINT "A = 3"
8	STOP
9	PRINT "B = 4"
10	STOP
11	PRINT "B – A = 1"
12	STOP

    (A) STOP
    (B) A = 3
    (C) B = 4
    (D) B – A = 1
    (E) B – A = –1

19. If $\ln x + \ln(x + 2) = \ln 3$, solve for x.
    (A) 1
    (B) 0
    (C) 2
    (D) e
    (E) e^2

20. If $f(x) = 2x - 1$ and $g(x) = 3x + 1$, then $g(f(x)) =$
    (A) $2x + 1$
    (B) $3x - 1$
    (C) $6x - 2$
    (D) x
    (E) $6x^2 - x - 1$

21. Find the lateral area of a right circular cone whose height is 10 and base radius is 2.
    (A) 400π
    (B) 20π
    (C) 40π
    (D) $2\sqrt{26}$
    (E) $4\pi\sqrt{26}$

22. Which is not an identity?

    (A) $\sin^2 2\theta + \cos^2 2\theta = 1$

    (B) $\dfrac{\tan 7x}{\sin 7x} = \sec 7x$

    (C) $\tan 3t + \cot 3t = 1$

    (D) $\dfrac{1}{\sin 4r} = \csc 4r$

    (E) $\tan^2 m^2 + 1 = \sec^2 m^2$

23. If $f(x) = x + \dfrac{1}{x}$, then $f\left(\dfrac{1}{x}\right) =$

    (A) $x^2 + 1$

    (B) $f(x)$

    (C) $x^2 + x$

    (D) $\dfrac{2}{x}$

    (E) $\dfrac{x^2 + 1}{x^2}$

24. Find the area between the graph of $y = 2x - x^2$ and the x-axis between the values of $x = 0$ and $x = 2$

    (A) $1\frac{1}{3}$

    (B) $1\frac{2}{3}$

    (C) $1\frac{5}{7}$

    (D) 2

    (E) $2\frac{1}{3}$

25. $\displaystyle \lim_{x \to -3} \dfrac{x^3 + 27}{x^2 - 9} =$

    (A) $\frac{3}{2}$

    (B) 0

    (C) $-\frac{3}{2}$

    (D) -2

    (E) $-\frac{9}{2}$

Test: Music Education (0110)

Time: 2 hours, comprised of a 40-minute listening section and an 80-minute written section

Number of Questions: 150

Format: 150 multiple-choice questions, 45 of which are based on taped musical excerpts

Purpose of the Test

Designed to measure the preparation of prospective kindergarten through twelfth grade music educators

Content Categories

- Music History and Literature—(20 percent)
- Music Theory—(21 percent)
- Performance Skills—(19 percent)
- Curriculum, Instruction, and Professional Concerns—(40 percent)

Category Descriptions

Music History and Literature

1. Music of all periods, with emphasis on eighteenth, nineteenth, and twentieth centuries
2. Style periods and their characteristics
3. Composers
4. Genres
5. Music literature
6. Performance media
7. Approximately half the music history questions are based on taped musical excerpts

Music Theory

1. Compositional organization and acoustics
2. Approximately half the music theory questions are based on taped musical excerpts

Performance Skills

1. Conducting
2. Interpretation of style and symbols
3. Improvisational techniques and performance literature
4. Critical listening and performance error recognition
5. Acoustical considerations involving rehearsal rooms and performance areas
6. Approximately half of the performance skills questions are based on taped musical excerpts

Curriculum, Instruction, and Professional Considerations

1. Course offerings from K-12

2. Course content including psychomotor, cognitive and affective behaviors, conceptual elements of music, learning sequence, grade-level performance skills, interdisciplinary aspects, student evaluation, pedagogical approaches, appropriate vocal and instrumental materials, and classroom management skills

3. Sociology, philosophy, psychology, and history of music education

4. Professional literature, practices, organizations, and ethics

5. Several curriculum, instruction, and professional concerns questions may be based on taped excerpts.

Music Education

Directions: Each question or incomplete statement is followed by five answer choices. For each question, circle the answer or completion that is best.

Sample Questions for the Taped Section (On the actual test, you will hear an excerpt from a well-known chorus.)

1. Name the composer.
   (A) J. S. Bach
   (B) W. A. Mozart
   (C) R. Schumann
   (D) G. F. Handel
   (E) L. Beethoven

2. Name the type of cadence used in this music.
   (A) Authentic
   (B) Half
   (C) Plagal
   (D) Deceptive
   (E) Imperfect

3. This example is part of a large work called
   (A) oratorio.
   (B) symphony.
   (C) tone poem.
   (D) opera.
   (E) sonata.

(On the actual test, you will hear a short excerpt from the following march.)

4. Name the composer of this famous march.

   (A) J. P. Sousa

   (B) K. L. King

   (C) P. Tchaikovsky

   (D) F. Mendelssohn

   (E) J. Brahms

Sample Questions for the Nontaped Section

5. Identify the most important form of early polyphonic music during the Middle Ages.

   (A) Trio sonata

   (B) Homophonic

   (C) Motet

   (D) Tone row

   (E) Quartet

6. The figured bass for a deceptive cadence is

   (A) V–I

   (B) II–V

   (C) I–VI

   (D) IV–I

   (E) V–VI

7. Pivot chords are used in

   (A) adagio.

   (B) augmentation.

   (C) atonal.

   (D) odd meter.

   (E) modulation.

8. Which of the following were not performed during the Baroque period?

   (A) Atonal

   (B) Cantata

   (C) Opera

   (D) Motet

   (E) Fugue

9. In order to produce a good characteristic tone, wind instrumental students must have the correct

   (A) rosin.

   (B) embouchure.

   (C) sticks.

   (D) music.

   (E) rhythm.

10. Classroom eurythmic activities would include

    (A) singing.

    (B) testing.

    (C) marching.

    (D) talking.

    (E) listening.

11. Which one of the following was a twentieth-century composer?

    (A) C. Ives

    (B) J. Brahms

    (C) C. P. E. Bach

    (D) F. Liszt

    (E) G. Verdi

12. The music of the Classical period includes the works of which composer?

    (A) S. Prokofiev

    (B) F. Haydn

    (C) A. Toscanini

    (D) S. Earnhart

    (E) A. Berg

13. In teaching beginning music reading, which of the following should be avoided?

    (A) Staff

    (B) Clef

    (C) Note values

    (D) Note names

    (E) Syncopation

14. The largest music educator's association is the
    (A) A.P.B.S.A.
    (B) N.A.R.D.
    (C) N.E.M.C.
    (D) N.A.S.A
    (E) D.O.T.

15. While conducting a fund-raising project, the music teacher should
    (A) deposit all money into a personal account.
    (B) delegate all responsibilities to the students.
    (C) expect compensation for the time spent fund-raising.
    (D) keep all money in the teacher's desk.
    (E) avoid using classroom time to conduct the project.

16. The main purpose for music education in the public schools is to
    (A) win contests.
    (B) prepare students for careers in music.
    (C) provide music for school functions.
    (D) provide experience for future music consumers.
    (E) teach discipline.

17. The first note a beginning violinist should play is
    (A) concert B flat.
    (B) middle C.
    (C) second space A.
    (D) first space F.
    (E) third line D.

18. One technique that can be used in teaching vocal sight reading is
    (A) a periodic chart.
    (B) solfeggio.
    (C) cantata.
    (D) madrigal.
    (E) arpeggio.

19. Which of the following scales does not share characteristics with the other four?
    (A) Major
    (B) Minor
    (C) Dorian
    (D) Mixolydian
    (E) Pentatonic

20. A curved line connecting two of the same note is called a
    (A) phrase marking.
    (B) tie.
    (C) slur.
    (D) staccato.
    (E) mistake.

21. The notations above are used to designate
    (A) chords.
    (B) glissandos.
    (C) arpeggios.
    (D) slurs.
    (E) staccatos.

22. The excerpt above is an example of
    (A) four-part harmony.
    (B) sotto voce.
    (C) elementary music.
    (D) polyrhythm.
    (E) lyre.

Credo in unum Deum, Patrem omni-potentem

23. The music above would have been performed during the
    (A) Gregorian period.
    (B) Baroque period.
    (C) Classical period.
    (D) Romantic period.
    (E) Modern period.

24. A capella vocal music should be performed
    (A) with a rhythm section only.
    (B) with a full orchestra.
    (C) with piano accompaniment.
    (D) with a cap.
    (E) unaccompanied.

25. Which of the following does not belong in an elementary classroom music curriculum?
    (A) Singing folksongs
    (B) Music reading
    (C) Music listening
    (D) Four-part dictation
    (E) Music writing

Test: Physics (0260)

Time: 2 hours

Number of Questions: 100

Format: Multiple-choice Questions

Purpose of the Test

Designed to measure the preparation of prospective junior and senior high school physics teachers

Content Categories

- Major Concepts, Heat and Thermodynamics, Environmental Issues —(28 percent)
- Mechanics—(25 percent)
- Electricity and Magnetism—(20 percent)
- Wave Motion, Atomic and Nuclear Physics—(27 percent)

Category Descriptions

Major Concepts, Heat and Thermodynamics, Environmental Issues

1. Nature and properties of matter
2. Interaction of energy and matter, including conservation, thermal effects, electrical effects, quantum effects, kinetic molecular theory, and nuclear reactions
3. Heat and thermodynamics: basic laws, friction, heat pumps, transfer, thermal properties, and expansion and contraction effects
4. Environmental issues

Mechanics

1. Motion: linear, curvilinear, and periodic
2. Dynamics, conservation, gravity
3. Fluid mechanics of noncompressible fluids
4. Relativistic mechanics related to special theory only

Electricity and Magnetism

Static electricity, electric current, and magnetic fields

Wave Motion, Atomic and Nuclear Physics

1. Wave motion: properties, models, phenomena, sound and vibrations in matter, electromagnetic radiation, and geometrical and physical optics
2. Atomic and nuclear physics: fundamental particles, quantum theory, models, and wave/particle duality

Physics

Directions: Each question or incomplete statement is followed by five answer choices. For each question, circle the answer or completion that is best.

1. The diagram represents a block sliding along a frictionless surface between points *A* and *G*.

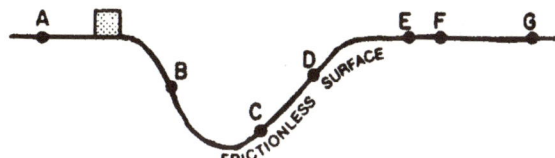

   As the block moves from point *A* to point *B*, the speed of the block will be

   (A) decreasing.

   (B) increasing.

   (C) constant, but not zero.

   (D) zero.

   (E) decrease and then increase.

2. A person travels 6 meters north, 4 meters east, and 6 meters south. What is the total displacement?

   (A) 16 m east

   (B) 6 m north

   (C) 6 m south

   (D) 4 m east

   (E) 4 m west

3. The diagram below shows a graph of distance as a function of time for an object in straight-line motion. According to the graph, the object most likely has

   (A) a constant momentum.

   (B) a decreasing acceleration.

   (C) a decreasing mass.

   (D) an increasing speed.

   (E) an increasing mass.

4. If an object's velocity changes from 25 meters per second to 15 meters per second in 2.0 seconds, the magnitude of the object's acceleration is

   (A) 5.0 m/s^2

   (B) 7.5 m/s^2

   (C) 13 m/s^2

   (D) 20 m/s^2

   (E) 25 m/s^2

5. Which vector below represents the resultant of the concurrent vectors *A* and *B* in the diagram at the right?

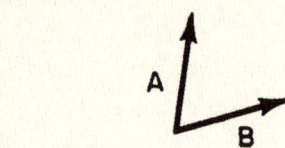

(A)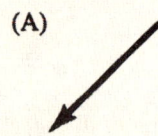

(B)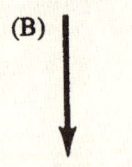

(C)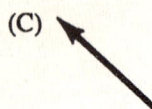

(D)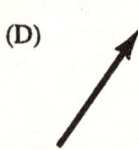

(E)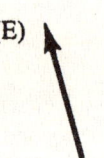

6. Four forces are acting on an object as shown in the diagram at the right. If the object is moving with a constant velocity, the magnitude of force *F* must be

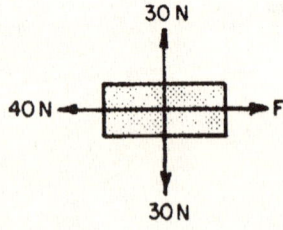

(A) 0 N
(B) 20 N
(C) 30 N
(D) 40 N
(E) 100 N

7. A force of 50 newtons causes an object to accelerate at 10 meters per second squared. What is the mass of the object?

(A) 500 kg
(B) 60 kg
(C) 5.0 kg
(D) 0.20 kg
(E) 0.10 kg

8. Which graph best represents the relationship between the mass of an object and its distance from the center of the Earth?

(A)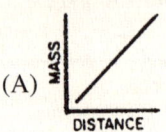

(B)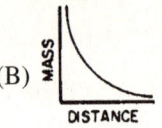

(C)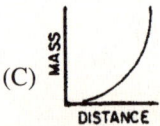

(D)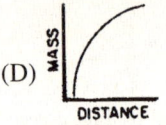

(E)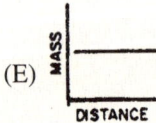

9. Gravitational force of attraction *F* exists between two point masses *A* and *B* when they are separated by a fixed distance. After mass *A* is tripled and mass *B* is halved, the gravitational attraction between the two masses is

(A) $\frac{1}{6} F$

(B) $\frac{2}{3} F$

(C) $\frac{3}{2} F$

(D) $\frac{9}{4} F$

(E) $6F$

10. Which terms represent scalar quantities?

    (A) Power and force

    (B) Work and displacement

    (C) Time and energy

    (D) Distance and velocity

    (E) Mass and acceleration

11. What is the approximate thickness of this piece of paper?

    (A) 10^2 m

    (B) 10^1 m

    (C) 10^0 m

    (D) 10^{-2} m

    (E) 10^{-5} m

12. A negatively charged object is brought near the knob of a negatively charged electroscope. The leaves of the electroscope will

    (A) move closer together.

    (B) move farther apart.

    (C) become positively charged.

    (D) become neutral.

    (E) be unaffected.

13. Which diagram below shows correct current direction in a circuit segment?

    (A)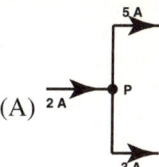

    (B)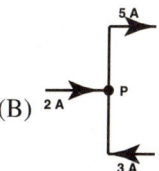

    (C)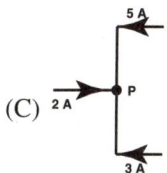

    (D)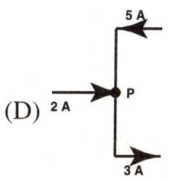

    (E)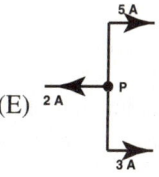

14. Which circuit segment has an equivalent resistance of 6 ohms?

    (A)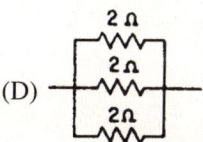

    (B)

    (C)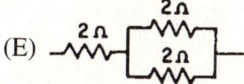

    (D)

    (E)

15. Which diagram best represents the magnetic field near the poles of a horseshoe magnet?

(A)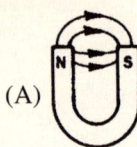

(B)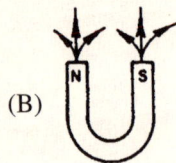

(C)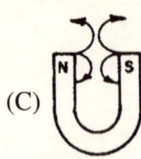

(D)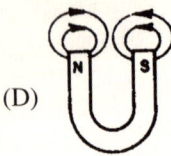

(E)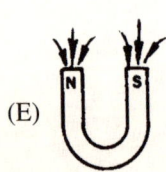

16. In the diagram below, ray *XO* is incident upon the concave (diverging) lens. Along which path will the ray continue?

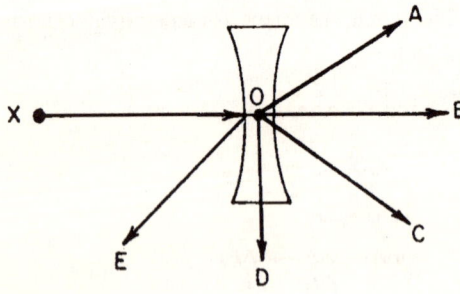

(A) *OA*

(B) *OB*

(C) *OC*

(D) *OD*

(E) *OE*

17. A beam of blue light causes photoelectrons to be emitted from a photoemissive surface. An increase in the intensity of the blue light will cause an increase in the

(A) maximum kinetic energy of the emitted photoelectrons.

(B) number of photoelectrons emitted per unit of time.

(C) charge carried by each photoelectron.

(D) work function of the photoemissive surface.

(E) frequency of the impinging light.

18. Which reaction is an example of nuclear fusion?

(A) $^{226}_{88}\text{Ra} \rightarrow ^{222}_{86}\text{Rn} + ^{4}_{2}\text{He} + Q$

(B) $^{214}_{83}\text{Bi} \rightarrow ^{214}_{84}\text{Po} + ^{0}_{-1}\text{e} + Q$

(C) $^{235}_{92}\text{U} + ^{1}_{0}\text{n} \rightarrow ^{92}_{36}\text{Kr} + ^{141}_{56}\text{Ba} + 3^{1}_{0}\text{n} + Q$

(D) $^{3}_{1}\text{H} + ^{1}_{1}\text{H} \rightarrow ^{4}_{2}\text{He} + Q$

(E) $^{235}_{92}\text{U} + ^{1}_{0}\text{n} \rightarrow ^{141}_{56}\text{Ba} + ^{92}_{36}\text{Kr} + 3^{1}_{0}\text{n} + Q$

19. In the reaction $^{24}_{11}\text{Na} \rightarrow ^{24}_{12}\text{Mg} + x$, what does x represent?

(A) An alpha particle

(B) A beta particle

(C) A neutron

(D) A positron

(E) A proton

20. The wavelength of the periodic wave shown in the diagram below is 4.0 meters. What is the distance from point *B* to point *C*?

(A) 1.0 m

(B) 2.0 m

(C) 3.0 m

(D) 4.0 m

(E) 5.0 m

21. The half-life of an isotope is 14 days. How many days will it take 8 grams of this isotope to decay to 1 gram?

    (A) 14

    (B) 21

    (C) 28

    (D) 42

    (E) 49

22. The diagram below shows an object traveling clockwise in a horizontal, circular path at constant speed. Which arrow best shows the direction of the centripetal acceleration of the object at the instant shown?

    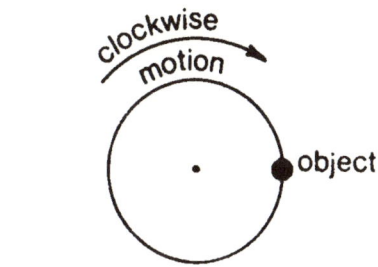

    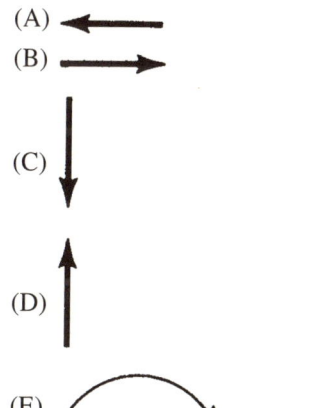

    (A) ⟵

    (B) ⟶

    (C) ↓

    (D) ↑

    (E) ⤵

23. The graph below represents the relationship between the temperature of a gas and the average kinetic energy (KE) of the molecules of the gas.

    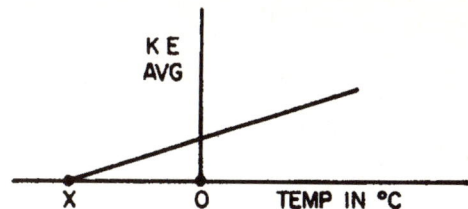

    The temperature represented at point X is approximately

    (A) 273°C

    (B) 0°C

    (C) –273°C

    (D) –373°C

    (E) –1000°C

24. What is the mass number of an atom with 9 protons, 11 neutrons, and 9 electrons?

    (A) 9

    (B) 18

    (C) 20

    (D) 23

    (E) 29

25. Which of the following electromagnetic waves has the *lowest* frequency?

    (A) Violet light

    (B) Green light

    (C) Yellow light

    (D) Red light

    (E) Blue light

Test: Reading Specialist (0300)

Time: 2 hours

Number of Questions: 145

Format: Multiple-choice Questions:

Purpose of the Test

Designed to measure the preparation of prospective supervisory or instructor positions in reading instruction K-12

Content Categories

- Linguistic and Cognitive Bases of the Reading Process—(15 percent)
- Comprehension—(20 percent)
- Word Identification—(15 percent)
- Vocabulary Development—(10 percent)
- Methodologies—(20 percent)
- Diagnosis and Program Improvement—(20 percent)

Category Descriptions

Linguistic and Cognitive Bases of the Reading Process

1. Language as a communication system (including relationships of listening, thinking, reading, writing, and speaking) and linguistic differences
2. Language and cognitive development, including abilities, major theories, learning styles, and sociolinguistics

Comprehension

1. Literal and interpretive: teaching strategies, content area integration, and signals
2. Critical and Evaluative: criteria for evaluation, propaganda, stereotyping, teaching styles, content area integration, and development of creative thinking
3. Reference and study skills, including SQ3R, reading rate, graphic interpretation, test-taking, and graphic organizers

Word Identification

1. Interrelatedness of identification skills and comprehension
2. Knowledge of word identification strategies
3. Knowledge of individual and group activities for mastery

Vocabulary Development

1. Interrelatedness of vocabulary development and comprehension
2. Strategies for teaching
3. Word origins

Methodologies

1. Research and theories on teaching and learning
2. Environment organization for diagnostic instruction
3. Special needs concerns
4. Fostering enjoyment and appreciation of reading

Diagnosis and Program Improvement

1. Prescription, organization, and implementation of instruction on the basis of individual or group diagnosis
2. Community interaction in the planning and development of a program
3. Curriculum development and instructional planning
4. Identification of needs and initiation and implementation of improvement in programs

Reading Specialist

Directions: Each question or incomplete statement is followed by five answer choices. For each question, circle the answer or completion that is best.

1. A reading-impaired student who cannot learn individual phonic sounds can be best taught using all of the following techniques *except:*

   (A) identifying word endings.

   (B) putting together and separating compound words.

   (C) teaching syllabication skills by emphasizing that each word part contains a vowel.

   (D) identifying separate diphthongs and r-controlled patterns.

   (E) identifying root prefixes and suffices.

2. A reading disability can best be defined as a

   (A) significant discrepancy between reading level and intellectual potential as measured by standardized tests.

   (B) gap of at least two years below grade level as measured by an Informal Reading Inventory.

   (C) significant discrepancy between literal comprehension and decoding ability.

   (D) problem caused by severe perceptual and neurologic deficits.

   (E) blockage primarily caused by a combination of emotional and cognitive factors.

3. Techniques for dealing with high school students who have low reading ability include all of the following *except*

   (A) introduce text by building concepts and developing new vocabulary.

   (B) ask many factual questions using a structured approach.

   (C) emphasize discussion and oral reading.

   (D) give students a great deal of independent seatwork.

   (E) give students high-interest/low-vocabulary supplementary material.

4. Which of the following are examples of mature reading material to use with a fifteen-year-old nonreader?

   I. Operation Alphabet

   II. Picture-word cards

   III. Merrill Linguistic Readers

   IV. Readers' Digest Skill Texts

   (A) I and II only

   (B) I, II, and IV only

   (C) I and IV only

   (D) III and IV only

   (E) II, III, and IV only

5. A student who reads up to grade level on standardized tests but is still not functioning to his potential is usually considered an underachiever. Often, this student lacks outside reading interests. Such a student usually has problems with higher-level reading skills in high school. Which is the *least* effective remedial technique for such an underachiever?

   (A) Choose material that will motivate the student to read further on his own.

   (B) Give comprehension exercises dealing with separate content area fields.

   (C) Increase vocabulary by developing a notebook of new words and sentences.

   (D) Teach Latin and Greek prefixes and roots.

   (E) Emphasize oral reading so the student hears what a story is about.

6. A teacher says groups of four words, three with the same sound. She says each group a second time and the children clap at the word that does not begin with the sound being taught. The instructor is trying to enhance

(A) auditory memory.

(B) auditory closure.

(C) auditory discrimination.

(D) auditory sequencing.

(E) auditory blending.

7. Which of these skills should be taught last?

(A) Syllabication

(B) Phrasing and expression

(C) Context clues

(D) Blending

(E) Nonphonetic words

8. A student glances over chapter headings and turns them into questions. Then the student answers these questions while looking away from the book while he writes down the information to review the lesson to understand its major points. The technique being described is

(A) advanced organizing.

(B) outlining.

(C) SQ3R.

(D) summarizing.

(E) semantic mapping.

9. In teaching initial consonants and blends to disabled readers, which of the following procedures should be followed?

I. Present them in uppercase and lowercase with pictures whose content is mature in format.

II. Teach four to five sounds in a single lesson.

III. Have children name each object pictured to avoid confusion.

IV. Choose letters that are similar in appearance and sound to enhance discrimination skills.

(A) I, II, and IV only

(B) IV only

(C) I, III, and IV only

(D) I, II, and III only

(E) II, III, and IV only

10. How would you lower the anxiety of a pupil taking a standardized reading test?

(A) Tell the student that the test will not count.

(B) Cut out hard questions.

(C) Read the test to him.

(D) Tell him that the questions will get easier during the session.

(E) Tell him to take the test slowly to avoid mistakes.

11. A high school student with a bright average IQ is reading at the second-grade level. He has extreme difficulty decoding words. All of the following are good techniques to use *except*

(A) use other media to reinforce learning.

(B) assign books at his independent reading level.

(C) use recorded audio books.

(D) introduce spelling and writing gradually and only when necessary.

(E) engage student in various shop activities to develop a technical vocabulary.

12. It is important to have poor readers read aloud alternating paragraphs with an instructor to help the student with

I. phrasing.

II. expression.

III. comprehension.

IV. learning new words.

(A) I, II, and IV only

(B) I, II, and III only

(C) II, III, and IV only

(D) II and III only

(E) I and II only

13. Poor high school readers need to develop test-taking skills. All of the following are ways to develop such skills *except*

(A) explain the purpose of various tests.

(B) start with short quizzes.

(C) relate questions directly to material covered.

(D) have pupils correct the test and de-emphasize marks.

(E) stress the rightness or wrongness of answers.

14. In remediating reading-disabled students, word recognition skills must be taught in a systematic and simplified fashion. Which skill should probably be taught first?

    (A) Long vowel sounds

    (B) Initial consonants

    (C) Sight words

    (D) Syllabication

    (E) Consonant diagraphs

15. What is the importance of developing a large sight vocabulary?

    (A) It teaches students to figure out words phonetically.

    (B) Failure to develop this prevents fluency.

    (C) It increases a student's comprehension of vocabulary concepts.

    (D) A large sight vocabulary prevents students from using configuration clues.

    (E) It is essential in developing alphabetization skills.

16. Which is an example of a visual-motor method in teaching irregular sight words?

    (A) Child looks at a word, tries to remember it with eyes closed, then writes it down

    (B) Teacher makes repetitive use of picture-word cards created from magazine photographs

    (C) Small groups engage in oral reading of stories at children's own level with teacher supplying missing words repeatedly until they are recognized by sight

    (D) Child looks at word, traces it with finger while pronouncing each sound, then writes word without a model

    (E) Teacher uses tachistoscope to mechanically flash sight words at shorter and shorter intervals

17. An approach to help a high school student who cannot read beyond the second-grade level would include

    (A) teaching blending skills using a newspaper.

    (B) teaching words from signs, labels, medicines, and menus.

    (C) teaching words using only capitals.

    (D) emphasizing syllabication skills in dealing with context-area vocabulary.

    (E) using cloze techniques at a student's potential reading level.

18. According to the latest research, the best prognosis for remediating nonreaders is when

    (A) emphasis is placed on pull-out programs.

    (B) focus is placed on structural analysis.

    (C) functional words are emphasized.

    (D) a multimodal approach is used.

    (E) remediation begins at a young age.

19. Library techniques must be taught to facilitate research skills. All of the following library skills should be taught *except*

    (A) use of reference material.

    (B) use of a computer database to search for specific authors, titles, or subjects.

    (C) use of microfiche material.

    (D) structure of the Dewey Decimal or Library of Congress systems.

    (E) how to find fiction books using a card catalog.

20. A student completes a whole story for the first time although he or she has struggled through decoding the words. The student feels proud of his or her accomplishment. The teacher's next step would be to

    (A) ask multiple questions about the content.

    (B) have the student look back in the story to substantiate specific facts.

    (C) find explanatory phrases to elaborate specific points.

    (D) encourage spontaneous discussion.

    (E) focus on answering main idea questions.

21. All are effective ways to help students improve their vocabularies *except*

    (A) using a dictionary to look up many unknown words.

    (B) teaching words that have multiple meanings.

    (C) reminding students to use context to figure out unknown words.

    (D) teaching the origin of words by using dramatic examples.

    (E) teaching technical vocabulary groups.

22. Which of the following skills would probably be taught *last*?

    (A) Pronunciation of words derived from foreign languages

    (B) Adjusting reading rate

    (C) Following directions

    (D) Drawing conclusions

    (E) Finding the main idea

23. Why is it advisable to postpone the teaching of the short *e* until the other vowels are learned?

    (A) The *e* sound can sometimes be silent.

    (B) There are many vowel sounds for *e*.

    (C) Many children have considerable difficulty distinguishing between the short sounds of *a* and *e*.

    (D) The short *e* should be taught in combination with blends and diagraphs.

    (E) It is best to teach the short *e* as a CVC combination.

24. Having students read cookbooks, magic books, math problems, and science experiments teaches them how to

    (A) find the main idea.

    (B) draw conclusions.

    (C) recall facts.

    (D) follow directions.

    (E) determine effective research skills.

25. Which is the *least* important factor interfering with comprehension of content area material?

    (A) Limited intelligence

    (B) Unfamiliarity with basic concepts of the subject matter

    (C) Lack of interest in the material

    (D) Meager vocabulary

    (E) Reading rate

Test: School Guidance and Counseling (0420)

Time: 2 hours

Number of Questions: 140 (45 based on listening section)

Format: Multiple-choice Questions, approximately one-third based on taped interactions

Purpose of the Test

Designed to measure the preparation of prospective public school counselors

Content Categories

- Counseling and Guidance—(55 percent)
- Consulting—(20 percent)
- Coordinating—(15 percent)
- Professional Issues—(10 percent)

Category Descriptions

Counseling and Guidance

Communication, special populations, appraisal, transition

Consulting

Indirect services to other students, including consultation with staff members, families, and community agencies

Coordinating

1. Management and organization
2. Information acquisition and dissemination
3. Program evaluation

Professional Issues

1. Legal and ethical concerns
2. Resources for professional development

School Guidance and Counseling

Directions: Each question or incomplete statement is followed by five answer choices. For each question, circle the answer or completion that is best.

1. After twelve weeks, a junior high counselor has to terminate counseling services to a student who initially was having difficulty adjusting to being in a departmentalized program. All are effective ways for the counselor to end counseling *except*

    (A) avoid discussing any new counseling material during the last two or three weeks.

    (B) leave on a positive note—celebrate the student's progress and gains.

    (C) tell the student he can come when he needs to even though they will not be meeting regularly.

    (D) forewarn the student how many sessions they have left.

    (E) ask the student's homeroom teacher to tell him that he no longer needs to come to counseling because he has adjusted well to junior high school.

2. The type of therapy that builds a positive relationship between client and therapist and then emphasizes that each person assumes responsibility for his own behavior by setting goals and making responsible decisions illustrates

    (A) reality therapy.

    (B) play therapy.

    (C) behavioral counseling.

    (D) rational-emotive therapy.

    (E) client-centered counseling.

3. Lawrence Kohlberg's research on moral development emphasizes a three-level, six-stage approach. Using his theory, if a student says that he will do something because his conscience tells him it is right, this student is at the

    (A) punishment and obedience stage.

    (B) law and order stage.

    (C) social contract stage.

    (D) universal ethics stage.

    (E) instrumental relativism stage.

4. Which of the following *least* describes the role of a guidance counselor?

    (A) He or she tries to develop school adjustment strategies.

    (B) He or she emphasizes personal and career development.

    (C) He or she should experiment in the use of different disciplinary techniques to control management problems in the classroom.

    (D) He or she develops structured learning activities or lessons that guide students to understand themselves and others.

    (E) He or she helps students understand and meet academic goals.

5. In the 1920s,

    (A) a guidance counselor's primary function was measurement of personality traits using standardized tests.

    (B) school counselors emphasized mental health due to rapid changes in society.

    (C) guidance encouraged talented youths to attend college if aptitude in math and science were shown.

    (D) school guidance focused primarily on developing vocational skills and choices.

    (E) school guidance coordinated the transition between school and the world of work for students with developmental delays.

6. The developmental approach to school guidance
    I. identifies certain skills and experiences students need to be successful in school.
    II. clarifies behaviors and tasks a student will need to facilitate adjustment.
    III. emphasizes the learning of tasks through a guidance curriculum.
    IV. develops interpersonal skills in students after crisis situations.

    (A) I and III only
    (B) II, III, and IV only
    (C) III only
    (D) I, II, and III only
    (E) I and II only

7. Which is a limitation of using teachers as guidance advisers in lieu of trained counselors?
    (A) Differential staffing makes better use of school personnel.
    (B) Such an approach depends on administrative as well as teacher knowledge and support.
    (C) It fosters a positive learning environment.
    (D) More students receive guidance services in the school.
    (E) It lowers counselor-student ratios dramatically.

8. In an elementary school, a guidance counselor does all of the following *except*
    (A) help develop guidance units that evolve from student needs.
    (B) consult with teachers and administrators about counseling interventions being done with various students.
    (C) serve as a resource to teachers about behavior changes a student may be having.
    (D) help identify students with special needs or problems and help find alternative educational or guidance services for them.
    (E) serve as a liaison between the school and public health and rehabilitation agencies.

9. This type of student needs less verbal counseling. He or she needs more concrete and operational forms of assistance. This student needs to gain insight by doing instead of talking. The student being described
    (A) is learning disabled.
    (B) has mental retardation.
    (C) has a conduct disorder.
    (D) has an attention deficit disorder.
    (E) is socially maladjusted.

10. A student describes to a guidance counselor several ways he has tried to harm his parents because they are abusive to him. It is the counselor's responsibility at this point to
    (A) keep the matter confidential.
    (B) refer the student to someone more qualified.
    (C) secretly inform the authorities.
    (D) tell the student he must inform the authorities for his own protection.
    (E) talk the student out of any further harmful actions.

11. Rational-emotive therapy is most associated with
    (A) Carl Rogers.
    (B) Albert Ellis.
    (C) Virginia Axline.
    (D) B. F. Skinner.
    (E) William Glasser.

12. The best way for a guidance counselor to begin to develop study skills and habits in underachieving students would be to
    (A) give out a list of effective study approaches.
    (B) have these underachieving students observe the study habits of excelling students.
    (C) drill such students in various study approaches.
    (D) encourage students to talk about study habits from their own experiences.
    (E) have them view filmstrips about various study approaches.

13. A student broke up with his girlfriend several days ago. He tells the school counselor that last night he thought about putting a pillow over his head. What should the counselor do at this point?

    (A) Engage in therapeutic-intervention techniques.

    (B) Refer the student to a mental health center.

    (C) Call the police to have the student hospitalized.

    (D) Immediately have the student suspended from school.

    (E) Refer the student for family therapy.

14. How are school counseling and psychotherapy different?

    (A) School guidance and psychotherapy utilize totally different theories of counseling.

    (B) Psychotherapy must be done by someone with a medical degree, while counseling can be done by lay personnel trained in various techniques.

    (C) School counseling deals with students who are within the normal range of functioning, while psychotherapy deals with people in a clinical setting who are very dysfunctional and need to gain insight into their problems through exploration of the past.

    (D) Psychotherapy uses a behavioral approach to change dysfunctional behaviors, while school counseling focuses more on a psychosexual model of therapy to help clients gain insight into the reasons for their behaviors.

    (E) There is no significant difference in approach between school counseling and psychotherapy.

15. All of the following contributed to the development of school guidance and counseling *except*

    (A) more humane care of the mentally disturbed, which began in the nineteenth century.

    (B) scientific methods in the study of affective behavior.

    (C) the concept that one's environment contributes to development.

    (D) John Dewey's emphasizing the importance of the student in the educational process.

    (E) Piaget's theory of child development.

16. School guidance at the primary level focuses on

    (A) the testing and evaluation of middle-grade students.

    (B) the setting up of school schedules and programming.

    (C) individual counseling of those students who are having academic difficulty.

    (D) intervening in order to avoid crisis situations.

    (E) developing a consultative role with teachers and administrators.

17. A student confides in her guidance counselor that she is having sex with her boyfriend. She is afraid that if her parents find out, they will severely punish her and try to end her relationship. How should the counselor deal with this situation?

    (A) Tell the student's parents about the problem in a nonjudgmental way.

    (B) Tell the student to abstain from sex to avoid catching a venereal disease or AIDS.

    (C) Show the student a filmstrip about the consequences of such immoral behavior.

    (D) Discuss with the student various methods of birth control.

    (E) Advise the student to seek the counsel of a priest, minister, or rabbi.

18. A leader in the vocational guidance movement in the early twentieth century was

    (A) Carl Rogers.

    (B) A. S. Neil.

    (C) Jesse B. Davis.

    (D) Fritz Redl.

    (E) Bruno Bettelheim.

19. There are four approaches to guidance and counseling in the schools: crisis, remedial, preventive, and developmental. Which of the following are examples of the developmental approach?

    I. Assisting in the development of life skills

    II. Acting as a mediator

    III. Teaching students how to interact in a positive manner

    IV. Helping in the development of interpersonal skills

    (A) I, III, and IV only

    (B) II, III, and IV only

    (C) I, II, and III only

    (D) II only

    (E) IV only

20. Individual counseling is considered the best approach for all of the following students *except*

    (A) a student who lacks self-confidence.

    (B) a student who feels others neither understand nor care about his situation.

    (C) a student who lacks social skills who is rejected by others.

    (D) a student whose siblings may be involved in illegal activities.

    (E) a class clown engaging in attention-seeking behavior.

21. A counselor has initiated counseling with a student who is being described by his teacher as uncooperative. The student pays no attention to classwork, constantly talks, and is sullen. How should this counselor initiate discussing the boy's problem?

    (A) State to the student that he is being seen because he is in trouble with his teacher.

    (B) State that the principal feels the student should be taken out of his present class.

    (C) Ask a series of open-ended questions pertaining to school.

    (D) Immediately describe to the student various strategies on how to improve class adjustment.

    (E) Threaten suspension if the student does not change his behavior.

22. In a developmental guidance curriculum, the goal of recognizing how one's self-esteem and attitude are related to the way in which a goal is approached describes

    (A) motivation.

    (B) study skills and habits.

    (C) self-assessment.

    (D) decision making and problem solving.

    (E) educational planning.

23. The theory focuses on goal orientation within a social context, emphasizing that people should see themselves as individuals who have the capacity to make decisions and choices and to gain insight into their behavior for the purpose of finding alternatives to solving problems. This describes

    (A) psychoanalytic theory.

    (B) Adlerian psychology.

    (C) transactional analysis.

    (D) Gestalt theory.

    (E) multimodal theory.

24. An adolescent coming from a ghetto environment has trouble relating to students and teachers. He has been suspended several times. Which is the best approach to deal with this student?

    (A) The counselor needs to discuss childhood conflicts with the student using the psychoanalytic approach.

    (B) The student should be involved in counselor-led group activities where interpersonal skills could be discussed and practiced.

    (C) The counselor should mediate any conflicts between the student and other school personnel.

    (D) The counselor should use play therapy so the student can act out his negative impulses in private.

    (E) The counselor should call in the student's mother to discuss a possible referral to an outside agency for the purpose of beginning family therapy.

25. Which of the following are either classroom guidance methods or programs?

    I. DUSO

    II. Magic Circle

    III. Classroom meetings

    IV. DISTAR

    (A) I only

    (B) I and II only

    (C) II, III, and IV only

    (D) I, II, and III only

    (E) IV only

Test: School Psychologist (0400)

Time: 2 hours

Number of Questions: 120

Format: Multiple-choice Questions:

Purpose of the Test

Designed to measure the preparation of prospective school psychiatrists

Content Categories

- Diagnosis and Fact Finding—(25 percent)
- Prevention and Intervention—(25 percent)
- Applied Psychological Foundations—(20 percent)
- Applied Educational Foundations—(12 percent)
- Ethical and Legal Considerations—(18 percent)

Category Descriptions

Diagnosis and Fact Finding

1. Initial fact gathering
2. Assessment of functioning levels, diagnostics, achievement, development, behavior, personality, self-concept, and performance-based
3. Assessment of special needs

Prevention and Intervention

1. Cognitive and behavioral: techniques and major research studies
2. Interventions with special populations
3. Academic: accommodations and modifications, research, discipline, classroom management, and remediation
4. Crisis intervention and prevention
5. Other skills: developmentally appropriate intervention for ages 0-21 years, adjustment techniques, social skills, data management, computer applications, therapy recommendation, stress management, conflict/resolution, decision making, problem solving, communication skills, group facilitation, and leadership skills

Applied Psychological Foundations

1. General psychological principles: biological bases, effects of commonly prescribed medications, substance abuse signs and symptoms, research findings, life span development, motivation, theories of intelligence, and language development
2. Knowledge of testing theory and principles

Applied Educational Foundations

Principle of learning and teaching, academic needs of exceptional students

Ethical and Legal Considerations

1. Ethical principles and professional standards
2. Laws, codes, and regulations governing the practice of school psychology, including rights, disabilities, legal liability, malpractice, negligence, and student records

School Psychologist

Directions: Each question or incomplete statement is followed by five answer choices. For each question, circle the answer or completion that is best.

1. Drug therapy has been effectively used in treating children with behavior problems. Of the following, the best type of medications for children who have personality disorders and psychoses are

    I. psychostimulant drugs.

    II. psychotropic drugs.

    III. antidepressant drugs.

    IV. anticonvulsant drugs.

    (A) I and III only

    (B) II only

    (C) I only

    (D) III and IV only

    (E) I, II, and III only

2. Psychological testing is used for all of the following *except*

    (A) detection of intellectual deficiencies for admission to special programs.

    (B) research on individual differences.

    (C) the determination of academic achievement.

    (D) the determination of potential intellectual ability.

    (E) selection and classification of personnel for various types of jobs.

3. A technique in which a psychologist compares two interpretations of a single set of behaviors—i.e., idealistic and real points of view—is called

    (A) peer nomination.

    (B) behavioral inventories or checklists.

    (C) task analysis of standardized tests of personality.

    (D) Q-Sort.

    (E) life-space interview.

4. A troublesome student is sent by a teacher to the school psychologist, along with a note. Which one of the notes below describes an inappropriate use of the psychologist's counseling services?

    (A) "The student is having a personal problem he wants to talk over."

    (B) "The child is afraid to walk into the class."

    (C) "I don't want him in my room. Keep him until the bell rings. He's out of control again."

    (D) "I've noticed excessive bruises on her arm. Please look further into this matter."

    (E) "This boy keeps falling asleep in class. Can you please see if he is having any problems? He won't open up to me at all."

5. A psychologist recommends a commercial program designed to teach affective skills. She recommends a program in which teacher-led discussions take place using a structured approach in order to help students develop skills in self-control, responsibility, and role expectations and in creating satisfactory peer relations. The clinician is describing

    (A) DUSO-R.

    (B) TAD.

    (C) Magic Circle.

    (D) TLC.

    (E) ACCESS.

6. A type of therapy that combines value clarification and social-skills learning using a modified behavioral approach has been developed by

    (A) Ellis.

    (B) Meichenbaum.

    (C) Glasser.

    (D) Coleman.

    (E) Wolfe and Moseley.

7. What is a major problem with intelligence tests, such as the WISC III and the Stanford Binet, as a measure of mental deficiency?

   (A) The tests are heavily loaded with verbal content.

   (B) Both tests are known to have poor reliability coefficients.

   (C) They have insufficient validity.

   (D) The content is not related to the needs of society.

   (E) These tests are culturally biased in favor of a middle-class population.

8. Planned ignoring, signal interference, and proximity control are techniques used in

   (A) operant conditioning.

   (B) managing surface behavior.

   (C) contracting.

   (D) managing temper tantrums.

   (E) life-space interviewing.

9. A seven-year-old student who has normal hearing and vision but cannot pronounce even initial sounds when attempting to talk needs to be evaluated for her intellectual potential. The best test to use is the

   (A) Vineland.

   (B) K-ABC.

   (C) McCarthy Scale.

   (D) WISC III.

   (E) Leiter Scale.

10. In which situation is a middle-grade student considered a danger to himself and to others?

   (A) Throwing temper tantrums

   (B) Arguing with another student

   (C) Using profanity

   (D) Talking at inappropriate times

   (E) Refusing to follow teacher directions

11. All of the following are steps in the consultation process *except*

   (A) identify the problem.

   (B) clarify the situation.

   (C) identify goals and outcomes.

   (D) observe and record behavior.

   (E) initiate the plan.

12. The classroom is out of control. The teacher constantly yells at her students in a hostile fashion, but the class is impossible to manage. The teacher has negative things to say about many students in the class. She wants you to help her find a way to improve her class. All of the following must be considered in such a situation *except*

   (A) the teacher may be resistant to change.

   (B) it can be correctly assumed that the problem rests wholly with the students.

   (C) more than one intervention may be needed.

   (D) the presenting problem may not be the real problem.

   (E) the responsibility for changing the students has to be shared.

13. Which author believed that tests of sensory discrimination could serve as a means of gauging a person's intellect?

   (A) Pearson

   (B) Galton

   (C) Binet

   (D) Sequin

   (E) Terman

14. All of the following are projective counseling techniques used by psychologists to help students express feelings they may not reveal in conversation *except*

   (A) puppetry.

   (B) role playing.

   (C) play therapy.

   (D) art and music therapy.

   (E) reality therapy.

15. An event that is imposed or occurs regularly after a behavior and increases the frequency or duration of that behavior is an example of

   (A) reinforcement.

   (B) punishment.

   (C) generalization.

   (D) shaping.

   (E) discrimination training.

16. Two students are given the WISC III. One has a full-scale IQ of 91, while the other has an IQ of 109. It can be concluded that

    (A) the second student has significantly higher intellectual ability.

    (B) intelligence cannot be measured by this test because the instrument has poor internal consistency.

    (C) both students are functioning in the average range of intellectual ability.

    (D) the first student is probably below average, while the second student has above-average potential.

    (E) another IQ test should be given to truly assess their intellectual potential.

17. Some weaknesses of self-reporting personality checklists are that

    I. individuals can hide or disguise feelings.

    II. results are highly subjective and dependent on the competence and experience of the examiner.

    III. all have poor internal consistency and stability.

    IV. many personality measures have built in lie scales.

    (A) III and IV only

    (B) II, III, and IV only

    (C) I and II only

    (D) I, II, and III only

    (E) I only

18. Which of these authors would favor an analytic approach to managing behavior?

    (A) Trieshman

    (B) Long and Newman

    (C) Algozzine

    (D) Thorndike

    (E) Redl

19. Which type of test determines whether students accept responsibility for their own behavior or assign responsibility for their behavior to other people?

    (A) Sentence-completion checklists

    (B) Locus-of-control tests

    (C) Stylistic tests

    (D) Thematic tests

    (E) Draw-a-person tests

20. An example of a peer-nominating technique is

    (A) class pictures in which a child chooses among photographs of students engaged in maladjusted or neutral behaviors.

    (B) TAT in which students describe pictures of various social events.

    (C) a technique describing how students act in different physical environments.

    (D) the use of interaction analysis to examine and analyze pupil-pupil relationships within a classroom.

    (E) the use of sociometric diagrams to determine a student's position within a class.

21. All are good ways to improve your own interview skills as a psychologist during counseling *except* to

    (A) videotape yourself in interview and have others evaluate your performance.

    (B) role play an interview.

    (C) monitor yourself for defensive behaviors or responses.

    (D) write an outline of the questions to be asked.

    (E) keep extensive notes during the interview of how you responded.

22. Which of the following are examples of good interview techniques to be employed by a clinician?

    I. Open the interview by asking nonthreatening questions.

    II. Avoid answering any direct questions posed by the respondent.

    III. Clarify unclear responses through further questioning.

    IV. Probe sensitive subject matter intensively.

    (A) I, II, and III only

    (B) I and III only

    (C) II and IV only

    (D) II, III, and IV only

    (E) I only

23. The purpose of a Rapid Deployment Team is to

    (A) evaluate students in crisis.

    (B) counsel individual students who are suicidal.

    (C) determine if a call to child welfare is necessary when abuse or neglect is suspected.

    (D) counsel students, parents, and staff in case of a death or fatal injury of a student or teacher.

    (E) counsel staff when problems in management arise.

24. This behavioral checklist is unique because it has five subscales that deal with behaviors that are indicative of the five components of the federal definition of emotional disturbance. This checklist is called the

    (A) Test of Early Socioemotional Development.

    (B) Behavior Evaluation Scale.

    (C) Behavior Rating Scale.

    (D) Thematic Apperception Test.

    (E) Bailey Scale.

25. The term describing the consistency of a test is

    (A) the objective measure of difficulty.

    (B) standardization.

    (C) validity.

    (D) norm sample.

    (E) reliability.

Test: Special Education (0350)

Time: 2 hours
Number of Questions: 150
Format: Multiple-choice Questions

Purpose of the Test

Designed to measure the preparation of prospective special education teachers for preschool through high school grade levels

Content Categories

- Understanding Exceptionality—(10 percent)
- Legal Aspects of Special Education—(10 percent)
- Assessment and Evaluation in Special Education—(20 percent)
- Service Delivery and Instruction—(37 percent)
- Classroom Management and Student Behavior—(23 percent)

Category Descriptions

Understanding Exceptionality

1. Major historical/social movements and trends that influence the delivery of services for exceptional children

2. Basic concepts relating to exceptionality: characteristics of various exceptionalities, degrees of severity, prevalence of exceptionalities in the national population, causation and prevention, early identification and early intervention, and service provisions throughout the life span

3. Major research findings and classroom implications of research

Legal Aspects of Special Education

1. Procedural rights of exceptional students and parents

2. Special Education legislation

3. Service delivery requirements of Individuals with Disabilities Act

Assessment and Evaluation in Special Education

1. Application of basic measurement concepts, such as validity, reliability, and standard deviation

2. Ethical use of tests: nondiscriminatory assessment, testing in the native language, use of multiple measures

3. Procedures for identifying and establishing students' eligibility for special education programs, such as multidisciplinary teams, the role of team members, complete and multifaceted assessment, observation procedures, and interpretation of formal assessment

4. Use of assessment and evaluation data to plan, implement, and monitor effectiveness

Service Delivery and Instruction

1. Individualized education programs

2. Curriculum and instruction

3. Career education, vocational planning, and post-school transitions

4. Skills related to teacher consultation

Classroom Management and Student Behavior

1. Classroom organization for exceptional students, including both physical and social environments

2. Techniques for managing student behavior: applied behavior analysis/behavior modification, self-management, behavioral and psycho-educational approaches to discipline

3. Teaching of social skills

4. Locating and using resources by working with a variety of individuals and groups: parents, auxiliary and related-services personnel and consultants, volunteers, paraprofessionals, tutors, and out-of-school resources

Special Education

Directions: Each question or incomplete statement is followed by five answer choices. For each question, circle the answer or completion that is best.

1. Which of the following best describes a noncategorical resource room program?

    (A) In this program, even gifted students can be accommodated.

    (B) This disability-based program allows the teacher to service various schools within a district.

    (C) This program services only learning-disabled students.

    (D) The teacher engages in team teaching within the regular classroom.

    (E) All classwork in this program is individualized and based on the particular academic needs of each student.

2. In determining the educational needs of a special education student, a variety of assessment techniques are used. Which of the following is *not* an effective assessment technique used in evaluating a student who may be in need of special services?

    (A) Direct observation

    (B) Testing

    (C) Teacher recommendation

    (D) Review of records

    (E) Product evaluation

3. An instructor uses prescriptive teaching to determine a pupil's knowledge of shapes. The pupil is able to match two or more shapes of different sizes. The student is also able to point to particular shapes named by the teacher. However, when asked, "What shape is this?" the pupil confuses three out of five common shapes. Which of the following describes the pupil's ability to recognize shapes?

    I. He is able to discriminate pictorial representations.

    II. The pupil has good expressive language concepts.

    III. The student's receptive understanding is adequate

    IV. He does not understand the concept of congruence

    (A) I, II, and IV only

    (B) II, III, and IV only

    (C) I and III only

    (D) I, III, and IV only

    (E) IV only

4. All of the following are examples of norm-referenced interpretations *except*

    (A) The student's Performance IQ is 92.

    (B) The pupil's intellectual development is two standard deviations below the mean.

    (C) The student received an 11.9 Age Equivalent Score on this measure of receptive language.

    (D) Given first-grade Dolch list, the student will correctly spell 80 percent of the words.

    (E) The student received a score above the 80th percentile on this achievement measure.

5. In this program, a teacher provides direct and indirect services to handicapped students. Although this teacher provides services to special education students, they are not the exclusive recipients of the program's benefits. Other students within a regular classroom benefit when this teacher and the general education instructor modify instruction for labeled students. The above statement is best describing

   (A) a categorical resource room.

   (B) consultant teaching.

   (C) an itinerant resource room.

   (D) a noncategorical resource room.

   (E) mainstreaming.

6. A student during informal conversation states the following: "Umm, I like the, umm *Cosby Show*. You know, it was, umm, interesting. Bill Cosby walked down the stairs and then, umm, he fell on the rug, then he did something to whatchamacallit..." How would you describe this student's difficulty with semantic language?

   (A) Poor understanding of indefinite pronouns

   (B) Repeated use of meaningless sounds or phrases

   (C) Roundabout descriptions or circumlocutions

   (D) Overuse of verbs and nouns

   (E) Redundancies and repetitions

7. All of the following describe strategies used by fluent readers *except* that the reader

   (A) shifts speed and approach to the type and purpose of reading.

   (B) predicts the endings of words and phrases.

   (C) reads to identify meaning rather than to identify letters and words.

   (D) notes the distinctive features in letters and words.

   (E) utilizes tactile reinforcement to distinguish between similar letters and words.

8. A major advantage of curriculum-based assessment is that

   (A) it connects testing with teaching.

   (B) it is based on a criterion-referenced measurement model.

   (C) national norms are being developed for this technique.

   (D) it tends to focus on anecdotal information on how a student is progressing.

   (E) these tests are informal in nature.

9. This norm-referenced reading test uses a modified cloze technique in which the student has to supply the missing word of a short sentence or passage. Which of the tests below is being described?

   (A) Woodcock Reading Mastery Test—Revised

   (B) Diagnostic Reading Scale

   (C) Gray Oral Reading Test

   (D) Informal Reading Inventory

   (E) Durrell Analysis of Reading Difficulty

10. Many special educators have to work with paraprofessionals or teacher's aides. This extra person in the classroom can be either an asset or a detriment. Which of the following are good ways to improve the effectiveness of such personnel in the classroom?

    I. Train teaching assistants in record keeping.

    II. Make sure teacher aides carry out specified remedial strategies developed and utilized by the teacher.

    III. Minimize direct teacher supervision of paraprofessionals.

    IV. Handle contradictory student-paraprofessional relationships strictly within the classroom.

    (A) I and III only

    (B) II only

    (C) I only

    (D) I and II only

    (E) All of the above

11. All of the following are effective techniques in facilitating parent involvement in a student's special education program *except*

    (A) schedule parent conferences to accommodate a parent's work responsibilities.

    (B) develop a parents' brochure illustrating how to help students with their homework.

    (C) keep parents informed by a newsletter about different school programs.

    (D) provide a resource room where parents may browse or borrow material.

    (E) inform parents of a student's progress by means of a monthly report card.

12. Computer technology is being used today to enhance the communication skills of various handicapped individuals. A device useful in helping someone who is visually impaired is a(n)

    (A) teletypewriter.

    (B) electronic page turner.

    (C) keyboard emulator.

    (D) lightpen.

    (E) viewscan.

13. Time management, listening, self-management of behavior, and the use of graphic aids are all examples of

    (A) adaptive living skills.

    (B) career education skills.

    (C) study skills.

    (D) socio-emotional skills.

    (E) content-area skills.

14. Most special education students do not possess adequate test-taking ability. All of the following are effective test-taking strategies *except:*

    (A) teaching test-making procedures to enhance a student's ability to understand different types of questions.

    (B) allowing unlimited time when taking standardized tests.

    (C) discussing different methods of studying for objective and essay tests.

    (D) reviewing completed tests with students in order to highlight test-taking errors.

    (E) ensuring that students know how much time is allotted for completion of a test.

15. A student continually called out answers in class. Her teacher decided to ignore this student's outbursts but rewarded her with a star every time she silently raised her hand and was called upon to give an answer. This behavior modification technique is called

    (A) discrimination training.

    (B) differential reinforcement.

    (C) punishment.

    (D) extinction.

    (E) modeling.

16. Long and Newman are best known for their

    (A) use of contracts for facilitating behavioral changes.

    (B) strategy in the management of temper tantrums.

    (C) development of life-space interviewing.

    (D) theories on counseling using projective techniques.

    (E) techniques for managing surface behavior.

17. A seventh-grade student has been placed in a resource room program. The student has problems in developing skills in mathematics. His assessment reveals that he is having problems in visual perception and visual memory. All of the following are effective strategies for this student *except*

    (A) reinforcing memorization of automatic multiplication and division facts to improve computational speed.

    (B) having frequent demonstrations, modeling, and rehearsal.

    (C) reading textbook instructions to the student.

    (D) minimizing the type or amount of information presented to the student.

    (E) allowing the student to make oral rather than written responses.

18. The *least* effective method to remediate a student who writes too small is to

    (A) rule a midline on standard writing paper and have lowercase letters touch the midline.

    (B) practice large writing on the chalkboard.

    (C) have the student copy a correct model of several words and have him or her evaluate the size.

    (D) have the student evaluate his own writing problem so he is aware of what must be corrected.

    (E) encourage the student to write more slowly, as speed tends to affect size.

19. Which is *not* a practical remedial technique in the teaching of spelling skills to a learning disabled student?

    (A) Have the student use a structured basal program such as *Riverside Spelling*, *Basic Goals in Spelling*, or *Silver Burdett Spelling*.

    (B) The teacher must provide a variety of writing activities that necessitate using the words learned.

    (C) Teach minimum-sized lists and use words that are of functional importance to the student.

    (D) Teach no more words than the pupil can successfully learn to spell.

    (E) Ask questions about the structural aspects of the words.

20. An eighth-grade student attending middle school has recently been evaluated. The student exhibits all the signs of learning disabilities and will be recommended for a self-contained classroom. The student is reading on the third-grade level and doing math also on the same level. Written expression is poor, and he has a low fund of general information. The student immigrated to the United States four years ago and is now somewhat proficient in both his native language and English. His mother is totally against the recommendation for this service. She does not want her child to be called a cripple, and she states that he is able to read better than she. What is the probable reason for the attitude of this parent?

    (A) The evaluation team is using too restrictive a label for this parent to tolerate.

    (B) The student was probably tested only in English and thus the evaluation is invalid.

    (C) The child's mother probably feels her due process rights have been violated.

    (D) The child study team may not have taken divergent cultural factors into consideration.

    (E) The child's scores better warrant a resource room program because he can probably function in a regular class for part of the day.

21. Which is *not* an example of an occupational-interest test for special education students taking career education courses in secondary school?

    (A) Career Assessment Inventory

    (B) Geist Inventory

    (C) Strong-Campbell Inventory

    (D) Kuder Survey

    (E) Career Ability Placement Survey

22. The Detroit Test of Learning Ability–3 measures all of the following skills *except*

    (A) visual memory.

    (B) visual problem-solving and reasoning.

    (C) auditory memory.

    (D) visual closure.

    (E) auditory discrimination.

23. A teacher presents a student with a list of words and a list of endings. She asks the student to make up as many *real* words as she can using the endings. This remedial technique is mainly used to address problems with

    (A) word discrimination.

    (B) compound words.

    (C) root words.

    (D) vocabulary development.

    (E) phonics.

24. In recent years, P.L. 94-142 has been amended by Congress and renamed. This federal law is now called

    (A) ADA.

    (B) P.L. 99-457.

    (C) IDEA.

    (D) Chapter 53.

    (E) Chapter I.

25. A special education teacher gave a student several multiplication examples. One example was done in this way:

$$\begin{array}{r} 367 \\ \times\ 25 \\ \hline 1535 \\ \underline{614} \\ 7675 \end{array}$$

In analyzing the error, how would you describe the problem this student is having?

    (A) Omitting steps

    (B) Format problems

    (C) Regrouping incorrectly

    (D) Wrong order of steps in computation process

    (E) Random response

Test: Speech Communication (0220)

Time: 2 hours
Number of Questions: 150
Format: Multiple-choice Questions

Purpose of the Test

Designed to measure the preparation of prospective speech communication teachers in junior or senior high school

Content Categories

- Interpersonal Communication—(17 percent)
- Small Group Communication—(13 percent)
- Public Speaking—(17 percent)
- Media and Their Influences—(10 percent)
- Play Production—(13 percent)
- Oral Interpretation—(13 percent)
- Forensics: Classroom and Curriculum Instruction—(10 percent)
- Assessment and Evaluation Issues—(7 percent)

Category Descriptions

Interpersonal Communication

1. Communication process and competence
2. Verbal and nonverbal
3. Listening
4. Goals, skills, and outcomes of interpersonal communication
5. Intercultural communication

Small Group Communication

1. Discussion principles
2. Problem solving/Decision making
3. Group roles and functions, including leadership
4. Conflict management

Public Speaking

1. Purposes, types, and forms
2. Audience analysis
3. Organizing strategies
4. Language and style
5. Delivery, including voice and diction, projection, and movement
6. Listening, feedback, and adaptation to audience
7. Criticism and evaluation of speeches

Media and Their Influences

1. Media: television, film, radio, computer technology
2. Critical analysis and evaluation
3. Social and technological influences and effects
4. Production techniques and audiovisual

Play Production

1. Dramatic theory and criticism
2. Acting, directing, design and construction, and theater management

Oral Interpretation

1. Readers' theater, storytelling, folklore, oral history, and creative dramatics
2. Aesthetic principles, universality, individuality, imagination, principles of text
3. Analysis: thinking involved in interpretation process
4. Performance techniques

Forensics: Classroom and Cocurricular Instruction

1. Argumentation and debate
2. Individual events
3. Program management

Assessment and Evaluation Issues

1. Teacher responsibilities
2. Curriculum: planning, development, appropriate assignments, textbook selection
3. Oral performance
4. Test construction

Speech Communication

Directions: Each question or incomplete statement is followed by five answer choices. For each question, circle the answer or completion that is best.

1. Little attention is paid in most classrooms to which areas of communication?

    I. Written language

    II. Listening

    III. Speaking

    IV. Reading

    (A) II and III only

    (B) III and IV only

    (C) I and IV only

    (D) II only

    (E) III only

2. A student can express positive and negative feelings. He can take the role of another person and take part in complex inferential communication. This student is most likely in

    (A) high school.

    (B) kindergarten.

    (C) an advanced private elementary school.

    (D) the upper-elementary grades.

    (E) middle school.

3. "Self-talk" is how we talk to ourselves so as to self-regulate our behavior and deploy strategies in routine tasks. All are examples of "self-talk" *except:*

    (A) finding the main idea in paragraphs.

    (B) going through the process of long division.

    (C) checking answers on tests.

    (D) memorizing a poem.

    (E) listening to foreign-language audiotapes.

4. Difficulties in listening and speaking often result in which of the following?

    I. Saying inappropriate things

    II. Being described as weird by peers

    III. Misinterpreting what other students and teachers say

    IV. Causing social isolation or rejection

    (A) I, II, and III only

    (B) II, III, and IV only

    (C) III only

    (D) IV only

    (E) I, II, III, and IV

5. The research of Otto and Smith identifies five levels of speaking competence seen in students. If a student appropriately uses regular and irregular verbs and eliminates double negatives, he or she is speaking

    (A) at the homely level.

    (B) at the illiterate level.

    (C) using standard informal English.

    (D) at the literacy level.

    (E) formal English.

6. A student who works to discern relationships among materials resulting in the ability to state the main idea and summarize is usually engaged in

    (A) active listening.

    (B) passive listening.

    (C) factual listening.

    (D) interpretive listening.

    (E) metacognitive listening.

7. A student says "tin" for "thin," "den" for "then," and "sin" for "sing." The most likely cause of this pupil's articulation errors is due to the fact that he

   (A) comes from a multicultural background.

   (B) speaks black English.

   (C) speaks a nonstandard regional dialect.

   (D) has little education.

   (E) comes from a lower-class group.

8. According to some theories, if a person articulates and pronounces very precisely, varying intonation patterns and using appeal tags, such as "isn't it?" or "don't you think?," this individual is probably

   (A) from the upper class.

   (B) well educated.

   (C) a woman.

   (D) an elderly man.

   (E) a teenager.

9. Using the linguistic model, the basic unit of language development is the

   (A) morpheme.

   (B) syllable.

   (C) kernel.

   (D) surface structure.

   (E) phoneme.

10. The set of rules for changing sentences into questions, imperatives, passives, or more complex sentences containing conjunctive clauses is the

    (A) transformational grammar system.

    (B) pragmatic language system.

    (C) psycholinguistic system.

    (D) structural language system.

    (E) auditory-symbolic system.

11. Study of egocentric language, in which a child's speech is manifested in such a way as not to make allowances for the perspective of the listener, characterizes the research of

    (A) Piaget.

    (B) Wiig.

    (C) Bloom.

    (D) Chomsky.

    (E) Hammill.

12. Effective speech and listening require linguistic, cognitive, and social prerequisites so as to establish coherent communication. Which are examples of a social prerequisite?

    I. Comprehension of technical information

    II. Teacher shifting vocabulary levels

    III. Knowing grammatical verbs for interpreting sentences

    IV. Articulation of speech sounds clearly and correctly

    (A) II and IV only

    (B) II, III, and IV only

    (C) III and IV only

    (D) I and II only

    (E) III only

13. Research describes three dimensions of language—linguistic content, use, and form. Which are examples of linguistic form?

    I. Semantics

    II. Syntax

    III. Morphology

    IV. Phonology

    (A) I, III, and IV only

    (B) II, III, and IV only

    (C) I, II, and III only

    (D) I only

    (E) IV only

14. Children from the age of three use various sentence types. The sentence "allgone nana" can be described as

    (A) the joining of elements to make sentences.

    (B) the development of subject-predicate sentences.

    (C) the expansion of the verb phrase.

    (D) an embedded element within a sentence.

    (E) the use of negative, declarative, and interrogative transformations.

15. Which is an example of the use of passive voice in a sentence?

    (A) "We will go to the movies."

    (B) "When can we leave?"

    (C) "We left for town on the railroad."

    (D) "If you're happy, then please smile."

    (E) "The building was destroyed by the explosion."

16. Which is an example of a bounded morpheme?

    (A) Con

    (B) Leave

    (C) Run

    (D) Book

    (E) Parties

17. Groups in which to place words relating to objects, actions, relationships, or events that share an essential feature are called

    (A) semantic categories.

    (B) syntactical categories.

    (C) object classes.

    (D) interjections.

    (E) coordinate categories.

18. Language during Piaget's concrete operational stage can best be described as

    (A) having meanings tied to concrete actions.

    (B) having more complex relationships along with broader meaning.

    (C) having meanings tied to the function performed by the word.

    (D) the discussion of complex processes from an abstract point of view.

    (E) having words used to declare, question, or exclaim.

19. It is expected that a young child would say "comed" instead of "came" and "bringed" instead of "brought." These are examples of a child's development of

    (A) phonological concepts.

    (B) morphological concepts.

    (C) syntactical concepts.

    (D) semantic concepts.

    (E) pragmatic concepts.

20. Pragmatics is the function or purpose of communication. An eight-year-old child would have which pragmatic skills?

    I. Protesting

    II. Increasing ability to express feelings appropriately

    III. Differential adaption to listeners' perspective and personality

    IV. Ability to judge and use speech of appropriate directness

    (A) I and III only

    (B) All of the above

    (C) I, III, and IV only

    (D) I and II only

    (E) II and IV only

21. An indirect way of speaking when someone cannot retrieve a specific word for an object, action, or event is called a(n)

    (A) counterfactive.

    (B) indefinite reference.

    (C) circumlocution.

    (D) fricative.

    (E) permutation.

22. All are examples of morphological functions *except:*

    (A) the use of comparatives and superlatives.

    (B) the use of affixes in sentences.

    (C) the use of regular and irregular plural forms.

    (D) usage of hard and soft *g*.

    (E) the conjugation of verbal forms.

23. The sentences "You nice" and "They bad" are found in

    I. black English.

    II. Southern white nonstandard.

    III. Appalachian.

    IV. nonstandard English.

    (A) I and II only

    (B) III and IV only

    (C) I only

    (D) II only

    (E) I, II, and IV only

24. The sentence "Driving cars can be dangerous" contains

    (A) a structural ambiguity.

    (B) ritualized reduplications.

    (C) a stereotypical starter.

    (D) passive reduplications.

    (E) omission of auxiliaries and modals.

25. The ability of a student to repeat sentences and words can be used as a measure of a student's short-term auditory memory.

    Many questions have been raised about the efficacy of such sentence-repetition tests. Such tests may not be a valid measure of auditory memory because

    (A) students may find too many associations among the words used.

    (B) dialectical differences may impact on a student's ability to recall cues accurately.

    (C) the syntax may be too simple for the student.

    (D) the number of perceptual units may be too small.

    (E) the vocabulary level of the sentence may be congruent with the student's ability.

Test: Speech-Language Pathology (0330)

Time: 2 hours
Number of Questions: 150
Format: Multiple-choice Questions

Purpose of the Test

Designed to measure the academic preparation in and knowledge of the field of Speech-Language Pathology

Content Categories

- Basic Human Communication Processes—(17 percent)
- Phonological and Language Disorders—(19 percent)
- Speech Disorders—(13 percent)
- Neurogenic Disorders—(19 percent)
- Audiology/Hearing—(5 percent)
- Clinical Management—(19 percent)
- Professional Issues/Psychometrics/Research—(8 percent)

Category Descriptions

Basic Human Communication Processes

1. Language acquisition and learning theory: normal development, theoretical models, behavior management and modification, cognitive development, developmental, motor, and linguistic processes
2. Language science: structure, phonetics, phonology, grammatical categories, morphology, syntax, semantics, and pragmatics
3. Learning theory: theoretical models related to disorders, models of behavior management and modification, and theories of cognitive development
4. Multicultural awareness: applications of theoretical models of language in society to a variety of linguistic and cultural groups; cultural and socioeconomic factors; communicative differences between speakers of the same language; and cultural differences in use of nonverbal communication
5. Speech science: speech perception, physiological phonetics, acoustic phonetics, related anatomy and physiology, and neural bases

Phonological and Language Disorders: Assessment and Treatment

1. Articulation disorders as influenced by anomalous, oral-motor, dental, learning, or behavioral factors
2. Language disorders: developmental, motor, and linguistic processes; differentiation of normal, delayed, and disordered language development; nature of expressive and receptive language disorders; treatment of language delays and language disorders

Speech Disorders: Identification, Assessment, Treatment, and Prevention

1. Fluency disorders, including theories, neurological, and psychological factors, assessment, treatment, and prevention
2. Resonance disorders as influenced by congenital anomalies, neuralgic disorders, disease, trauma, and behavioral factors
3. Assessment, treatment, and prevention of resonance disorders
4. Phonation of voice disorders as influenced by respiratory, laryngeal, and airway problems
5. Alaryngeal speech
6. Assessment, treatment, and prevention of voice disorders

Neorogenic Disorders

1. Neurological disorders: aphasia, progressive disorders, motor speech disorders, traumatic brain injury, and cognitive communication disorders
2. Dysphagia: process, cause, effect, assessment, and treatment of swallowing disorders

Audiology/Hearing

1. Principles, anatomy, and physiology of hearing
2. Cogenital and acquired hearing loss in children and adults
3. Audiological assessment: screening, interpretation of audiograms and tympanograms, and referrals
4. Auditory habilitation and rehabilitation

Clinical Management

1. Assessment, use, and determining candidacy for alternative/augmentative communication devices
2. Communication of assessment and treatment plans, progress, and results to clients and appropriate professionals
3. Interpersonal communication and counseling techniques
4. Documentation and monitoring client progress, including using other agencies; communication to other professionals; data gathering and interpretation; determining termination; procedures for referral and follow-up; and writing reports
5. Efficacy in demonstration of results and determining and communicating information
6. Instrumentation used
7. Purpose, use, and applications of technological developments
8. Speech-language assessment: establishing clients' past and present status, recommendations, identifying at-risk individuals, screening, selection and administration of standard and nonstandard evaluation procedures
9. Speech-language intervention: diagnostic; activities appropriate to age; sociocultural membership and disorder; remediation methods and strategies
10. Basic principles of relevant genetics
11. Syndromic and nonsyndromic inherited and developmental conditions and their influences

Professional Issues/Psychometrics/Research

1. Ethical practices: standards for professional conduct, referrals, obtaining permissions, client records, client privacy, and handling staff issues

2. Research methodology/psychometrics: criteria for selection of test materials; determining reliability of assessment procedures; models of research design; test construction principles

3. Standards and laws: designing appropriate assessment and treatment; federal laws and regulations; reporting requirements to government agencies

Speech-Language Pathology

Directions: Each question or incomplete statement is followed by five answer choices. For each question, circle the answer or completion that is best.

1. All are examples of organic causes of disorders in rhythm and speech flow *except*

   (A) a predisposition to break down easily under emotional stress, thereby losing fluency.

   (B) a parent's causing the child to stutter more by labeling a normal dysfluency as defective.

   (C) a child's lack of cerebral dominance resulting in stuttering.

   (D) dysphemia, which is a neuromuscular condition characterized by nerve impulses that are poorly timed in coordinating speech musculatures.

   (E) an epileptic type of condition resulting in a series of small seizures which interrupt speech.

2. A receptive language disorder in which a child repeats words and sentences in a parrot-like fashion is usually found in

   (A) learning-disabled children.

   (B) emotionally disturbed children.

   (C) mentally retarded children.

   (D) autistic children.

   (E) hearing-impaired children.

3. Twenty years ago, specialists dealing with communication disorders focused primarily on which of the following problems?

   I. Inability to articulate sounds

   II. Lisps

   III. Dysfluencies

   IV. Delayed speech

   (A) II and III only

   (B) I and IV only

   (C) I, II, and III only

   (D) II, III, and IV only

   (E) I, III, and IV only

4. According to most research, deaf children

   (A) develop language and speech in the same sequential manner as hearing students.

   (B) develop as many concepts as hearing students but take a longer time to do so.

   (C) in terms of nonverbal functioning can have as high an IQ as hearing children.

   (D) have intelligence test scores three to four years below those of hearing children.

   (E) are taught using methods similar to those used with learning disabled students.

5. A child speaks using excessive speed, resulting in disorganized sentences. The speech is garbled with syllables and sounds that are slurred or omitted. The student tends to make excessive repetitions when vocalizing. The problem described is called

   (A) cluttering.

   (B) hypernasality.

   (C) stuttering.

   (D) dysphasia.

   (E) aphasia.

6. The remediation of language deficits will take into account all of the following factors *except*

   (A) vocabulary.

   (B) voice intensity.

   (C) word meaning.

   (D) concept formation.

   (E) development of grammatical rules.

7. Which language systems are usually set before the age of six?

I. Semantics

II. Morphology

III. Syntax

IV. Phonology

(A) II and III only

(B) III and IV only

(C) I, II, and III only

(D) I, III, and IV only

(E) II, III, and IV only

8. The *least* effective technique to use with a child who has speech apraxia is to

(A) have the child feel vibrations of sound by touching the teacher's face and throat.

(B) use a computer to mimic speech sounds.

(C) have the child observe mouth movements and shaping during the production of sound.

(D) exercise the child's speech muscles by smiling, chewing, blowing, and laughing.

(E) have the child practice tongue movements in front of a mirror.

9. Pronouncing /s/ in "said" as /z/ is an example of a

(A) distortion.

(B) addition.

(C) substitution.

(D) omission.

(E) lalling.

10. All of the following either are or contain oral language tests *except*

(A) Carrow.

(B) EOWPVT-R.

(C) PPVT.

(D) Vocabulary subtest of the WISC III.

(E) Word Opposites subtest of the DTLA-3.

11. A child has an expressive language delay in which he cannot remember words to be expressed. He may use words like "thing" for objects he cannot recall, or he may attempt to use circumlocutions. The child is suffering from

(A) dyslexia.

(B) dysnomia.

(C) apraxia.

(D) aphasia.

(E) echolalia.

12. The concept that language is learned through imitation and reinforcement comes from the

(A) linguistic view.

(B) language arts view.

(C) pathological view.

(D) psycholinguistic view.

(E) behavioral view.

13. Which author is most associated with the psycholinguistic view of language?

(A) Myklebust

(B) Chomsky

(C) Piaget

(D) Vygotsky

(E) Roswell

14. Which of the following children would be diagnosed with a language disorder rather than a language deficit?

(A) A student who often omits subjects when speaking

(B) A student who often uses inappropriate words when speaking

(C) A child who is speaking in one-word utterances in kindergarten

(D) A seventh-grader who uses many circumlocutions while conversing

(E) A student who has poor pragmatic language skills

15. Acquired aphasia is

    (A) the loss of ability to speak due to brain damage as a result of an accident.

    (B) a language disorder primarily affecting children.

    (C) the inability to develop receptive language skills.

    (D) a neurological dysfunction causing delays in speech.

    (E) primarily a problem in communication beginning after the age of two.

16. Children who have difficulty with pitch, stress, and juncture usually

    (A) cannot discriminate syllables.

    (B) speak in monotone and without expression.

    (C) mix up sentence order.

    (D) demonstrate considerable skill in vocabulary acquisition.

    (E) have good understanding of morphological units.

17. Which of the following describe language of inner-city children?

    I. Nonstandard language has divergencies in vocabulary, dialect, and grammatical structure.

    II. Nonstandard language can be considered as a different but equal language system.

    III. Research shows that inner-city language is functionally inadequate and structurally unsystematic.

    IV. There is frequently a mismatch between the child's language and that used by teachers.

    (A) I only

    (B) II and III only

    (C) I, II, and IV only

    (D) I and III only

    (E) I and IV only

18. All are possible organic causes of speech disorders *except*

    (A) a significant hearing loss.

    (B) oral-facial abnormalities.

    (C) poor coordination of speech musculature.

    (D) dyslalia caused by parents' not stimulating speech.

    (E) high and narrow palate that leaves little room for the tongue to move.

19. According to research, the sound which is *least* misarticulated in children

    (A) /s/

    (B) /r/

    (C) /d/

    (D) /th/

    (E) /sh/

20. Which is the basic morphemic generalization of inner-city or ghetto dialect to denote plurality?

    (A) The use of the /z/ sound added to nouns

    (B) Omission of irregular plurals

    (C) The use of appropriate quantitative adjectives without pluralizing the noun

    (D) Adding /s/ to all nouns and adjectives in a sentence

    (E) The use of qualitative adjectives without pluralizing the noun

21. All of the following are techniques you might use in teaching auditory perception and discrimination of language sounds *except*

    (A) make bingo cards with consonant blends in the squares and then read words while asking the child to cover the blend that begins each word.

    (B) say three words, two of which have the same initial sound, and then ask the child to identify the word that begins with a different sound.

    (C) use sound boxes by putting toys, pictures, and objects in a box representing a consonant sound.

    (D) ask a child to substitute an initial sound to make a new word.

    (E) use gestures and exaggeration to help children understand the meaning of a word that symbolizes an object.

22. Which is probably the *least* common speech problem among school-age children?

    (A) Articulation difficulty

    (B) Stuttering

    (C) Speech problems due to hearing impairment

    (D) Cerebral palsy speech

    (E) Retarded speech development

23. John often speaks omitting verb inflections when conjugating. His problem is best described as a

    (A) communication disorder.

    (B) language disorder.

    (C) developmental aphasic response.

    (D) language disability.

    (E) language difference.

24. A student is asked to verbally list different vegetables. His list includes peas, beans, salads, orange, and fruit. The student's problem is mainly

    (A) caused by delayed speech.

    (B) in vocabulary.

    (C) in concept formation.

    (D) in the misapplication of grammatical rules.

    (E) due to problems in language comprehension.

25. Which of the following statements describe the language of a four-year-old child?

    I. She uses compound and complex sentences.

    II. Reversals of sounds are typically the most frequent error, with repetitions rarely present.

    III. Hesitations and repetitions are still present although the voice is usually well controlled.

    IV. Medial consonants are often slighted.

    (A) I and II only

    (B) III and IV only

    (C) All of the above

    (D) I and III only

    (E) II, III, and IV only

Answer Key for Specialty Area Tests

Biology and General Science

1. C	6. A	11. A	16. A	21. E
2. A	7. A	12. C	17. B	22. C
3. E	8. D	13. D	18. C	23. D
4. B	9. D	14. A	19. E	24. C
5. B	10. C	15. B	20. B	25. B

Business Education

1. D	6. C	11. D	16. A	21. B
2. C	7. D	12. D	17. D	22. C
3. B	8. A	13. B	18. C	23. B
4. B	9. B	14. D	19. A	24. B
5. B	10. B	15. A	20. B	25. C

Chemistry

1. C	6. D	11. A	16. C	21. C
2. B	7. B	12. C	17. C	22. A
3. D	8. C	13. D	18. A	23. D
4. C	9. C	14. C	19. D	24. D
5. B	10. E	15. D	20. C	25. D

Early Childhood Education

1. C	6. A	11. E	16. B	21. E
2. C	7. E	12. D	17. C	22. A
3. D	8. A	13. D	18. C	23. A
4. E	9. D	14. E	19. E	24. D
5. D	10. A	15. D	20. B	25. B

Education in the Elementary School

1. B	6. C	11. A	16. B	21. E
2. A	7. A	12. E	17. C	22. E
3. C	8. C	13. C	18. A	23. B
4. A	9. B	14. E	19. A	24. E
5. C	10. E	15. B	20. B	25. D

Education of Students with Mental Retardation

1. A	6. C	11. D	16. E	21. B
2. E	7. B	12. E	17. E	22. A
3. B	8. A	13. B	18. A	23. B
4. D	9. A	14. C	19. B	24. B
5. C	10. E	15. E	20. B	25. D

Educational Leadership: Administration and Supervision

1. B	6. C	11. C	16. C	21. A
2. D	7. D	12. B	17. A	22. B
3. D	8. C	13. C	18. D	23. C
4. B	9. B	14. D	19. B	24. D
5. B	10. A	15. C	20. B	25. A

Family and Consumer Sciences

1. D	6. E	11. B	16. A	21. D
2. C	7. E	12. B	17. C	22. A
3. E	8. B	13. D	18. E	23. C
4. C	9. E	14. B	19. A	24. B
5. B	10. C	15. A	20. A	25. D

Introduction to the Teaching of Reading

1. A	6. E	11. D	16. C	21. C
2. B	7. D	12. A	17. E	22. A
3. B	8. B	13. B	18. B	23. B
4. D	9. E	14. C	19. A	24. C
5. E	10. B	15. B	20. B	25. C

Mathematics

1. B	6. B	11. D	16. A	21. E
2. D	7. B	12. D	17. D	22. C
3. C	8. A	13. B	18. B	23. B
4. A	9. E	14. E	19. A	24. A
5. C	10. A	15. C	20. C	25. E

Music Education

Taped Section

1. D
2. C
3. A
4. D

Nontaped Section

5. C	10. C	15. E	20. B	25. D
6. E	11. A	16. D	21. C	
7. E	12. B	17. C	22. D	
8. A	13. E	18. B	23. A	
9. B	14. C	19. E	24. E	

Physics

1. B	6. D	11. E	16. B	21. D
2. D	7. C	12. B	17. B	22. A
3. D	8. E	13. B	18. D	23. C
4. A	9. C	14. C	19. B	24. C
5. D	10. C	15. A	20. B	25. D

Reading Specialist

1. D	6. C	11. B	16. A	21. A
2. A	7. B	12. A	17. B	22. B
3. D	8. C	13. E	18. E	23. C
4. B	9. D	14. C	19. E	24. D
5. E	10. A	15. B	20. D	25. E

School Guidance and Counseling

1. E	6. D	11. A	16. E	21. C
2. A	7. B	12. D	17. D	22. A
3. D	8. E	13. B	18. C	23. B
4. C	9. B	14. C	19. A	24. B
5. D	10. D	15. B	20. E	25. D

School Psychologist

1. B	6. B	11. E	16. C	21. E
2. C	7. A	12. B	17. C	22. B
3. E	8. B	13. B	18. E	23. D
4. C	9. E	14. E	19. B	24. B
5. C	10. A	15. A	20. A	25. E

Special Education

1. A	6. B	11. E	16. E	21. E
2. C	7. E	12. E	17. A	22. E
3. C	8. A	13. C	18. E	23. C
4. D	9. A	14. B	19. A	24. C
5. B	10. D	15. D	20. D	25. A

Speech Communication

1. A	6. D	11. A	16. A	21. C
2. A	7. A	12. D	17. A	22. D
3. E	8. C	13. B	18. C	23. A
4. E	9. A	14. A	19. C	24. A
5. C	10. A	15. E	20. D	25. B

Speech-Language Pathology

1. B	6. B	11. B	16. B	21. E
2. D	7. E	12. E	17. C	22. D
3. C	8. B	13. B	18. D	23. E
4. D	9. A	14. C	19. C	24. C
5. A	10. A	15. A	20. C	25. A

Multiple Subjects Assessment for Teachers

Multiple Subjects Assessment for Teachers
Content Knowledge

The Content Knowledge test of the Multiple Subjects Assessment for Teachers is intended to measure knowledge and critical-thinking abilities for prospective elementary school teachers. The test contains 120 multiple-choice questions, and you are given 2 hours to complete this section.

The seven subtests are:

    I.   Literature and Language Studies

    II.   Mathematics

    III.   Visual and Performing Arts

    IV.   Physical Education

    V.   Human Development

    VI.   History/Social Sciences

    VII.   Science

Each subtest contains multiple-choice questions with four choices per question. You are to select the best answer for each question and blacken the corresponding space on the answer sheet.

MSAT Content Knowledge Test scores are based on the number of questions answered correctly. Since there is no penalty for wrong answers, it is better to guess at an answer than to leave it blank.

MSAT: Content Knowledge Test

Start with number 1 for each new section. If a section has fewer than 25 questions, leave the extra answer spaces blank.

SECTION 1

1 Ⓐ Ⓑ Ⓒ Ⓓ Ⓔ
2 Ⓐ Ⓑ Ⓒ Ⓓ Ⓔ
3 Ⓐ Ⓑ Ⓒ Ⓓ Ⓔ
4 Ⓐ Ⓑ Ⓒ Ⓓ Ⓔ
5 Ⓐ Ⓑ Ⓒ Ⓓ Ⓔ
6 Ⓐ Ⓑ Ⓒ Ⓓ Ⓔ
7 Ⓐ Ⓑ Ⓒ Ⓓ Ⓔ
8 Ⓐ Ⓑ Ⓒ Ⓓ Ⓔ
9 Ⓐ Ⓑ Ⓒ Ⓓ Ⓔ
10 Ⓐ Ⓑ Ⓒ Ⓓ Ⓔ
11 Ⓐ Ⓑ Ⓒ Ⓓ Ⓔ
12 Ⓐ Ⓑ Ⓒ Ⓓ Ⓔ
13 Ⓐ Ⓑ Ⓒ Ⓓ Ⓔ
14 Ⓐ Ⓑ Ⓒ Ⓓ Ⓔ
15 Ⓐ Ⓑ Ⓒ Ⓓ Ⓔ
16 Ⓐ Ⓑ Ⓒ Ⓓ Ⓔ
17 Ⓐ Ⓑ Ⓒ Ⓓ Ⓔ
18 Ⓐ Ⓑ Ⓒ Ⓓ Ⓔ
19 Ⓐ Ⓑ Ⓒ Ⓓ Ⓔ
20 Ⓐ Ⓑ Ⓒ Ⓓ Ⓔ
21 Ⓐ Ⓑ Ⓒ Ⓓ Ⓔ
22 Ⓐ Ⓑ Ⓒ Ⓓ Ⓔ
23 Ⓐ Ⓑ Ⓒ Ⓓ Ⓔ
24 Ⓐ Ⓑ Ⓒ Ⓓ Ⓔ
25 Ⓐ Ⓑ Ⓒ Ⓓ Ⓔ

SECTION 2

1 Ⓐ Ⓑ Ⓒ Ⓓ Ⓔ
2 Ⓐ Ⓑ Ⓒ Ⓓ Ⓔ
3 Ⓐ Ⓑ Ⓒ Ⓓ Ⓔ
4 Ⓐ Ⓑ Ⓒ Ⓓ Ⓔ
5 Ⓐ Ⓑ Ⓒ Ⓓ Ⓔ
6 Ⓐ Ⓑ Ⓒ Ⓓ Ⓔ
7 Ⓐ Ⓑ Ⓒ Ⓓ Ⓔ
8 Ⓐ Ⓑ Ⓒ Ⓓ Ⓔ
9 Ⓐ Ⓑ Ⓒ Ⓓ Ⓔ
10 Ⓐ Ⓑ Ⓒ Ⓓ Ⓔ
11 Ⓐ Ⓑ Ⓒ Ⓓ Ⓔ
12 Ⓐ Ⓑ Ⓒ Ⓓ Ⓔ
13 Ⓐ Ⓑ Ⓒ Ⓓ Ⓔ
14 Ⓐ Ⓑ Ⓒ Ⓓ Ⓔ
15 Ⓐ Ⓑ Ⓒ Ⓓ Ⓔ
16 Ⓐ Ⓑ Ⓒ Ⓓ Ⓔ
17 Ⓐ Ⓑ Ⓒ Ⓓ Ⓔ
18 Ⓐ Ⓑ Ⓒ Ⓓ Ⓔ
19 Ⓐ Ⓑ Ⓒ Ⓓ Ⓔ
20 Ⓐ Ⓑ Ⓒ Ⓓ Ⓔ
21 Ⓐ Ⓑ Ⓒ Ⓓ Ⓔ
22 Ⓐ Ⓑ Ⓒ Ⓓ Ⓔ
23 Ⓐ Ⓑ Ⓒ Ⓓ Ⓔ
24 Ⓐ Ⓑ Ⓒ Ⓓ Ⓔ
25 Ⓐ Ⓑ Ⓒ Ⓓ Ⓔ

SECTION 3

1 Ⓐ Ⓑ Ⓒ Ⓓ Ⓔ
2 Ⓐ Ⓑ Ⓒ Ⓓ Ⓔ
3 Ⓐ Ⓑ Ⓒ Ⓓ Ⓔ
4 Ⓐ Ⓑ Ⓒ Ⓓ Ⓔ
5 Ⓐ Ⓑ Ⓒ Ⓓ Ⓔ
6 Ⓐ Ⓑ Ⓒ Ⓓ Ⓔ
7 Ⓐ Ⓑ Ⓒ Ⓓ Ⓔ
8 Ⓐ Ⓑ Ⓒ Ⓓ Ⓔ
9 Ⓐ Ⓑ Ⓒ Ⓓ Ⓔ
10 Ⓐ Ⓑ Ⓒ Ⓓ Ⓔ
11 Ⓐ Ⓑ Ⓒ Ⓓ Ⓔ
12 Ⓐ Ⓑ Ⓒ Ⓓ Ⓔ
13 Ⓐ Ⓑ Ⓒ Ⓓ Ⓔ
14 Ⓐ Ⓑ Ⓒ Ⓓ Ⓔ
15 Ⓐ Ⓑ Ⓒ Ⓓ Ⓔ
16 Ⓐ Ⓑ Ⓒ Ⓓ Ⓔ
17 Ⓐ Ⓑ Ⓒ Ⓓ Ⓔ
18 Ⓐ Ⓑ Ⓒ Ⓓ Ⓔ
19 Ⓐ Ⓑ Ⓒ Ⓓ Ⓔ
20 Ⓐ Ⓑ Ⓒ Ⓓ Ⓔ
21 Ⓐ Ⓑ Ⓒ Ⓓ Ⓔ
22 Ⓐ Ⓑ Ⓒ Ⓓ Ⓔ
23 Ⓐ Ⓑ Ⓒ Ⓓ Ⓔ
24 Ⓐ Ⓑ Ⓒ Ⓓ Ⓔ
25 Ⓐ Ⓑ Ⓒ Ⓓ Ⓔ

SECTION 4

1 Ⓐ Ⓑ Ⓒ Ⓓ Ⓔ
2 Ⓐ Ⓑ Ⓒ Ⓓ Ⓔ
3 Ⓐ Ⓑ Ⓒ Ⓓ Ⓔ
4 Ⓐ Ⓑ Ⓒ Ⓓ Ⓔ
5 Ⓐ Ⓑ Ⓒ Ⓓ Ⓔ
6 Ⓐ Ⓑ Ⓒ Ⓓ Ⓔ
7 Ⓐ Ⓑ Ⓒ Ⓓ Ⓔ
8 Ⓐ Ⓑ Ⓒ Ⓓ Ⓔ
9 Ⓐ Ⓑ Ⓒ Ⓓ Ⓔ
10 Ⓐ Ⓑ Ⓒ Ⓓ Ⓔ
11 Ⓐ Ⓑ Ⓒ Ⓓ Ⓔ
12 Ⓐ Ⓑ Ⓒ Ⓓ Ⓔ
13 Ⓐ Ⓑ Ⓒ Ⓓ Ⓔ
14 Ⓐ Ⓑ Ⓒ Ⓓ Ⓔ
15 Ⓐ Ⓑ Ⓒ Ⓓ Ⓔ
16 Ⓐ Ⓑ Ⓒ Ⓓ Ⓔ
17 Ⓐ Ⓑ Ⓒ Ⓓ Ⓔ
18 Ⓐ Ⓑ Ⓒ Ⓓ Ⓔ
19 Ⓐ Ⓑ Ⓒ Ⓓ Ⓔ
20 Ⓐ Ⓑ Ⓒ Ⓓ Ⓔ
21 Ⓐ Ⓑ Ⓒ Ⓓ Ⓔ
22 Ⓐ Ⓑ Ⓒ Ⓓ Ⓔ
23 Ⓐ Ⓑ Ⓒ Ⓓ Ⓔ
24 Ⓐ Ⓑ Ⓒ Ⓓ Ⓔ
25 Ⓐ Ⓑ Ⓒ Ⓓ Ⓔ

SECTION 5   SECTION 6   SECTION 7

SECTION 5	SECTION 6	SECTION 7
1 Ⓐ Ⓑ Ⓒ Ⓓ Ⓔ	1 Ⓐ Ⓑ Ⓒ Ⓓ Ⓔ	1 Ⓐ Ⓑ Ⓒ Ⓓ Ⓔ
2 Ⓐ Ⓑ Ⓒ Ⓓ Ⓔ	2 Ⓐ Ⓑ Ⓒ Ⓓ Ⓔ	2 Ⓐ Ⓑ Ⓒ Ⓓ Ⓔ
3 Ⓐ Ⓑ Ⓒ Ⓓ Ⓔ	3 Ⓐ Ⓑ Ⓒ Ⓓ Ⓔ	3 Ⓐ Ⓑ Ⓒ Ⓓ Ⓔ
4 Ⓐ Ⓑ Ⓒ Ⓓ Ⓔ	4 Ⓐ Ⓑ Ⓒ Ⓓ Ⓔ	4 Ⓐ Ⓑ Ⓒ Ⓓ Ⓔ
5 Ⓐ Ⓑ Ⓒ Ⓓ Ⓔ	5 Ⓐ Ⓑ Ⓒ Ⓓ Ⓔ	5 Ⓐ Ⓑ Ⓒ Ⓓ Ⓔ
6 Ⓐ Ⓑ Ⓒ Ⓓ Ⓔ	6 Ⓐ Ⓑ Ⓒ Ⓓ Ⓔ	6 Ⓐ Ⓑ Ⓒ Ⓓ Ⓔ
7 Ⓐ Ⓑ Ⓒ Ⓓ Ⓔ	7 Ⓐ Ⓑ Ⓒ Ⓓ Ⓔ	7 Ⓐ Ⓑ Ⓒ Ⓓ Ⓔ
8 Ⓐ Ⓑ Ⓒ Ⓓ Ⓔ	8 Ⓐ Ⓑ Ⓒ Ⓓ Ⓔ	8 Ⓐ Ⓑ Ⓒ Ⓓ Ⓔ
9 Ⓐ Ⓑ Ⓒ Ⓓ Ⓔ	9 Ⓐ Ⓑ Ⓒ Ⓓ Ⓔ	9 Ⓐ Ⓑ Ⓒ Ⓓ Ⓔ
10 Ⓐ Ⓑ Ⓒ Ⓓ Ⓔ	10 Ⓐ Ⓑ Ⓒ Ⓓ Ⓔ	10 Ⓐ Ⓑ Ⓒ Ⓓ Ⓔ
11 Ⓐ Ⓑ Ⓒ Ⓓ Ⓔ	11 Ⓐ Ⓑ Ⓒ Ⓓ Ⓔ	11 Ⓐ Ⓑ Ⓒ Ⓓ Ⓔ
12 Ⓐ Ⓑ Ⓒ Ⓓ Ⓔ	12 Ⓐ Ⓑ Ⓒ Ⓓ Ⓔ	12 Ⓐ Ⓑ Ⓒ Ⓓ Ⓔ
13 Ⓐ Ⓑ Ⓒ Ⓓ Ⓔ	13 Ⓐ Ⓑ Ⓒ Ⓓ Ⓔ	13 Ⓐ Ⓑ Ⓒ Ⓓ Ⓔ
14 Ⓐ Ⓑ Ⓒ Ⓓ Ⓔ	14 Ⓐ Ⓑ Ⓒ Ⓓ Ⓔ	14 Ⓐ Ⓑ Ⓒ Ⓓ Ⓔ
15 Ⓐ Ⓑ Ⓒ Ⓓ Ⓔ	15 Ⓐ Ⓑ Ⓒ Ⓓ Ⓔ	15 Ⓐ Ⓑ Ⓒ Ⓓ Ⓔ
16 Ⓐ Ⓑ Ⓒ Ⓓ Ⓔ	16 Ⓐ Ⓑ Ⓒ Ⓓ Ⓔ	16 Ⓐ Ⓑ Ⓒ Ⓓ Ⓔ
17 Ⓐ Ⓑ Ⓒ Ⓓ Ⓔ	17 Ⓐ Ⓑ Ⓒ Ⓓ Ⓔ	17 Ⓐ Ⓑ Ⓒ Ⓓ Ⓔ
18 Ⓐ Ⓑ Ⓒ Ⓓ Ⓔ	18 Ⓐ Ⓑ Ⓒ Ⓓ Ⓔ	18 Ⓐ Ⓑ Ⓒ Ⓓ Ⓔ
19 Ⓐ Ⓑ Ⓒ Ⓓ Ⓔ	19 Ⓐ Ⓑ Ⓒ Ⓓ Ⓔ	19 Ⓐ Ⓑ Ⓒ Ⓓ Ⓔ
20 Ⓐ Ⓑ Ⓒ Ⓓ Ⓔ	20 Ⓐ Ⓑ Ⓒ Ⓓ Ⓔ	20 Ⓐ Ⓑ Ⓒ Ⓓ Ⓔ
21 Ⓐ Ⓑ Ⓒ Ⓓ Ⓔ	21 Ⓐ Ⓑ Ⓒ Ⓓ Ⓔ	21 Ⓐ Ⓑ Ⓒ Ⓓ Ⓔ
22 Ⓐ Ⓑ Ⓒ Ⓓ Ⓔ	22 Ⓐ Ⓑ Ⓒ Ⓓ Ⓔ	22 Ⓐ Ⓑ Ⓒ Ⓓ Ⓔ
23 Ⓐ Ⓑ Ⓒ Ⓓ Ⓔ	23 Ⓐ Ⓑ Ⓒ Ⓓ Ⓔ	23 Ⓐ Ⓑ Ⓒ Ⓓ Ⓔ
24 Ⓐ Ⓑ Ⓒ Ⓓ Ⓔ	24 Ⓐ Ⓑ Ⓒ Ⓓ Ⓔ	24 Ⓐ Ⓑ Ⓒ Ⓓ Ⓔ
25 Ⓐ Ⓑ Ⓒ Ⓓ Ⓔ	25 Ⓐ Ⓑ Ⓒ Ⓓ Ⓔ	25 Ⓐ Ⓑ Ⓒ Ⓓ Ⓔ

Section 1: Literature and Language Studies

24 questions

Directions: Each question or incomplete statement is followed by four answer choices. For each question, select the answer or completion that is best and blacken the corresponding space on the answer sheet.

Questions 1–2 refer to the following quote.

The wolf also shall dwell with the lamb, and the leopard shall lie down with the kid.

They shall beat their swords into ploughshares, and their spears into pruning-hooks:

nation shall not lift sword against nation, neither shall they learn war any more.

1. The lines above are taken from

   (A) a sonnet by William Wordsworth.

   (B) a poem by Shakespeare.

   (C) the Old Testament.

   (D) a poem by Dylan Thomas.

2. The lines above describe

   (A) a mythical state.

   (B) the Messianic age.

   (C) a child's fairy tale.

   (D) the author's fervent wishes.

Questions 3–5 refer to the following.

(A) O Captain! my Captain! our fearful trip is done,

    The ship has weathered every rack, the prize we sought is won,

    The port is near, the bells I hear, the people all exulting.

    While follow eyes the steady keel, the vessel grim and daring;

    But O heart! heart! heart!

    O the bleeding drops of red,

    Where on the deck my Captain lies,

    Fallen cold and dead.

(B) Hain't we got all the fools in town on our side? And Hain't that a big enough majority in any town?

(C) One catches more flies with a spoonful of honey than with twenty casks of vinegar.

(D) Is life so dear or peace so sweet as to be purchased at the price of chains and slavery? Forbid it, Almighty God! I know not what course others may take; but as for me, give me liberty, or give me death!

3. Which is a political speech?

4. Which uses colloquial speech?

5. Which upholds flattery as a means to an end?

6. *Don Giovanni, Eine kleine Nachtmusik,* and *The Magic Flute* are works by
   (A) Ludwig van Beethoven.
   (B) Gian-Carlo Menotti.
   (C) Wolfgang Amadeus Mozart.
   (D) Henry Purcell.

Questions 7–9 refer to the following.

   (A) There was an Old Man with a beard,
       Who said, "It is just as I feared!
       Two Owls and a Hen,
       Four Larks and a Wren,
       Have all built their nests in my beard!"

   (B) I hold that if the Almighty had ever made a set of men that should do all the eating and none of the work, He would have made them with mouths only and no hands; and if he had ever made another class that He intended should do all the work and no eating, He would have made them with hands only and no mouths.

   (C) Her feet beneath her petticoat,
       Like little mice, stole in and out,
       As if they feared the light.

   (D) Pale Death, with impartial step, knocks at the poor man's cottage and the palaces of kings.

7. Which uses a metaphor?

8. Which is an example of a limerick?

9. Which poem uses a simile?

Questions 10–11 refer to the following poem.

   Gather ye rosebuds while ye may,
   Old time is still a-flying:
   And this same flower that smiles today
   Tomorrow will be dying.
   The glorious lamp of heaven, the sun,
   The higher he's a-getting,
   The sooner will his race be run,
   And nearer he's to setting.

10. Which of the following best describes the theme of the poem?
    (A) Father Time is destructive.
    (B) Time marches on.
    (C) God is waiting.
    (D) Races are to be won.

11. The poet uses the examples of the sun and the flowers to show
    (A) love of nature.
    (B) love of humanity.
    (C) the fleeting nature of life.
    (D) the arbitrary death of natural things.

Questions 12–14 refer to the following.

   (A) Knowledge is the only instrument of production that is not subject to diminishing returns.

   (B) All happy families resemble one another; every unhappy family is unhappy in its own way.

   (C) If my theory of relativity is proven successful, Germany will claim me as a German and France will declare that I am a citizen of the world. Should my theory prove untrue, France will say that I am a German and Germany will declare that I am a Jew.

   (D) Lost, yesterday, somewhere between Sunrise and Sunset, two golden hours, each set with sixty diamond minutes. No reward is offered for they are gone forever.

12. Which describes prejudice?

13. Which uses metaphor to show the value of time?

14. Which gives a sociological perspective?

Question 15 refers to the following.

The apparition of these faces in the crowd:
Petals on a wet, black bough.

15. Which of the following describes the lines above?
    (A) Blank verse
    (B) A tercet
    (C) A triolet
    (D) A quatrain

16. The part of the word *convivial* that means "life" is
    (A) con.
    (B) convi.
    (C) ial.
    (D) viv.

17. The literal meaning of the prefix *ab-* in the word *abnormal* is
    (A) toward.
    (B) away from.
    (C) within.
    (D) under.

18. Which *mis-* has a meaning different from the *mis-* of the three other given words?
    (A) Misanthrope
    (B) Misspell
    (C) Misguided
    (D) Misinformed

19. "I was never so humiliated in all my days!"

    This sentence is an example of
    (A) hyperbole.
    (B) hypodermic.
    (C) hypertrophy.
    (D) hypocrisy.

20. A phrase can NEVER be a
    (A) fragment of a sentence.
    (B) modifier.
    (C) complete thought.
    (D) noun.

21. If someone has *deep pockets*, she has
    (A) apparel with large pockets.
    (B) large amounts of money.
    (C) a long family tree.
    (D) a scarred face.

22. If someone is described as *fly-by-night*, he is
    (A) an evening traveller.
    (B) impermanent.
    (C) like a bat.
    (D) evil.

23. The Greek suffix *logy* means
    (A) study of.
    (B) writing.
    (C) cylindrical.
    (D) life.

24. The following quote is from a speech by Bertrant Barere, given in 1792.

    The tree of liberty grows only when watered by the blood of tyrants.

    This quotation is an example of
    (A) simile.
    (B) metaphor.
    (C) onomatopoeia.
    (D) redundancy.

Section 2: Mathematics

24 questions

Directions: Each question or incomplete statement is followed by four answer choices. For each question, select the answer or completion that is best and blacken the corresponding space on the answer sheet.

1. A nonstop flight from Atlanta to London leaves Atlanta at 8:30 p.m. Eastern Standard Time and arrives in London at 8:15 a.m. Greenwich Mean Time. There is 5-hour difference in the time between Atlanta and London. Therefore the amount of time spent in flight was

   (A) 3 hours 30 minutes

   (B) 6 hours 45 minutes

   (C) 11 hours 45 minutes

   (D) 13 hours 30 minutes

2. Finishing time for the last three runners in the mini-marathon is as follows:

Runner	Hours	Minutes
#1	2	10
#2	2	13
#3	1	55

   How many minutes would Runner #2 have had to take off his time in order to win the race?

   (A) 4

   (B) 6

   (C) 7

   (D) Insufficient data is given to solve the problem.

3.

   If the area of a square postage stamp is .64 inches, what is the length of one of its sides in inches?

   (A) .0008

   (B) .008

   (C) .08

   (D) .8

4.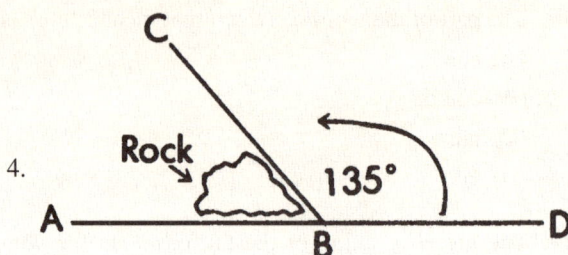

   A gate, (BC), can swing open only 135 degrees because of a rock that is wedged behind it. Without the rock, the gate could swing all the way back against the fence, (AD), to form a straight angle. Find the number of degrees that the gate is prevented from opening (angle ABC in the diagram above).

   (A) 45

   (B) 55

   (C) 60

   (D) 135

Questions 5 and 6 refer to the following information.

A family has a monthly income of $3600. Their monthly expenditures are as shown in the graph below.

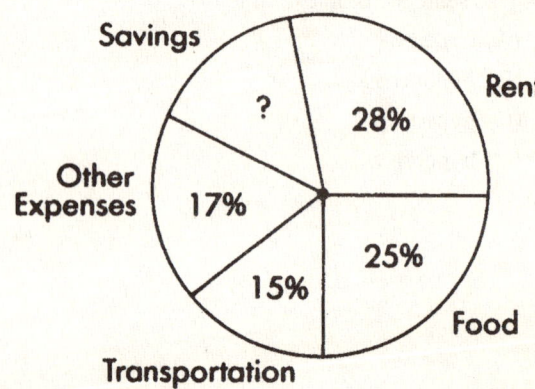

5. How much money does the family save in a year?

   (A) $6000

   (B) $6320

   (C) $6480

   (D) $6900

6. What is the cost of rent each month?

   (A) $612

   (B) $750

   (C) $1000

   (D) $1008

7. A part-time worker at a fast-food restaurant is paid $4.50 per hour. If he works 4 hours on Monday, 3 hours on Tuesday, 5 hours on Wednesday, 4 hours on Thursday, and 4 hours on Saturday, his income could be expressed algebraically as $x =$

   (A) $(4 + 3 + 5 + 4 + 4) + 4.50$

   (B) $(4.50)(4 \times 3 \times 5 \times 4 \times 6)$

   (C) $(4.50)(24)$

   (D) $(4 + 3 + 5 + 4 + 4)(4.50)$

Questions 8–10 are based on the following graph.

CO$_2$ Production by Yeast from Four Different Sugar Solutions at 40°C.

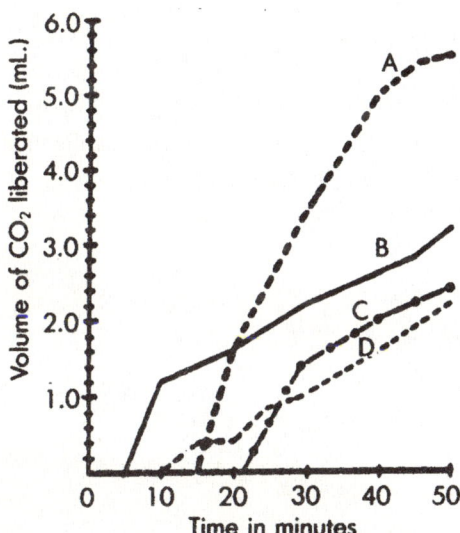

8. From which solution was CO$_2$ liberated first?

   (A) A

   (B) B

   (C) C

   (D) D

9. In how many minutes was the same volume of CO$_2$ liberated from solution A and solution B?

   (A) 1.1

   (B) 1.6

   (C) 6

   (D) 20

10. From which solution was the most CO$_2$ liberated at the end of 30 minutes?

    (A) A

    (B) B

    (C) C

    (D) D

11. A statement that is always true whether its premises are true or false is called a(n)

    (A) syllogism.

    (B) tautology.

    (C) equivalence.

    (D) paradox.

12. Two numbers are relatively prime if their greatest common divisor is 1. Which pair of numbers is relatively prime?

    (A) 3 and 12

    (B) 15 and 28

    (C) 25 and 30

    (D) 18 and 36

13. The sum of 2 coins of value x and 3 coins of value y is 50 cents. If the value of y is 10 cents, which of the following equations can be used to express this relationship?

    (A) $x + y = 5$

    (B) $x + 3y = 50$

    (C) $2x = 50 - 3y$

    (D) $x = 50 - y$

14. 11 to the fourth power may be expressed correctly as

    (A) $11 + 11 + 11 + 11$

    (B) 4^{11}

    (C) $4\sqrt{11}$

    (D) $11(11)(11)(11)$

15. $\dfrac{6464}{32}$

    (A) .2

    (B) 2

    (C) 20

    (D) 202

16. Express the integer 30 as a percent.

    (A) 3000%

    (B) 300%

    (C) 30%

    (D) 3%

17. How many 25-passenger buses are required to transport 105 people?

    (A) 3

    (B) 4

    (C) 5

    (D) 6

18. At 30 mph a trip from Town A to Town B takes 6 hours. If the speed were doubled, how many hours would the trip take?

    (A) 18

    (B) 12

    (C) 6

    (D) 3

19. $21(73 \times 26)$ is equivalent to all the following *except*

    (A) $21(73) \times 26$

    (B) $21 \times (73)(26)$

    (C) $(21)(73)(26)$

    (D) $21(73) + 21(26)$

20. Simplify the equation:

    $$5x + 5y + 5z = 5$$

    (A) $x + y + z = 1$

    (B) $21x = 5$

    (C) $5x + 11y + 5z = 1$

    (D) $11x + 5y + 5z = 5$

21. What is the product of all the consecutive integers from −5 to +5?

    (A) −120

    (B) −15

    (C) 0

    (D) +15

22. What is the mode of the following numbers?

    1,2,2,3,3,3,4,4,4,5,5,5,5,5

    (A) 1

    (B) 2

    (C) 3

    (D) 5

23. 10% of 13 is equivalent to all of the following *except*

    (A) $\dfrac{10}{100}$

    (B) 2% of 5% of 13

    (C) $10\left(\dfrac{13}{100}\right)$

    (D) 13% of 10

24. The scale of a map represents 12 miles as 1 inch. If the distance between two cities on the map is $2\frac{3}{4}$ inches, what is the actual distance, in miles, between the cities?

    (A) 28

    (B) 30

    (C) 33

    (D) 35

Section 3: Visual and Performing Arts

12 questions

Directions: Each question or incomplete statement is followed by four answer choices. For each question, select the answer or completion that is best and blacken the corresponding space on the answer sheet.

1. The painting *Bananas and Grapefruit*, shown above, is an example of

   (A) Cubism.

   (B) Pop Art.

   (C) Impressionism.

   (D) Op Art.

2. Which of the following is *not* true regarding the sculpture shown above?

   (A) Solid intertwined forms make up the sculpture.

   (B) Frailty of the figures is demonstrated by the medium used.

   (C) A family unit is suggested by the figures portrayed.

   (D) The texture of the sculpture appears slick.

Questions 3–5 refer to the following.

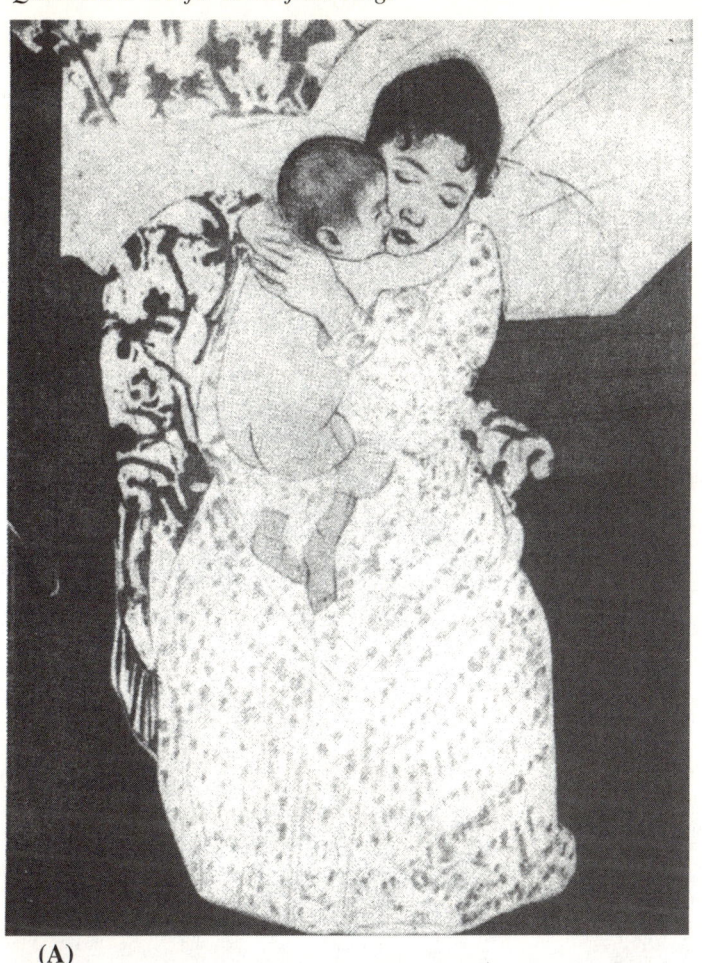

(A)

(B)

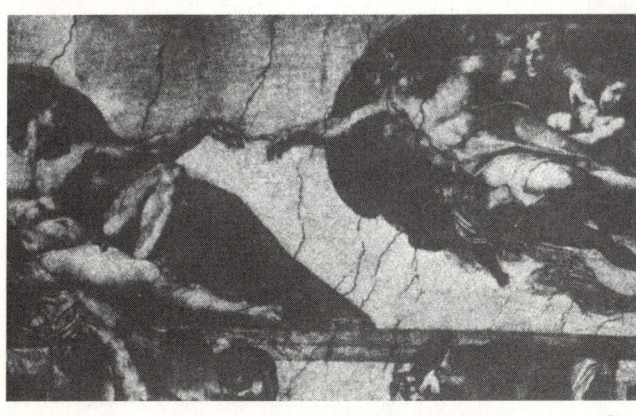

(C)

(D)

3. Which is by Michelangelo?   4. Which is by Mary Cassatt?   5. Which is by Rubens?

Questions 6 and 7 refer to the following.

(A)

(B)

(C)

(D)

6. Which is by Renoir?

7. Which is a surrealist painting?

8. The novel *Don Quixote* was the inspiration for the musical

    (A) *The Wiz.*

    (B) *West Side Story.*

    (C) *Man of La Mancha.*

    (D) *Evita.*

9. Which is not associated with Greek theater?

    (A) Masks

    (B) Deus ex machina

    (C) Chorus

    (D) Scene changes

10. All of the following were contemporaries of Shakespeare, except

    (A) Raleigh.

    (B) Bacon.

    (C) Marlowe.

    (D) Milton.

11. Woody Allen was the major force behind all of the following films *except*

    (A) *Annie Hall.*

    (B) *Sleeper.*

    (C) *All That Jazz.*

    (D) *Interiors.*

12. The "King of Ragtime Composers" was

    (A) Ferdinand "Jelly Roll" Morton.

    (B) Scott Joplin.

    (C) Edward "Duke" Ellington.

    (D) William "Count" Basie.

Section 4: Physical Education

8 questions

Directions: Each question or incomplete statement is followed by four choices. Select the best answer and blacken the corresponding space on the answer sheet.

1. Which of the following terms includes all the activities required to keep an organism alive?

    (A) Growth

    (B) Excretion

    (C) Metabolism

    (D) Nutrition

2. Humans breathe more rapidly during exercise than before because during exercise the blood contains

    (A) an increased level of oxygen.

    (B) a decreased number of red blood cells.

    (C) an increased level of carbon dioxide.

    (D) a decreased amount of hemoglobin.

3. Smoking may damage the respiratory system because deposits from smoke can

    (A) interfere with ciliary action in the trachea.

    (B) trigger the release of antigens by the alveoli.

    (C) block the transmission of impulses that regulate breathing.

    (D) lower blood pressure in the mucous membranes of the bronchioles.

4. Which portion of the central nervous system coordinates motor activities and aids in maintaining balance?

    (A) Cerebrum

    (B) Cerebellum

    (C) Medulla

    (D) Spinal cord

5. One factor that contributes to the fatigue of a long-distance runner is the accumulation of lactic acid molecules in muscle cells. This lactic acid is produced most directly as a result of

    (A) digestion.

    (B) aerobic respiration.

    (C) photosynthesis.

    (D) anaerobic respiration.

6. In humans, food is moved down the esophagus into the stomach by means of

    (A) peristalsis.

    (B) cyclosis.

    (C) active transport.

    (D) hydrolytic enzymes.

7. Which statement concerning hormones is true?

    (A) Hormones are produced by every cell of an organism.

    (B) Hormones are produced only by the pituitary gland.

    (C) Hormones produced by endocrine glands travel through ducts to various organs.

    (D) Hormones produced in one part of the body may affect the action of another part of the body.

Suggested Desirable Weights for Heights and
Ranges for Adult Males and Females

Height (inches)	Weight (pounds)			
	Men		Women	
58			102	(92-119)
60			107	(96-125)
62	123	(112-141)	113	(102-131)
64	130	(118-148)	120	(108-138)
66	136	(124-156)	128	(114-146)
68	145	(132-166)	136	(122-154)
70	154	(140-174)	144	(130-163)
72	162	(148-184)	152	(138-173)
74	171	(156-194)		
76	181	(164-204)		

Heights and Weights of Selected Adults

Jane	64 inches	150 pounds
Jeff	72 inches	165 pounds
Bill	68 inches	130 pounds
Sara	68 inches	130 pounds
Paul	70 inches	150 pounds

8. Based on the Table of Desirable Weights, which of the following adults should gain some weight?

(A) Jane

(B) Jeff

(C) Bill

(D) Sara

Section 5: Human Development

8 questions

Directions: Each question or incomplete statement is followed by four choices. Select the best answer and blacken the corresponding space on the answer sheet.

1. A child with problems in spatial relations will have difficulty

   (A) understanding one-to-one correspondence.

   (B) visualizing geometric shapes and doing horizontal and vertical examples.

   (C) counting using ordinal numbers.

   (D) learning the communicative properties of multiplication and addition.

2. A child who is inattentive and distractible usually has difficulty developing

   (A) expressive language concepts.

   (B) spatial concepts.

   (C) multiplication facts.

   (D) an understanding of coin values.

3. The concept that cognitive performance is primarily determined by general ability, or "g," is based on a theory developed by

   (A) Horn and Cattell.

   (B) Woodcock and Mather.

   (C) Salvia and Ysseldyke.

   (D) Hammill and Bartell.

4. Which is *not* a component of intelligence or cognitive development?

   (A) Quantitative ability

   (B) Short-term memory

   (C) Graphomotor skills

   (D) Processing speed

5. Which of the following factors tends to inhibit cognitive development in children?

   I. Personality style

   II. Physical health

   III. Anxiety

   IV. Family structure

   (A) I, II, and IV only

   (B) II, III, and IV only

   (C) I and III only

   (D) I, II, and III only

6. This author believes in the role experience plays in intellectual development. He feels the school environment should match the individual student. He attacks the concepts of fixed intelligence, predetermined development, and the unimportance of early experience. These views primarily express the ideas of

   (A) Jensen.

   (B) Piaget.

   (C) Bruner.

   (D) Hunt.

7. A student with this problem cannot participate in a traditional academic program. This student can learn skills primarily through the use of behavior modification. These statements *best* describe a student who is

   (A) learning disabled.

   (B) mentally retarded.

   (C) emotionally disturbed.

   (D) orthopedically handicapped.

8. Peer relations become increasingly active. Communication expands to include a wide array of nonverbal and verbal responses. Identification with and imitation of models is responsible for rapid social development at this stage. Achievement-oriented behavior develops, depending upon the prompts and reinforcement received. This best describes social-emotional development occurring during which of the following age spans?

(A) Birth to one year

(B) One to three years

(C) Three to six years

(D) Six to thirteen years

Section 6: History/Social Sciences

22 questions

Directions: Each question or incomplete statement is followed by four answer choices. For each question, select the answer or completion that is best and blacken the corresponding space on the answer sheet.

1. Social psychology is a field of study concerned with
   (A) the effect of group membership on the individual.
   (B) human behavior in crowds or mobs.
   (C) changes in values and attitudes over the individual's life span.
   (D) the process of learning the traditions of one's culture.

2. Sociological research is likely to include all of the following *except*

   (A) independent variables.
   (B) dependent variables.
   (C) operational definitions.
   (D) haphazard sampling.

Questions 3–5 refer to the figure below.

3. Which of the following groups or situations does the restaurant in the cartoon represent?
   (A) The fast-food industry
   (B) Worldwide poverty and hunger
   (C) The oil crisis
   (D) The American people

4. Which of the following is a hypothesis suggested by this cartoon?
   (A) Americans eat out a great deal, especially at inexpensive fast-food restaurants.
   (B) Americans are unwilling to accept newcomers easily. As a result, immigrants tend to live in isolated groups.
   (C) Americans have become much more open to dietary innovations.
   (D) A wide variety of nationalities make up American culture.

5. Which of the following statements is best supported by evidence presented in this cartoon?
   (A) There is a wide variety of foods offered at fast-food restaurants.
   (B) The United States is made up of immigrants from many nations.
   (C) The cost of food keeps rising.
   (D) American food is imported from Europe.

6. The social scientist examining social stratification would be *least* interested in which of the following?
   (A) The impact of education on upward mobility
   (B) The distribution of property in a given society
   (C) Which occupations are thought to be most prestigious
   (D) The impact of race on mortality and fertility

7. The Napoleonic Code was
   (A) a military strategy.
   (B) a style of politics.
   (C) a style of etiquette.
   (D) a legal system.

8. The *Bay of Pigs* refers to which of the following events?
   (A) A vote in Congress to permit the bombing of North Vietnam
   (B) An anti-Castro invasion of Cuba
   (C) The invasion of Cambodia by South Vietnamese troops
   (D) The American refusal to permit the building of Soviet missiles in the Western Hemisphere

Questions 9–11 refer to the following statement.

Nations sent early explorers for three reasons: gold, glory, and God. Later explorers were sent out for raw materials, trading posts, and places to colonize.

9. According to this statement, which of the following could be considered an early explorer or exploration?
   (A) The Dutch East India Company trading with the Indians for fur
   (B) Sieur de la Salle setting up trading posts
   (C) James Oglethorpe settling in Savannah, Georgia
   (D) Francisco Coronado searching for the Seven Cities of Cíbola in Arizona and New Mexico

10. According to this statement, which of the following could be considered a later explorer or exploration?
    (A) Cortés stealing the Incas' treasures from the Yucatán
    (B) Sir Francis Drake returning to England with a cargo of Spanish silver
    (C) Lewis and Clark's mapping of the territory west of the Mississippi acquired in the Louisiana Purchase
    (D) Ponce de León searching for the Fountain of Youth

11. According to this passage, which of the following motivated early explorers?
    (A) Hopes of fame and fortune
    (B) A desire for better living conditions
    (C) A need for religious freedom
    (D) A belief that the monarchy was always right

12. *Business cycle* refers to
    (A) profits and losses of a corporation over a one-year period.
    (B) fluctuations in corporate profits in a given region.
    (C) upswings and downswings in the economy.
    (D) the life span of a business or corporation.

Questions 13 and 14 are based on the following graph.

Growth of Population
in the United States, 1870–1910

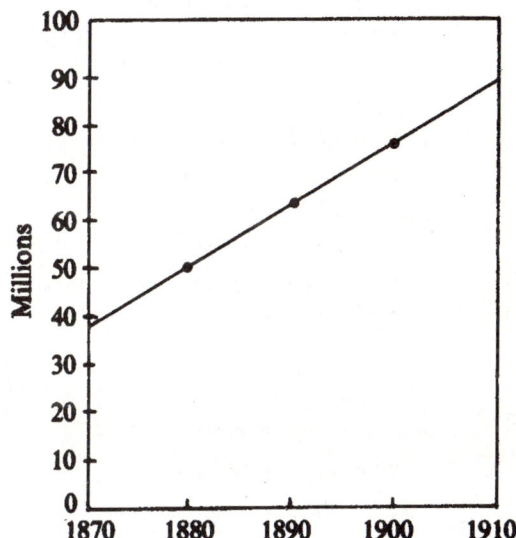

13. Between 1870 and 1910, it would be most accurate to say that the population of the United States
    (A) more than doubled.
    (B) almost doubled.
    (C) increased by 40 percent.
    (D) increased by 50 percent.

14. According to the information given above, which of the following statements is true?

 (A) The rate of population increase between 1870 and 1880 was approximately the same as the rate of population increase between 1890 and 1900.

 (B) The percentage of foreign-born Americans in the United States between 1900 and 1910 was greater than the percentage of foreign-born Americans in the United States from 1870 to 1880.

 (C) Between 1880 and 1890 immigration accounted for approximately 10 percent of the population.

 (D) The rate of population increase grew steadily from 1870 to 1910.

Questions 15–18 refer to the following information.

Throughout American history, people have been selected for positions within the government and in private companies in several ways. Some of these ways are still used today; others have fallen into disfavor. Listed below are five methods that have been used for candidate evaluation and promotion.

 1. The spoils system—

 Candidates are selected for positions based on their membership in a political party and/or for supporting their candidate's election bid.

 2. The merit system—

 An impartial body tests and evaluates job applicants.

 3. The "Old Boy" network—

 People are placed in high-status jobs because they are members of the upper-middle and upper class.

 4. Nepotism—

 Positions are awarded based on a candidate's relationship to a person within the company.

 5. Networking—

 People look for positions through social contacts.

Each of the following statements describes an aspect of the application-review process. Choose the system in which the process would most likely occur. The categories may be used more than once in the set of items, but no one question has more than one best answer.

15. In 1883 Congress passed the Pendleton Act, setting up the Civil Service Commission. This impartial body was to test and rate applicants for federal jobs. Which system did this Act establish?

 (A) The spoils system

 (B) The merit system

 (C) The "Old Boy" network

 (D) Nepotism

16. Joshua Seth's father is the president of a major oil company. His mother is active in many charitable organizations. In addition, his parents are friends with many socially important people. Joshua, like his father and grandfather, attended the exclusive and expensive preparatory high school, Wooded Hills. When Joshua graduated from an Ivy League college, his father's friend told him about an excellent position in an investment banking firm. Under which system did Joshua receive his job?

 (A) The spoils system

 (B) The merit system

 (C) The "Old Boy" network

 (D) Nepotism

17. In 1939 Congress passed the Hatch Act, providing that federal employees may not be asked for political contributions and may not actively participate in political affairs. The act was passed to lessen the influence of

 (A) the spoils system.

 (B) the merit system.

 (C) the "Old Boy" network.

 (D) nepotism.

18. Jessica Dawn was a loyal volunteer for Senator Halloway's campaign. After the senator won reelection, Jessica Dawn was given a well paying position on the senator's staff. Which system was the senator using to justify giving Jessica Dawn a job?

 (A) The spoils system

 (B) The merit system

 (C) The "Old Boy" network

 (D) Nepotism

Questions 19–21 refer to the following paragraph and chart.

The following chart shows how the United States government supported scientific research and development (R&D) over an eleven-year period and how that money was distributed among the various states. The bars indicate differences during three time periods.

Federal R&D support to the 10 states leading in such support in 1986 for selected years

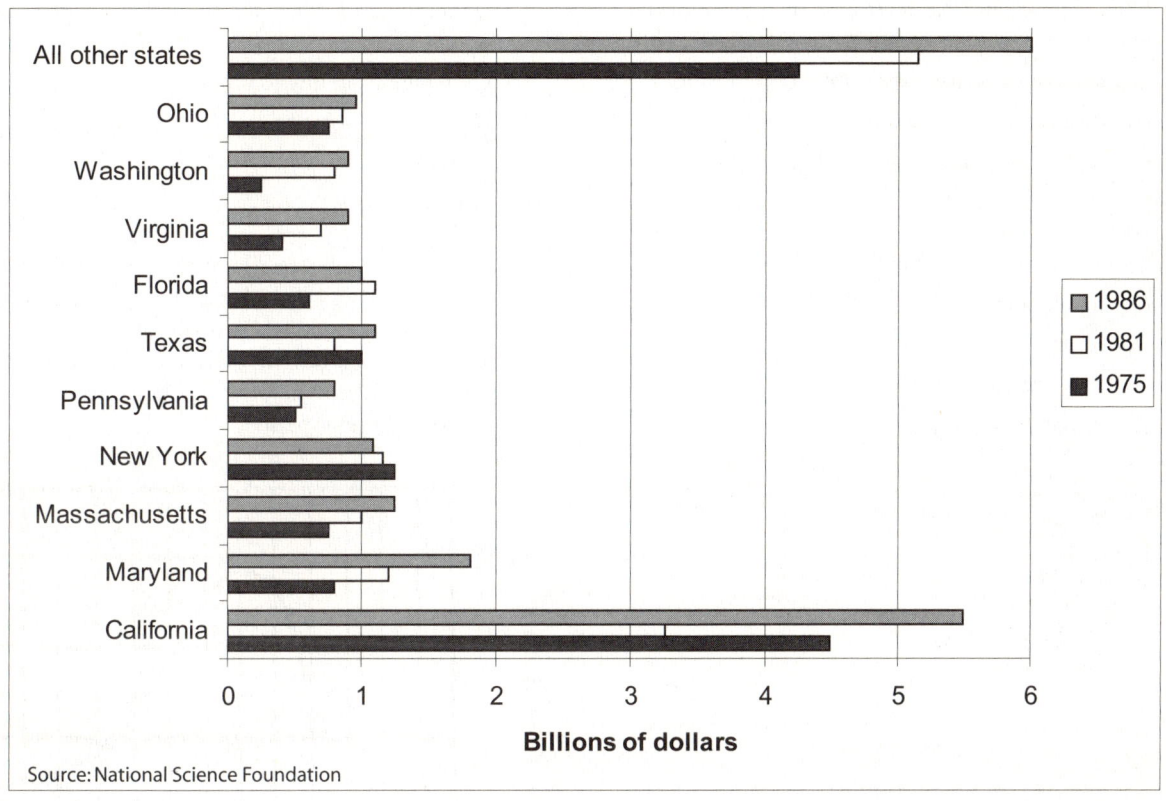

Source: National Science Foundation

19. Based on this chart, what happened to money for scientific research and development over the time period shown?

 (A) It increased dramatically.

 (B) It decreased dramatically.

 (C) It probably just kept up with inflation.

 (D) It enabled dramatic scientific breakthroughs.

20. Which combination of states had the largest share of funds in 1981?

 (A) California, Pennsylvania, and Texas

 (B) Maryland, Massachusetts, and New York

 (C) California, Florida, and Texas

 (D) Pennsylvania, Texas, and Florida

21. Which state had the largest percentage decline in funds over the time period of the chart?

 (A) Florida

 (B) New York

 (C) California

 (D) Texas

22. The caste system of social stratification connotes all of the following *except* that

 (A) caste membership is hereditary.

 (B) caste membership is permanent.

 (C) marriage within one's caste is required.

 (D) an individual can change caste by gaining wealth.

Section 7: Science

22 questions

Directions: Each question or incomplete statement is followed by four answer choices. For each question, select the answer or completion that is best and blacken the corresponding space on the answer sheet.

1. Human interferon can be used to fight viral infections. This means that interferon may be helpful in curing

    (A) diseases that are responsible for deformities.

    (B) diseases that are genetic in origin.

    (C) problems related to psychological stress.

    (D) the common cold.

2. "Opposites attract" is the fundamental law of

    (A) momentum.

    (B) forces.

    (C) magnetism.

    (D) gravitation.

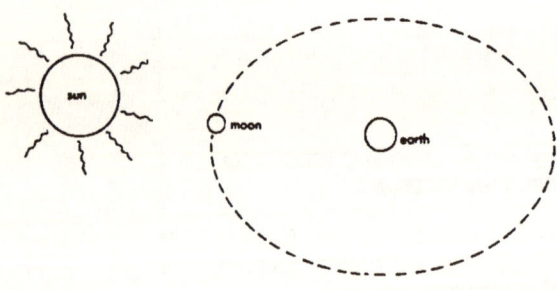

3. The illustration above is an example of

    (A) the phases of the moon.

    (B) the seasons of the year.

    (C) a lunar eclipse.

    (D) a solar eclipse.

4. All the following tend to purify water *except*

    (A) bacteria.

    (B) oxidation.

    (C) sedimentation.

    (D) chlorination.

5. Cyclic changes occur at a definite rate and are repeated regularly. All of the following are examples of cyclic changes *except*

    (A) change from day to night.

    (B) change of seasons.

    (C) tides.

    (D) earthquakes.

6. Below is a graph describing the results of an experiment that was done by a biologist. The scientist put live bacteria and growth medium (food for bacteria to live on) into a closed container and then counted the number of live bacteria every half hour for a 16-hour period.

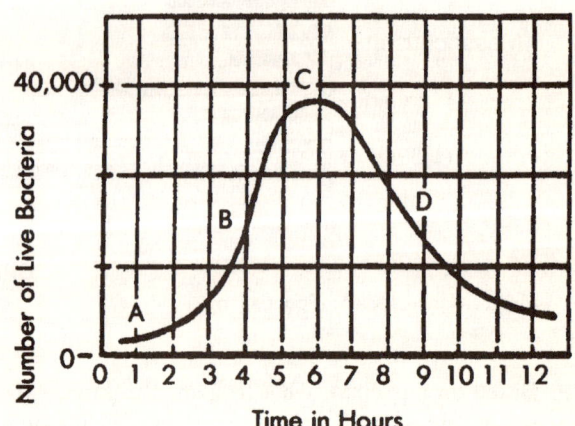

Which of the following can be inferred from the results of this experiment?

    (A) Bacteria can grow anywhere, anytime.

    (B) Bacteria can be easily eliminated with cleaners.

    (C) It takes a very long time for bacteria to grow.

    (D) It is important to store leftover food correctly.

Questions 7 and 8 are based on the information below.

Few areas in the United States are free from thunderstorms and their attendant hazards, but some areas have more storms than others. The map below shows the incidence of thunderstorm days—days on which thunderstorms are observed—for the United States.

Incidence of Thunderstorms

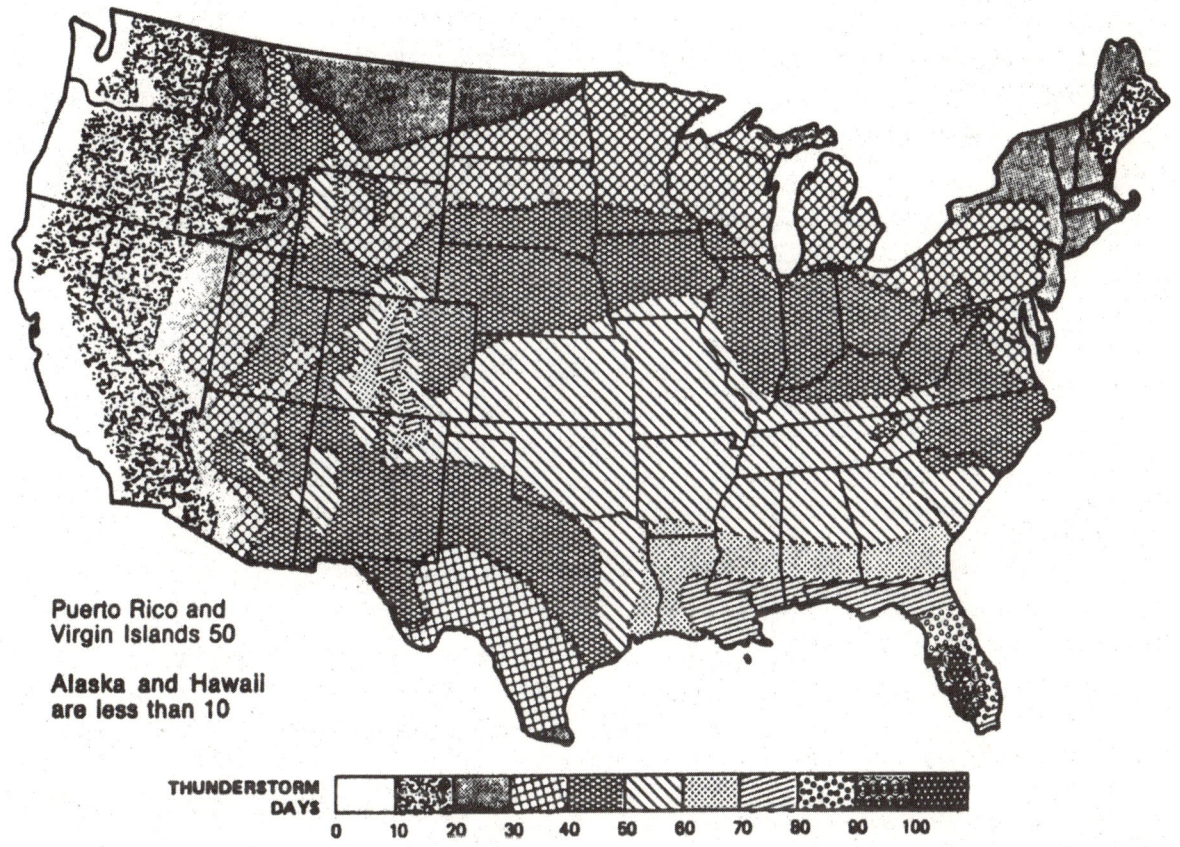

Puerto Rico and
Virgin Islands 50

Alaska and Hawaii
are less than 10

THUNDERSTORM DAYS
0   10   20   30   40   50   60   70   80   90   100

7. The Garcias are looking forward to a carefree camping vacation. They would like to avoid the frequent thunderstorms that spoiled their last camping trip. Based on the information in the map above, which region of the country would they be *least* likely to choose for their next vacation?

 (A) California, Oregon, Washington

 (B) Florida, Georgia, Alabama

 (C) Kentucky, Virginia, West Virginia

 (D) Missouri, Iowa, Illinois

8. If they are caught in a thunderstorm despite their careful planning, they should do any of the following *except*

 (A) stay inside a solid building.

 (B) remain in an all-metal automobile.

 (C) stand under a tall tree.

 (D) go to a low place such as a ravine or valley.

9. Which of the following processes is responsible for clothes drying on the line on a warm summer day?

   (A) Freezing

   (B) Condensation

   (C) Sublimation

   (D) Evaporation

10. Conductors are materials through which electrons can flow freely. Most metals make good electrical conductors, but of all, silver is the best. Next to silver, copper is a good conductor, with aluminum following closely behind.

    Which of the following best explains why copper is the metal most widely used in electrical wiring?

    (A) It is the best conductor of electricity.

    (B) It has a high resistance to electricity.

    (C) It is cheaper than aluminum.

    (D) It is a better conductor than aluminum and cheaper than silver.

11. Species that practice internal fertilization are characterized by a

    (A) fetus that develops entirely in the oceans.

    (B) wide degree of care for their young.

    (C) parental noninterest once the eggs have been laid.

    (D) diminished potency as they reach maturity.

12. As an object sinks in water, the pressure on the object

    (A) decreases.

    (B) increases.

    (C) remains the same.

    (D) first increases then decreases.

13. Which of the following offers the best summary of the Second Law of Thermodynamics?

    (A) Energy transformations are not 100 percent efficient.

    (B) The ultimate energy source in the biosphere is our sun.

    (C) Energy cannot be created or destroyed.

    (D) For each action there exists an equal and opposite reaction.

14. Consider the following three pieces of evidence.

    I. Identical fossil species of terrestrial plants and animals, older than Carboniferous, are found in Africa, South America, India, and Australia.

    II. The Cape Mountains of South Africa are the same type of folded mountain and made up of the same type rocks as the mountains south of Buenos Aires in South America.

    III. The rock on the crests of the midoceanic ridges is younger than the rock on either side of the crest.

    Based upon this evidence, which of the following is the most probable conclusion?

    (A) The Earth has been formed by the shrinking and cooling of an originally molten mass; this process ended prior to the Carboniferous.

    (B) Radioactive heat has caused thermal convection currents in the mantle of the Earth.

    (C) Since its creation, the Earth's surface has changed little.

    (D) Prior to the Carboniferous, all the land on the surface of the Earth was one great continent, which subsequently began to split apart.

15. A white-cell count is helpful in determining whether a patient has

    (A) an infection.

    (B) antitoxins.

    (C) diabetes.

    (D) heart disease.

16. If a doctor describes a patient as dehydrated, the patient

    (A) has a contagious disease.

    (B) needs insulin.

    (C) cannot manufacture chlorophyll.

    (D) has lost a great deal of water.

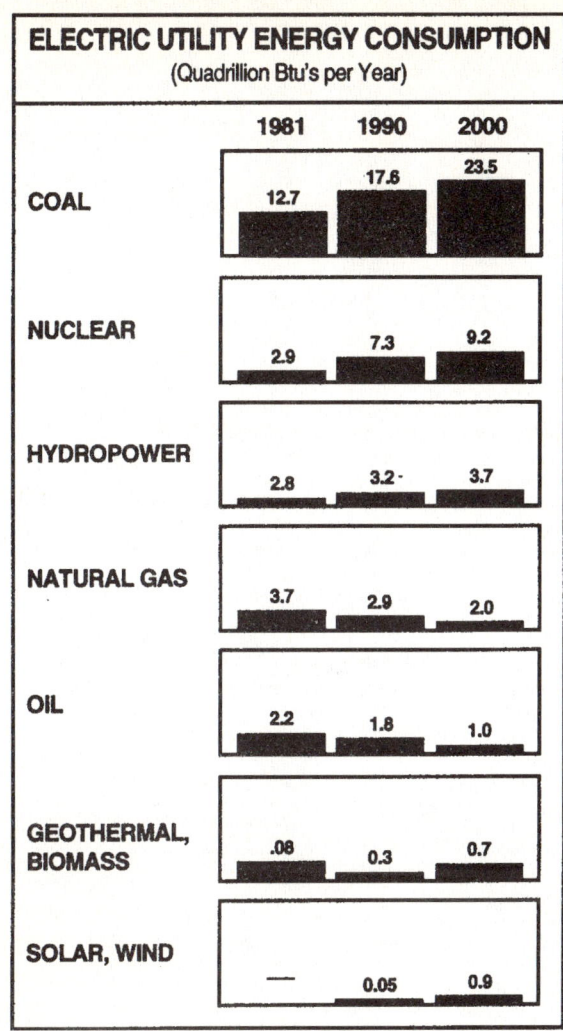

ELECTRIC UTILITY ENERGY CONSUMPTION
(Quadrillion Btu's per Year)

	1981	1990	2000
COAL	12.7	17.6	23.5
NUCLEAR	2.9	7.3	9.2
HYDROPOWER	2.8	3.2	3.7
NATURAL GAS	3.7	2.9	2.0
OIL	2.2	1.8	1.0
GEOTHERMAL, BIOMASS	.06	0.3	0.7
SOLAR, WIND	—	0.05	0.9

NORMAL TEMPERATURE DURING JANUARY FOR SELECTED CITIES

	MAXIMUM	MINIMUM
San Francisco, CA	55°	42°
Los Angeles, CA	67	48
Phoenix, AZ	65	39
Denver, CO	43	16
Miami, FL	75	59
Atlanta, GA	51	33
Chicago, IL	29	14
New Orleans, LA	62	43
Boston, MA	36	23
St. Paul, MN	20	2
New York City, NY	37	26
Portland, OR	44	34
Philadelphia, PA	39	24
Houston, TX	62	41

17. Based on the chart above, the fuel that supplies the greatest amount of energy is

    (A) nuclear.

    (B) natural gas.

    (C) coal.

    (D) hydropower.

18. This planet revolves around the sun in an orbit between that of Venus and Mars. It is known to be covered by oceans and some land; it has but a single moon. Name the planet.

    (A) Jupiter

    (B) Saturn

    (C) Earth

    (D) Mercury

19. A travel agent uses the chart above to advise clients about weather conditions in the cities they plan to visit. Based on this temperature chart and the travel plans that follow, which of the travel agent's clients can expect to experience the widest range of temperatures on the trip scheduled?

    (A) Pat, who will spend the week of January 12 in New York, Chicago, and Denver

    (B) Julie, who will spend the first two weeks of January in Miami, Atlanta, and New Orleans

    (C) Joe, who will tour New Orleans, Phoenix, and Houston the last week of January

    (D) Mike, whose travel plans include visits to Phoenix, Los Angeles, and San Francisco in mid-January

20. Which of the following common electrical devices contains an electromagnet?

    (A) Iron

    (B) Telephone

    (C) Water heater

    (D) Toaster

21. When all the colors of the spectrum are fused, the resulting light is

    (A) red.

    (B) white.

    (C) blue.

    (D) yellow.

22. The moon rotates once while going around the Earth once. As a result,

    (A) the moon follows an elliptical path.

    (B) the sun is eclipsed by the moon every seven years.

    (C) only one side of the moon faces the Earth.

    (D) every fourth year is a leap year.

This is the end of the Content Knowledge Test.

Multiple Subjects Assessment for Teachers Content Area Exercises

The Multiple Subjects Assessment for Teachers Content Area Exercises consists of 3 hours of short essay questions. There are eighteen essays. A nonprogrammable calculator is allowed.

Content areas include:

- I. Literature and Language Studies
- II. Mathematics
- III. Visual and Performing Arts
- IV. Physical Education
- V. Human Development
- VI. History/Social Sciences
- VII. Science

These essays are scored from 0 (totally incorrect) to 3 (best possible score).

I. Literature and Language Studies

Question 1 refers to the following paragraph:

Professor William J. Requin is presently developing a new theory about gene mutation. He was born in Elmsford, Maryland, on January 24, 1953. He graduated from the University of Maryland in 1975. He received a medical degree in 1980. He helped map the structure of DNA molecules from 1983 to 1987. The experience greatly enhanced his present research in gene mutation.

1. Describe three ways in which the author can edit this paragraph so as to have fewer choppy and monotonous sentences.

2. Using any fictional literary work, describe how the author used contemporary sources to develop three themes within his or her written work.

Question 3 refers to the following poem:

First, Nature builds the body.

A house with doors of sense.

Wherein a strange child, the Spirit is born.

Tools he finds and uses at his pleasure.

Leaving the house, it crumbles,

But the architect always builds anew

And beckons the heavenly guest again to earthly accommodation.

—Friedrich Ruckert

3. Describe the basic theme of this poem in terms of its view of death. Focus on the author's philosophical view of death.

II. Mathematics

1. If the diagonals of a two-dimensional parallelogram are perpendicular and congruent, then how can we describe the shape of this geometric form?

Question 2 refers to the following equation:

$$c(a \times b) = ca \times cb$$

2. Describe what is wrong with this equation in terms of the mathematical property or properties being used.

3. When rolling a die, the probability of getting a six is 1/6, while the probability of rolling another number is 5/6. If you roll the die twenty times, how can we determine the probability of rolling a six exactly eight times?

III. Visual and Performing Arts

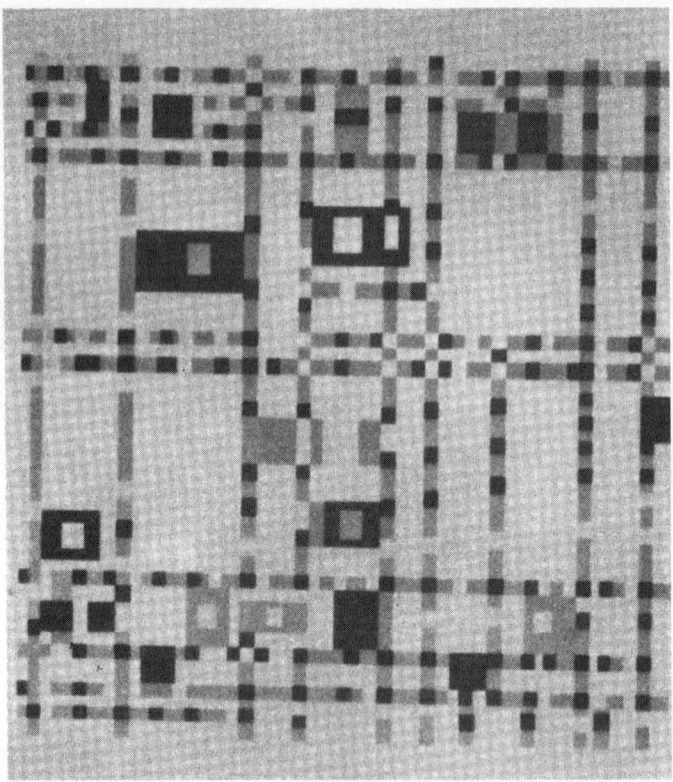

1. Briefly discuss the stylistic elements and principles of design used in the painting above.

2. Discuss the importance and uses of flying buttresses. Include structural and aesthetic purposes.

IV. Physical Education

1. Define and give two examples of open skills.
2. Describe two different goals of a physical education program on the elementary level and how to reach them.

V. Human Development

1. Discuss, describe, and analyze two differences between the Freudian and behavioral approaches to child development.

2. Even though a child has the ability to do well in school, he or she may fail because of the concept of the "self-fulfilling prophecy." Describe this concept and how it affects a student's behavior and achievement.

VI. History/Social Sciences

Question 1 refers to the following quotation:

> A well regulated Militia, being necessary to the security of a free state, the right of the people to keep and bear arms shall not be infringed.

—Second Amendment, U.S. Constitution

1. Use this amendment to create arguments to justify and oppose gun-control legislation. Give specific historical or legal precedents to justify each argument.

2. Describe how geography affected Japan and China historically. Discuss geographic influences upon social, economic, and religious developments.

Question 3 refers to the following graph:

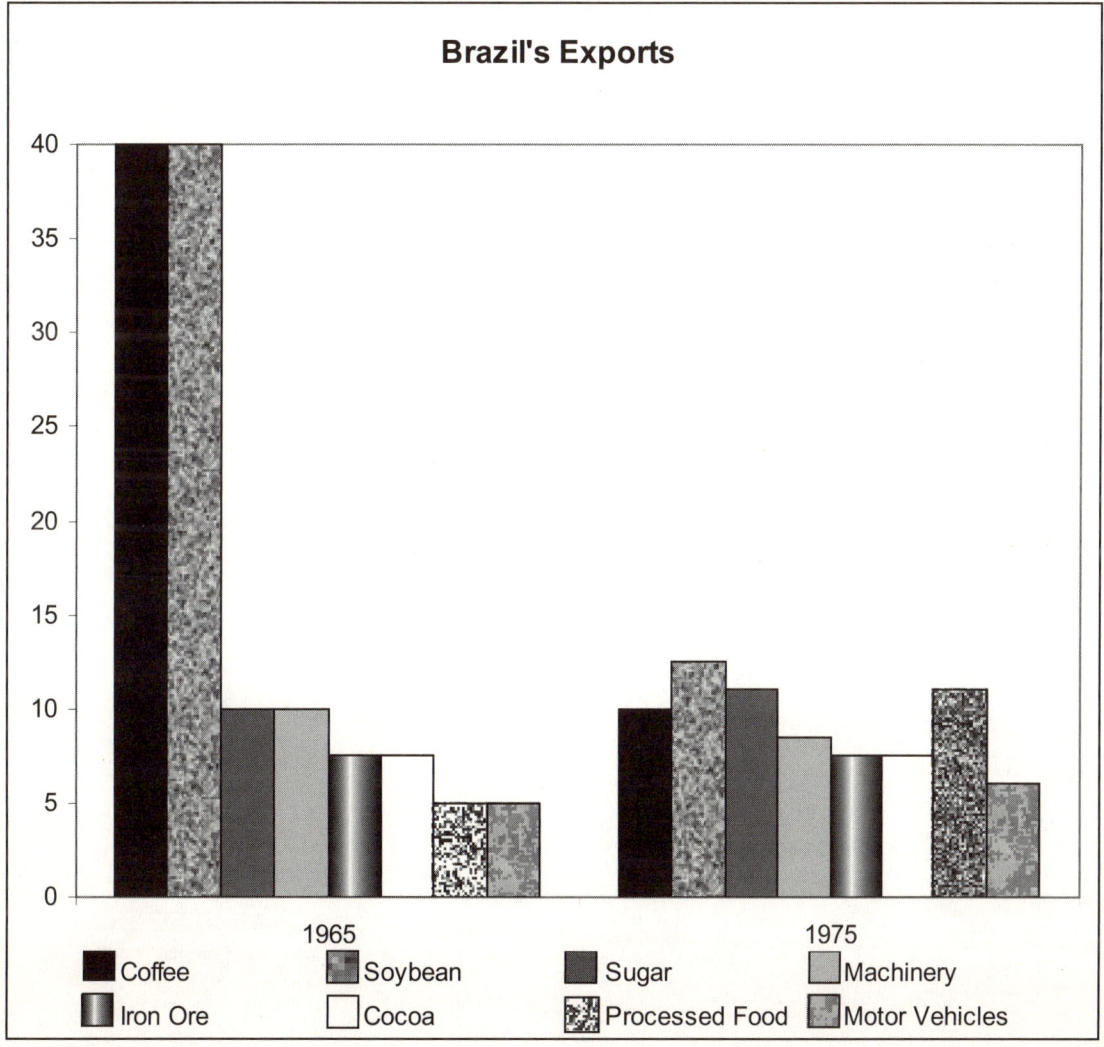

3. Describe three possible reasons for the change in Brazil's exports from 1965 to 1975. Discuss geographic, social, and economic factors.

VII. Science

1. Describe how scientists use radioactive isotopes to determine the age of various geographic forms. Identify and discuss two practical applications of radiometric dating.

2. Using the concepts of nuclear fusion and gravity, describe the formation and lifecycle of a sun-like star.

3. Describe how effort and resistance turn energy into work in the simple machines listed below.

> lever
> pulley
> inclined plane

Illustrate practical applications for one of these machines.

This is the end of the Content Area Exercises.

MSAT: Content Knowledge Test Answer Key

Section 1: Literature and Language Studies

1. C	7. D	13. D	19. A
2. B	8. A	14. B	20. C
3. D	9. C	15. A	21. B
4. B	10. B	16. D	22. B
5. C	11. C	17. B	23. A
6. C	12. C	18. A	24. B

Section 2: Mathematics

1. B	7. D	13. C	19. D
2. D	8. B	14. D	20. A
3. D	9. D	15. D	21. C
4. A	10. A	16. A	22. D
5. C	11. B	17. C	23. B
6. D	12. B	18. D	24. C

Section 3: Visual And Performing Arts

1. B	4. A	7. B	10. D
2. B	5. D	8. C	11. C
3. C	6. D	9. D	12. B

Section 4: Physical Education

1. C	3. A	5. D	7. D
2. C	4. B	6. A	8. C

Section 5: Human Development

1. B	3. A	5. D	7. B
2. C	4. C	6. C	8. C

Section 6: History/Social Sciences

1. A	7. D	13. A	19. C
2. D	8. B	14. A	20. C
3. D	9. D	15. B	21. B
4. D	10. C	16. C	22. D
5. B	11. A	17. A	
6. D	12. C	18. A	

Section 7: Science

1. D	7. B	13. A	19. B
2. C	8. C	14. D	20. B
3. D	9. D	15. A	21. B
4. A	10. D	16. D	22. C
5. D	11. B	17. C	
6. D	12. B	18. C	

MSAT: Content Knowledge Test Answer Explanations

Section 1: Literature and Language Studies

1. **The correct answer is (C).** These lines come from the prophet Isaiah in the Old Testament.

2. **The correct answer is (B).** The lines describe a total peace that will exist when the Messiah comes.

3. **The correct answer is (D).** Patrick Henry's famous oration is a political speech from Revolutionary War times.

4. **The correct answer is (B).** Mark Twain's use of "hain't we got . . ." is an example of colloquial speech.

5. **The correct answer is (C).** Catching more flies with honey (flattery) than vinegar (punishment) is using flattery as a means to an end.

6. **The correct answer is (C).** Mozart (1756–91) was an Austrian whom many consider to be the greatest composer of all time. He began composing at the age of five and wrote his first symphony at nine. In all, he wrote more than 600 works, and his mastery of all classical forms makes his work the epitome of classical music.

7. **The correct answer is (D).** A metaphor is a figure of speech that compares one thing to another without the use of "like" or "as." Death is portrayed as knocking upon the door of the poor and the rich alike.

8. **The correct answer is (A).** A limerick is a light or humorous poem of five lines.

9. **The correct answer is (C).** A simile is a figure of speech that compares one thing to another using the terms "like" or "as."

10. **The correct answer is (B).** The poet is telling readers to appreciate things while they last, because time moves quickly and nothing lasts forever.

11. **The correct answer is (C).** The fact that flowers die and the sun sets shows that life's pleasures do not last.

12. **The correct answer is (C).** Einstein states that if he is proved wrong, each nationality will disavow him and claim he belonged elsewhere.

13. **The correct answer is (D).** "Two golden hours, each set with sixty diamond minutes . . ." is used to show how valuable time is. It can never be recaptured.

14. **The correct answer is (B).** Tolstoy, in the first sentence of his classic work *Anna Karenina*, discusses the sociology of families.

15. **The correct answer is (A).** The lines are blank verse, unrhymed iambic pentameter.

16. **The correct answer is (D).** The Latin root *viv* means "life."

17. **The correct answer is (B).** The prefix *ab-* means "away from." *Abnormal* is literally "away from the norm."

18. **The correct answer is (A).** The *mis* in *misanthrope* means "hated." The *mis* in the remaining choices means "wrong."

19. **The correct answer is (A).** Hyperbole is an exaggeration.

20. **The correct answer is (C).** A phrase cannot be a complete thought. A clause, on the other hand, can be a complete thought.

21. **The correct answer is (B).** *Deep pockets* refers to large amounts of available money.

22. **The correct answer is (B).** *Fly-by-night* means "impermanent."

23. **The correct answer is (A).** *Logy* means "study of something." Thus biology is the study of life.

24. **The correct answer is (B).** A metaphor is a comparison between two things without the use of "like" or "as."

Section 2: Mathematics

1. **The correct answer is (B).** Add the time difference (5 hours) to the starting time:

    8:30 p.m. EST + 5 hours = 1:30 a.m. GMT

    1:30 a.m. to 8:15 a.m. = 6 hours 45 minutes

2. **The correct answer is (D).** To find out how much faster Runner #2 must run, we need to know the time of the winner. Without this, there is insufficient information to solve the problem.

3. **The correct answer is (D).** Know the squares of the numbers from 1 to 10. Here, 8 squared is 64. Reversing this, the square root of 64 is 8. And the square root of .64 is .8.

4. **The correct answer is (A).** Angle ABC and Angle DBC (135°) are supplementary angles. That means the sum of these two angles is 180°.

    Angle ABC + 135° = 180°

    Angle ABC = 180° – 135° = 45°

5. **The correct answer is (C).** First calculate the amount spent on known items: 28 + 25 + 15 + 17 = 85%. Subtract this figure from 100% to find out how much was saved: 100 – 85 = 15%. Multiply by total income, $3600: .15 × 3600 = $540 in 1 month, and 12 × 540 = $6480 in 1 year.

6. **The correct answer is (D).** Since 28% is spent on rent, the cost of rent each month is .28 × $3600 = $1008.

7. **The correct answer is (D).** Hourly Wage × Hours Worked = Total Income ($4.50)(4 + 3 + 5 + 4 + 4) = Total Income. The actual numerical solution is not asked for, just the equation you would use to solve the problem, which is choice (D).

8. **The correct answer is (B).** The curve for solution B (the solid line) shows that CO_2 was liberated after about 5 minutes, well before any of the other solutions showed CO_2 production.

9. **The correct answer is (D).** The curves for solution A and solution B intersect at a point before 20 minutes. At this point, 1.6 ml of CO_2 was liberated by both solutions. This can be determined by drawing a line horizontally from the point of intersection to the scale at the left.

10. **The correct answer is (A).** At the end of 30 minutes, the most CO_2 was liberated from solution A. Draw a horizontal line from this point to the scale at the left. The volume of liberated CO_2 is 3.4 ml.

11. **The correct answer is (B).** A statement that is true independently of the truth of its premises is a tautology.

12. **The correct answer is (B).** The greatest common divisor (gcd) of 3 and 12 is 3, the gcd of 25 and 30 is 5, the gcd of 18 and 36 is 18, and the gcd of 35 and 60 is 5. Because 15 and 28 have no common divisors other than 1, their gcd is 1 and they are relatively prime.

13. **The correct answer is (C).** Write the equation for the information given:

    2 coins of value $x = 2x$

    3 coins of value $x = 3y$

    $$2x + 3y = 50 \text{ cents}$$

    Therefore, $2x = 50 - 3y$

14. **The correct answer is (D).** $11^4 = 11(11)(11)(11)$

15. **The correct answer is (D).** $\dfrac{6464}{32} = 202$

16. **The correct answer is (A).** To get percent, multiply by 100.

    $$30(100) = 3000\%$$

17. **The correct answer is (C).** $\dfrac{105}{25} = 4.2$. Therefore 5 buses are required.

18. **The correct answer is (D).** Doubling the speed makes the trip take half the time.

19. **The correct answer is (D).** Multiplication does *not* distribute over multiplication.

20. **The correct answer is (A).** Divide both sides of the equation by 5:

    $$\frac{5x+5y+5z}{5} = \frac{5}{5}$$

    $x + y + z = 1$

21. **The correct answer is (C).**

    $$-5(-4)(-3)(-2)(-1)(0)(1)(2)(3)(4)(5) = 0$$

22. **The correct answer is (D).** The mode is the most frequent number.

23. **The correct answer is (B).**

$$2\% \text{ of } 5\% = \frac{2}{100} \cdot \frac{5}{100} = \frac{10}{10000} = .1\%, \text{ not } 10\%$$

24. **The correct answer is (C).** $2\frac{3}{4} \times 12 = 33$

Section 3: Visual and Performing Arts

1. **The correct answer is (B).** Lichtenstein's *Bananas and Grapefruit* (1972) is an example of Pop Art.

2. **The correct answer is (B).** All the answers are applicable to the sculpture pictured except choice (B). In this sculpture by Henry Moore, titled *Family Group*, the medium is bronze, and its use suggests anything but frailty.

3. **The correct answer is (C).** Michelangelo: *Creation of Man*, Sistine Chapel (1508–12)

4. **The correct answer is (A).** Mary Cassatt: *Maternal Caress* (1891)

5. **The correct answer is (D).** Rubens: *An Allegory of Peace and War* (1629)
   The other work shown is:
   (B) Leonardo Da Vinci: *Mona Lisa* (c. 1503–05)

6. **The correct answer is (D).** Pierre-Auguste Renoir: *On The Terrace* (1881)

7. **The correct answer is (B).** Yves Tanguy: *The Sun in its Casket* (1937)
   The other works shown are:
   (A) James Abbott McNeill Whistler: *Carlyle* (1872)
   (C) Claude Monet: *The Cliff at Fécamp* (1881)

8. **The correct answer is (C).** *Don Quixote*, Miguel de Cervantes' (1547–1616) masterpiece, contains the characters Don Quixote, Sancho Panza, and Dulcinea, as well as the broken-down horse, Rocinante.

9. **The correct answer is (D).** The Greek dramatists observed the unity of place and therefore did not employ changes of scene.

10. **The correct answer is (D).** The English poet John Milton, author of *Paradise Lost*, lived from 1608–74; Shakespeare lived from 1564–1616.

11. **The correct answer is (C).** *All That Jazz* is associated with Bob Fosse, as are *Sweet Charity* and *Cabaret*.

12. **The correct answer is (B).** Scott Joplin (1868–1917), the pianist-songwriter who composed *Maple Leaf Rag*, *Wall Street Rag*, and *Sugar Cane Rag*, was the major ragtime composer of his time.

Section 4: Physical Education

1. **The correct answer is (C).** Metabolism is the term used to incorporate all processes designed to keep an organism alive.

2. **The correct answer is (C).** During exercise, the rate of respiration increases. Carbon dioxide is a waste product produced during cellular respiration.

3. **The correct answer is (A).** Cilia move mucus with foreign material out of the trachea. Smoking incapacitates the cilia.

4. **The correct answer is (B).** The cerebellum is that part of the brain that coordinates motor activities and helps maintain balance.

5. **The correct answer is (D).** Anaerobic respiration produces the lactic acid in the muscles of a long-distance runner.

6. **The correct answer is (A).** Peristalsis is the name for the muscular contractions by which food moves down the esophagus into the stomach.

7. **The correct answer is (D).** The endocrine glands produce hormones, which then travel through the bloodstream to particular organs.

8. **The correct answer is (C).** The desirable weight for a man 68 inches tall is 145. At 130, Bill is underweight.

Section 5: Human Development

1. **The correct answer is (B).** Choice (A) is wrong because this concept has to do with the ability to learn how to count in a meaningful fashion. Choice (C) is related to one-to-one correspondence and not spatial relations. Choice (D) is wrong because this skill is related to the concept of reversibility.

2. **The correct answer is (C).** A child who is inattentive and distractible usually will have difficulty developing multiplication facts. This skill requires concentration and memory. Choice (B) is obviously incorrect because students with attention deficit disorders may have no difficulty with perception and fine-motor ability. Understanding coin value does not necessitate a high degree of concentration and attention. Choice (A) has nothing to do with the problem at hand.

3. **The correct answer is (A).** The concept of "g" theory comes from the work of Horn and Cattell. Woodcock and Mather do utilize "g" theory in the development of their achievement and cognitive batteries, but they did not develop the theory per se. Choice (C) is wrong because these two authors are closely associated with their critical research pertaining to educational and psychological testing. Hammill and Bartell, choice (D), are best known for describing remedial techniques for students who have learning problems.

4. **The correct answer is (C).** Most intelligence tests do not consider handwriting to be a measurable component of intelligence. The other choices are usually assessed when given a standardized intelligence test.

5. **The correct answer is (D).** Personality style (Item I) is known to inhibit cognitive development—especially if the child tends to respond impulsively rather than carefully. It is obvious that Item II also inhibits cognitive development. A child in poor health would have a great deal of difficulty in learning. It is also obvious that a child with high levels of anxiety may become blocked and do poorly on a standardized test (Item III). Item IV is not a correct response because research demonstrates that family structure has very little to do with the development of cognitive skills.

6. **The correct answer is (C).** The views described are most closely associated with Hunt. Using twin and animal studies, Hunt concluded that experience plays a critical role in the development of cognitive ability. On the other hand, both Piaget, choice (B), and Bruner, choice (C), believe in fixed biological stages of cognitive development. Choice (A) is wrong because Jensen believed that genetics played a major role in determining intelligence.

7. **The correct answer is (B).** A severely mentally retarded student is being described. Such a student cannot do traditional academic work and is usually taught through the use of task analysis and behavior modification. Students with the other three handicapping conditions can usually be taught a traditional academic program with modifications.

8. **The correct answer is (C).** The passage best describes social-emotional development from three to six years. Choice (A) is obviously wrong because at this stage a child is helpless and dependent. Choice (B) is incorrect because language is simple at this stage and socially aggressive behaviors are often manifested. Choice (D) is also wrong because at this latter stage moral development continues and a child begins to identify with ethnic, racial, and religious groups.

Section 6: History/Social Sciences

1. **The correct answer is (A).** Choice (D) describes the process of socialization. The other answers are inappropriate.

2. **The correct answer is (D).** Haphazard sampling is unlikely to yield useful results. In the sample survey, sociologists select a sample that is representative of a larger population.

3. **The correct answer is (D).** The restaurant represents the American population with its many different kinds of people.

4. **The correct answer is (D).** The cartoon suggests America is made up of a number of different nationalities, as indicated by foods representative of each culture.

5. **The correct answer is (B).** The different foods indicate the United States has been settled by people from many other countries.

6. **The correct answer is (D).** The researcher examining social stratification is interested in the distribution of power, property, and prestige within a society. These factors are mentioned in all answer options except choice (D).

7. **The correct answer is (D).** The Napoleonic Code, derived from Roman law, went into effect in 1805 and remained a lasting monument to Napoleonic rule. Its five sections covered all areas of civil law, from domestic relations to property rights and commercial life.

8. **The correct answer is (B).** In 1961, about 1,000 Cuban exiles, who had left Cuba during its revolution, staged a brief, unsuccessful invasion of Cuba with the assistance of the Central Intelligence Agency. The Bay of Pigs was the site of the invasion. The exiles had been led to believe that the Cuban people would welcome them as liberators, but this never occurred. Instead, the Bay of Pigs fiasco increased Castro's animosity toward the United States and caused further tensions between the two nations.

9. **The correct answer is (D).** Francisco Coronado was looking for gold in the American Southwest. The Seven Cities of Cíbola were reported by Indians to be rich in gold, a precious metal sought by explorers.

10. **The correct answer is (C).** Mapping land already acquired implies Lewis and Clark were seeking raw

materials and places to colonize. Choices (A) and (B) sought treasure; choice (D) sought fame.

11. **The correct answer is (A).** "Glory" is fame and fortune.

12. **The correct answer is (C).** *Business cycle* refers to fluctuations in the economy as a whole.

13. **The correct answer is (A).** Between 1870 and 1910 the population of the United States rose from almost 40 million to approximately 90 million, or more than doubled.

14. **The correct answer is (A).** From 1870 to 1880 the population rose from about 40 million to about 50 million, for about a 25 percent rate of population increase. From 1890 to 1900 the population rose from about 60 million to about 75 million, with again approximately a 25 percent rate of population increase. The rate of population increase did not grow steadily, as suggested in choice (D). Choices (B) and (C) cannot be supported by the information provided in the graph.

15. **The correct answer is (B).** The Pendleton Act established the merit system.

16. **The correct answer is (C).** Awarding a job to a candidate because of social standing is an example of the "Old Boy" network in action.

17. **The correct answer is (A).** The Hatch Act greatly decreased the effects of the spoils system.

18. **The correct answer is (A).** Jessica Dawn got her job as a result of the spoils system.

19. **The correct answer is (C).** By observation we can see that there was probably less than a 50 percent increase in available funds over the eleven years. The only possible option among all the answers is choice (C).

20. **The correct answer is (C).** The 1981 bar shows that Florida and Texas combined had more funding than Pennsylvania and Texas combined. Add California, and you have the largest combination.

21. **The correct answer is (B).** Only New York showed a consistent decline over the eleven-year period.

22. **The correct answer is (D).** A caste system is a hierarchy of endogamous divisions, which means that people are required to choose marriage partners from the same division or caste. Caste membership is hereditary and permanent. It is "ascribed" in that it is determined by forces that an individual is unable to change.

Section 7: Science

1. **The correct answer is (D).** Since the common cold is a virus infection, interferon might be helpful in curing it.

2. **The correct answer is (C).** The like poles of different magnets repel each other, and the unlike poles attract each other.

3. **The correct answer is (D).** During a solar eclipse the moon travels between the sun and the Earth, blocking out the view of the sun totally or partially on at least some part of the Earth.

4. **The correct answer is (A).** The more bacteria in the water, the less pure it is.

5. **The correct answer is (D).** Earthquakes are changes that occur suddenly after long periods of inactivity. All of the other changes are examples of regular or cyclic change.

6. **The correct answer is (D).** The bacteria flourished in a growth medium (food). In the same way, we can infer that incorrectly stored food provides a breeding ground for bacteria.

7. **The correct answer is (B).** Based on the map, Florida shows the highest incidence of thunderstorm activity, up to 100 thunderstorm days per year.

8. **The correct answer is (C).** Standing under a tall tree or telephone pole or on the top of a hill creates a natural lightning rod. In a forest, seek shelter under a thick growth of small trees. In open areas, go to a low place such as a ravine or valley.

9. **The correct answer is (D).** Evaporation is described by the following: Water (liquid) $\rightarrow$ Water (gas)

10. **The correct answer is (D).** Copper is the metal most widely used in electrical wiring because it is almost as good a conductor of electricity as silver and considerably less expensive.

11. **The correct answer is (B).** Internal fertilization is important in terrestrial forms, many of which provide no care for their young, while others provide extensive care for their young.

12. **The correct answer is (B).** Water pressure increases with depth. For every foot of depth in fresh water, the pressure increases 62.5 pounds, while in salt water it increases 64 pounds for each foot of depth.

13. **The correct answer is (A).** According to the First Law of Thermodynamics, energy is neither created nor destroyed but is transformed from one type to another. When energy changes form, according to the Second Law of Thermodynamics, some energy is always dispersed or lost. Thus the transformation is not 100 percent efficient.

14. **The correct answer is (D).** From the evidence given it is most probable that all the land on the surface of the earth was once connected.

15. **The correct answer is (A).** The function of white cells is to remove unwanted organisms from the bloodstream and surrounding tissue. Of the choices given, only an infection indicates the presence of unwanted organisms. The white-cell count in this case would go up.

16. **The correct answer is (D).** To dehydrate something is to deprive it of water.

17. **The correct answer is (C).** Coal shows the highest bar for each year.

18. **The correct answer is (C).** Earth is the planet between Venus and Mars.

19. **The correct answer is (B).** Find the difference between the lowest and highest temperatures expected for the cities named for each traveler. Julie will experience temperatures ranging from a low of 33° in Atlanta to a high of 75° in Miami. This is a range of 42°, which is the widest range of the five scheduled trips.

20. **The correct answer is (B).** The telephone is the only one of the five electrical devices that uses an electromagnet, which produces a force field.

21. **The correct answer is (B).** White is the result of the fusion of many colors of the spectrum.

22. **The correct answer is (C).** The moon revolves around the Earth over the same amount of time as it rotates. This means that the same side of the moon faces the Earth at all times. The side away from us is referred to as the dark side of the moon.

Notes

Notes

Notes

Notes

Notes

Management Team

Contents

Overview

What We Do: The "Big Three"

Finances, Organization, and Accountability

Looking Back/ Looking Ahead

The IMF's financial year is May 1 through April 30.

The analysis and policy considerations expressed in this publication are those of the IMF Executive Directors.

The unit of account of the IMF is the SDR; conversions of IMF financial data to U.S. dollars are approximate and provided for convenience. On April 30, 2015, the SDR/U.S. dollar exchange rate was US$1 = 0.71103, and the U.S. dollar/SDR exchange rate was SDR 1 = US$1.40642. The year-earlier rates (April 30, 2014) were US$1 = SDR 0.645290 and SDR 1 = US$1.54969.

"Billion" means a thousand million; "trillion" means a thousand billion; minor discrepancies between constituent figures and totals are due to rounding.

As used in this Annual Report, the term "country" does not in all cases refer to a territorial entity that is a state as understood by international law and practice. As used here, the term also covers some territorial entities that are not states but for which statistical data are maintained on a separate and independent basis.

About the IMF

The International Monetary Fund is the world's central organization for international monetary cooperation. With 188 member countries, it is an organization in which almost all of the countries in the world work together to promote the common good. The IMF, which oversees the international monetary system to ensure its effective operation, has among its key purposes to promote exchange rate stability and to facilitate the expansion and balanced growth of international trade. This enables countries (and their citizens) to buy goods and services from one another and is essential for achieving sustainable economic growth and raising living standards.

All of the IMF's member countries are represented on its Executive Board, which discusses the national, regional, and global consequences of each member's economic policies and decides the IMF's lending to help member countries address temporary balance-of-payments problems, as well as capacity-building efforts. This Annual Report covers the activities of the Executive Board and IMF management and staff during the financial year May 1, 2014, through April 30, 2015. Some figures on lending to Greece were updated after the end of the financial year. The contents reflect the views and policy discussions of the IMF Executive Board, which has actively participated in preparation of this Annual Report.

The IMF's main activities

The key roles of the IMF are to:

Provide advice to members on adopting policies that can help them achieve macroeconomic stability, thereby accelerating economic growth and alleviating poverty.

Make financing temporarily available to member countries to help them address balance-of-payments problems, that is, when they find themselves short of foreign exchange because their external payments exceed their foreign exchange earnings.

Offer technical assistance and training to countries, at their request, to help them build the expertise and institutions they need to implement sound economic policies.

The IMF is headquartered in Washington, D.C., and, reflecting its global reach and close ties with its members, also has offices around the world.

Additional information on the IMF and its member countries can be found on the IMF's website, www.imf.org.

Message from the Managing Director

The past year has been a time of unexpected challenges for the international community. Amid the continued focus on spurring stronger and more inclusive growth and strengthening global cooperation, the IMF faced economic developments that required rapid adjustments.

First was the sudden, steep decline of oil prices. For most of our members, lower prices proved beneficial, supporting growth amid concerns about a new mediocre in the world economy. But oil producers faced difficult adjustments. These developments placed a premium on the IMF's analytical work and policy advice.

The second challenge was posed by the Ebola pandemic in Guinea, Liberia, and Sierra Leone. This outbreak was a matter of life and death, and the IMF moved quickly to ensure the three governments could respond to the crisis and get their economies moving again. The IMF provided more than $400 million of aid and debt relief, including by redesigning our disaster-response facility.

The third challenge during the past year was to assist several member countries addressing difficult economic and financial circumstances through IMF-supported programs. The IMF remains committed to helping these countries, along with all members, through this period of turmoil.

It was a year of innovation across the institution: pilot programs aimed at embedding in our country work the research on inclusive growth and gender that has been conducted in recent years; online training courses available to both officials and the wider public; the launch of a free data initiative; and cooperation with member countries on Islamic finance.

We continued to engage with our membership to implement the 2010 IMF quota and governance reforms as soon as possible. Our members reaffirmed the importance and urgency of these reforms for the IMF's credibility, legitimacy, and effectiveness.

The year provided an opportunity to look back to the achievements of the past 25 years in eastern and central Europe, and to the 70th anniversary of the IMF. It also was a time to plan for the future by building on the achievements of the United Nations Millennium Development Goals and supporting climate policy by getting energy prices right. In 2015 the international community will put in place the goals and policies aimed at reducing poverty and strengthening inclusive growth by 2030.

With the 2015 Annual Report, we highlight the IMF's work in these and other areas with a new approach that blends essays and graphics. As always, the report emphasizes the work of the IMF's Executive Board, whose policy guidance is central to the efforts to ensure global financial stability and growth.

Yours sincerely,

Christine Lagarde

FY2015 Key IMF Activities

The IMF established a new emergency relief fund and continued to provide financial assistance to members The Catastrophe Containment and Relief Trust (CCRT), established in response to the Ebola crisis, provides grants for debt relief to the poorest and most vulnerable countries hit by natural or public health disasters that have the potential to spread to other countries. The IMF provided $95 million in grants to Guinea, Liberia, and Sierra Leone to relieve eligible debt burdens. The IMF also augmented the program under the Extended Credit Facility for Guinea, Sierra Leone, and Liberia by $63.6 million, $111.7 million, and $48.2 million, respectively, and provided access to the Rapid Credit Facility to Guinea and Liberia in the amount of $39.8 million and $45.5 million, respectively.

Successor arrangements for Mexico and Poland under the Flexible Credit Line totaling $88 billion and for Morocco under the Precautionary Credit Line totaling $4.5 billion were approved. New arrangements were also approved for Georgia, Honduras, Kenya, Serbia, Seychelles, and Ukraine involving a resource commitment of $19.4 billion. New disbursements under the Rapid Credit Facility were approved for the Central African Republic, Gambia, Guinea, Guinea-Bissau, Liberia, Madagascar, and St. Vincent and the Grenadines, for a total of $117 million (see all support to low-income developing countries in Table 2.4). An augmentation to Bosnia and Herzegovina's Stand-By Arrangement in the amount of $118.9 million was also approved.

A number of major policy reviews were completed Follow-up work to the 2014 Triennial Surveillance Review (TSR) is under way. The Managing Director's action plan covers all core operational areas of surveillance, including risks and spillovers, and macro-financial and macrocritical structural issues.

A review of the Financial Sector Assessment Program found that reforms implemented in 2009 had strengthened the focus, effectiveness, and traction of the assessments.

Reforms to the IMF's Debt Limit Policy were adopted. The new policies, effective end-June 2015, provide countries with more flexibility to finance productive investments while containing risks to medium-term sustainability.

Following the Independent Evaluation Office's (IEO's) recommendation, a review of the IMF's work on trade issues was completed. The assessment covered macrocritical trade issues underlying a work agenda for the IMF for the next five years.

Staff published guidance notes to strengthen the IMF's advice on macroprudential policy in surveillance. The notes factor the work of international standard setters and evolving country experiences with macroprudential policy—that is, government policies designed to ensure the health and soundness of a financial system.

In response to the IEO's suggestion and building on previous work, a new framework for determining the appropriate level of international reserves held by member countries has been developed that is more country-specific than previous methods of assessing reserve adequacy.

Activities summarized from the Managing Director's Global Policy Agenda. See end Notes for details.

Analytical and policy work focused on challenges facing the membership

Work on underlying macrocritical issues covered topics such as productivity-enhancing reforms in advanced economies, female labor force participation, drivers of income inequality, economic diversification in the Gulf Cooperation Countries, and youth unemployment in European advanced economies. Analysis of monetary and financial sector policies focused on the role of exchange rate interventions, and implications of Islamic finance. Policy and analytic work on fiscal issues included revenue mobilization and tax compliance, and public investment efficiency in the Middle East and North Africa and Caucasus and Central Asia oil-exporting countries.

Intensive capacity development continued through technical assistance and training

Capacity building—helping countries develop more effective institutions, legal frameworks, and policies to promote economic stability and inclusive growth—focused on low-income developing countries. The regional technical assistance office in Thailand also was pivotal in rapidly responding to demand for technical assistance and training in Myanmar and Lao P.D.R. Other highlights included the creation of the Somalia Trust Fund for Capacity Development and the official launch of the IMF–Middle East Center for Economics and Finance in Kuwait, the IMF's first regional training institute in the Middle East. Two new massive open online courses on debt sustainability analysis and energy subsidy reform further extended the reach of IMF training.

IMF Policy Priorities in 2015

Priorities set out in the Managing Director's Global Policy Agenda were:

Members

Euro area
Provide effective demand support
Implement labor and product market reforms

United States
Ensure smooth monetary normalization
Establish medium-term fiscal consolidation plan

Japan
Implement fiscal and structural reforms
Enhance monetary policy transmission

China
Manage demand rebalancing
Address vulnerabilities in overinvested sectors

Emerging market economies
Address external vulnerabilities
Lift potential growth

Low-income developing countries
Strengthen policy frameworks
Rebuild fiscal and external buffers

IMF

Monetary policy
Assess impact of policy divergence
Analyze monetary policy and financial stability links

Financial sector policies
Deepen macro-financial analysis
Provide guidance on macroprudential policy

Fiscal policy
Examine how policy can boost long-term growth
Strengthen advice on frameworks and institutions

Structural reforms
Bolster advice on structural reforms
Advise on measures to improve investment efficiency

The Global Policy Agenda

The Managing Director's *Global Policy Agenda* (GPA) is a document presented twice a year to the International Monetary and Financial Committee (IMFC), which is the IMF's policy-guiding body. The GPA identifies the policy challenges faced by the IMF membership, assesses progress since the previous GPA, outlines the policy responses needed at the global and country levels, and lays out how the IMF can support those policy responses.

The GPA is regarded as an important blueprint for the IMF and its membership. It is also a key element of the IMF's multilateral surveillance work—as highlighted in the 2014 Triennial Surveillance Review (TSR) and the Managing Director's Action Plan for Strengthening Surveillance, which was issued along with the TSR. The GPA is discussed by the members of the IMF Executive Board in an informal session.

The April 2015 GPA—Confront Global Challenges Together—states: "Promoting balanced, sustained growth requires an integrated policy package that bolsters today's actual and tomorrow's potential output, diminishes risks, and confronts emerging global challenges."

Among the report's recommendations:

Lifting today's growth: Boosting growth and jobs requires continued monetary accommodation and supportive fiscal policies, where appropriate. But improving policy effectiveness and securing financial stability is crucial. This includes tackling debt overhang and encouraging productive investment rather than excessive financial risk-taking. The approaching increase in U.S. interest rates and large currency movements call for proactive policies to manage risks and growing leverage. Stronger fiscal frameworks can make revenue and spending more growth-friendly and contain fiscal risks.

Fortifying tomorrow's prospects: Structural reforms are lagging compared with other areas of the GPA. Targeted structural reforms can boost investment and productivity. While bottlenecks vary, priorities include advancing energy subsidy reforms to take advantage of lower oil prices, financial deepening, upgrading infrastructure, increasing employment, removing distortions in product markets, and improving the business environment. Trade reforms in traditional areas and emerging ones such as services and regulations can complement and augment other structural reforms.

Working together for the future: The impact of asynchronous monetary policies on currencies and capital flows underscores the need to make the international monetary system more resilient, promote the continuing integration of dynamic emerging economies, and ensure an adequate and cohesive global safety net. Anchored by three major international conferences, 2015 marks an unprecedented opportunity for the world to chart the course for sustainable development for the next decade and a half, and beyond (see Part 2).

What the IMF will do: The GPA states that the IMF will help members deliver on the policy agenda by providing flexible financing arrangements to members facing pressing challenges. It also committed the IMF to closely link policy advice and capacity development, highlight priorities such as implementing growth-friendly fiscal policies and macrocritical financial and structural reforms, and address debt overhang. The GPA also states that the IMF will take stock of challenges facing the international monetary system, embrace the 2015 global development agenda, and tailor its work to meet members' evolving needs.

Spotlights

Impact of Falling Oil Prices on the IMF Membership

The unexpectedly steep drop in oil prices over the past year—falling by more than one-half from September 2014 to January 2015—has had a significant impact across the IMF membership. The decline, which is part of a broader trend of declining commodities prices, has provided a boost to global growth and benefited many oil importers, but it also has weighed on economic activity among oil-exporting nations.

The falling prices were driven by production increases (in members of the Organization of Petroleum Exporting Countries [OPEC] and non-OPEC countries) and a significant slowdown in the growth of global oil demand—particularly from Europe and the Asia-Pacific region.

The depth of the price decline took forecasters and markets by surprise: the October 2014 *World Economic Outlook* (WEO) showed the average price of oil at $99.36 a barrel in 2015 based on the assumed price on futures markets, while the April 2015 WEO showed the assumed price for 2015 at $58.14 and $65.65 in 2016. The WEO contained a detailed analysis of commodity market developments and forecasts, with a focus on investment in an era of low oil prices.

Broad implications for the IMF's work

The impact of oil prices across the IMF's membership had broad implications for the work of the IMF. Bilateral and multilateral surveillance activities all adjusted to the rapidly changing environment. Article IV consultations, *Regional Economic Outlooks*, and the IMF's flagship publications—the WEO, *Global Financial Stability Report* (GFSR), and *Fiscal Monitor*—all devoted considerable attention to issues related to oil prices.

While the IMF assessed the overall macroeconomic impact as positive, other reports highlighted the risks. The April 2015 GFSR, for example, stated that "the speed and magnitude of the movement in oil prices raise questions about how stress can be transmitted through the financial sector." It cited channels through which lower prices could "spawn financial vulnerabilities," including "a self-reinforcing cycle of rising credit risk and deteriorating refinancing conditions for countries and companies, a decline in oil surplus recycling in world funding markets, and strains on the financial market infrastructure's ability to accommodate prolonged heightened energy price volatility."

Country-by-country trends

The IMF Executive Board has been deeply involved in reviewing the reports and documents that analyze the impact of falling oil prices. Beyond detailed discussion of the analysis contained in the flagship publications, it also has reviewed the trends on a country-by-country basis. For example, an analysis of the Executive Board's press releases on Article IV consultations during the period January 1–March 31, 2015, showed that 58 percent of the 21 Article IV Board's assessments contained references to the impact of lower oil prices—with a more detailed focus on the implications for oil-producing countries.

IMF Economic Counselor Olivier Blanchard and Rabah Arezki, head of the commodities team in the Research Department, posted an article on the oil price decline on *iMFdirect*, the IMF's blog. The article, titled "Seven Questions about the Recent Oil Price Slump," examined the mechanics of the oil market, the implications for various groups and for financial stability, and steps policymakers could take to address the impact on their economies. It attracted the largest readership of any item posted on the blog during the year.

Oil Prices
(U.S. dollars per barrel)

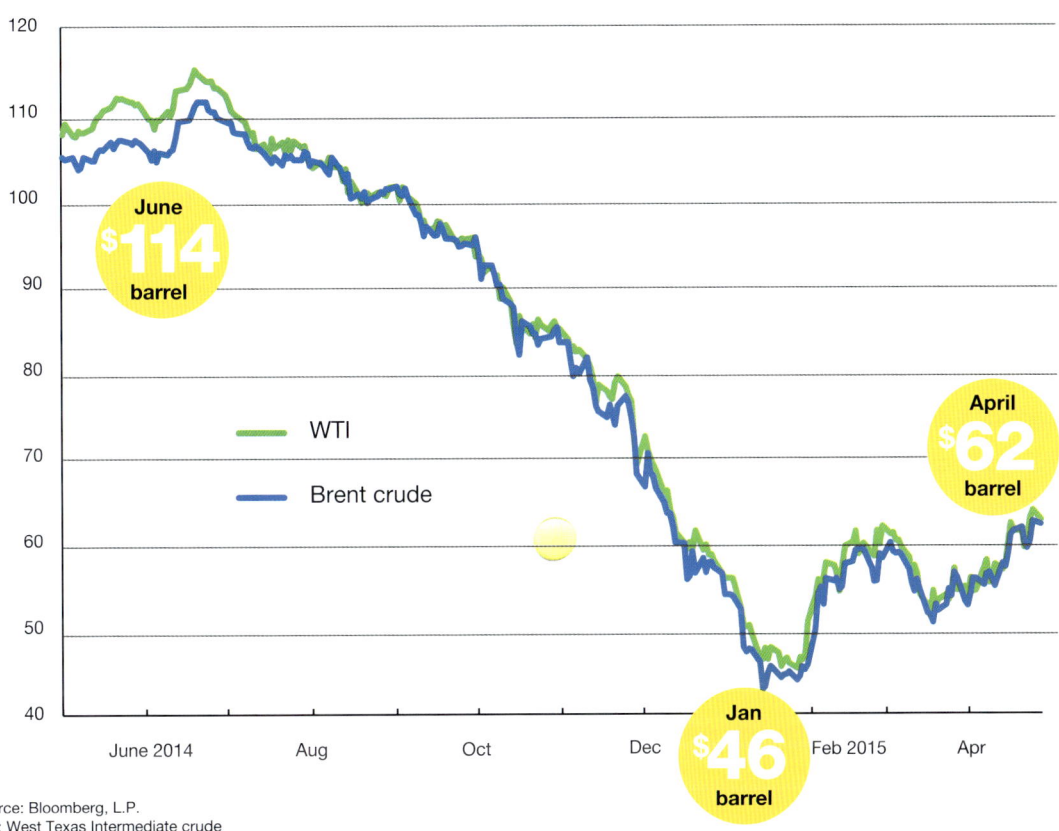

June $114 barrel

April $62 barrel

Jan $46 barrel

— WTI
— Brent crude

Source: Bloomberg, L.P.
WTI: West Texas Intermediate crude

Fiscal implications of falling oil prices

The fall in international oil prices also has significant implications for oil importers and exporters in terms of public finances. The April 2015 *Fiscal Monitor* highlighted this element of the impact of oil prices, saying that importers were likely to benefit while exporters could be hurt.

The *Fiscal Monitor* said: "The impact could be large, but whereas the gains will be spread across many economies, the adverse fiscal effects will be concentrated in relatively few. Although oil exporters account for a lower share of global GDP than oil importers, exporters face a much larger shock given that oil has a much bigger weight in their economies and budgets."

For many exporters, the *Fiscal Monitor* said, vulnerabilities were building before prices began falling; revenues from higher prices paid for large increases in current and capital expenditures. As a result, the

fiscal break-even price for oil increased in most exporting countries in the Middle East, and most exporters need prices considerably above the $58 projected for 2015 to cover budgetary spending.

A major element of the fiscal impact of falling oil prices lies in the area of fuel subsidies and the structure of energy taxation. The *Monitor* concluded that the higher the "pass-through" of fuel prices to consumers, the lower the fiscal savings would be. For example, oil importers that provide no subsidies but earn revenues from oil tariffs and other taxes could see revenue deterioration. On the other hand, if the entire decline

in oil prices is passed on to consumers, there could be stronger aggregate demand and revenues.

IMF area departments—through Article IV consultations and regional surveillance activities—identified a window of opportunity for both importing and exporting countries to reform fuel subsidies and taxation regimes that would strengthen fiscal balances to create space for increasing priority expenditures. Public finances in many oil-importing low-income developing countries are expected to improve as declining oil prices reduce energy subsidies.

The Response to Ebola
Emergency Funding and a New Instrument

"Our membership has demonstrated great commitment in coming together to respond to the Ebola crisis. I am particularly gratified at the support for approving the new Catastrophe Containment and Relief Trust, which will make a difference to the people of Guinea, Liberia, and Sierra Leone—and other countries in the future."

IMF Managing Director Christine Lagarde, February 5, 2015

first multilateral institution to deliver on 100 percent of its commitments to the Ebola-stricken countries.

The financial assistance to combat the epidemic fits within the IMF's mandate to support its member countries with balance-of-payments support in times of economic and social stress. Each step of the response was carefully considered by the Executive Board, which approved all requests for financing and the creation of the CCRT by reforming the Post-Catastrophe Debt Relief Trust.

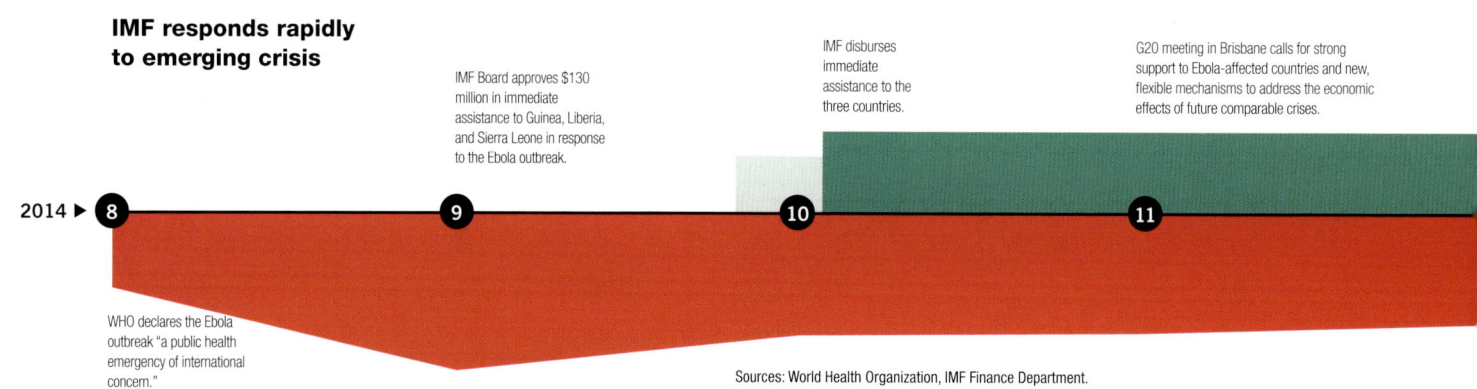

IMF responds rapidly to emerging crisis

IMF Board approves $130 million in immediate assistance to Guinea, Liberia, and Sierra Leone in response to the Ebola outbreak.

IMF disburses immediate assistance to the three countries.

G20 meeting in Brisbane calls for strong support to Ebola-affected countries and new, flexible mechanisms to address the economic effects of future comparable crises.

2014 ▶ 8   9   10   11

WHO declares the Ebola outbreak "a public health emergency of international concern."

Sources: World Health Organization, IMF Finance Department.

The Ebola outbreak in West Africa presented the international community with an unprecedented public health crisis. The spread of the pandemic through Guinea, Liberia, and Sierra Leone infected nearly 26,000 people and killed more than 10,600. It brought economic activity in the three countries virtually to a halt and raised the specter of a broader crisis.

The IMF response was rapid and flexible, committing about $404 million of financing that went directly to the governments of the three countries to meet the many new financing demands posed by Ebola. Emergency assistance was first provided on an accelerated basis in September 2014. Then, as the scale of the disaster became clear, the IMF augmented its assistance in early 2015 with additional financing under the Poverty Reduction and Growth Trust and debt relief under a new Catastrophe Containment and Relief Trust (CCRT).

Managing Director Christine Lagarde announced the additional financing in a proposal to the G20 Heads of State at their November 2014 Summit in Brisbane, Australia. By following up on the Brisbane proposal, the IMF became the

Concessional lending: The IMF provided $309 million of expedited assistance at zero interest rates to the three Ebola-stricken countries. The lending was provided under the Rapid Credit Facility and Extended Credit Facility. The money was disbursed immediately, providing the countries with urgently needed resources to help tackle the crisis.

Debt relief: A unique feature of the IMF response was the decision to create the CCRT. The three Ebola-affected countries (Guinea, Liberia, and Sierra Leone) were provided with $95 million in grants for debt relief in FY2015 to ease pressures on their balance of payments.

Policy advice: After the epidemic hit, GDP contracted in all three countries. A key element of IMF policy advice was to support expansionary macroeconomic policies—including budget deficits to fight the epidemic and avoid an even larger recession. IMF staff interaction with the authorities of each country was maintained throughout the pandemic, and as the crisis began to abate, discussions turned to the longer-term challenge of rapidly restoring growth.

IMF support to Ebola-afflicted countries: $404 million
IMF financing (in millions of U.S. dollars)

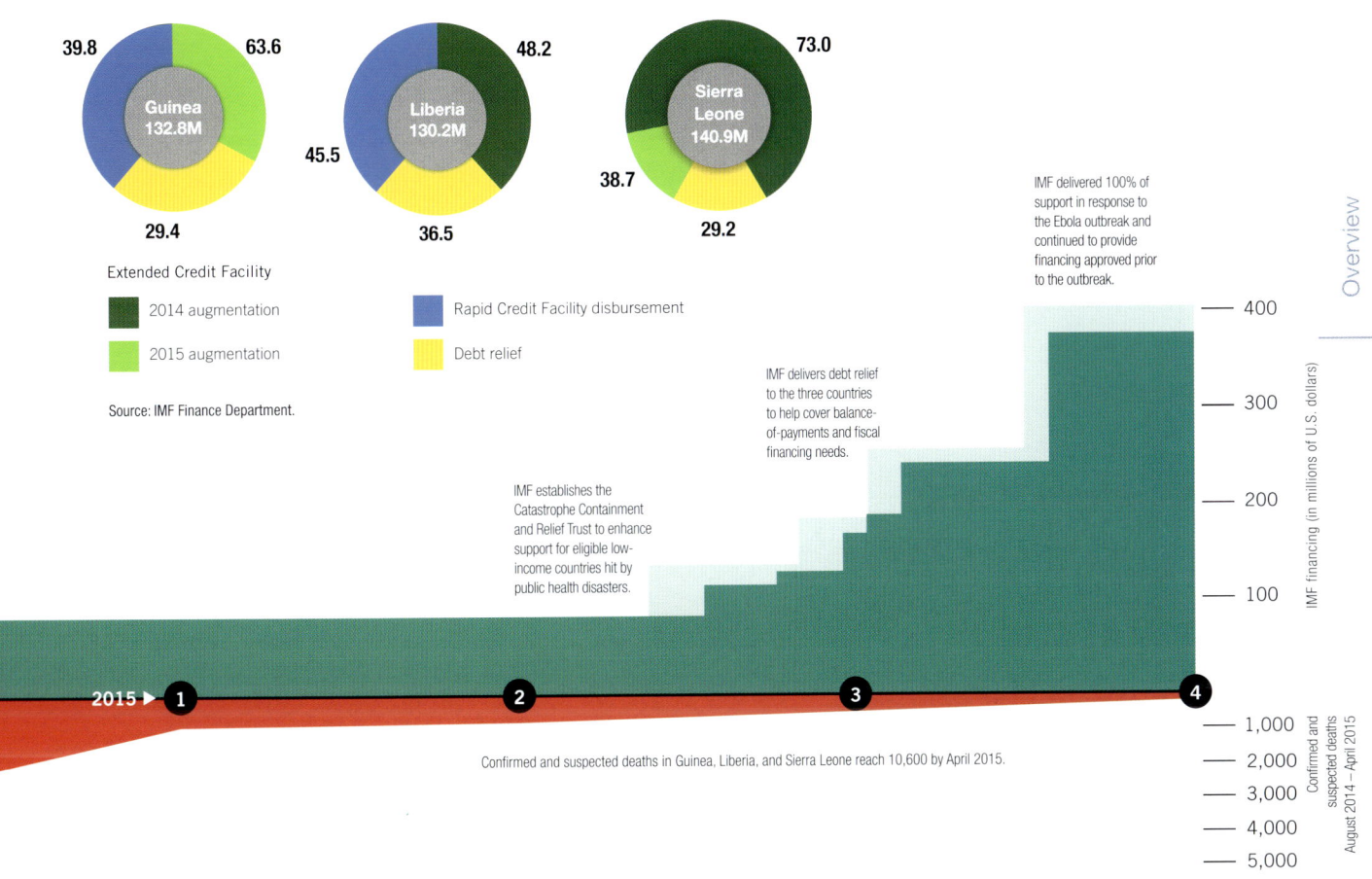

Guinea 132.8M — 39.8, 63.6, 29.4, 45.5

Liberia 130.2M — 48.2, 36.5, 45.5

Sierra Leone 140.9M — 73.0, 29.2, 38.7

Extended Credit Facility

- 2014 augmentation
- 2015 augmentation
- Rapid Credit Facility disbursement
- Debt relief

Source: IMF Finance Department.

IMF establishes the Catastrophe Containment and Relief Trust to enhance support for eligible low-income countries hit by public health disasters.

IMF delivers debt relief to the three countries to help cover balance-of-payments and fiscal financing needs.

IMF delivered 100% of support in response to the Ebola outbreak and continued to provide financing approved prior to the outbreak.

IMF financing (in millions of U.S. dollars) — 400, 300, 200, 100

Confirmed and suspected deaths August 2014 – April 2015 — 1,000, 2,000, 3,000, 4,000, 5,000

2015 ► ① ② ③ ④

Confirmed and suspected deaths in Guinea, Liberia, and Sierra Leone reach 10,600 by April 2015.

The Catastrophe Containment and Relief Trust

In February 2015 the IMF established a Catastrophe Containment and Relief Trust (CCRT). This instrument allows the IMF to provide grants for debt relief to the poorest and most vulnerable countries hit by catastrophic natural disasters or public health disasters, including epidemics. The new trust is intended to complement donor financing and the IMF's concessional lending. The relief on debt service payments frees up additional resources to meet exceptional balance-of-payments needs created by the disaster, and for containment and recovery efforts.

The CCRT was created by transforming the Post-Catastrophe Debt Relief Trust, which was established in 2010 following the terrible earthquake in Haiti. The CCRT has two windows: (1) a Post-Catastrophe Relief window, to provide exceptional assistance in the wake of a natural disaster such as an earthquake or typhoon; and (2) a Catastrophe Containment window, to provide assistance in containing the spread of a public health disaster.

The introduction of a Catastrophe Containment window acknowledges that poor countries with weak health systems have limited capacity to contain the wider threat posed by a public health disaster, and that the international community has a strong interest in providing extensive support to such countries. Eligible low-income countries that are hit by public health disasters would receive up-front grants to immediately pay off upcoming debt service to the IMF. The amount of grant support is capped at 20 percent of a country's quota, with additional debt relief possible under exceptional circumstances.

Assistance through the CCRT is available to 38 low-income developing countries that are eligible for concessional borrowing and that also have either a per capita income below $1,215 or, for small states with a population below 1.5 million, a per capita income below $2,430.

The Two Windows of CCRT

Post-Catastrophe Relief Window

Provides exceptional assistance in the wake of a natural disaster like an earthquake or typhoon.

Catastrophe Containment Window

Provides assistance in containing the spread of a public health disaster.

IMF Support for Ukraine

On March 11, 2015, the IMF Executive Board approved a four-year, $17.5 billion Extended Fund Facility (EFF) arrangement for Ukraine, with immediate disbursement of about $5 billion.

The program has challenging goals: to put the economy on the path to recovery, restore external sustainability, strengthen public finances, support economic growth by advancing structural and governance reforms, and protect the country's most vulnerable citizens.

After independence in 1991, Ukraine entered into several IMF-supported programs—including after the 2008 financial crisis—but none achieved the objective of prompting sustained reform. The 2010 program ended unsuccessfully, and Ukraine's macroeconomic problems intensified. Wages and production costs rose, but productivity did not. Eventually competitiveness slipped so much that the economy stopped growing and exports stagnated.

Rapid deterioration in 2014

The new government that took office in February 2014 embarked on a program to secure macroeconomic and financial stability. However, the situation deteriorated rapidly after the armed conflict in the East intensified. In the fourth quarter of 2014, GDP contracted 14.8 percent from the year before, and additional financing needs surged. The foreign exchange market was destabilized, and banks came under stress.

The government responded with a more ambitious and comprehensive program supported by substantial new financing from the international community, including the IMF. The first step of the new IMF-supported program is to stabilize Ukraine's finances. It covers Ukraine's external financing needs, estimated at about $40 billion over 2015–18, along with other international assistance and a debt-restructuring operation. The country's official reserves are expected to triple to about $18 billion by end-2015. Subdued by a tight monetary stance, inflation should recede toward single digits by early 2017.

Tackling deficits, protecting the vulnerable

In addition, lower deficits can help to reduce financing needs and public debt. This includes raising energy tariffs to restrain the state-owned gas monopoly's quasi-fiscal deficit. To protect the most vulnerable from the impact of these measures and build support for the reforms, total spending on social assistance

programs is targeted to reach 4.1 percent of GDP in 2015, an increase of 30 percent from 2014, with assistance for energy bills rising fourfold.

The next step is to revive growth by restoring competitiveness, starting with a flexible exchange rate. In addition, the banking system is to be brought back to health with recapitalization and liquidation efforts so that credit growth can resume.

Addressing corruption and vested interests

Equally important, decisive measures are to be taken to address structural impediments preventing sustained growth that can raise living standards to that of Ukraine's neighbors, including deregulation and reform of tax administration, transparency, improvements in public financial management, and reforms of state-owned enterprises. Finally, corruption is targeted with strengthened legislation, measures to enhance the effectiveness of the judiciary, and steps to curb the potentially distorting influence of vested interests in Ukraine.

The Ukrainian authorities have made determined efforts in recent months to address deep-rooted problems and make a break from the unsustainable policies of the past. The IMF and the international community are supporting Ukraine's pursuit of its reform program.

IMF Interaction with Greece during FY2015

IMF interactions with Greece continued on several fronts during FY2015, focusing on progress on implementing an economic program supported by an extended arrangement under the EFF and provision of technical assistance and training to the authorities in order to strengthen administrative capacity across a range of public functions.

In May 2014, the IMF Executive Board completed the fifth review of Greece's performance under the extended arrangement. The completion of the review enabled the disbursement of about $4.24 billion under the arrangement, bringing total disbursements under the EFF to about $14.38 billion. In completing the review, the Executive Board approved a waiver of nonobservance of the performance criterion on domestic arrears.

As the year progressed, there were extensive interactions among the Greek authorities, senior Fund officials, and high-level representatives of euro area member governments, the European Commission, and the European Central Bank. These interactions addressed a range of issues related to the progress in reaching understandings that could pave the way to completion of the sixth review. These interactions continued after national elections in January 2015 that led to the formation of a coalition government led by the Syriza Party.

An important element of the IMF's interaction with Greece came in the area of capacity development. The areas covered included tax administration, public financial management, regulation and supervision of the banking system, and other key areas of public administration. Policy discussions are continuing in FY2016.

After the end of FY2015, Greece went into arrears to the IMF as its economic crisis deepened. These were cleared July 20, 2015. The IMF remains committed to helping Greece through this period of economic turmoil.

Jobs and Growth

Creating jobs and fostering inclusive growth have become increasingly important themes in the work of the IMF over the past five years.

Countries are facing these challenges at a time of technological change, globalization, and shifting demographic trends—as well as macroeconomic challenges growing out of the global financial crisis of 2008–09, which caused millions of people to lose their jobs and unemployment to rise sharply.

The work on inequality was spurred by research conducted by the IMF Research and Fiscal Affairs Departments on the topic, including papers on "Inequality and Unsustainable Growth: Two Sides of the Same Coin?," "Redistribution, Inequality, and Growth," and "Income Inequality and Fiscal Policy." In February 2014, the Board discussed a paper prepared by staff on "Fiscal Policy and Income Inequality." The paper focused on fiscal policy—the primary tool that governments can use to affect income distribution. It surveyed available tax and expenditure options and how they can be designed to minimize unfavorable effects on work and income growth. The staff will continue to operationalize the IMF's recent analytical work on inequality, including in the context of annual consultations.

A staff paper prepared for Board discussion in 2013 on "Jobs and Growth: Analytical and Operational Considerations for the IMF" discussed the role of the IMF in helping countries devise strategies to meet the job creation and inclusive growth. It concluded that there was scope to improve the analysis of trends in this area and to strengthen policy advice.

Integrating jobs and growth into IMF operations

Since publication of the 2013 Board paper, the process of integrating a focus on jobs and economic growth into operations has begun, and research has continued to expand, with guidance from an interdepartmental advisory group. Area departments have identified pilots to include the work on jobs and growth in Article IV consultations. As this Article IV work proceeds, it becomes part of the Executive Board's assessment of the respective countries. Several country consultations are scheduled to include it in FY2016.

The 2014 Triennial Surveillance Review (TSR) — recommended further strengthening work on jobs and growth. Among its recommendations, the TSR suggested increasing attention to the impact of fiscal policy and financial sector developments on growth, expanding advice on labor market policies to support member countries' job creation objectives, and taking into account more fully country authorities' goals and constraints to better tailor advice to individual country circumstances. The TSR survey of Article IV consultations supported the finding that jobs and growth increasingly have entered into this area of operations. Contributing factors were the strengthening of surveillance tools, improvements in labor statistics, and training.

Research and surveillance

In the area of research, the wide range of issues where analytical work is being conducted includes:

Growth: quantifying gains from reforms to the structure of the economy, the role of access to finance in supporting growth, and the importance of economic diversification.

Jobs: youth unemployment in Europe, the role of wage moderation in the euro area, the impact of labor market reforms, and the informal sector in emerging and developing economies.

Inclusion and income distribution: enhancing the participation of women in the labor force, and evaluating the impact on income distribution of fiscal policies, labor market institutions, and capital account liberalization.

In the area of regional surveillance, the African Department's April 2014 *Regional Economic Outlook* contained a chapter that looked at how economic policy efforts to promote job creation can help make growth more inclusive in sub-Saharan Africa. Those findings were presented at the Mozambique conference in May 2014, which had a major focus on employment and inclusive growth.

The May 2014 conference in Amman, Jordan, also addressed the issues of jobs and growth in the Middle East and Central Asia.

Women and work

A crucial element of jobs and inclusive growth is the role of women in the workplace. Women make up more than half the world's population, but their contributions to measured economic activity, growth, and well-being fall far short of potential. This has serious consequences in terms of losses to an individual country's GDP.

Despite significant progress in recent decades, labor markets across the world remain divided along gender lines, and progress toward gender equality seems to have stalled. In a speech in September 2014 on "The Economic Power of Women's Empowerment," IMF Managing Director Christine Lagarde described the barriers working women face worldwide: "When women do participate, they tend to be stuck in low-paying, low-status jobs. Globally, women earn only three-quarters as much as men—this is true even with the same level of education and in the same occupation."

Building upon the 2012 IMF Working Paper "Can Women Save Japan?," analysis on women and work has expanded rapidly. Area departments have put in place pilot assessments of the issues related to working women in the context of Article IV consultations across a range of countries, with the goal of building expertise, facilitating collaboration with other institutions, and sharing knowledge.

As the assessments have been completed, they have become part of the Executive Board discussions of the pilot countries. A cross-country study of women's economic participation in European countries will inform Article IV consultations of some of those countries.

A Staff Discussion Note entitled "Fair Play: More Equal Laws Boost Female Labor Force Participation," released in February 2015, examined the effect of gender-based legal restrictions and other policies, and of demographic characteristics on labor market outcomes.

IMF Training Expands through Online Courses

The IMF has entered an exciting new phase in its approach to training, with the adoption of new online learning courses designed in partnership with edX, the nonprofit online learning initiative founded by Harvard University and the Massachusetts Institute of Technology. The partnership enables the IMF to expand the reach of its training program to more member country officials and to offer the wider public audience access to its courses through so-called massive open online courses (MOOCs).

The new courses—created by the Institute for Capacity Development in collaboration with other IMF departments—are designed with short video segments interspersed with quizzes and hands-on exercises, and include a discussion forum to allow participants to network and discuss course content. The use of computer grading saves on instructor time and means that the IMF can allow virtually unlimited enrollment. Since the launch of the program in late 2013, these courses—free and open to anyone with an Internet connection—have attracted more than 10,000 active participants, of whom about 6,000 earned a certificate of completion.

New opportunities for low-income developing countries

Online learning is creating training opportunities for a wider range of country officials. Forty percent of online graduates to date are government officials, boosting IMF training by four percentage points in FY2015. The most numerous recipients of this training have been officials in sub-Saharan Africa, serving to shift the distribution of training toward the region. Online training is also shifting to officials in low-income developing countries, who received almost half of it in FY2015, compared with slightly less than 40 percent of face-to-face training.

MOOCs are serving as an important channel for IMF outreach: four-fifths of participants agree that the courses have increased their understanding of the IMF and its work. The courses have been well received, with participants expressing appreciation to the IMF for making this training openly available. By engaging

See for yourself

The free courses are online at:
https://www.edx.org/school/imfx

The new IMF courses have achieved worldwide participation.
Active students (light blue); students already achieving passing grade (dark blue)

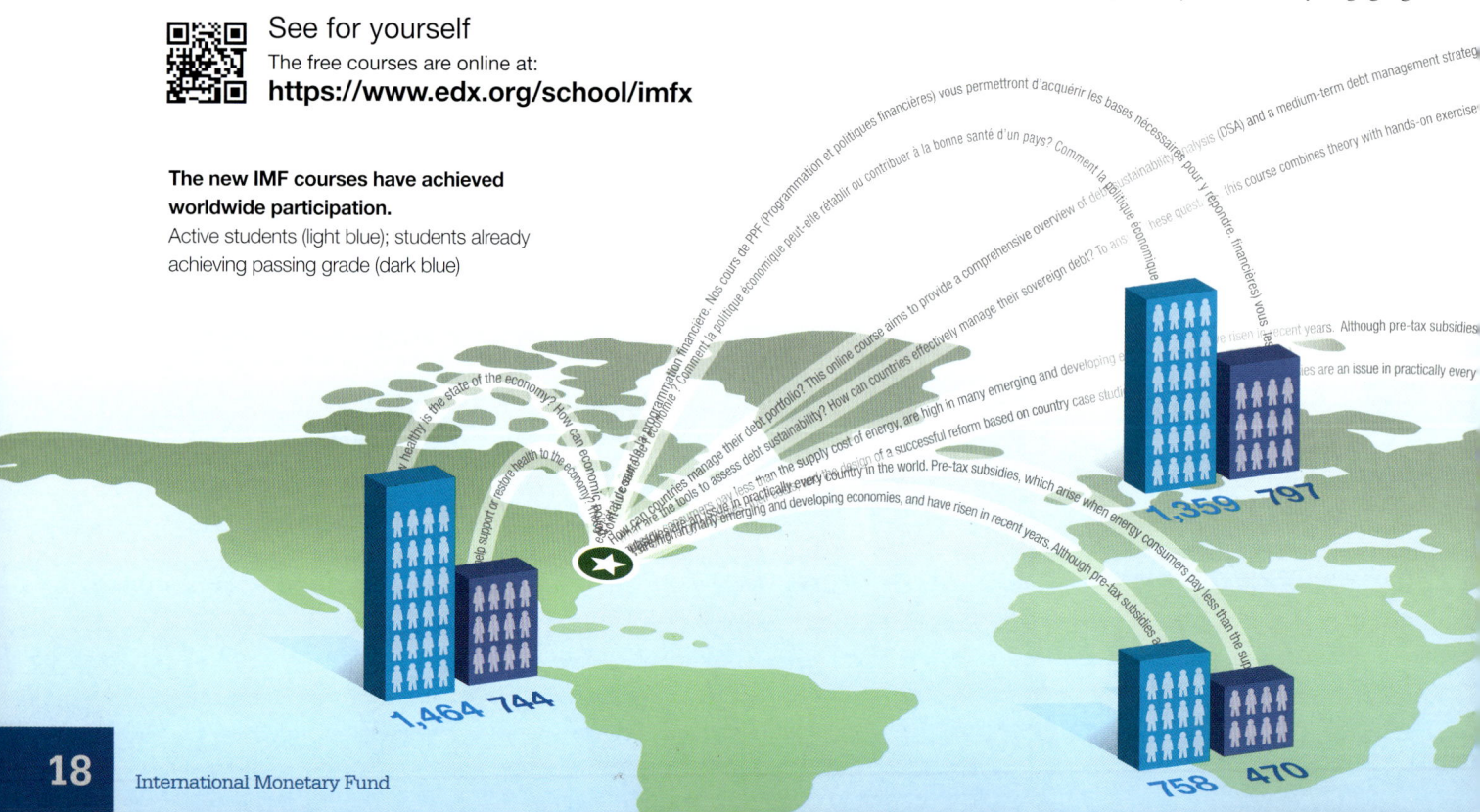

youth (one-quarter of participants are students) and sharing knowledge, MOOCs help a diverse global audience better understand economic policies in their own countries and around the world.

Online courses to date include the following:

Financial Programming and Policies, Part 1: Macroeconomic Accounts and Analysis (FPP.1x) provides an introduction to financial programming, presenting the principal features of the accounts of the four main sectors that comprise the macroeconomy (real, fiscal, external, and monetary) and their interrelations.

Debt Sustainability Analysis (DSAx) gives a comprehensive overview of debt sustainability analysis and a medium-term debt management strategy framework as adopted by the IMF and the World Bank.

Energy Subsidy Reform (ESRx) builds on an extensive cross-country analysis, which is reported in the recently published IMF book *Energy Subsidy Reform: Lessons and Implications*, to make recommendations on how best to implement reforms aimed at reducing state subsidies on energy.

Upcoming courses include Macroeconomic Forecasting; Financial Programming and Policies, Part 2: Program Design; and Financial Market Analysis. FPP, Part 1 has already been translated into French and will be translated into Spanish and Russian during FY2016.

MOOC participation by occupation

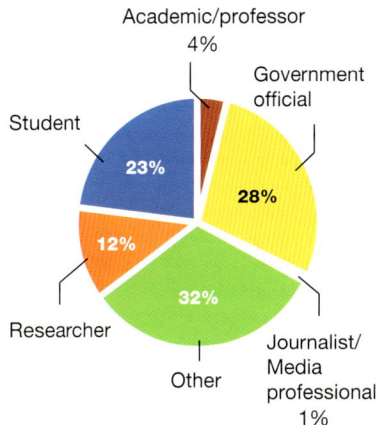

- Academic/professor 4%
- Government official 28%
- Student 23%
- Researcher 12%
- Other 32%
- Journalist/Media professional 1%

Training of government officials, MOOC top 10 countries in FY2015

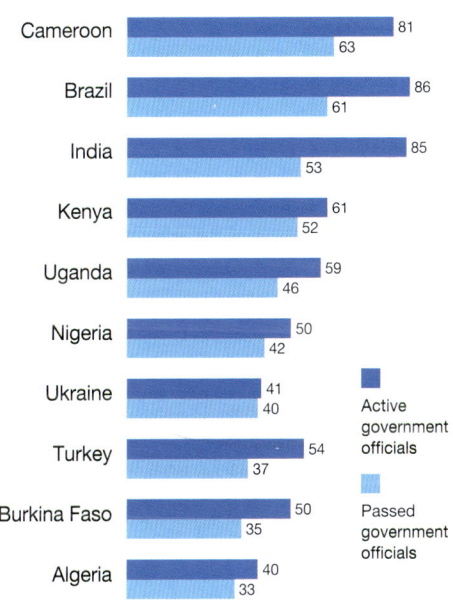

Country	Active government officials	Passed government officials
Cameroon	81	63
Brazil	86	61
India	85	53
Kenya	61	52
Uganda	59	46
Nigeria	50	42
Ukraine	41	40
Turkey	54	37
Burkina Faso	50	35
Algeria	40	33

MOOC participation by region

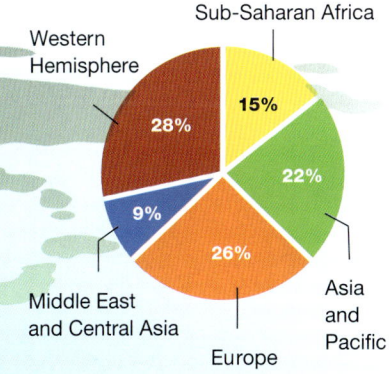

- Sub-Saharan Africa 15%
- Western Hemisphere 28%
- Asia and Pacific 22%
- Europe 26%
- Middle East and Central Asia 9%

446   250

1,162   592

The Free Data Initiative

"The free data program will help all those who draw on our data to make better use of this vital statistical resource—from budget numbers to balance-of-payments data, debt statistics to critical global indicators."

IMF Managing Director Christine Lagarde
Second IMF Statistical Forum
November 18–19, 2014

See for yourself
The free data are online at:
http://www.imf.org/data

Accurate, timely statistics are the lifeblood of economic policymaking and analysis. Good data can help policymakers identify and manage macroeconomic and financial vulnerabilities and can greatly enhance policy transparency.

Over the years, policymakers and investors generally have had access to reliable and timely economic data, but large segments of the public in member countries have not been able to benefit from data that help identify emerging economic risks requiring policy adjustments.

Cross-country databases often have been the domain of international organizations. In many instances, these databases have been available only by subscription. That approach is now changing with a global shift toward free data.

Data free of charge for all users

In January 2015, the IMF made its online statistical data available free of charge to all users. While these data had previously been available for free to users from low-income countries, the IMF now grants everyone access to a wealth of macroeconomic data covering all economic sectors across a large part of the IMF's membership.

During the first three months of the free data regime at the IMF, the average monthly user base rose by more than 90 percent to more than 262,000 users from 185 countries.

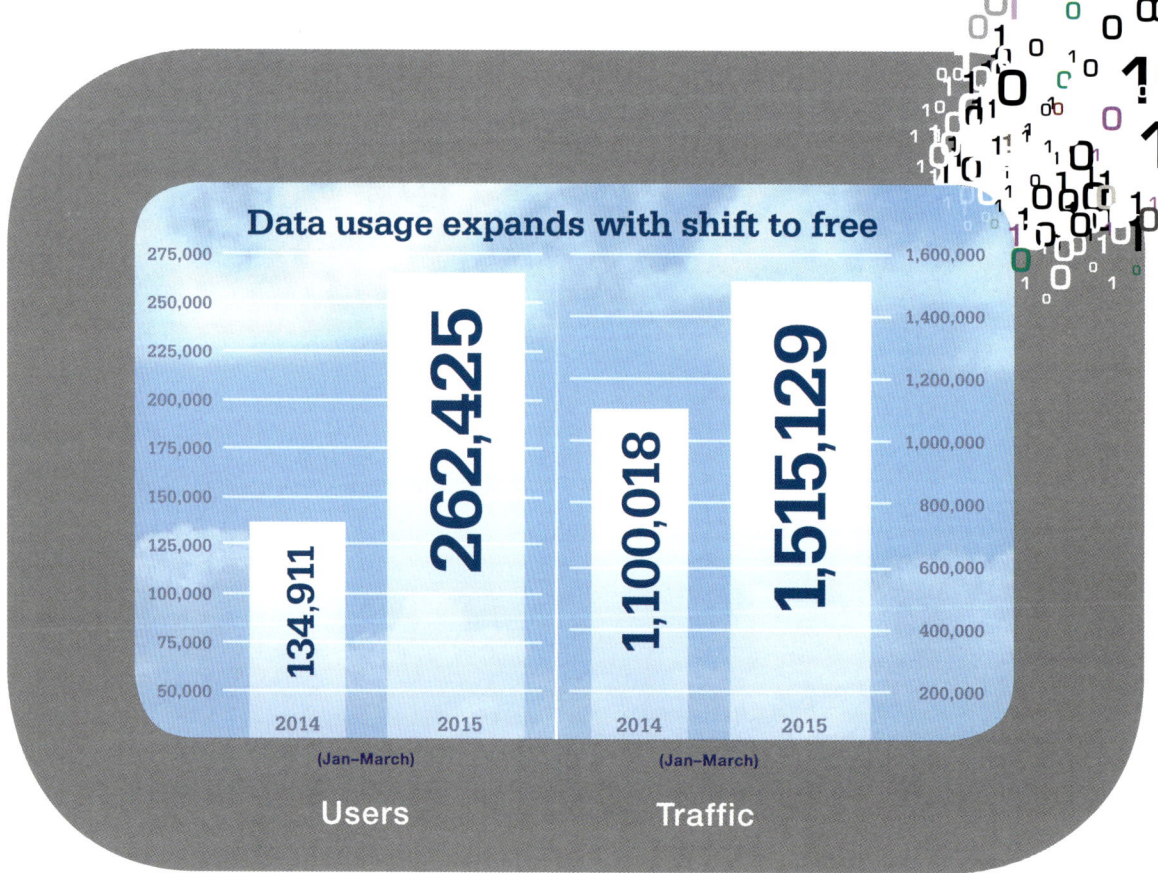

Data usage expands with shift to free

	Users		Traffic	
	2014 (Jan–March)	2015 (Jan–March)	2014 (Jan–March)	2015 (Jan–March)
	134,911	262,425	1,100,018	1,515,129

The databases that were made free of charge include:

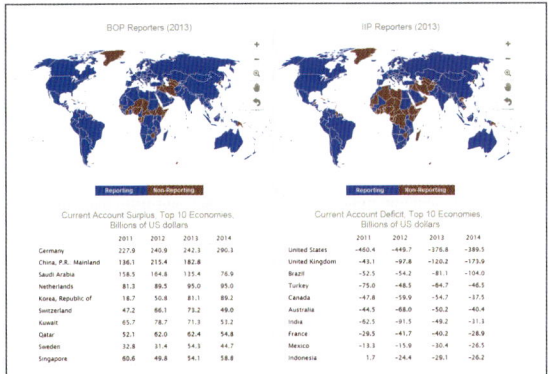

International Financial Statistics

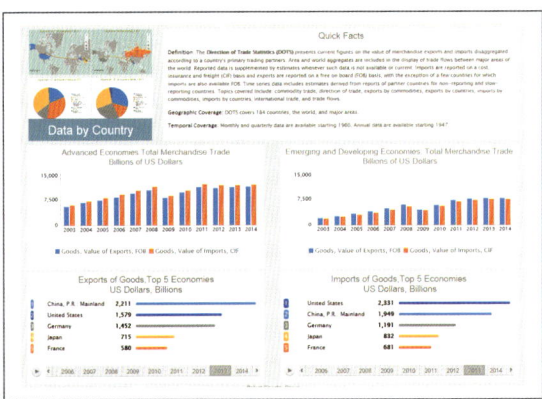

Balance-of-Payments Statistics

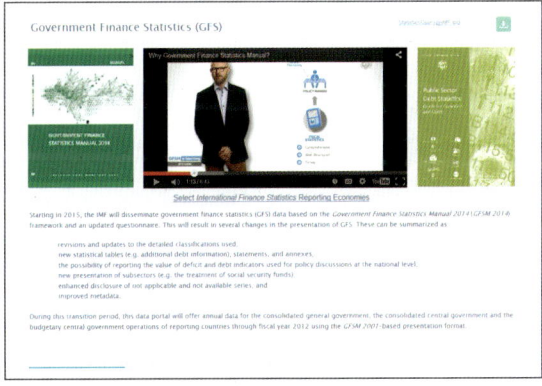

Government Finance Statistics

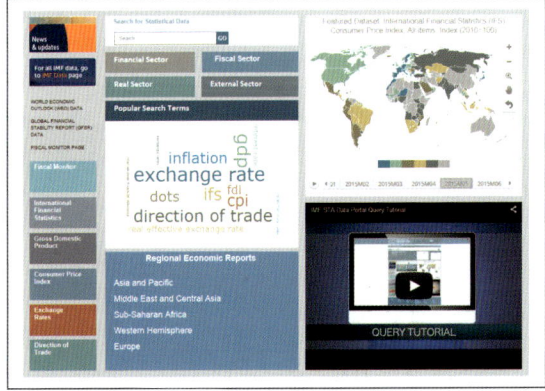

Directions of Trade Statistics

This generated an overall increase in monthly traffic of close to 40 percent.

The policy was introduced along with technological improvements, including a new online data portal and an enhanced dissemination platform. The platform provides greater capability for dynamic data visualization, downloading, and sharing.

The databases that were made free of charge include:

International Financial Statistics: A library of continuously updated statistics on all aspects of international and domestic finance.

Balance-of-Payments Statistics: Balance-of-payments and international investment position data of individual countries, jurisdictions, and other reporting entities, and regional and world totals for major components of the balance of payments, with history to 1960.

Government Finance Statistics: Comprehensive annual data covering various levels of government—including general, central, state, and local governments, with history to 1990.

Directions of Trade Statistics: Database of exports and imports between countries and areas with their trading partners, with history to 1980.

IMF capacity development activities have expanded rapidly to meet demand from member countries across the globe. The maps below show the amount of technical assistance and training provided in FY2015, measured in the equivalent of a year's worth of full-time work by one expert and a week's worth of full-time coursework for one student, respectively.

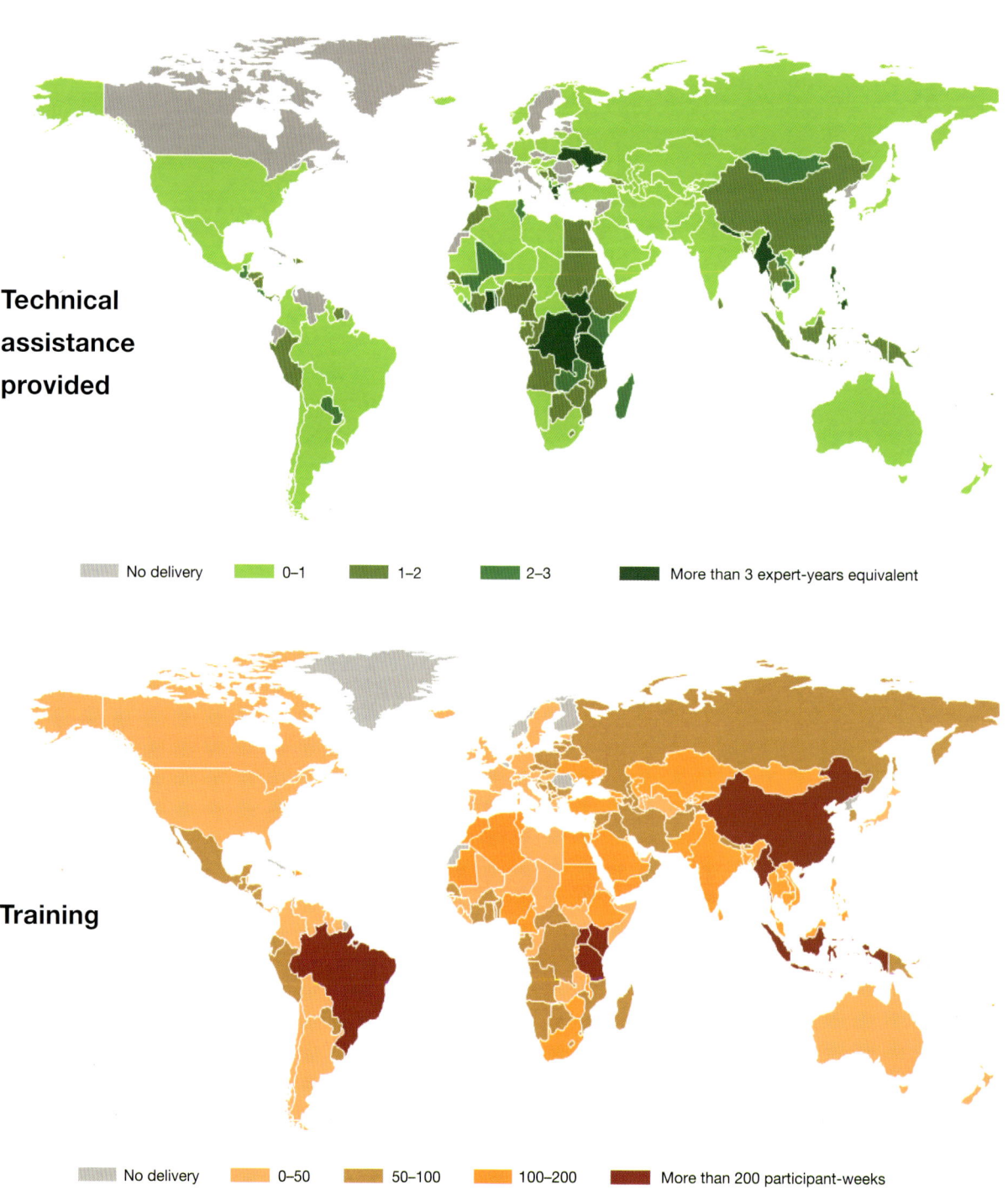

Technical assistance provided

No delivery   0–1   1–2   2–3   More than 3 expert-years equivalent

Training

No delivery   0–50   50–100   100–200   More than 200 participant-weeks

Part 2   What We Do: The "Big Three"

The IMF has three main roles

Economic Surveillance

131 country health checks

The IMF oversees the international monetary system and monitors the economic and financial policies of its 188 member countries. As part of this surveillance process, which takes place both at the global level and in individual countries, the IMF highlights possible risks to stability and advises on needed policy adjustments.

Lending

$112B to 9 countries, plus $2.7 billion in low- or zero-interest loans to 17 of its low-income developing member countries

The IMF provides loans to member countries experiencing actual or potential balance-of-payments problems to help them rebuild their international reserves, stabilize their currencies, continue paying for imports, and restore conditions for strong economic growth, while correcting underlying problems.

Capacity Development

$242M for expert advice and training

The IMF helps its member countries design economic policies and manage their financial affairs more effectively by strengthening their human and institutional capacity through expert advice and training, which it calls capacity development.

Economic Surveillance

Surveillance is the catch-all term encompassing the process by which the IMF oversees the international monetary system and global economic developments, and monitors the economic and financial policies of its 188 member countries. As part of this annual financial health check, known as surveillance, the IMF highlights possible risks to stability and advises on the necessary policy adjustments. In this way, it helps the international monetary system serve its essential purpose of facilitating the exchange of goods, services, and capital among countries, thereby sustaining sound economic growth.

There are two main aspects to the IMF's surveillance: **bilateral surveillance**, or the appraisal of and advice on the policies of each member country, and **multilateral surveillance**, or oversight of the world economy. By integrating bilateral and multilateral surveillance, the IMF can ensure more comprehensive, consistent analysis of "spillovers"—how one country's policies may affect other countries.

The centerpiece of bilateral surveillance is the so-called Article IV consultation, named after the article of the IMF's Articles of Agreement that requires a review of economic developments and policies in each of the IMF's 188 member countries. The consultations cover a range of issues considered to be of macrocritical importance—fiscal, financial, foreign exchange, monetary, and structural—focusing on risks and vulnerabilities and policy responses. Hundreds of IMF economists are involved in the Article IV process.

The consultations are a two-way policy dialogue with the country authorities, rather than the IMF assessing a country. The IMF team typically meets with government and central bank officials, as well as other stakeholders such as parliamentarians, business representatives, civil society, and labor unions, to help evaluate the country's economic policies and direction. The staff presents a report to the IMF's Executive Board, normally for discussion, after which the consultation is concluded and a summary of

the meeting is transmitted to the country's authorities. In the vast majority of cases, the Board's assessment is published as a press release, along with the Staff Reports, with agreement of the member country in question. In FY2015, the IMF conducted 131 Article IV consultations (see Web Table 2.1).

The IMF has also conducted financial sector surveillance since the Asian crisis, with special emphasis on the need to strengthen it following the 2008 global financial crisis.

Multilateral surveillance involves monitoring global and regional economic trends and analyzing spillovers from members' policies onto the global economy. The flagship reports on multilateral surveillance are published twice a year: the *World Economic Outlook* (WEO), *Global Financial Stability Report* (GFSR), and *Fiscal Monitor* (FM). The WEO provides detailed analysis of the state of the world economy, addressing issues of pressing interest, such as the current global financial turmoil and economic downturn. The GFSR provides an up-to-date assessment of global financial markets and prospects, and highlights imbalances and vulnerabilities that could pose risks to financial market stability. The FM updates medium-term fiscal projections and assesses developments in public finances. The IMF also publishes *Regional Economic Outlook* (REO) reports, as part of its World Economic and Financial Surveys.

The "Big Three"

The 2014 Triennial Surveillance Review

The latest major review of IMF surveillance practices and effectiveness, known as the Triennial Surveillance Review (TSR), was completed in September 2014. The findings and recommendations were informed by diverse analyses and perspectives, including: surveys of stakeholders; a review of recent IMF surveillance products; staff background studies; and extensive external inputs—analytical studies, commentaries, interviews with stakeholders, and a consultation with civil society. The review also received input and scrutiny from an independent External Advisory Group and benefited from independent commentaries.

The Executive Board discussed the TSR in September 2014.

The overarching theme of the 2014 TSR was how to tailor surveillance to support sustainable growth in a still deeply interconnected postcrisis world.

The review found that significant progress has been made since 2011 but stressed that strengthening surveillance is an ongoing and dynamic process. Accordingly, the review focused on ways to build on recent reforms while continuing to adapt surveillance to the challenges developing across the membership.

Three key themes emerged from the review:

First, the review identified scope to further integrate and deepen risk and spillover analysis, particularly to build a deeper understanding of how risks map across

---

The Article IV Process: The Annual Economic Policy Assessment

The Article IV process unfolds over a period of several months, beginning with an internal review of key policy issues and surveillance priorities across departments and management, set out in a briefing document known as the Policy Note.

The Policy Note elaborates on key economic policy directions and recommendations to be discussed with the government. Review of the Policy Note with other departments to build consensus about a country ahead of the consultation culminates in a Policy Consultation Meeting, and then the Policy Note goes to IMF management for approval. After Policy Note approval, the team travels to the country for its meetings with government officials and stakeholders. Upon returning to IMF Headquarters, a Staff Report is prepared that again proceeds through departmental and management review before being considered by the IMF Executive Board.

countries and spillovers spread across sectors. **Second, the review highlighted the need for policy advice to be more tailored and expert,** including in new policy areas such as macroprudential and macro-structural analysis, and deliver more cohesive analysis and advice that better leverages the IMF's knowledge of cross-country experiences.

Third, the review emphasized the importance of looking beyond analytical approaches and tools to achieve greater impact. The review concluded that, despite making good strides, the IMF still has room for more client-focused, yet candid, communication, while evenhandedness remains a critical ingredient for legitimacy and effective surveillance.

The Executive Board supported the main conclusions and most of the recommendations of the review. Accordingly, it endorsed five operational priorities for 2014–19: (1) risks and spillovers; (2) macro-financial surveillance; (3) macrocritical structural policy advice; (4) cohesive and expert policy advice; and (5) a client-focused approach to surveillance.

The Managing Director issued an Action Plan for Strengthening Surveillance in December 2014, with specific proposals in each of these priority areas. In particular, the plan includes actions to revive and adapt balance sheet analysis, fully embed macro-financial analysis in surveillance, and lay the groundwork for stronger and more focused structural policy advice.

Given that implementation of surveillance reforms will take some time, the Executive Board agreed to move from a three- to a five-year surveillance review cycle. Accordingly, the next regular comprehensive surveillance review is scheduled to take place in 2019.

Box 2.1 Injecting the financial perspective

A key element of the Triennial Surveillance Review (TSR) was macro-financial surveillance—a big-picture view of national and regional financial issues. The review determined that more could be done to incorporate this area of work into the IMF's core macroeconomic analysis. It recommended that macro-financial surveillance be mainstreamed with better tools and new practices. It also called for strengthened surveillance of macroprudential policies.

The Managing Director's Action Plan for Strengthening Surveillance, which accompanied the TSR, pointed to the need for greater understanding of macro-financial linkages. The plan committed to undertaking a focused effort to identify themes in this area for diverse countries, and to provide interdepartmental support to develop and reflect this analysis in Article IV consultations with the aim of developing leading practices into Fund analysis and policy advice. This initiative will be supported by increased efforts to disseminate user-friendly toolkits to supplement the IMF's analytical work.

The plan also undertook to build capacity in area departments and identify networks of internal macro-financial experts to support the diffusion of learning practices across IMF staff, including through a training program and by sharing good practices.

To strengthen macroprudential surveillance, a guidance note was prepared for staff based on the 2013 Executive Board paper on "Key Aspects of Macroprudential Policy" and on country experiences. The note details a range of macroprudential tools and discusses the implementation of macroprudential policies, including in low-income countries.

The IMF continues to deepen its financial sector surveillance and integrate it more systematically into the Fund's macroeconomic analysis, including through focused efforts in recently completed and upcoming Article IV consultations with a sample range of IMF member countries.

Review of Financial Sector Assessments

The Financial Sector Assessment Program (FSAP) is an element that informs IMF surveillance in the area of financial sector stability. Established in 1999, the FSAP assessment is an in-depth analysis of a country's financial sector and in recent years became an integral part of surveillance for members with systemically important financial sectors, that is, in which financial instability could have a major impact on other countries.

In developing and emerging market countries, FSAP assessments are usually conducted jointly with the World Bank and include two components: a financial stability assessment that is the main responsibility of the IMF, and a financial development assessment that is overseen by the World Bank. At the IMF, in addition to the FSAP report, the staff produces a Financial System Stability Assessment report, which focuses on issues of relevance to IMF surveillance and is discussed by the IMF Executive Board, normally together with a country's Article IV consultation's staff report.

The IMF's policy on FSAPs is assessed every five years, and the latest review took place in September 2014. A core purpose of this review was to assess far-reaching reforms put in place after the 2009 review, including clarification of the respective roles of the IMF and World Bank and the introduction of an optional modular approach. In 2010, the financial stability assessment under the FSAP became a mandatory part of Article IV consultations for 25 members with systemically important financial sectors—to take place every five years. That number was expanded to 29 jurisdictions in 2013. For all other jurisdictions, FSAP participation continues to be voluntary.

In its assessment of the 2014 review, the Executive Board agreed that the 2009 reforms had considerably improved the FSAP, strengthening the focus, effectiveness, and traction of the assessments.

The Board said that a clearer definition of content had proved effective in disciplining and focusing assessments, and the delineation of Fund and Bank responsibilities had bolstered institutional accountability. The analysis of vulnerabilities has benefited from the introduction of a Risk Assessment Matrix, the expansion of stress tests to cover a broader set of risks, the ongoing progress in the analysis of spillovers, and the coverage of macroprudential frameworks and financial safety nets.

Going forward, the Board encouraged further improvements in the risk assessment, including by expanding the coverage of stress tests to the nonbank sector and strengthening the analysis of interconnectedness, cross-border exposures, and spillovers. It supported more systematic evaluations of institutional arrangements for micro and macroprudential supervision and financial safety nets, and asked staff to explore ways to focus standards assessments on key areas critical to financial stability.

On the matter of mandatory financial stability assessments, Executive Directors recognized that this prioritization may limit the availability of FSAP assessments to nonsystemic countries because of Fund resource constraints. They agreed that for such cases other forms of engagement should be used, including improved coverage of financial sector issues in Article IV consultations and multi-topic technical assistance.

The wider impact of large economies

The IMF's "Third Pilot External Sector Report"—issued in June 2014—presented a multilaterally consistent assessment of the largest economies' external sector positions and policies for 2013 and the first part of 2014.

The report integrated the analysis from the IMF's bilateral and multilateral surveillance to provide a consistent assessment of exchange rates, current accounts, reserves, capital flows, and external balance sheets. Together with the Spillover Report and Article IV consultations (with their heightened focus on spillovers),

the External Sector Report was part of a continuous effort to ensure that the IMF is in a good position to address the possible effects of spillovers from members' policies on global stability, and to monitor the stability of members' external sectors in a comprehensive manner.

The Executive Board discussed the report in an informal session, and no decisions were made.

Implications of monetary policy normalization

The report determined that external sector dynamics in 2013 were shaped by several interrelated developments. A stronger though uneven recovery in advanced economies began, resulting in first steps toward monetary policy normalization. The beginning of the exit from unconventional monetary policy in the United States initiated a tightening of global financial conditions and a round of capital flow volatility and substantial emerging market depreciations. With a subsequent recovery of demand for emerging market assets, supported in part by policy responses, many emerging market currencies strengthened again.

The report found that over a number of years, the global pattern of current account balances has narrowed but also rotated gradually into a new composition. The relative importance of excess imbalances of the world's largest economies has diminished. Among other economies, some cases of new excess imbalances have emerged, and in the past few years cases of excess deficits have grown in terms of number and size.

Policy actions to narrow excess imbalances

The report stated that policy actions required to further narrow excess imbalances varied but included medium-term fiscal consolidation, limiting financial excesses, structural reforms to facilitate adjustment in deficit economies, and various policies that support stronger domestic demand in surplus economies. More broadly, the report said, policy actions are needed on both sides of excess imbalances. Many economies have their own roles to play, and policy adjustments by all would be mutually supporting, with benefits in terms of growth and reducing financial risks.

How policies spill over to affect other economies

As part of the broad effort to strengthen the surveillance process, the IMF has implemented more systematic coverage of spillovers from member countries' economic and financial policies. The process—growing out of the Integrated Surveillance Decision adopted in 2012—takes place in the context of the Article IV consultations. It aims to better integrate bilateral and multilateral surveillance.

The spillover reports—begun in 2011—are issued on an annual basis, with the 2014 report issued in July 2014 after an Executive Board informal session.

The "Big Three"

The Early Warning Exercise (EWE) is an important element of the IMF's surveillance toolkit. It combines analysis of economic, financial, fiscal, and external risks as well as cross-sector and cross-border spillovers. The EWE is conducted semiannually, in close coordination with the IMF's flagship publications: the *World Economic Outlook*, *Global Financial Stability Report*, and *Fiscal Monitor*.

The EWE examines unlikely, but plausible, risks that would necessitate policy recommendations that could differ from those related to baseline projections presented in the flagships. However, it does not attempt to predict crises.

Rather, it seeks to identify the vulnerabilities and triggers that could precipitate systemic crises, and identifies risk-mitigating policies, including those that would require international cooperation. The EWE is prepared in collaboration with the Financial Stability Board, which represents experts and policymakers from financial supervisory agencies and central banks in member countries.

Each EWE is discussed by the IMF Executive Board, after which it is presented to senior officials during the IMF–World Bank Spring and Annual Meetings. The findings are considered market sensitive and are not released publicly.

The reports allow the IMF to discuss with its members the full range of spillovers from their policies on domestic and global stability, and encourage discussion of spillover-related issues in multilateral forums to foster policy attention and dialogue. Until 2013, the reports focused on the external effects of domestic policies in five systemically important economies: China, euro area, Japan, the United Kingdom, and the United States.

Beginning with the 2014 report, the IMF shifted to a more thematic approach, focusing on key issues chosen on their relevance from a spillover perspective.

The 2014 report stated that global spillovers had entered a new phase.

With crisis-related spillovers and risks fading, changing growth patterns had become the main source of spillovers in the global economy.

The paper highlighted two key trends:

First, the paper pointed to signs of self-sustaining recovery in some advanced economies—led by the United States and United Kingdom—that indicated that the unwinding of exceptional monetary accommodation will proceed and lead to a tightening of global financial conditions in the coming years. However, the paper said, an uneven recovery suggested that normalization will proceed at different times in different countries, with possible spillover implications.

Second, the report underlined that growth in emerging markets was slowing on a broad basis since its precrisis peak and could carry noticeable spillover effects at the global level, with a gradual, synchronized, and protracted slowdown likely to weigh on global growth through trade as well as finance.

The report also described how key spillover risks can intersect and interact. It said the two risks highlighted in the report can be interrelated because markets may reassess growth prospects in emerging markets amid renewed bouts of financial turbulence and capital outflows. The report described a downside scenario of sharply tighter financial conditions alongside a further weakening of emerging market growth that could lower output by about 2 percent.

The paper stated that the 2014 spillover risks warranted stronger policy action at both the national and global levels.

Stronger actions at the national level in both source and recipient countries of spillovers would align with better outcomes at the global level. With incentive problems and tradeoffs, the report said, stronger national actions alone might not be sufficient to address spillover consequences. That meant that collaboration took on renewed importance in mitigating potential downside risks and providing support for more vulnerable economies, if certain key risks were to materialize.

The 2016 Spillover Report is to be incorporated into the *World Economic Outlook* as part of broader initiatives to streamline, mainstream, and integrate the various strands of IMF work.

Macroeconomic developments in low-income developing countries

The IMF released a new report addressing trends in low-income developing countries (LIDCs) during 2014 in order to broaden the institution's analysis of a group of nations that represents an increasingly dynamic part of the global economy.

The 2014 report examined the strong economic performance achieved by the bulk of LIDCs since 2000 and assessed their short-term prospects. It also analyzed the economic risks and vulnerabilities they face amid an uneven global recovery and the evolution of their public debt levels in recent years.

The Executive Board discussed the report in an informal session. The report is to be produced on an annual basis.

The key messages of the 2014 report included the following:

Most LIDCs have recorded strong economic growth over the past 15 years, but based primarily on factor accumulation rather than productivity growth. Growth has been faster than in previous decades and on par with growth performance in emerging markets. This performance has been underpinned by external factors, sound macroeconomic management, and wide-ranging market-oriented reforms. But growth has not been very deep or transformative. In addition, many countries affected by conflict and fragile states failed to increase the level of output per capita.

The share of LIDCs that are assessed to be highly vulnerable declined slightly to about 10 percent of the total, and most are fragile states. Weak fiscal positions are typically the most important source of vulnerability. Analysis of selected shock scenarios flags the significant adverse impact on LIDCs of a protracted period of slower growth in advanced and emerging market

economies. To enhance resilience, policy actions to rebuild fiscal and external buffers are a priority in many countries. As frontier market economies expand their links to the global financial system, they face new risks: rapid credit growth and the expansion of foreign credit warrant close monitoring in some cases.

Public debt is at relatively low levels in a majority of LIDCs, but fiscal institutions should be strengthened to pre-empt the buildup of new imbalances. Strong growth, low interest rates, and comprehensive external debt relief have contributed to relatively low levels of public debt. Nevertheless, in a third of LIDCs, debt levels are high and/or have increased significantly in recent years. The changing external financial landscape has enabled an increasing number of LIDCs to access international financial markets and nontraditional official creditors have also significantly expanded their provision of project finance. Countries tapping new sources of funding need to give attention to where these funds go and how efficiently they are used. Also, with new risks such as bunching of repayments and rollover risk, efforts to strengthen public debt management are an imperative.

Global Housing Watch: On the Front Lines of Crisis Prevention

Housing is an essential sector of every country's economy. But it also can be a source of instability for financial institutions and countries—witness the roots of the 2008 global financial crisis in advanced economy housing markets. As a result, understanding the drivers of housing price cycles, and how to moderate these cycles, has become important for economic stability and for the work of the IMF.

As research and policy advice in this area has become more central to the IMF, an effort has been made to bring together the institution's work in this area. This enables IMF economists to better keep track of boom and bust cycles worldwide, and to work together with policymakers to take early action to address housing booms.

Among the IMF's initiatives in this area are the following:

Global Housing Watch: A web page was launched in 2014 to help track developments across housing markets, enable more transparent cross-country and historical comparisons, and discuss the policy tools being developed to address market cycles. The page features the Global House Price Index, which is a compilation of average housing prices in different countries to highlight global prices trends. These data give IMF country teams an indication of how their country compares on these metrics to other countries.

"Cluster Report on Housing Recoveries": The November 2014 paper, produced by the European Department, on the experiences of Denmark, Ireland, the Netherlands, and Spain, covered countries that experienced large declines in housing prices in recent years and shared a similar institutional environment. It explored how policies can best support economic recovery in the wake of a price bust.

Conference on Housing Markets, Financial Stability, and Growth: This event in Bangalore, India, in December 2014 provided a forum for discussing crucial macroeconomic topics related to housing markets. Cohosted with the Indian Institute of Management, the conference addressed such issues as macroprudential policies, the drivers of house prices, and housing markets and monetary policy. In a related blog post, IMF Deputy Managing Director Min Zhu highlighted the challenges of housing price booms in emerging markets; the article was one of the most widely read items on the IMF blog, *iMFdirect*.

Conference on Housing Markets and the Macroeconomy: Cosponsored by the IMF, Deutsche Bundesbank, and the German Research Foundation, this June 2014 gathering examined the challenges housing markets present for monetary policy and financial stability.

The Role of Trade in the Work of the IMF

Trade has become an essential element of the policy agenda to spur global growth. A revival of trade growth, which has been slowing in recent years, has the potential to significantly affect growth in individual economies and the global economy as a whole. Trade-related reforms can enhance the benefits of other economic reforms, spurring increased growth.

That was a core message of the IMF's five-yearly review of the role of trade in the work of the IMF, during which the IMF takes stock of the changing trends in trade and trade policy, and discusses key issues for the institution's work agenda. The review, discussed by the Executive Board in February 2015, followed Board-endorsed recommendations and an implementation plan arising from the 2009 IEO evaluation of IMF Involvement in International Trade Policy Issues.

Implications of a changing trade landscape

The staff paper provided a broad overview of the role of trade and trade policy issues in the work of the IMF over the past five years and discussed how to integrate and make operational the implications of the changing global trade landscape, including the changing drivers of trade—such as global value chains—and the movement of the focus of trade policy from multilateral rounds to regional and multilateral deals.

During the Board's discussion, Executive Directors broadly agreed with the paper's main findings, noting that there are potentially large global gains to be derived from further trade liberalization and integration.

Tailoring surveillance to countries' needs

Directors emphasized that the IMF's work on trade should remain within the institution's mandate, addressing trade issues deemed macrocritical and taking into account resource constraints and limited trade expertise. This would require careful prioritization and continued collaboration with other international institutions, including the World Trade Organization and the World Bank.

They also emphasized that coverage of trade issues should be tailored to the needs of individual countries, and agreed that better embedding trade in the IMF's surveillance work would require a concerted effort on several fronts.

For advanced economies, a key issue would be the implications of their efforts to pioneer and advance new trade policy areas such as services, regulations, and investment.

For emerging market economies, traditional liberalization and anchoring to global supply chains still provide benefits. For low-income countries, greater integration requires sustained efforts to reduce trade costs, including upgrading trade infrastructures and improving economic institutions both at national and regional levels, supported by relevant technical assistance.

POLICY ADVICE

From Banking to Sovereign Stress: Implications for Public Debt

An increasing amount of IMF research has been conducted in recent years on the linkages between banks and sovereign debt, particularly since the global financial crisis of 2008. The period witnessed accumulated banking sector vulnerabilities, which in some cases triggered full-blown banking crises that contributed to significant increases in public debt, partly resulting from government interventions.

A staff paper, "From Banking to Sovereign Stress: Implications for Public Debt," was published in March 2015 after an informal session for Executive Directors. The paper explored how banking sector developments and characteristics influence the propagation of risks from the banking sector to sovereign debt, including how they affect the extent of fiscal costs of banking crises.

An interdepartmental study

The paper was prepared by an interdepartmental team from the Strategy Policy and Review Department, Fiscal Affairs Department, Monetary and Capital Markets Department, and Research Department. It presented new empirical work on the ways in which banking sector developments can affect macroeconomic and fiscal outcomes.

Systemic banking crises have contributed to large increases in public debt.

Over the period 2007–11, the median increase in public debt four years after the beginning of a crisis was 12 percentage points of GDP. And in many countries, public debt increased by more than 20 percentage points of GDP.

The paper found several factors that affect the bank-sovereign link. These include the extent of banks' balance sheet expansion, leverage, and reliance on wholesale external funding; the strength of precrisis institutional settings and crisis resolution policies; and the extent of banks' holdings of their own government debt—also known as "home bias."

The paper proposed practices and policies for fiscal authorities to help manage the risks and enhance crisis preparedness. It determined that efforts to strengthen financial sector regulation and supervision are the preferred approach to preserve the health of the banking sector and minimize the risk that taxpayer funds may be exposed to losses due to banks' failures. In this respect, policy priorities should include macroprudential measures aimed at: (1) reducing excessive procyclicality in banking systems; (2) higher bank loss-absorbing capacities; and (3) effective resolution powers and planning.

Approaches for fiscal authorities

On the fiscal side, the paper suggested that although the specific policy recommendations to deal with banking sector risks depend on country-specific circumstances, fiscal authorities should:

Have in place an institutional framework that strengthens the ability to identify and monitor risks emanating from the banking sector.

Develop fiscal buffers during banking booms that would allow for appropriately sized countercyclical policies during downturns. The adoption of fiscal rules that constrain the spending of unsustainable increases in tax revenue associated with credit booms, including particular reliance on real estate–related sources of revenues, would be beneficial in this regard.

Balance the benefits and risks associated with reliance on domestic banks as a source of public financing. Excessive reliance on domestic bank financing may lead to distortions, a false sense of debt sustainability, and a deeper bank-sovereign nexus.

Consider tax policies that reduce the bias toward debt financing and the attractiveness of leverage. Removing tax incentives to borrow and introducing a Financial Stability Contribution tax could lower banking sector risks and help build fiscal buffers when vulnerabilities increase.

The Cross-Border Impact of Banking Crises

Developing an effective framework for cross-border resolution is an important priority in international regulatory reform. Large bank failures during the global financial crisis highlighted the need for tools to resolve "too-big-to-fail" institutions.

A key achievement in the reform agenda has been the establishment of an international standard for the resolution of systemically important financial institutions.

The Financial Stability Board's (FSB) Key Attributes of Effective Resolution Regimes for Financial Institutions has established an agreed set of principles and best practices, and FSB member countries have committed to implement the rules by the end of 2015. The Key Attributes call for countries to put in place resolution regimes that give the authorities comprehensive resolution powers while establishing effective mechanisms for cross-border cooperation and for the allocation of losses to private stakeholders.

A progress report prepared by the IMF Monetary and Capital Markets and Legal Departments and released in June 2014 described the status of efforts to put the rules in place. The Executive Board discussed the paper in an informal session.

The paper determined that considerable additional work remains to establish an effective regime for cross-border resolution. Areas in need of attention include:

■ **National resolution regimes:** Several jurisdictions have adopted far-reaching legal reforms, but the reforms are complex and progress has been mixed overall. While some countries have made progress, many still lack comprehensive resolution powers for banks and other financial institutions, and effective mechanisms for the recognition of foreign resolution measures.

■ **Firm-specific operational resolution strategies:** Reaching agreement between home and host supervisors on how to resolve systemic, cross-border institutions has been difficult, in particular because of legal impediments to cross-border cooperation and the complexities of operational and financial structures.

■ **Loss absorbency:** The Key Attributes call for the burden of bank failure to fall on private creditors of banks. The credibility of this commitment depends on ensuring that banks have sufficient liabilities to absorb losses without destabilizing the financial system. The FSB is expected to finalize a new standard on total loss-absorbing capacity for global systemically important banks later this year.

■ **Harmonization of creditor hierarchies:** Differences across countries in the ranking of creditor claims in liquidation or resolution is an important impediment to the cooperative resolution of cross-border bank failures.

■ **Use of public funds:** The risk that public funds will be needed to preserve financial stability cannot be ruled out and creates powerful incentives for unilateral action that can undermine cooperation. Achieving prior agreement on the location of buffers and loss allocation, resolution strategies, and aligning group structure accordingly will be critical.

■ **Smaller jurisdictions/entities:** Many cross-border banks are not globally systemic, but their resolution, if disorderly, could undermine financial stability in home and host countries. Reforms to resolution frameworks will need to take account of the different degrees of complexity of financial systems and ensure that incentives are aligned so that resolution strategies can minimize financial stability risks in small as well as core jurisdictions for the entity in resolution.

Sovereign Debt Restructuring

In May 2013, the Executive Board discussed a staff paper, "Sovereign Debt Restructuring—Recent Developments and Implications for the IMF's Legal and Policy Framework," and endorsed a work program focused on strengthening market-based approaches to resolving sovereign debt crises. The program comprised four elements: (1) reforming the IMF's lending framework; (2) strengthening collective action clauses in sovereign bond contracts; (3) reviewing the framework for official sector involvement; and (4) assessing the effectiveness of the IMF's lending-into-arrears policy.

The "Big Three"

On the lending framework, in June 2014 the Board discussed the staff paper "The IMF's Lending Framework and Sovereign Debt—Preliminary Considerations." The primary focus of the paper was the Fund's exceptional access framework—the context in which the IMF most likely will have to make difficult judgments about whether a member's debt is sustainable (with high probability). With the principal objective of reducing the costs of crisis resolution for creditors and debtors, and for the system as a whole, the paper presented two possible directions for reforms: the introduction of a "debt reprofiling" option to make the lending framework more flexible where debt is assessed as sustainable but not with high probability, and the elimination of the systemic exemption.

No decision was made on the suggested reforms, but the Board asked staff to prepare an additional paper to be discussed in FY2016.

On collective action clauses, in October 2014 the Board discussed the staff paper "Strengthening the Contractual Framework to Address Collective Action Problems in Sovereign Debt Restructuring." The paper contained recommendations to further improve the contractual, market-based approach to dealing with collective action problems.

The Board endorsed the key features of modified pari passu and enhanced collective action clauses in international sovereign bond contracts to reduce their vulnerability to holdout creditors in case of a debt restructuring. The recommended reforms resulted from a process of consultation with public and private stakeholders. The Board also supported an active role for the IMF in promoting the inclusion of these provisions in new international sovereign bond issuances. However, the Board also noted that a large portion of the significant stock of outstanding international sovereign bonds, which do not contain the new clauses, will only mature in the next 10 years and could pose a risk to orderly restructurings.

The Board encouraged staff to engage in further discussions with stakeholders on ways to minimize this remaining risk to orderly restructurings and looked forward to periodic progress reports on the status of inclusion of the proposed contractual provisions in international sovereign bonds. Since October 2014, several member countries have incorporated modified clauses that include the key features endorsed by the IMF in new bond issuances.

Work on official sector involvement and the lending-into-arrears policy is expected to follow the Board's discussion of the "lending framework" paper in FY2016.

Spillovers in International Corporate Taxation

The world is focusing on cross-border tax issues, with work in this area receiving greatly increased attention. In May 2014, IMF staff issued a paper, "Spillovers in International Corporate Taxation," which received considerable notice.

The paper, which was discussed by the Executive Board in an informal session, explored the nature, significance, and policy implications of spillovers—the effects of one country's rules and practices on others—with a focus on developing countries.

The paper complemented initiatives focused on reducing tax avoidance by multinational corporations, particularly the G20–Organisation for Economic Co-operation and Development (OECD) project on Base Erosion and Profit Shifting (BEPS). The spillover paper drew on IMF experience with broader international tax issues across the membership, including experience gained through technical assistance.

Allegations of multinational tax avoidance

The IMF study went beyond OECD BEPS to explore the broader macroeconomic and development impact of corporate tax spillovers, including wider issues of tax competition among national governments. The BEPS action plan aims—in the context of the existing, informally

agreed, international tax architecture—to alter some of the technical global guidelines and standards for taxation of cross-border activities and reduce opportunities for tax avoidance and profit shifting.

The IMF work determined that tax spillovers can have implications for macroeconomic performance.

Capital account data are clearly influenced by taxation, and considerable evidence shows that taxation powerfully affects the behavior of multinational enterprises. The results confirmed that spillover effects on corporate tax bases and rates are significant.

The analysis also found that spillovers are especially marked for *developing economies*, which typically derive a greater proportion of their revenue from corporate taxes. The paper noted that technical assistance experience provides many examples in which the sums at stake in international tax issues are large relative to countries' overall revenues—sometimes equal to 10–15 percent of total revenue.

Limiting spillovers on developing nations

The study argued that limiting adverse spillovers on developing economies requires not only capacity building, but also addressing weaknesses in domestic law and international arrangements. It made specific suggestions in areas that IMF technical assistance has found to be especially problematic for developing economies. The paper flags, for instance, the risk that countries run by signing bilateral tax treaties, such as forgone revenue from withholding taxes and base erosion through treaty shopping. It also draws attention to the ambiguities in many tax laws regarding the taxation of offshore capital gains, often related to extractive industries. And many countries fail to provide protection against excessive debt finance or manipulation of transfer pricing.

The institutional framework for addressing international tax spillovers is weak, the paper concluded, so as the strength and pervasiveness of tax spillovers become increasingly apparent, the case for an inclusive and less piecemeal approach to international tax cooperation grows.

Subsequent work and developments

At the November 2014 G20 Summit, IMF staff was asked to work with the OECD and other international organizations to better include developing countries in the BEPS decision-making and deliberative processes; staff have so engaged, through technical assistance interactions and outreach events, including an International Tax Dialogue with Developing Countries at the 2015 Spring Meetings and in the Fiscal Affairs Department's annual tax conference for Asian countries. The G20 also asked the IMF to take the lead in producing a report on "Efficient and Effective Use of Tax Incentives in Low-Income Countries," and to work with OECD staff on a report on taxation of offshore capital gains.

Assessing Reserve Adequacy

The foreign exchange reserves held by central banks occupy an important place in the policy toolkit of most economies.

Together with sound policies, they can help reduce the likelihood of balance-of-payments crises and preserve economic and financial stability.

To help support IMF's member countries, IMF staff has undertaken a series of studies on reserve adequacy, with a 2011 paper, "Assessing Reserve Adequacy," which assessed approaches to reserve accumulation, and a second paper in 2013 that explored the role of reserves in preventing and mitigating crises and considered how IMF guidance on the topic might need to be augmented. Both papers were discussed by the Executive Board.

In January 2015, the Board assessed a follow-up paper drawing on this work and outlining a framework for discussing reserve adequacy issues in the context of Article IV consultations. The paper was intended, in part, to help provide guidance on the desirable level of reserve holdings for a given country by providing tools for quantifying risks to help governments determine this level.

The new framework classifies countries based on the strength of market access, the depth and

liquidity of their markets, and the flexibility of their economies.

For each country group, the paper proposes frameworks to help assess the appropriate level of reserves based on its circumstances. To achieve this, the report also provides further reserve assessment guidance for specific country types

within these categories. For example, within the set of deepening or emerging market economies, the paper refines the guidance for those with capital flow management measures, commodity-intensive countries, and dollarized economies.

In its assessment of the paper, which was released in April 2015, the Executive Board agreed that

reserves, in conjunction with sound policies and fundamentals, can bring significant benefits in reducing the likelihood of balance-of-payments crises and preserving economic and financial stability.

Most Executive Directors supported a systematic discussion of reserve adequacy issues in IMF surveillance reports, which could help enrich staff's analysis and policy advice.

Executive Directors agreed that the depth and emphasis of the discussion should depend on country circumstances and reflect the aspects that are relevant for a country's external stability as well as global stability. In this regard, they said, the discussion should reflect the adequacy of reserves for precautionary purposes, the authorities' stated precautionary and nonprecautionary objectives for holding reserves, and the cost of reserves.

To make the agreed framework operational, most Executive Directors supported the preparation of a staff guidance note, in line with management's planned response to the findings of the IEO's 2012 evaluation of "International Reserves—IMF Concerns and Country Perspectives."

Revising the Fiscal Transparency Code

Fiscal transparency is essential for effective fiscal management and accountability. It ensures that governments have an accurate picture of their fiscal position and prospects when making economic decisions, including of the long-term costs and benefits of policy changes and potential risks to public finances. It also provides legislatures, citizens, and markets with the information they need to hold governments accountable.

The IMF's new Fiscal Transparency Code and Evaluation are part of its ongoing efforts to help Fund member countries strengthen their fiscal policymaking, monitoring, and accountability. A paper approved by the Executive Board in 2014 presented the new code and evaluation that replace the 2007 Code and the related fiscal module of the IMF's Reports on the Observance of Standards and Codes initiative.

Transparency will strengthen fiscal surveillance

The work is part of ongoing efforts by the Fiscal Affairs Department, in cooperation with other departments, to strengthen the IMF's fiscal surveillance and capacity development.

The new code and evaluation reflect the lessons of the global financial crisis, incorporate developments in international standards, and build on feedback from stakeholder consultations.

The Fiscal Transparency Code is the global standard for disclosure of information about public finances. It consists of a set of principles built around four "pillars": (1) fiscal reporting; (2) fiscal forecasting and budgeting; (3) fiscal risk analysis and management; and (4) resource revenue management.

For each principle, the code differentiates between basic, good, and advanced practices to provide countries with clear milestones toward full compliance with the code and ensure its applicability to the full range of IMF member countries. Pillars 1–3 have been issued, and pillar 4 is expected to be finalized in FY2016. Pillar 4 will complement the first three pillars for resource-rich countries and will reflect feedback from consultations with stakeholders and the public.

Fiscal Transparency Evaluations assess country compliance with the code. They provide countries with a comprehensive assessment of their fiscal transparency practices against the standard established by the code; quantified analyses of the scale and sources of fiscal vulnerability, based on a set of fiscal transparency indicators; an accessible summary of the fiscal transparency strengths and reform practices through heat maps; and the option of a sequenced fiscal transparency action plan to help countries address those reform priorities. The evaluation also allows for modular assessments focused on the new code's individual pillars for addressing the most pressing transparency issues. Feedback from country authorities and other stakeholders on these evaluations has been very positive.

A new Fiscal Transparency Manual

A new two-volume Fiscal Transparency Manual is expected to be issued by end-FY2016, providing more detailed guidance on implementation of the new Fiscal Transparency Code's principles and practices. Volume I will cover the code's first three pillars and replace the 2007 Manual on Fiscal Transparency, while Volume II will focus on Pillar 4—covering resource revenue management—and integrate the previously separate 2007 Guide on Resource Revenue Transparency.

The "Big Three"

The IMF's Work with Small States

"The IMF stands ready to work with small states to help them overcome their development challenges and build a prosperous future."

IMF Deputy Managing Director Min Zhu
September 3, 2014

The IMF has 42 member countries with populations of fewer than 1.5 million, 33 of which are classified as small developing economies. In recent years, this group of developing nations has come to be known as "small states," although they also include a subcategory of "micro" states with populations under 200,000 as of 2011.

Small states do not enjoy the benefits of economies of scale, which hampers their ability to provide public goods and services, or produce goods for global trade. Their economic growth has lagged larger peers over the past decade, and micro states have seen considerable economic volatility due to climatic and other shocks. Given the special economic needs of this group of countries, the IMF has responded by reviewing how best to engage with them and provide support.

This process was launched in 2013 with a staff paper, "Macroeconomic Issues in Small States and Implications for Fund Engagement," and an associated Executive Board discussion. In May 2014, a Staff Guidance Note on the IMF's engagement with small states was issued, consolidating the lessons from the 2013 staff paper and Board discussion. Five key thematic areas identified by the acronym G.R.O.W.T.H. have been identified as central to the policy dialogue with small states: growth and job

creation, resilience to shocks, overall competitiveness, workable fiscal and debt sustainability options, and thin financial sectors.

At the third United Nations International Conference on Small Island Developing States, held in Samoa in September 2014, IMF Deputy Managing Director Min Zhu pledged the IMF's continued support to those countries in their pursuit of sustainable economic development.

With many small states clustered in the Caribbean and Pacific, the IMF's regional departments and technical assistance centers play a lead role in serving small states' needs.

To better communicate with their smaller members, the IMF's Asia-Pacific Department and Western Hemisphere Department have recently launched periodic bulletins—the "Caribbean Corner" and "Asia & Pacific Small States Monitor," respectively. Following on the issuance of the Staff Guidance Note, the Asia-Pacific Department introduced a training course for mission chiefs engaged in surveillance of small states.

Policy analysis prepared by the two departments was also included in a March 2015 paper on "Macroeconomic Developments and Selected Issues in Small Developing States," prepared in collaboration with two other departments. This paper, discussed by the Board in March, provided a summary of recent developments and Fund staff projections, as well as thematic chapters on the challenges of fiscal management in small states, the impact of currency devaluations, and levels of financial inclusion.

Data and Data Standards Initiatives

The quality of data provided by member countries under the Articles of Agreement is essential to the success of IMF surveillance.

Data dissemination standards help enhance the availability of timely and comprehensive statistics, which is critical to the pursuit of sound macro-economic policies.

The Special Data Dissemination Standard (SDDS) was established in 1996 to guide members in the provision of their economic and financial data to the public. The General Data Dissemination System (GDDS), established the following year, provides a framework to help countries evaluate their needs and sets priorities for improving their statistical systems.

In 2012, the SDDS Plus was created to help address data gaps identified during the global financial crisis. The SDDS Plus is aimed at countries with systemically important financial sectors, although all SDDS subscribers are encouraged to adhere. An initial cluster of eight countries adhered to the SDDS Plus in FY2015.

There were no new subscribers to the SDDS in FY2015, with the number of subscribing economies standing at 63 as of the end of the financial year, following the graduation of eight countries to the SDDS Plus (Seychelles subscribed on May 1, 2015). The Cook Islands and Micronesia began participation in the GDDS, bringing the total number of GDDS participants to 113 at the end of the year (excluding the economies that have graduated from the GDDS to the SDDS over the years).

More than 97 percent of the IMF's member countries participate in the GDDS, SDDS, or SDDS Plus. There are 113 participants in the GDDS, 63 SDDS subscribers, and 8 SDDS Plus adherents.

The Statistics Department has partnered with the African Development Bank and the World Bank to develop and promote the so-called Open Data Platform aimed at facilitating dissemination of data (including Sustainable Development Goals) by country authorities. Several countries in Africa have already successfully implemented this new tool.

The G20 Data Gaps Initiative (DGI) was initiated after the global financial crisis, in response to a request to the IMF and FSB by the G20 Finance Ministers and Central Bank Governors (FMCG). The 20 recommendations to close data gaps were endorsed by the International Monetary and Financial Committee. Six years after the start of the project, significant progress has been made in closing the gaps. The data emerging from the DGI are seen as enhancing the support to policy work, including financial stability and debt analysis, and promoting a better understanding of domestic and international interconnectedness. In September 2014, the G20 FMCG asked the FSB Secretariat and IMF staff to report back in September 2015 with a proposal for a second phase of the DGI as well as a final progress report on the implementation of Phase 1 of the Initiative.

The "Big Three"

Lending

IMF loans are meant to help member countries tackle balance-of-payments problems, stabilize their economies, and restore sustainable economic growth. This crisis resolution role is at the core of IMF lending. At the same time, the recent global financial crisis has highlighted the need for effective global financial safety nets to help countries cope with adverse shocks. A key objective of recent lending reforms has therefore been to complement the traditional crisis resolution role of the IMF with additional tools for crisis prevention. Unlike development banks, the IMF does not lend for specific projects.

In broad terms, the IMF has two types of lending — money provided at nonconcessional interest rates and loans provided to poorer countries on concessional terms, where interest rates are low or in some cases zero.

NONCONCESSIONAL FINANCING ACTIVITY

In FY2015, the Executive Board approved nine arrangements under the IMF's nonconcessional financing facilities, for a gross total of SDR 80 billion ($112 billion not netted for canceled arrangements, and converted to United States dollars at the SDR/$ exchange rate on April 30, 2015 of 0.71103 (see Table 2.1). Six precautionary arrangements under the Flexible Credit Line (FCL) and Precautionary and Liquidity Line (PLL) accounted for more than 84 percent of these commitments, including an FCL with access amounting to SDR 47 billion ($67 billion) for Mexico. The two FCL arrangements approved for Mexico and Poland and the PLL arrangement approved for Morocco were successors to previous arrangements that were expiring. The remaining three precautionary arrangements were Stand-By Arrangements with Honduras, Kenya, and the Republic of Serbia totaling SDR 1.4 billion ($1.9 billion), which were treated as precautionary by the authorities upon approval of the programs. In addition, the Board approved an extended arrangement under the EFF for Ukraine with exceptional access amounting to SDR 12.348 billion or $17.5 billion to support the authorities' adjustment program.

By end-April 2015, disbursements under financing arrangements from the General Resources Account (GRA), referred to as "purchases," totaled SDR 12.0 billion ($16.9 billion), with purchases by Ukraine amounting to SDR 6.5 billion ($9.2 billion) or 54 percent. Total repayments, termed "repurchases," for the financial year amounted to SDR 38.0 billion ($53.4 billion). Of these, advance repurchases from Ireland and Portugal during the period amounted to SDR 20.8 billion ($29 billion). Sizable repurchases and stalled purchases associated with off-track programs resulted in the

Table **2.1**

Arrangements approved in the General Resources Account in FY2015

(Millions of SDRs)

Member	Type of arrangement	Effective date	Amount approved
NEW ARRANGEMENTS			
Georgia	36-month Stand-By	July 30, 2014	100.0
Honduras	36-month Stand-By	December 3, 2014	77.7
Kenya	12-month Stand-By	February 2, 2015	352.8
Mexico	24-month Flexible Credit Line	November 26, 2014	47,292.0
Morocco	24-month Precautionary and Liquidity Line	July 28, 2014	3,235.1
Poland, Republic of	24-month Flexible Credit Line	January 14, 2015	15,500.0
Serbia, Republic of	36-month Stand-By	February 23, 2015	935.4
Seychelles	36-month Extended Fund Facility	June 4, 2014	11.4
Ukraine	36-month Extended Fund Facility	March 11, 2015	12,348.0
Subtotal			**79,852.5**
AUGMENTATIONS OF ARRANGEMENTS¹			
Bosnia and Herzegovina	33-month Stand-By	June 30, 2014	84.6
Subtotal			**84.6**
Total			**79,937.0**

Source: IMF Finance Department.

¹For augmentation, only the amount of the increase is shown.

Learn more: see *IMF Financial Operations 2014*

The "Big Three"

Table **2.2**

Financial terms under IMF General Resources Account credit

This table shows major nonconcessional lending facilities. Stand-By Arrangements have long been the core lending instrument of the institution. In the wake of the 2007–09 global financial crisis, the IMF strengthened its lending toolkit. A major aim was to enhance crisis-prevention instruments through the creation of the Flexible Credit Line (FCL), the Precautionary and Liquidity Line (PLL), and the Rapid Financing Instrument (RFI).

Credit facility (year adopted)[1]	Purpose	Conditions	Phasing and monitoring
CREDIT TRANCHES AND EXTENDED FUND FACILITY[3]			
Stand-By Arrangements (SBAs) (1952)	Short- to medium-term assistance for countries with short-term balance-of-payments difficulties	Adopt policies that provide confidence that the member's balance of payments difficulties will be resolved within a reasonable period	Generally quarterly purchases (disbursements) contingent on observance of performance criteria and other conditions
Extended Fund Facility (EFF) (1974) (Extended Arrangements)	Longer-term assistance to support members' structural reforms to address long-term balance-of-payments difficulties	Adopt up to 4-year program, with structural agenda and annual detailed statement of policies for the next 12 months	Quarterly or semiannual purchases (disbursements) contingent on observance of performance criteria and other conditions
Flexible Credit Line (FCL) (2009)	Flexible instrument in the credit tranches to address all balance-of-payments needs, potential or actual	Very strong ex ante macroeconomic fundamentals, economic policy framework, and policy track record	Approved access available up front throughout the arrangement period, subject to a midterm review after 1 year
Precautionary and Liquidity Line (PLL) (2011)	Instrument for countries with sound economic fundamentals and policies	Sound policy frameworks, external position, and market access, including financial sector soundness	Large frontloaded access, subject to semiannual reviews (for 1- to 2-year PLL)
SPECIAL FACILITIES			
Rapid Financing Instrument (RFI) (2011)	Rapid financial assistance to all member countries facing an urgent balance of payments need	Efforts to solve balance of payments difficulties (may include prior actions)	Outright purchases without the need for full-fledged program or reviews

[1] The IMF's lending through the General Resources Account (GRA) is primarily financed from the capital subscribed by member countries; each country is assigned a quota that represents its financial commitment. A member provides a portion of its quota in Special Drawing Rights (SDRs) or the currency of another member acceptable to the IMF and the remainder in its own currency. An IMF loan is disbursed or drawn by the borrower's purchase of foreign currency assets from the IMF with its own currency. Repayment of the loan is achieved by the borrower's repurchase of its currency from the IMF with foreign currency.

[2] The rate of charge on funds disbursed from the GRA is set at a margin over the weekly SDR interest rate (currently 100 basis points). The rate of charge is applied to the daily balance of all outstanding GRA drawings during each IMF financial quarter. In addition, a one-time service charge of 0.5 percent is levied on each drawing of IMF resources in the GRA, other than reserve tranche drawings. An up-front commitment fee (15 basis points on committed amounts of up to 200 percent of quota; 30 basis points for amounts in excess of 200 percent and up to 1,000 percent of quota; and 60 basis points for amounts in excess of 1,000 percent of quota) applies to the amount that may be drawn during each (annual) period under a Stand-By Arrangement, Flexible Credit Line, Precautionary and Liquidity Line, or Extended Arrangement; this fee is refunded on a proportionate basis as subsequent drawings are made under the arrangement.

Access limits[1]	Charges[2]	Repayment schedule (years)	Installments
Annual: 200% of quota; cumulative: 600% of quota	Rate of charge plus surcharge (200 basis points on amounts above 300% of quota; additional 100 basis points when outstanding credit remains above 300% of quota for more than 3 years)[4]	3¼–5	Quarterly
Annual: 200% of quota; cumulative: 600% of quota	Rate of charge plus surcharge (200 basis points on amounts above 300% of quota; additional 100 basis points when outstanding credit remains above 300% of quota for more than 3 years)[4]	4½–10	Semiannual
No preset limit	Rate of charge plus surcharge (200 basis points on amounts above 300% of quota; additional 100 basis points when outstanding credit remains above 300% of quota for more than 3 years)[4]	3¼–5	Quarterly
250% of quota for 6 months; 500% of quota available upon approval of 1- to 2-year arrangements; total of 1,000% of quota after 12 months of satisfactory progress	Rate of charge plus surcharge (200 basis points on amounts above 300% of quota; additional 100 basis points when outstanding credit remains above 300% of quota for more than 3 years)[4]	3¼–5	Quarterly
Annual: 50% of quota; cumulative: 100% of quota	Rate of charge plus surcharge (200 basis points on amounts above 300% of quota; additional 100 basis points when outstanding credit remains above 300% of quota for more than 3 years)[4]	3¼–5	Quarterly

[3] Credit tranches refer to the size of purchases (disbursements) as a proportion of the member's quota in the IMF; for example, disbursements up to 25 percent of a member's quota are disbursements under the first credit tranche and require members to demonstrate reasonable efforts to overcome their balance-of-payments problems. Requests for disbursements above 25 percent are referred to as upper-credit-tranche drawings; they are made in installments as the borrower meets certain established performance targets. Such disbursements are typically associated with a Stand-By or Extended Arrangement.

[4] Surcharges were introduced in November 2000. A new system of surcharges took effect August 1, 2009, replacing the previous schedule: 100 basis points above the basic rate of charge on amounts above 200 percent of quota, and 200 basis points on amounts above 300 percent of quota. A member with credit outstanding in the credit tranches or under the Extended Fund Facility on, or with an effective arrangement approved before, August 1, 2009, had the option to elect between the new and the old system of surcharges.

Table **2.3**
Concessional lending facilities

Three concessional lending facilities for low-income countries are available.

	Extended Credit Facility (ECF)	Standby Credit Facility (SCF)	Rapid Credit Facility (RCF)
Objective	Help low-income countries achieve and maintain a stable and sustainable macroeconomic position consistent with strong and durable poverty reduction and growth	Very strong ex ante macroeconomic fundamentals, economic policy framework, and policy track record	Approved access available up front throughout the arrangement period, subject to a midterm review after 1 year
Purpose	Address protracted balance-of-payments problems	Resolve short-term balance of payments needs	Low-access financing to meet urgent balance-of-payments needs
Supersedes	Poverty Reduction and Growth Facility (PRGF)	Exogenous Shocks Facility–High- Access Component (ESF-HAC)	Exogenous Shocks Facility–Rapid Access Component (ESF-RAC), subsidized Emergency Post-Conflict Assistance (EPCA), and Emergency Natural Disaster Assistance (ENDA)
Eligibility	Countries eligible under the Poverty Reduction and Growth Trust (PRGT)	Efforts to solve balance-of-payments difficulties (may include prior actions)	Outright purchases without the need for full-fledged program or reviews
Qualification	Protracted balance of payments problem; actual financing need over the course of the arrangement, though not necessarily when lending is approved or disbursed	Potential (precautionary use) or actual short-term balance-of-payments need at the time of approval; actual need required for each disbursement	Urgent balance-of-payments need when upper- credit-tranche (UCT) program is either not feasible or not needed[1]
Poverty Reduction and Growth Strategy	IMF-supported program should be aligned with country-owned poverty-reduction and growth objectives and should aim to support policies that safeguard social and other priority spending			
	Submission of Poverty Reduction Strategy (PRS) document by second review	Submission of PRS document not required; if financing need persists, SCF user would request an ECF with associated PRS documentation requirements	Submission of PRS document not required; move to ECF facilitated in cases of repeated use by preparation of a Poverty Reduction Strategy Paper (PRSP)
Conditionality	UCT; flexibility on adjustment path and timing	UCT; aim to resolve balance-of-payments need in the short term	No UCT and no conditionality based on ex post review; track record used to qualify for repeat use (except under shocks window)

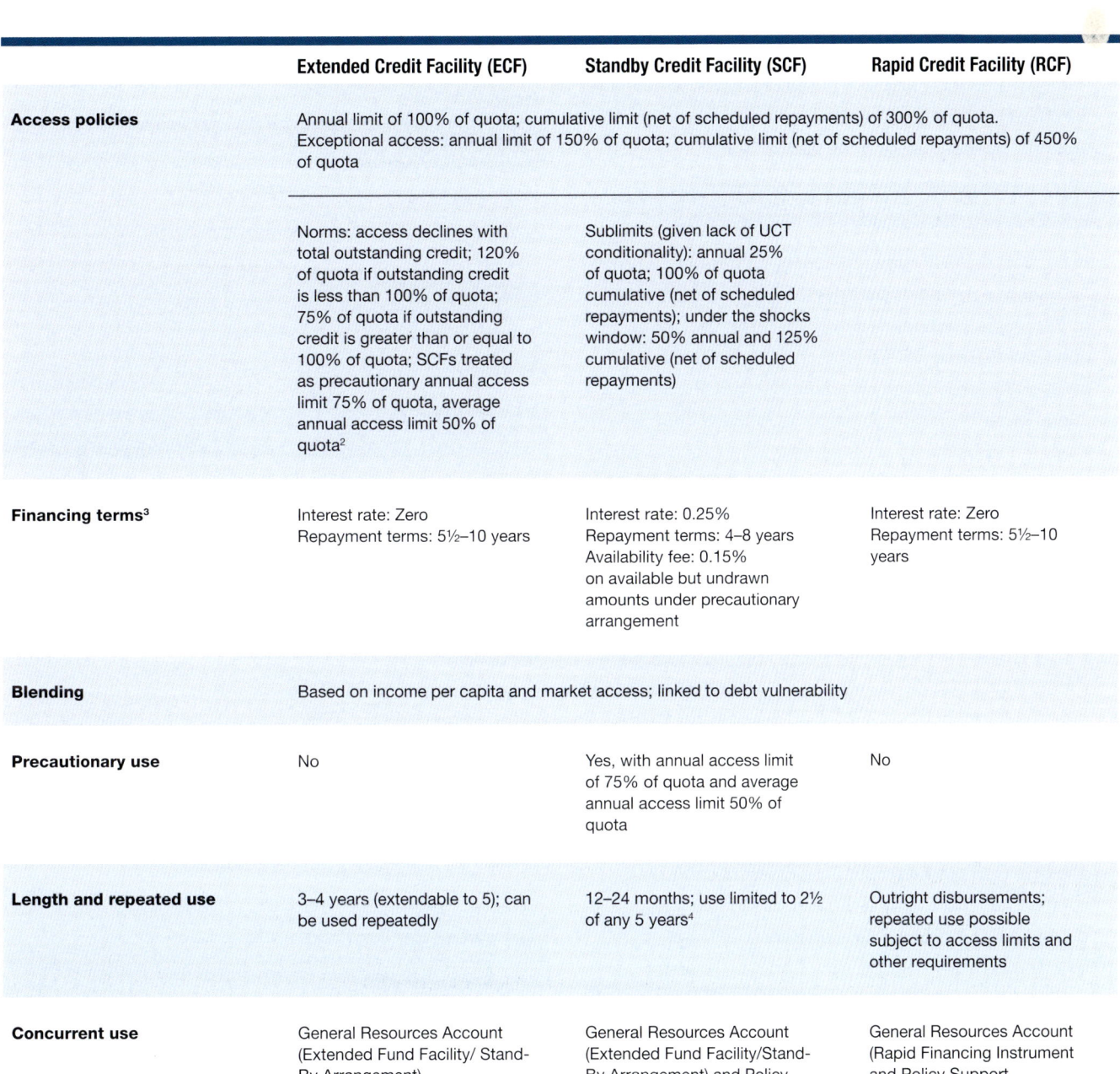

	Extended Credit Facility (ECF)	Standby Credit Facility (SCF)	Rapid Credit Facility (RCF)
Access policies	Annual limit of 100% of quota; cumulative limit (net of scheduled repayments) of 300% of quota. Exceptional access: annual limit of 150% of quota; cumulative limit (net of scheduled repayments) of 450% of quota		
	Norms: access declines with total outstanding credit; 120% of quota if outstanding credit is less than 100% of quota; 75% of quota if outstanding credit is greater than or equal to 100% of quota; SCFs treated as precautionary annual access limit 75% of quota, average annual access limit 50% of quota[2]	Sublimits (given lack of UCT conditionality): annual 25% of quota; 100% of quota cumulative (net of scheduled repayments); under the shocks window: 50% annual and 125% cumulative (net of scheduled repayments)	
Financing terms[3]	Interest rate: Zero Repayment terms: 5½–10 years	Interest rate: 0.25% Repayment terms: 4–8 years Availability fee: 0.15% on available but undrawn amounts under precautionary arrangement	Interest rate: Zero Repayment terms: 5½–10 years
Blending	Based on income per capita and market access; linked to debt vulnerability		
Precautionary use	No	Yes, with annual access limit of 75% of quota and average annual access limit 50% of quota	No
Length and repeated use	3–4 years (extendable to 5); can be used repeatedly	12–24 months; use limited to 2½ of any 5 years[4]	Outright disbursements; repeated use possible subject to access limits and other requirements
Concurrent use	General Resources Account (Extended Fund Facility/ Stand-By Arrangement)	General Resources Account (Extended Fund Facility/Stand-By Arrangement) and Policy Support Instrument	General Resources Account (Rapid Financing Instrument and Policy Support Instrument)

Source: IMF Finance Department.

[1] UCT standard conditionality is the set of program-related conditions intended to ensure that IMF resources support the program's objectives, with adequate safeguards to the IMF resources.

[2] Access norms do not apply when outstanding concessional credit is above 200% of quota. In those cases, access is guided by consideration of the access limit of 300% of quota, expectation of future need for IMF support, and the repayment schedule.

[3] The IMF reviews interest rates for all concessional facilities under the PRGT every 2 years; the next review is expected at the end of 2014. The Executive Board has approved a temporary interest waiver on concessional loans through the end of December 2014 in view of the global economic crisis (Box 3.5).

[4] SCFs treated as precautionary do not count toward the time limits.

stock of GRA credit falling from SDR 81.2 billion ($114.2 billion) to SDR 55.2 billion ($78 billion) in FY2015. Table 2.1 details the arrangements approved during the year, and Figure 2.1 the arrangements approved over the past 10 years. Tables 2.2 and 2.3 provide general information about the IMF's financing instruments and facilities, with Figure 2.2 offering information on nonconcessional financing amounts outstanding over the past 10 years.

CONCESSIONAL FINANCING ACTIVITY

In FY2015, the IMF committed loans amounting to SDR 1.8 billion to its low-income developing member countries under programs supported by the Poverty Reduction and Growth Trust (PRGT). Total concessional loans outstanding of 58 members amounted to SDR 6.3 billion at end-April 2015. Table 2.4 provides detailed information on new arrangements and augmentations of access under the IMF's concessional financing facilities, and Table 2.5 on IMF support to Ebola-afflicted countries. Figure 2.3 illustrates amounts outstanding on concessional loans over the past decade.

The IMF provided grants to be used as debt relief to eligible countries through the newly created Catastrophe Containment and Relief Trust (CCRT), transforming the Post-Catastrophe Debt Relief (PCDR) Trust. The CCRT, established in February 2015, expanded the circumstances under which the IMF can provide exceptional assistance to its low-income members to include public health disasters that could spread rapidly across borders. The CCRT provides exceptional support to countries confronting major natural disasters, including life-threatening, fast-spreading epidemics with the potential to spread to other countries, but also other types of catastrophic disasters such as massive earthquakes. As of end-April 2015, the IMF had provided grants under this Trust to cover debt relief of SDR 68 million to the three countries worst hit by the Ebola epidemic (Guinea, SDR 21.42 million; Liberia, SDR 25.84 million; and Sierra Leone, SDR 20.74 million).

Apart from CCRT relief, the IMF had also provided a total of SDR 5.2 billion of debt relief to eligible countries as of end-April 2015. This includes assistance under the Heavily Indebted Poor Countries (HIPC) Initiative of SDR 2.6 billion to 36 countries, debt relief under the

Table **2.4**

Arrangements approved and augmented under the Poverty Reduction and Growth Trust in FY2015
(Millions of SDRs)

Member	Effective date	Amount approved
NEW THREE-YEAR EXTENDED CREDIT FACILITY[1] ARRANGEMENTS		
Chad	August 1, 2014	79.9
Ghana	April 3, 2015	664.2
Grenada	June 26, 2014	14.0
Kyrgyz Republic	April 8, 2015	66.6
Yemen	September 2, 2014	365.3
Subtotal		**1,190.0**
AUGMENTATIONS OF EXTENDED CREDIT FACILITY ARRANGEMENTS[2]		
Burundi	March 23, 2015	10.0
Chad	April 27, 2015	26.6
Côte d'Ivoire	December 5, 2014	130.1
Guinea	February 11, 2015	45.1
Liberia	September 26, 2014	32.3
Sierra Leone	September 26, 2014	25.9
Sierra Leone	March 2, 2015	51.9
Subtotal		**321.9**
NEW STANDBY CREDIT FACILITY ARRANGEMENTS		
Honduras	December 3, 2014	51.8
Kenya	February 2, 2015	135.7
Subtotal		**187.5**
DISBURSEMENTS UNDER RAPID CREDIT FACILITY		
Central African Republic	May 14, 2014	8.4
Central African Republic	March 18, 2015	5.6
Gambia	April 2, 2015	7.8
Guinea	September 26, 2014	26.8
Guinea-Bissau	November 3, 2014	3.6
Liberia	February 23, 2015	32.3
Madagascar	June 18, 2014	30.6
St. Vincent and the Grenadines	August 1, 2014	2.1
Subtotal		**117.0**
TOTAL		**1,816.4**

Source: IMF Finance Department.

[1] Previously Poverty Reduction Growth Facility.

[2] For augmentation, only the amount of the increase is shown.

Table **2.5**

IMF support to Ebola-afflicted countries, June 2014–April 2015

(Millions of SDRs or otherwise noted)

	Approval date	Amount committed in SDR	Disbursement date	Amount disbursed in SDR
GUINEA				
RCF disbursement	October 2, 2014	26.8	October 2, 2014	26.8
ECF augmentation[1]	February 11, 2015	45.1	February 18, 2015	26.8
Debt relief	March 18, 2015	21.4	March 19, 2015	21.4
Total		93.3		75.0
LIBERIA				
RCF disbursement	February 27, 2015	32.3	February 27, 2015	32.3
ECF augmentation	September 26, 2014	32.3	October 2, 2014	32.3
Debt relief	February 23, 2015	25.8	February 24, 2015	25.8
Total		90.4		90.4
SIERRA LEONE				
ECF augmentation	September 26, 2014	25.9	October 2, 2014	25.9
ECF augmentation[2]	March 2, 2015	51.9	March 6, 2015	51.9
Debt relief	March 2, 2015	20.7	March 3, 2015	20.7
Total		98.5		98.5
TOTAL		282.3		263.9

Source: IMF Finance Department.

Note: Total amounts disbursed to Guinea on February 18, 2015 and Sierra Leone on March 6, 2015 include augmentations and regular tranches of previously approved ECFs.

RCF: Rapid Credit Facility.

ECF: Extended Credit Facility.

[1] Guinea's ECF augmentation is disbursed in two tranches, with the second one planned for a forthcoming review.

[2] The augmentation responded to financing needs arising from the Ebola epidemic as well as an adverse commodities shock.

Multilateral Debt Relief Initiative (MDRI) of SDR 2.3 billion to 30 countries, "beyond HIPC" debt relief to Liberia, and debt relief under the PCDR Trust to Haiti. All countries that reached the completion point under the enhanced HIPC Initiative, and those with per capita incomes below $380 and outstanding debt to the IMF at end-2004, also received debt relief under the MDRI. Afghanistan, Comoros, Haiti, and Togo did not have MDRI-eligible debt with the IMF, while Chad, Côte d'Ivoire, and Guinea had fully repaid MDRI-eligible debt to the IMF by the completion point date. These countries, therefore, did not receive debt relief under the MDRI from the IMF.

More Flexible Public Debt Limits

The Board began discussing reform of the IMF's policy on the use of conditionality on public external debt in Fund-supported programs—also known as the "debt limits policy"—in March 2013. The discussion took place against a backdrop of lower-income countries seeking to boost growth through higher public investment levels, targeted in particular at large infrastructure gaps, while facing both a wider range of financing opportunities and limits on the supply of traditional concessional financing.

The "Big Three"

Figure **2.1**

Arrangements approved during financial years ended April 30, 2006–15

(Billions of SDRs)

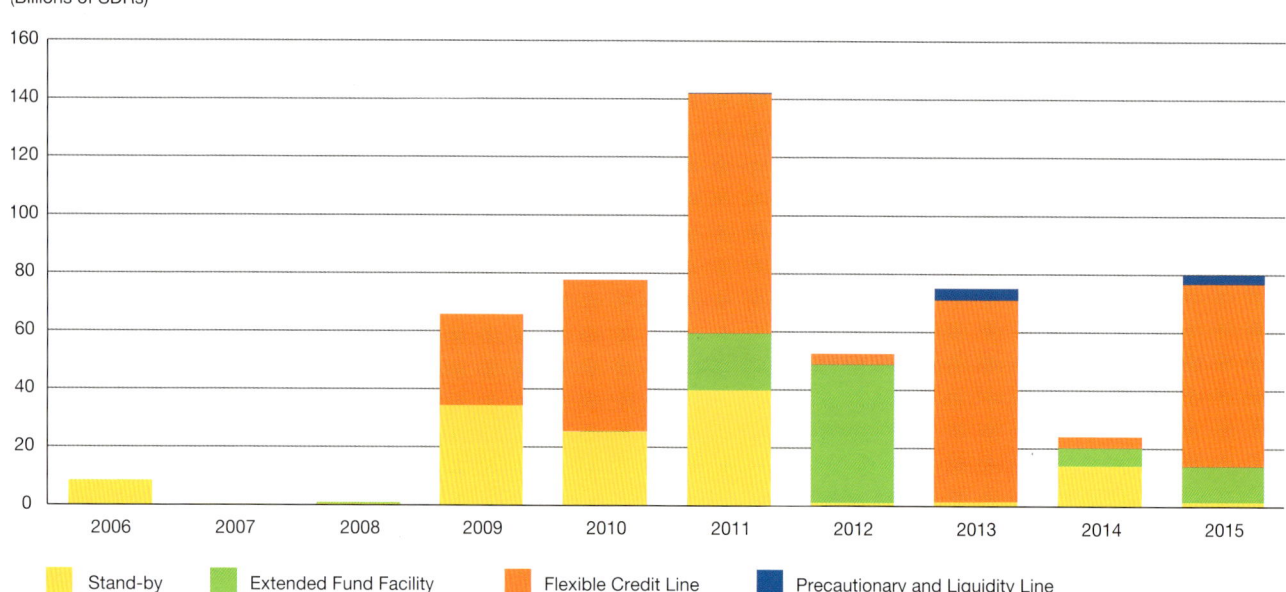

Source: IMF Finance Department.

Figure **2.2**

Nonconcessional loans outstanding FY2006–15

(Billions of SDRs)

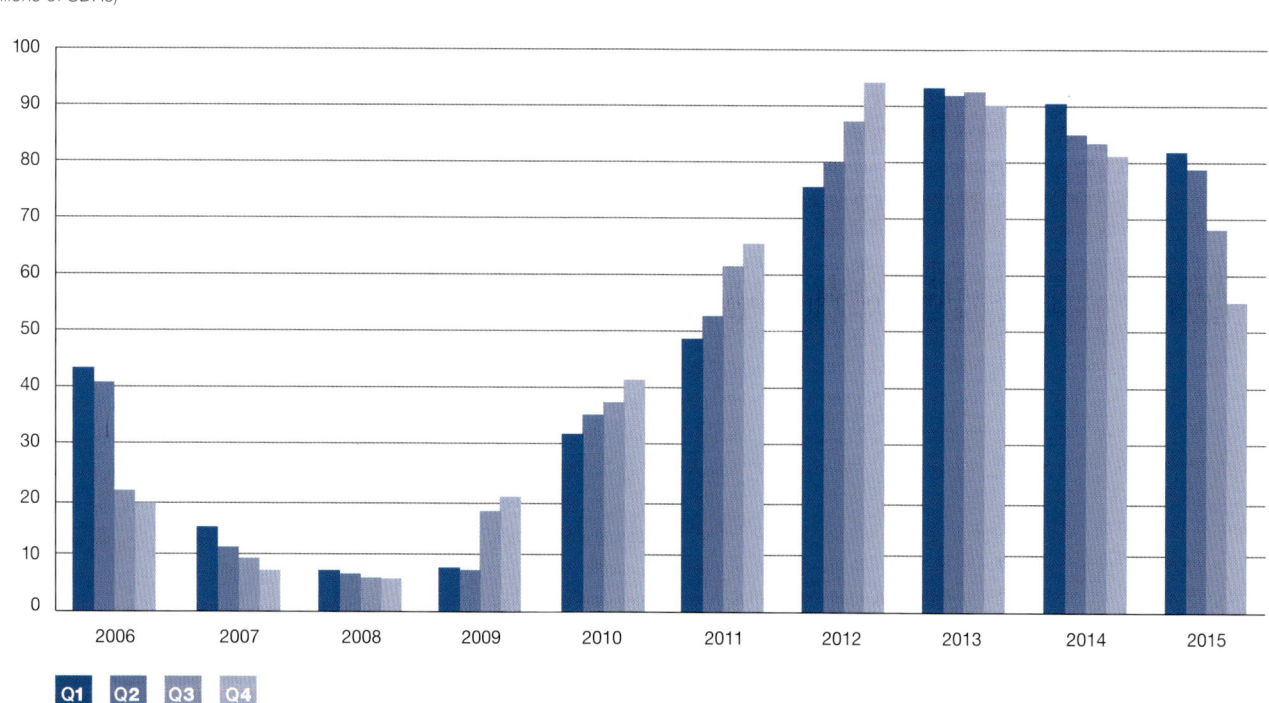

Source: IMF Finance Department

Figure **2.3**
Concessional loans outstanding FY2006–15
(Billions of SDRs)

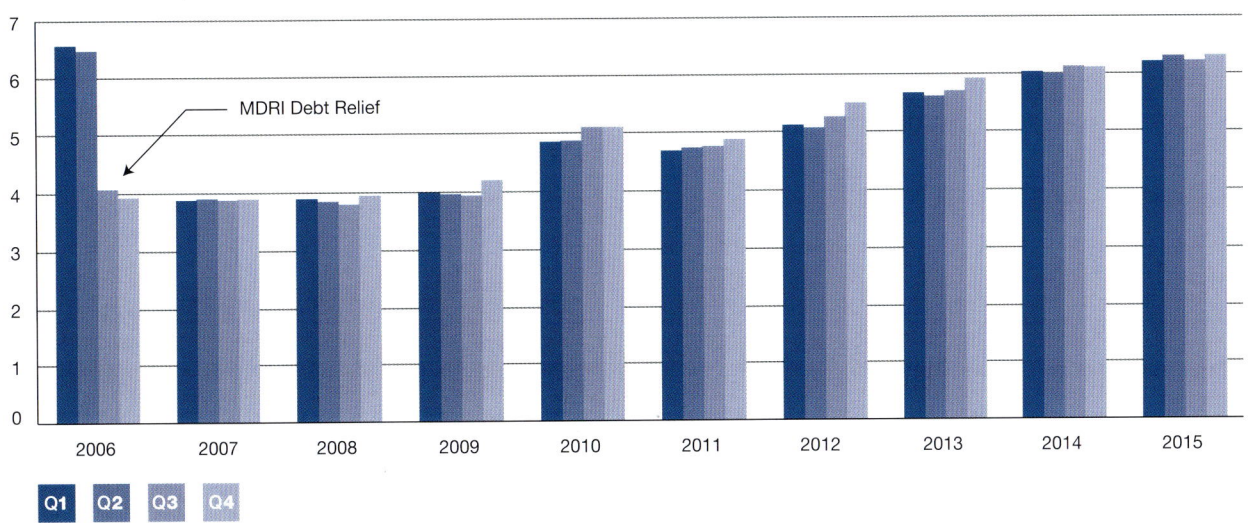

Source: IMF Finance Department.
Note: MDRI: Multilateral Debt Relief Initiative

Box 2.3 Supporting Tunisia's revival

After Tunisia's January 2011 revolution and a period in which growth declined sharply, the country's economy embarked on a moderate recovery despite a difficult political transition and an uncertain international economic environment.

Throughout the political transition to new elections, the country made progress on reforms needed to achieve short-term macroeconomic stabilization and address the challenges of widespread social and economic disparities and a fragile banking sector. The successful end of the political transition and the installation of a post-transition government with broad support in parliament provide an opportunity to push further ahead with reforms needed to address these challenges. Key elements of the government's program are to:

Build up fiscal and external buffers with appropriate fiscal, monetary, and exchange rate policies.

Support growth by addressing critical vulnerabilities in the banking sector and improving the investment climate through reforms of the tax and investment regimes.

Strengthen social safety nets to protect the vulnerable.

The authorities also reduced regressive energy subsidies, creating room to increase social and investment spending. This included increased social transfers to vulnerable households and the introduction of a social electricity tariff that protects poorer households.

In support of the reform agenda, in June 2013 the Executive Board approved a 24-month Stand-By Arrangement (SBA) amounting to about $1.75 billion. In December 2014, the Board completed the fifth review under the SBA, bringing total disbursements to $1.15 billion, and in May 2015, approved a seven-month extension of the SBA to December 31, 2015.

The IMF also supports Tunisia by providing technical assistance for tax policy and revenue administration, improving public financial management, strengthening the central bank's supervision capacity and collateral framework, and improving the production of monetary statistics.

The reform of the IMF's policy on debt conditionality in 2009 was a first step to accommodate these new realities. But experience with the 2009 reforms pointed to the need for more fundamental reforms to provide countries with greater flexibility to finance productive investments while containing risks to medium-term debt sustainability.

In December 2014, the Executive Board endorsed the new Policy on Public Debt Limits in Fund-Supported Programs. In a press release, the Executive Board agreed that the new debt limits policy should take effect at end-June 2015.

The paper discussed at the Board sought to accommodate a number of concerns emphasized by Executive Directors and other stakeholders, including: (1) ensuring even-handedness across the membership in the application of the policy, consistent with the principle of uniformity of treatment; (2) ensuring that the coverage of debt limits is unified and comprehensive, covering both concessional and nonconcessional borrowing; and (3) ensuring that there are incentives for creditors to provide, and borrowers to seek, financing on concessional terms.

Executive Directors welcomed the opportunity to revisit debt conditionality in Fund-supported programs. They emphasized that reforms to the policy should balance debt sustainability and borrowing requirements for investment and growth. They agreed that the coverage of debt limits should be unified and comprehensive, covering both concessional and nonconcessional debt, and supported the principle that debt conditionality should cover all public debt. They also agreed that there should be incentives for creditors to provide, and for borrowers to seek, financing on concessional terms.

Directors agreed that the use of debt conditionality in Fund-supported programs is warranted when a member faces significant debt vulnerabilities, and that debt sustainability analysis should continue to play the key role in identifying debt vulnerabilities. Directors emphasized that the broad principles that will guide the new debt limits policy should be applied in a transparent and even-handed manner, and that the particular form of debt conditionality adopted should reflect country-specific circumstances and program goals.

Box 2.4 Zero-interest-rate policy for low-income countries

In December 2014 the Executive Board approved the third extension of the exceptional waiver on interest payments for IMF concessional loans through the end of 2016.

The Executive Board initially endorsed temporary relief of interest payments on all outstanding concessional loans to Poverty Reduction and Growth Trust (PRGT)-eligible members in 2009, waiving all interest payments on PRGT loans through December 2011. Three subsequent extensions of the exceptional interest rate waiver were approved by the Board, first to end-December 2012, then to end-2014, and the latest to end-2016.

The PRGT has three facilities: the Extended Credit Facility to provide flexible medium-term support, the Stand-By Credit Facility to address short-term and precautionary needs, and the Rapid Credit Facility to provide emergency support.

POLICY SUPPORT INSTRUMENTS

Policy Support Instruments (PSIs) offer low-income countries that do not want—or need—IMF financial assistance a flexible tool that enables them to secure Fund advice and support without a borrowing arrangement. This nonfinancial instrument is a valuable complement to the IMF's lending facilities under the PRGT. PSIs help countries design effective economic programs that deliver clear signals to donors, creditors, and the general public on the strength of a member's policies.

In July 2014, the Executive Board approved a new three-year PSI for Tanzania. The IMF had previously concluded the final review of the country's economic performance under a Stand-By Credit Facility arrangement and under a previous PSI, together with the Article IV consultation with the country in April. The PSI for Tanzania aims to support the authorities' medium-term objectives, which include maintaining macroeconomic stability, preserving debt sustainability, and promoting more equitable growth and job creation.

As of April 2015, the Executive Board had approved 17 PSIs for seven members: Cabo Verde, Mozambique, Nigeria, Rwanda, Senegal, Tanzania, and Uganda.

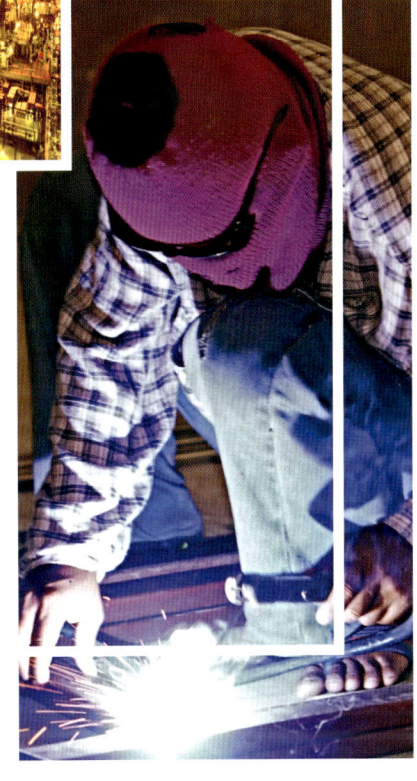

Capacity Development

The IMF shares its expertise with officials in member countries and provides training to them—what it calls "capacity development"—to help countries build strong institutions and boost skills to formulate and implement sound macroeconomic and financial policies. Capacity development is closely linked to the IMF's surveillance and lending activities and highly appreciated by member countries.

Technical assistance and training activities have expanded rapidly to meet member countries' extensive demands.

Capacity development represented about a quarter of the IMF's administrative expenditures in FY2015.

Most of this spending was on technical assistance, which represents 22 percent, while training accounts for 4 percent (see Figure 2.4).

Following an informal meeting of the IMF's Executive Board in April 2014, a new statement on IMF Policies and Practices on Capacity Development was approved by the Board in September 2014. The statement superseded the 2001 Policy Statement on IMF Technical Assistance, while incorporating the principles outlined in the 2013 capacity development strategy paper also approved by the Executive Board.

The strong growth in IMF capacity development activities supported by donor funding since 2009 tapered off in FY2015, mainly reflecting institutional and resource constraints. Total direct spending on capacity development activities (externally and IMF-financed) was $242 million in FY2015, compared with $237 million in FY2014, a growth of 2 percent (Figure 2.5). Growth of externally funded capacity development slowed to 1.7 percent in FY2015 from 7.2 percent in FY2014 and 17.4 percent in FY2013.

TECHNICAL ASSISTANCE

Technical assistance delivery increased in FY2015, mainly in the sub-Saharan African, Asia-Pacific, and Western Hemisphere regions (Figure 2.6).

About half of all IMF technical assistance continued to go to low-income developing countries (Figure 2.7).

Figure **2.4**
Share of costs of major IMF activities, FY2015

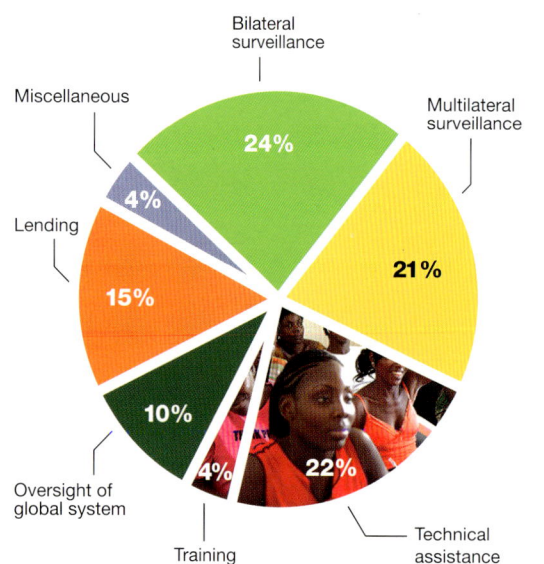

Source: Office of Budget and Planning, Analytic Costing and Estimation System (ACES).

Figure **2.5**
Spending on capacity development, FY2012–15
(Millions of U.S. dollars)

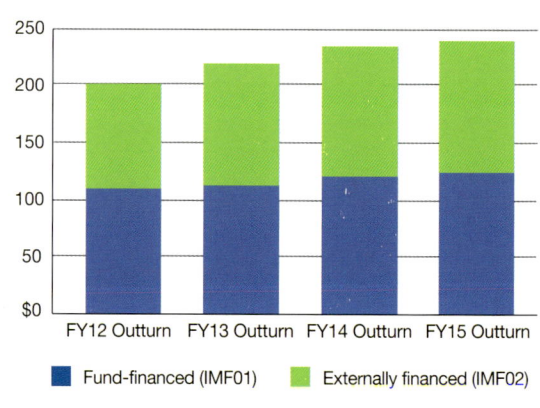

Source: IMF Office of Budget and Planning, Analytic Costing and Estimation System (ACES).

Figure **2.6**
Technical assistance delivery by region, FY2012–15
(Person-years of field delivery)

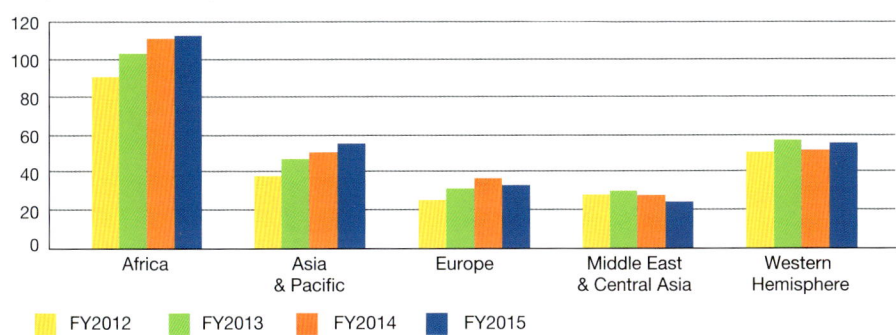

Source: IMF Travel Information Management System.

In FY2015, sub-Saharan Africa accounted for the largest share of technical assistance, reflecting the high number of low-income developing countries in this region.

Delivery of technical assistance on monetary and financial topics and on statistical topics has been increasing recently, in response to demand from the membership (Figure 2.8). Fiscal topics continued to be the main area of technical assistance provided by the IMF. The IMF has also been developing a suite of fiscal assessment tools to strengthen the analytical basis for fiscal surveillance, guide structural fiscal reforms, and set priorities for technical assistance. Seven main fiscal assessment tools are currently operational or undergoing testing (see Box 2.5).

Highlights of fiscal capacity building
The IMF continued to respond swiftly to meet both longer-term capacity development and more urgent technical assistance needs in a broad set

Figure **2.7**
Technical assistance delivery by income group, FY2012–15
(Person-years of field delivery)

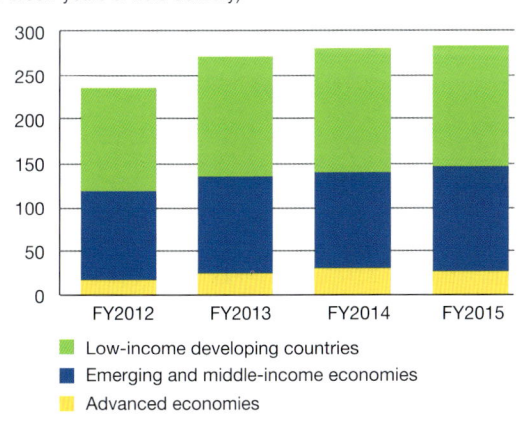

Source: IMF Travel Information Management System.

Figure **2.8**
Technical assistance delivery by topic, FY2012–15
(Person-years of field delivery)

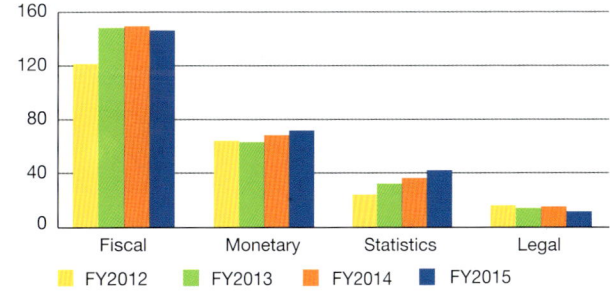

Source: IMF Travel Information Management System.

Box 2.5: Fiscal assessment tools

The IMF's standardized fiscal assessment tools review the fiscal institutional frameworks that countries have in place and help identify priorities for fiscal reform and technical assistance.

Revenue Administration Fiscal Information Tool (RA-FIT) gathers and analyzes tax and customs information, and establishes baseline indicators relating to administration performance. A first report based on the submissions of 85 countries in the first round of data gathering was prepared in 2014. A second round of data gathering was conducted in 2014 and 2015 via an online data-capture portal. Collaboration with other international organizations is proceeding with the goal of making RA-FIT the standard platform for capture, analysis, and dissemination of revenue administration information.

Revenue Administration Gap Analysis Program (RA-GAP) estimates the gap between current and potential revenue collections. Detailed gap estimates for value-added tax were broadened to eight countries from four countries during FY2015.

Tax Administration Diagnostic Assessment Tool (TADAT) provides a framework for standardized assessments of tax administration performance to help improve prioritization and sequencing of reforms; it is designed and governed in close cooperation with international partners. TADAT is still in the piloting phase, and four additional country pilots were successfully concluded in FY2015. The framework will be tested in about seven more countries before being rolled out for public use in November 2015. An online course is being launched in mid-May 2015 to train prospective TADAT assessors.

Fiscal Transparency Evaluations (FTEs) replace the fiscal module of the Reports on the Observance of Standards and Codes. They offer a four-pillar structure for assessing the quality of published information with a strong focus on identifying and managing fiscal risks. Five new FTEs were published in FY2015, and further FTEs are scheduled for FY2016. The framework is to be finalized in FY2016 with the completion of pillar 4 on resource revenue management and a *Fiscal Transparency Manual*.

Fiscal Analysis of Resource Industries (FARI) is a modeling framework to perform fiscal analysis of extractive industries (EIs). FARI provides a powerful tool for evaluating, comparing, and designing fiscal regimes for EIs by analyzing how annual project cash flows over the life of an EI project are shared between investors and the government, through detailed modeling of a particular fiscal regime.

Public-Private Partnership Fiscal Risk Assessment Model (P-FRAM) is an analytical tool to assess potential fiscal costs and risks arising from public-private partnerships. It is designed to provide a structured and guided process for gathering relevant data, quantifying the impact on deficit and debt, and performing sensitivity analysis to changes in key macroeconomic and project-specific parameters.

Public Investment Management Assessment (PIMA) is a framework designed to evaluate the strength of public investment management practices in a comprehensive manner. It evaluates institutions shaping decision-making at three key stages: planning, allocating, and implementing investment. PIMAs assess institutional strengths and weaknesses, and provide practical recommendations to improve public investment management institutions. The PIMA framework will be piloted in FY2016.

of countries. In **Ukraine**, the IMF has in place a broad-based technical assistance program that has supported, among other projects, reforms aimed at strengthening the authorities' long-term capacity to formulate and implement sound macroeconomic and financial sector policies, as well as reforms of the pension system and energy subsidies, developing a framework for managing state-owned enterprises, reviewing public financial management systems, and evaluating tax policy issues, including taxation of high-wealth individuals, establishing an institutional framework to prevent corruption, social security contributions, agricultural and international taxation, and subnational taxation powers. In **Egypt** and **Tunisia**, the IMF provided support for public financial management, and tax and revenue administration reforms.

The IMF has been providing advice in resource-rich countries aimed at reducing revenue volatility and broadening the revenue base.

In **Angola**, the IMF delivered technical assistance on fuel subsidy reform and modernizing revenue administration. In **Tanzania**, the IMF supported the preparation of a fiscal and budget policy

framework for the management of revenues from natural gas production. In **Kenya**, the IMF assisted in the design and implementation of the new petroleum fiscal regime. Mongolia was one of the first countries to benefit from a new natural resource revenue template that the IMF has developed to enhance transparency of these revenue flows and help mobilize domestic revenue. The template has been endorsed by the Extractive Industries Transparency Initiative, a global standard to promote open and accountable management of natural resources. In **Lebanon**, the IMF has held various interactive workshops with the authorities on tax policy issues for the country's nascent gas sector. The IMF also helped introduce a new consumer price index that reflects significantly improved compilation methods, including expanded coverage.

In response to the **Ebola outbreak in West Africa**, the IMF delivered urgently required technical assistance remotely from headquarters and the African Regional Technical Assistance Centers AFRITAC West 2 Regional Technical Assistance Center (RTAC). This assistance included advice to Liberia on the final phase of implementing a semi-autonomous revenue authority and planning for the introduction of a value-added tax. Remote technical assistance delivery was also provided to

Sierra Leone to improve the tax administration's capacity to assess and collect revenues from the extractive industry, as well as to Guinea to maintain capacity in public financial management and further improve national accounts statistics.

Highlights of monetary and financial sector capacity building

In the monetary and financial sector areas, the IMF deepened its engagement as well and launched new technical assistance programs to promote financial stability in low- and middle-income countries. Comprehensive technical assistance programs were implemented bilaterally and regionally to identify and manage financial sector vulnerabilities, strengthen regulatory and supervisory frameworks, support IMF lending programs, and build institutional capacities.

For example, banking supervision technical assistance in Cambodia, Myanmar, Nepal, and the Philippines helped establish the fundamental supervisory and regulatory infrastructure to safeguard financial stability.

Myanmar also received support in monetary operations, foreign exchange market operations, and central bank financial management. Countries in the Caribbean received technical assistance in the area of banking supervision and bank resolution; Barbados, Belize, Jamaica, and Suriname received assistance to improve the functioning of their domestic debt markets, and in central banking. Monetary and financial sector support to fragile and postconflict countries was provided in Democratic Republic of Congo, Somalia, and South Sudan.

In **South Sudan**, technical assistance aimed at supporting financial and macroeconomic stability through strengthening the Bank of South Sudan's institutional capacity and frameworks continued to progress despite a break due to security issues in the country. In **Somalia**, with the support of a new donor trust fund (see section on donor support below), assistance focused on establishing core activities of the central bank and building capacity for financial sector oversight and surveillance. In the **Democratic Republic of the Congo**, a multiyear program continued to make progress in strengthening financial sector supervision and regulation and implementing the central bank's modernization program.

Highlights of statistics capacity building

The IMF's technical assistance in **macroeconomic statistics** has increased significantly during the past few years (FY2012–15), posting a 76 percent increase. This growth was made possible through strengthened partnerships with donors, enabling the IMF to respond to the rising demand for capacity development compounded by the impact of the global financial crisis.

For example, in the Asia-Pacific region, 15 countries started to compile and disseminate balance-of-payments and international investment position (IIP) statistics in line with the *Balance of Payments and International Investment Position Manual* (BPM6), while 11 countries have for the first time submitted balance-of-payments or IIP statistics to the IMF for publication. Furthermore, 11 Asian countries started to report annual government finance statistics to the IMF with nine reporting high frequency data. Six countries began participating in the IMF–World Bank quarterly public sector debt database.

In the area of real sector statistics, notable outcomes include the implementation of the *System of National Accounts 2008*, the latest version of the international statistical standard for the national accounts, adopted by the United Nations, in Belarus, Bosnia, Macedonia, Moldova, Montenegro, and Serbia; the development of quarterly national accounts in Bosnia, Moldova, and Montenegro; and advances in the quality of price and merchandise trade statistics in some beneficiary countries.

Demand for legal technical assistance in both program and nonprogram countries continued in FY2015 in the areas of anti-money laundering and combating the financing of terrorism, financial and fiscal law, insolvency, and judicial reform. On tax law, new fields such as legal underpinnings for tax administration and natural resource taxation expanded in FY2015.

RTACs are instrumental in providing hands-on and longer-term reform implementation support and guidance to country authorities in a range of fiscal, macroeconomic statistics, and financial sector areas, including public financial management, tax administration, macro-fiscal analysis, national accounts and price statistics, external sector statistics, government finance statistics, banking supervision and regulation, monetary and foreign exchange operations, and debt management.

Technical assistance provided by the IMF through RTACs reached a peak of 38.3 percent of the total delivered in FY2015 (Figure 2.9).

Currently, nine centers serve countries in Africa, the Caribbean, Central America, the Middle East, and the Pacific.

Figure **2.9**
Technical assistance delivery through Regional Technical Assistance Centers (RTACs), FY2012–15
(Person-years of field delivery)

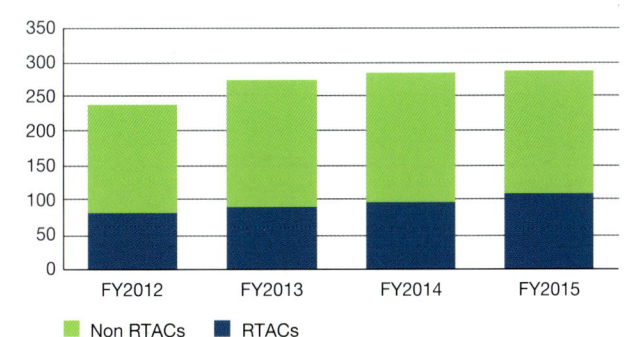

Source: IMF Travel Information Management System (TIMS).

The IMF's training program is an integral part of the IMF's capacity development mandate and strives to respond to evolving global macroeconomic developments and policy challenges, membership demands, and technological innovations. Last year, the IMF's Institute for Capacity Development added new topics of strategic importance for the IMF's membership, such as debt sustainability and energy subsidy reforms. The courses provide theoretical lectures, analytical tools, and hands-on workshops. The IMF's online learning courses, which are free and open to anyone with an Internet connection, continued to grow, with the addition of one course on Energy Subsidy Reform and the translation into French of the Financial Programming and Policies, Part 1 course. Online training grew sharply by 38 percent to 13 percent of total IMF training in FY2015.

During FY2015, 345 training events were delivered by the IMF to its members, with some 11,315 officials attending them. Emerging market economies received the largest volume of IMF training, at about 53 percent of the total for the year (Figure 2.10). In terms of regional distribution, sub-Saharan Africa, Asia and the Pacific, and the Middle East and Central Asia received the largest volume of IMF training during the year (Figure 2.11).

DONOR SUPPORT FOR CAPACITY DEVELOPMENT

Donor support continues to bolster the IMF's ability to deliver technical assistance and training to member countries. New contributions totaling $145 million were received during FY2015, and activities financed by donors totaled $152 million. The IMF leverages external support for capacity development through several vehicles, including RTACs, Regional Training Centers, Topical Trust Funds, and bilateral partnerships.

Multidonor vehicles have been effective in delivering technical assistance and training to low- and lower-middle-income countries. The network of nine RTACs in the Pacific, the Middle East, Africa, the Caribbean, and Central America provided hands-on technical assistance and training. With the support of these centers, member countries achieved tangible results in reforming their economic and financial institutions. Topical Trust Funds offer specialized advice based on the latest research and draw on

Figure **2.10**
IMF training participation by income group, FY2012–15
(Participant-weeks of training)

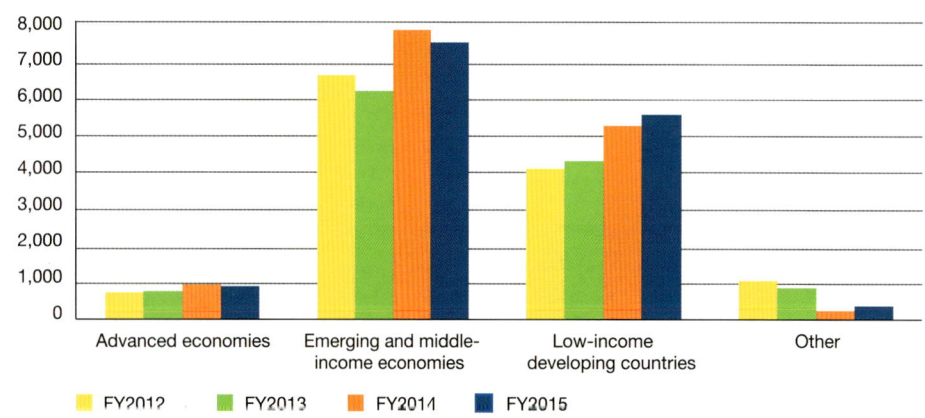

Source: Participant and Applicant Tracking System (PATS).

the IMF's global experiences. There are now two country-focused and seven thematic Topical Trust Funds.

In FY2015, the Somalia Trust Fund for Capacity Development was successfully launched with $6.6 million in donor commitments. With the receipt of a $3.1 million contribution from Norway during the year, the South Sudan Trust Fund's $10.2 million program is now fully funded. A second five-year phase of the trust fund for Anti-Money Laundering and Combating the Financing of Terrorism began in May 2014. The new Tax Administration Diagnostic Assessment Tool Trust Fund contributes to improving tax administration functions in member countries.

Independent mid-term evaluations of five RTACs, the Tax Policy and Administration Topical Trust Fund, and the Managing Natural Resources Wealth Topical Trust Fund found that these vehicles are delivering relevant, effective, and high-quality capacity development services.

The IMF expanded partnerships with longstanding donors on bilaterally funded projects. The top five donors to IMF capacity building are Japan, the European Union, Canada, the United Kingdom, and Switzerland. Japan, the

largest donor, made new contributions totaling $29.6 million to finance technical assistance and training, including two scholarship programs.

The IMF and the United Kingdom's Department for International Development (DFID) agreed on a new project to improve macroeconomic statistics in 44 countries in Africa and the Middle East under which DFID will provide about $9.3 million to support capacity development over the next five years.

The previous Enhanced Data Dissemination Initiative project was the first phase of a DFID-funded statistics project for Africa that was implemented by the IMF during 2010–15. It achieved many concrete results, helping numerous countries to produce for the first time quarterly national accounts, IIP statistics, and financial soundness indicators; rebase their national accounts; expand coverage in monetary statistics; increase the frequency and accuracy of government finance statistics; expand data dissemination by publishing national summary data pages and advance release calendars; and add more countries to the IMF's General Data Dissemination System and Special Data Dissemination Standard.

The "Big Three"

Figure **2.11**
IMF training participation by region, FY2012–15
(Participant-weeks of training)

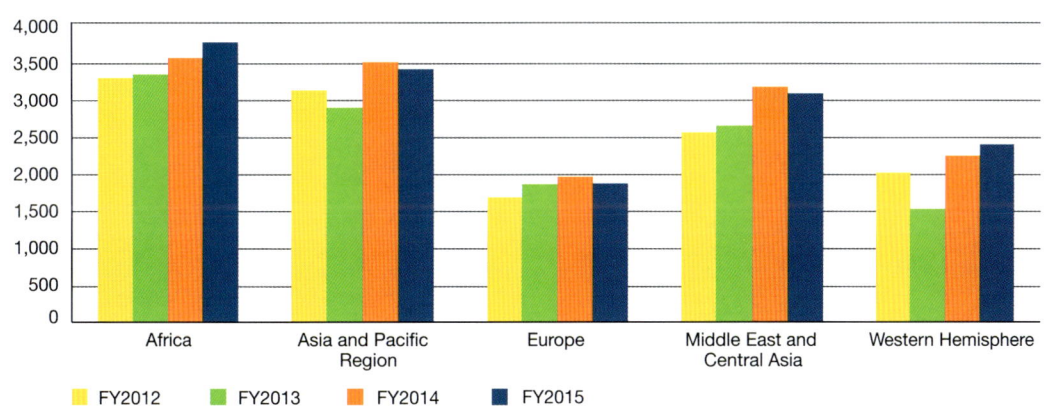

Source: Participant and Applicant Tracking System (PATS).

IMF Organization Chart

as of April 30, 2015

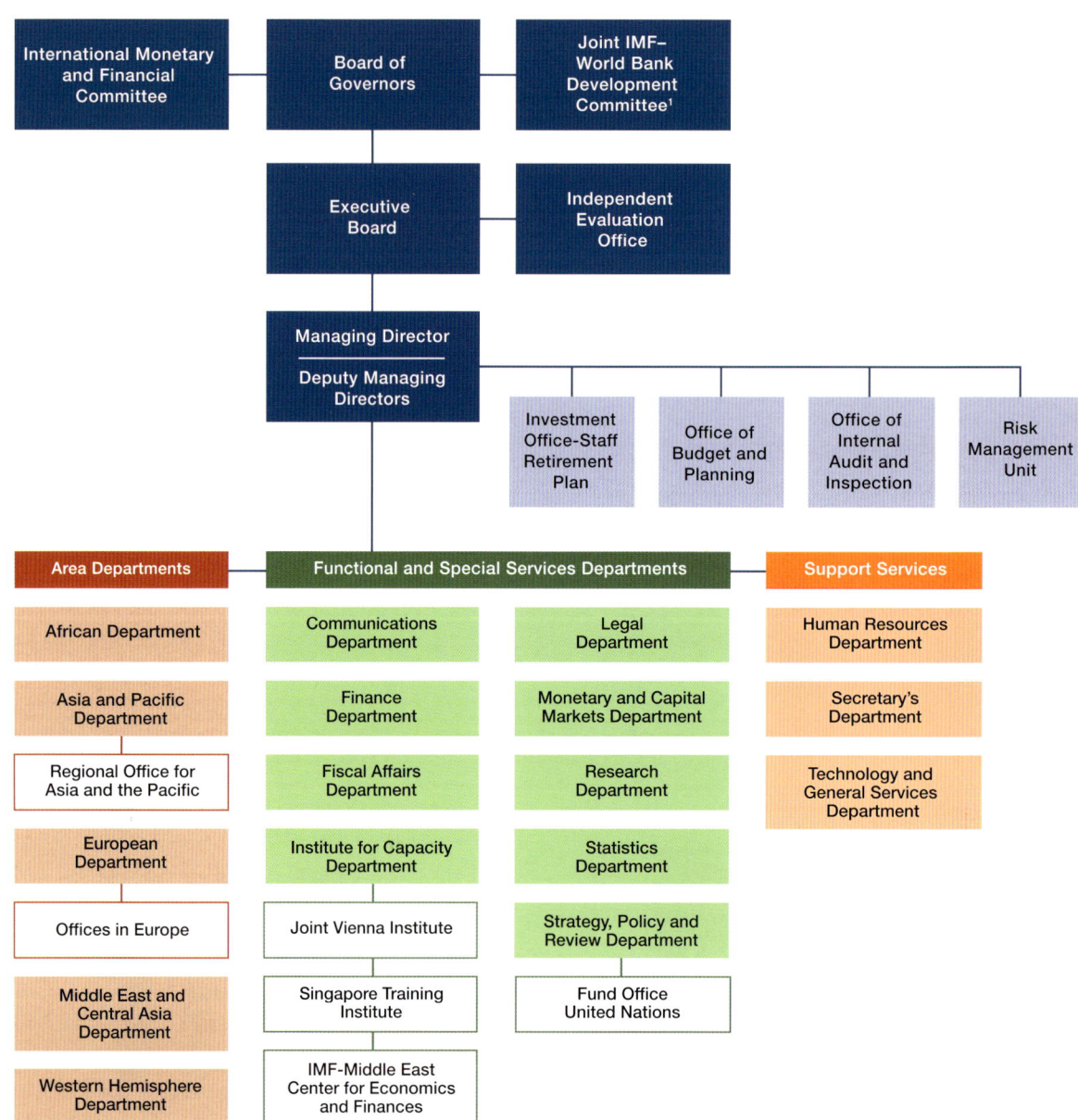

[1] Known formally as the Joint Ministerial Committee of the Boards of Governors of the Bank and the Fund on the Transfer of Real Resources to Developing Countries.

Part 3   Finances, Organization, and Accountability

The IMF's 24-member Executive Board takes care of the daily business of the IMF. Together, the 24 Board members represent all 188 member countries. Large economies, such as the United States and China, have their own seat at the table, but most countries are grouped in constituencies representing four or more countries. The largest constituency includes 23 countries.

formal board meetings

242

The Board usually meets several times each week. It carries out its work largely on the basis of papers prepared by IMF management and staff. The Board discusses everything from the annual health checks of member countries' economies to economic policy issues relevant to the global economy.

at the IMF

54 years

The IMF Executive Board during FY2015 celebrated the distinguished IMF career of its outgoing Dean, Mr. Shakour Shaalan, who represented Bahrain, Iraq, Jordan, Kuwait, Lebanon, Libya, Maldives, Oman, Qatar, Syria, United Arab Emirates, Yemen, and his native Egypt for 22 years at the Board. This followed a career as member of the Fund staff that began in 1961—for a total of 54 years at the IMF.

As Executive Director, Mr. Shaalan made important contributions to the work of the institution, especially in the realm of surveillance, quota and voice, and in calling for evenhanded treatment of members. He became Dean of the Executive Directors in 2007 and retired in October 2014.

board meetings on countries

179

The Board normally makes decisions based on consensus but sometimes formal votes are taken. Informal discussions may be held to discuss complex policy issues still at a preliminary stage.

Finances, Organization, and Accountability

In FY2015, the IMF operated within an unchanged budget envelope in real terms. This was the third year in row. Greater utilization and reallocation of the budget enabled the IMF to meet new demands. The IMF's income is generated primarily through its lending and investment activities. The IMF has in place a comprehensive audit framework, which comprises complementary, yet distinct, roles of the external audit, internal audit, and External Audit Committee. The IMF's staff of 2,611 come from 147 countries.

BUDGET AND INCOME

Medium-term budget

In April 2014, in the context of the FY2015–17 medium-term budget, the Executive Board authorized a total net administrative budget appropriation for FY2015 of $1,027 million. The Board also approved a limit on gross expenditures of $1,265 million, including up to $42 million in carry-forward of unspent FY2014 resources for possible spending in FY2015 (Table 3.1). It also approved capital expenditures of $52 million for building facilities and information technology capital projects.

The IMF work during the year continued to focus on supporting the still-weak global recovery in a sustainable way, a membership-wide priority covering advanced economies, particularly in Europe, emerging markets, and low-income developing countries. Actual administrative expenditures in FY2015 totaled $1,010 million, $17 million below the total net budget. The "underspend" continued the downward trend from the prior year and reflected greater utilization of the available budget. With vacancies declining, staffing expenses rose; separately the operating costs for the Annual and Spring Meetings increased due in part to the HQ1 building renovation; and physical security at overseas offices and information technology security costs grew.

Capital budget expenditures for facilities and information technology totaled $136 million, including amounts appropriated in prior years. Information technology spending totaled $29 million for core infrastructure replacements and upgrades, data management projects, and IT security. Progress continued on the multiyear HQ1 Renewal program, an occupied renovation in the construction phase.

For financial reporting purposes, the IMF administrative expenditures are accounted for on an accrual basis in accordance with International Financial Reporting Standards (IFRS). Those standards require accounting on an accrual basis and the recording and amortizing of employee benefit costs based on actuarial valuations. Table 3.2 provides a detailed reconciliation between the FY2015 net administrative budget outturn of $1,010 million and the IFRS-based administrative expenses of $1,262 million (SDR 857 million) reported in the IMF's audited financial statements for the year.

In April 2015, the Board approved a budget for FY2016, including net administrative expenditures of $1,052 million and a limit on gross expenditures of $1,290 million, including up to $43 million in carry-forward of unspent FY2015 resources. Indicative budgets for FY2017 and FY2018 were also presented to the Board. For the fourth year in a row, the limit on net administrative expenditures, excluding the carry-forward, remained unchanged in real terms relative to the prior year. The capital budget was set at $42 million, comprising $28 million for information technology and $14 million for building facilities projects. Budget formulation emphasized organizational efficiency as a means of accommodating new and ongoing strategic priorities. Departments stepped up efforts to reallocate resources away from lower priority activities and to achieve efficiency gains to help meet, within a flat budget envelope, the new priorities highlighted in the Global Policy Agenda.

Income, charges, remuneration, burden sharing, and a review of the IMF's charges and maturities

Income model

Since its establishment, the IMF's financing has relied primarily on its lending activities but has in recent years diversified its sources of income. Beginning in 2006, the IMF has invested its reserves to generate additional income. In 2008, the IMF Executive Board endorsed the

Table **3.1**

Budget by major expenditure category, FY2014–18

(Millions of U.S. dollars)

	FY2014		FY2015		FY2016	FY2017	FY2018
	Budget	**Outturn**	**Budget**	**Outturn**	**Budget**	**Budget**	**Budget**
ADMINISTRATIVE EXPENDITURES							
Personnel	861	829	893	862	910	934	960
Travel[1]	123	117	128	112	131	125	126
Buildings and other	190	203	196	204	197	200	204
Contingency reserves	12	...	7	...	10	10	10
Total gross expenditures	**1,186**	**1,149**	**1,224**	**1,177**	**1,248**	**1,269**	**1,300**
Receipts[2]	-179	-160	-197	-167	-196	-200	-205
Total net budget	**1,007**	**989**	**1,027**	**1,010**	**1,052**	**1,070**	**1,095**
Carry-forward[3,4]	42	...	42	...	43		
Total net budget including carry-forward	**1,049**	**989**	**1,069**	**1,010**	**1,094**	**1,070**	**1,095**
Capital[5]							
Facilities and Information Technology	41	144	52	136	42	47	49
of which: HQ1 Renewal				**96**			

Source: IMF Office of Budget and Planning.

Note: Figures may not add to totals due to rounding.

[1] FY2016 include travel to the Annual Meetings held abroad.

[2] Includes donor-financed activities, cost-sharing arrangements with the World Bank, sales of publications, parking, and other miscellaneous revenue.

[3] Unspent resources are carried forward from the prior year under established rules.

[4] The carry-forward, along with the approved budget, define the limit on gross expenditures.

[5] Capital budget expenditures are generally available to be spent over a three-year period. A major building project like HQ1 Renewal is an exception, with spending expected to take place over a five-year period.

new income model that includes the establishment of an endowment funded from the profits from the sale of a limited portion of the institution's gold holdings. As the Fifth Amendment of the IMF's Articles of Agreement, another key element of the new income model became effective in February 2011, the IMF's investment authority was also broadened enabling the IMF to adapt its investment strategy over time and to enhance the expected return on its investments.

Charges

Reflecting the high levels of lending activities, the IMF's main source of income continues to come from charges levied on the outstanding use of credit. However, the relative contribution to the IMF's income from investment earnings, and in particular earnings on the investment of resources held in the endowment, which will be phased over a three-year period (funding to the endowment's strategic asset allocation started in March 2014), will increase over time. The basic rate of charge (the interest rate) on IMF nonconcessional financing comprises the SDR interest rate plus a margin expressed in basis points. For FY2015 and FY2016, the Executive Board agreed to keep the margin for the rate of charge at 100 basis points. Under the rule adopted by the Executive Board in December 2011, the margin is set so as to cover the IMF's lending-related intermediation costs and allow for a buildup of its reserves. In addition, the rule includes a cross-check to ensure that the rate of charge maintains a reasonable alignment against long-term credit market conditions.

Surcharges of 200 basis points are levied on the use of large amounts of credit (above 300 percent of a member's quota) in the credit tranches* and under Extended Fund Facility Arrangements; these are referred to as level-based surcharges. The IMF also levies time-based surcharges of 100 basis points on the use of large amounts of credit (with the same threshold as above) that remains outstanding for more than 36 months.

In addition to basic charges and surcharges, the IMF also levies service charges, commitment fees, and special charges. A service charge of 0.5 percent is levied on each drawing, except for reserve tranche drawings, from the General Resources Account (GRA). A refundable commitment fee is charged on amounts available under GRA arrangements, such as Stand-By Arrangements, as well as Extended, Flexible Credit Line, and Precautionary Liquidity Line Arrangements, during each 12-month period. Commitment fees are levied at 15 basis points on amounts available for drawing up to 200 percent of quota, 30 basis

points on amounts in excess of 200 percent and up to 1,000 percent of quota, and 60 basis points on amounts over 1,000 percent of quota. The fees are refunded when the arrangement is drawn upon, in proportion to the drawings made. The IMF also levies special charges on overdue principal payments and on charges that are past due by less than six months.

Remuneration and interest

On the expenditure side, the IMF pays interest (remuneration) to members on their creditor positions in the GRA (known as reserve tranche positions). The Articles of Agreement provide that the rate of

Table **3.2**

Administrative expenses reported in the financial statements, FY2015

(Millions of U.S. dollars, unless otherwise indicated)

FY2015 NET ADMINISTRATIVE BUDGET OUTTURN	1,010
TIMING DIFFERENCES	
Pension and postemployment benefits costs	247
Capital expenditure—amortization of current and prior years' expenditure	46
AMOUNTS NOT INCLUDED IN THE ADMINISTRATIVE BUDGET	
Capital expenditure—items expensed immediately in accordance with International Financial Reporting Standards	41
Reimbursement to the General Department (from the Poverty Reduction and Growth Trust, Post-Catastrophe Debt Relief Trust, and Special Drawing Rights Department)	(82)
Total administrative expenses reported in the audited financial statements	1,262
MEMORANDUM ITEM	
Total administrative expenses reported in the audited financial statements (millions of SDRs)	857

Sources: IMF Finance Department and Office of Budget and Planning.

Note: Components may not sum exactly to totals because of rounding. Conversions are based on the effective weighted average FY2015 U.S. dollar/SDR exchange rate for expenditures of about 1.47.

---

* Credit tranches refer to the size of a member's purchases (disbursements) in proportion to its quota in the IMF. Disbursements up to 25 percent of a member's quota are disbursements under the first credit tranche and require members to demonstrate reasonable efforts to overcome their balance-of-payments problems. Disbursements above 25 percent of quota are referred to as upper-credit-tranche drawings; they are made in installments, as the borrower meets certain established performance targets. Such disbursements are normally associated with Stand-By or Extended Arrangements (and also the new Flexible Credit Line). Access to IMF resources outside an arrangement is rare and expected to remain so.

remuneration shall be not more than the SDR interest rate, or less than 80 percent of that rate. The rate of remuneration is currently set at the SDR interest rate. The IMF also pays interest, at the SDR interest rate, on its outstanding borrowings under the bilateral loans and note purchase agreements, and the enlarged and expanded New Arrangements to Borrow.

Burden sharing

The rates of charge and remuneration are adjusted under a burden-sharing mechanism that distributes the cost of overdue financial obligations equally between debtor and creditor members. Income loss due to unpaid interest charges that are overdue for six months or more is recovered via burden sharing by increasing the rate of charge and reducing the rate of remuneration. The amounts thus collected are refunded when the unpaid charges are settled.

In FY2015, the adjustments for unpaid quarterly interest charges averaged less than 1 basis point, reflecting the current levels of overdue obligations and lending, and the prevailing low interest rate environment. The adjusted rates of charge and remuneration averaged 1.06 percent and 0.06 percent, respectively, in FY2015.

Net income

The IMF's net income in FY2015 was SDR 1.6 billion, reflecting primarily income from the high levels of lending activity and income from its investments held in the Investment Account. As required by International Financial Reporting Standards (amended International Accounting Standard 19, *Employee Benefits*), the net income for the financial year includes a loss of SDR 0.5 billion arising from the immediate recognition of the effects of changes in actuarial assumptions used in determining the IMF's defined benefit obligation of post-employment employee benefit plans.

Rule for Setting the SDR Interest Rate

In October 2014, the Executive Board amended the rule for setting the SDR interest rate in order to address issues surrounding the fact that the SDR rate had reached historic lows and to prevent it from moving toward a negative rate, by introducing a floor of 0.050 percent (5 basis points) and changing the rounding convention for calculating the SDR interest rate from two to three decimal places. The Executive Board also made a corresponding change in the rounding convention for the burden-sharing mechanism and reduced the minimum burden sharing adjustment from 1 basis point to 0.1 basis point.

The SDR interest rate provides the basis for calculating the interest charged to members on nonconcessional IMF loans from the IMF's general resources, the interest paid to IMF members on their remunerated creditor positions in the IMF (reserve tranche positions), interest paid to lenders on their outstanding claims under borrowing agreements, and the interest paid to lenders on their SDR holdings and charged on their SDR allocations. The SDR interest rate is determined weekly and is based on a weighted average of representative interest rates on short-term financial debt instruments in the money markets of the SDR basket currencies, subject to a floor of 0.050 percent.

Extension of the 2012 Borrowing Agreements

In September 2014, the Executive Board approved a one-year extension of the 2012 Borrowing Agreements. These agreements have played a key role in ensuring that the IMF has adequate resources to meet members' potential needs in the event that tail risks were to materialize.

Box 3.1: Safeguards assessments: policy and activity

When the IMF provides financing to a member country, a safeguards assessment is carried out to obtain reasonable assurances that its central bank is able to adequately manage the resources received from the IMF and provide reliable program monetary data. Safeguards assessments are diagnostic reviews of central banks' governance and control frameworks, and complement the IMF's other safeguards, which include limits on access, conditionality, program design, measures to address misreporting, and post-program monitoring. They involve an evaluation of central bank operations in five areas: the external audit mechanism, the legal structure and autonomy, the financial reporting framework, the internal audit mechanism, and the system of internal controls.

As of April 2015, 272 assessments had been conducted, covering 96 central banks, 13 assessments of which were completed in FY2015. In addition, safeguards activities include monitoring of progress in addressing recommendations and other developments in central banks' safeguards frameworks for as long as IMF credit remains outstanding. About 70 central banks are currently subject to monitoring.

An increased focus on collaboration with key stakeholders has raised awareness of safeguards issues. Two safeguards seminars, which covered the safeguards policy and its application, were conducted at the IMF–Singapore Regional Training Institute and with the Joint Partnership for Africa in Tunis. In addition, a high-level forum on central bank governance was held in Dubai in December 2014, with participants from 43 countries in Africa, Europe, and the Middle East. The forum, organized in partnership with the Hawkamah Institute for Corporate Governance, provided a platform for a cross-regional dialogue on challenges and leading practices in audit oversight, governance, and risk management at central banks.

In accordance with a five-year review cycle, the IMF Executive Board will review the safeguards policy in October 2015, with a view to assessing the policy's effectiveness and identifying areas for further improvement.

In 2012, a number of member countries committed to increase IMF resources through bilateral borrowing agreements. Following Executive Board approval of the modalities for the 2012 Borrowing Agreements, 35 agreements for a total of about $396 billion (SDR 282 billion) were approved by the Executive Board, of which 33 agreements are now effective for a total of $381 billion (SDR 271 billion). The 2012 Borrowing Agreements are designed as a second line of defense after quota and New Arrangements to Borrow resources and have so far not been activated for use in financing operations. Each agreement has an initial two-year term, and may be extended by up to two additional one-year periods.

After this decision, which followed consultations with lenders, the initial two-year term of the agreements was extended by one year.

Arrears to the IMF

Overdue financial obligations to the IMF fell from SDR 1,295.5 million at end-April 2014 to SDR 1,290.8 million at end-April 2015 (Table 3.3). Sudan accounted for about 76 percent of remaining arrears, and Somalia and Zimbabwe for 18 and 6 percent, respectively. At end-April 2015, all arrears to the IMF were protracted (outstanding for more than six months); one-third consisted of overdue principal, and the remaining two-thirds, of overdue charges and interest. More than four-fifths represented arrears to the GRA, and the remainder to the Trust Fund and the PRGT. Zimbabwe is the only country with protracted arrears to the PRGT. Thanks to the SDR allocations in August/September 2009, all protracted cases have remained current in the SDR Department.

Under the IMF's strengthened cooperative strategy on arrears, remedial measures have been taken to address the protracted arrears. At the end of the fiscal year, Somalia and Sudan remained ineligible to use GRA resources. Zimbabwe is not able to access GRA resources until it fully settles its arrears to the PRGT. A declaration of noncooperation, the partial suspension of technical assistance, and the removal from the list of PRGT-eligible countries remain in place as remedial measures related to Zimbabwe's outstanding arrears to the PRGT.

On June 30 and July 13, 2015, Greece did not settle repurchase obligations falling due amounting to SDR 1,232 million and SDR 360 million, respectively. While the overdue obligations were outstanding, Greece was not permitted to receive any further IMF financing. Charges continued to accrue on all obligations. Greece subsequently settled these overdue obligations on July 20, 2015.

Audit mechanisms

The IMF's audit mechanisms comprise an external audit firm, an internal audit function, and an independent External Audit Committee (EAC) that, under the IMF's By-Laws, exercises general oversight over the annual audit.

External Audit Committee

The three members of the EAC are selected by the Executive Board and appointed by the Managing Director. Members serve three-year terms on a staggered basis and are independent of the IMF. EAC members are nationals of different member countries and must possess the expertise and qualifications required to carry out the oversight of the annual audit. Typically, EAC members have significant experience in international public accounting firms, the public sector, or academia.

The EAC selects one of its members as chair, determines its own procedures, and is independent of the IMF's management in overseeing the annual audit. It meets in Washington, D.C., each year, normally in January or February to oversee the planning for the annual audit,

Box 3.2: HQ1 building renovation progress

The renovation of the older of the two IMF headquarters buildings (HQ1) in downtown Washington, D.C., continued in FY2015. The project is designed to replace aging building systems nearing the end of their useful lives and in need of replacement or refurbishment. The renewal will enable more energy-efficient and sustainable operations, provide more natural light throughout the building, and promote institutional collaboration through the introduction of modern work areas and meeting spaces.

The renovation began on May 1, 2013, and much of the initial work took place on the lower levels and public spaces. In FY2015, staff returned to offices in portions of the below-ground levels after renovation of that space, and work progressed on floors one to four of the building. The project has experienced some challenges due to unexpected and complex technical conditions, as well as the discovery of additional asbestos. More time has been and will be needed to remove this material in the other floors, in accordance with the health and safety protocols being followed.

The project aspires to LEED (Leadership in Energy and Environmental Design) certification and incorporates green building design and construction practices that are intended to have a lower impact on the environment and will help lay the foundation for ongoing sustainable operations and maintenance.

in June after the completion of the audit, and in July to brief the Executive Board. The IMF staff and the external auditors consult with EAC members throughout the year. The 2015 EAC members were Gonzalo Ramos (chair), the secretary general of the Public Interest Oversight Board; Daniel Loeto, a chartered accountant and the chief accountant of the Bank of Botswana; and Mary Barth, a professor of accounting at Stanford University.

Table 3.3. Arrears to the IMF of countries with obligations overdue by six months or more and by type, as of April 30, 2015

(Millions of SDRs)

	Total	General Department (including Structural Adjustment Facility)	Trust Fund	Poverty Reduction and Growth Trust
Somalia	235.7	227.4	8.3	-
Sudan	975.2	893.1	82.1	-
Zimbabwe	79.9	-	-	79.9
Total	1,290.8	1,120.5	90.4	79.9

Source: IMF Finance Department.

External audit firm

The external audit firm, which is selected by the Executive Board in consultation with the EAC and appointed by the Managing Director, is responsible for conducting the IMF's annual external audit and expressing an opinion on the IMF's financial statements, including the accounts administered under Article V, Section 2(b), of the Articles of Agreement and the Staff Retirement Plan. At the conclusion of the annual audit, the EAC briefs the Executive Board on the results of the audit and transmits the report issued by the external audit firm, through the Managing Director and the Executive Board, for consideration by the Board of Governors.

The external audit firm is appointed for a term of five years, which may be renewed for up to an additional five years. PricewaterhouseCoopers (PwC) was appointed as the IMF's external audit firm in November 2014, following the mandatory rotation of Deloitte & Touche LLP after 10 years. The external audit firm can perform certain consulting services, subject to a blacklist of prohibited services and robust safeguards to protect the audit firm's independence. These safeguards involve the IMF's External Audit Committee and, for consulting fees above a certain limit, the Executive Board.

Office of Internal Audit and Inspection

The IMF's internal audit function is assigned to the Office of Internal Audit and Inspection (OIA), which independently examines the effectiveness of the IMF's risk management, control, and governance processes. OIA's audit coverage includes the IMF staff, the Executive Board, offices of the Executive Directors, and the Independent Evaluation Office and its staff. In line with best practices, OIA reports to IMF management and to the EAC, thus ensuring its objectivity and independence.

In FY2015, OIA completed assurance and advisory engagements to assess the adequacy of controls and procedures in order to mitigate risks to achievement of the IMF's institutional and departmental goals. Engagements were in the areas of financial audits on the adequacy of controls to safeguard and administer the IMF's financial assets and accounts, information technology audits to evaluate the adequacy of information technology management and the effectiveness of security measures, and operational audits of work processes and associated controls supporting the IMF's core operations.

The Risk Management Unit (RMU) was established on June 9, 2014, to replace the Advisory Committee on Risk Management (ACRM). Previously OIA served as Secretariat to the ACRM. In this capacity, OIA coordinated the production of an annual risk management report to the Board and supported informal briefings of the Board on risk management. OIA's last report on risk management was issued on June 20, 2014. In March 2015, the RMU presented the outline for a proposed risk management framework to the Executive Board for discussion in an informal Board session. More work in this area is to follow in FY2016.

The Board is informed of OIA activities twice a year by means of an activity report that includes information on audit results and the status of audit recommendations. The last informal Board briefing on these matters in FY2015 took place in January 2015.

HUMAN RESOURCES POLICIES AND ORGANIZATION

Human resources

To be effective in the global economy, the IMF must recruit and retain a highly qualified international staff. In FY2015, the IMF introduced a new employment framework to ensure flexibility and fairness in the hiring rules for new staff and contractual employees, and revised benchmark targets for the geographic and gender diversity of staff.

Workforce characteristics

As of April 30, 2015, the IMF employed 2,156 professional and managerial staff, and 455 support staff. A list of the institution's senior officers is on page 82 and its organizational chart can be found on page 62.

Recruitment of 174 total new staff in 2014 was similar to the 2013 level of 176. The IMF requires economists with advanced analytical and policymaking experience, and in 2014 recruited 27 top university graduates through the Economist Program (EP) and 56 experienced mid-career economists. Two-thirds of mid-career hires were macroeconomists, and the rest experts in fiscal policy and the financial sector. In 2014, 490 contractual employees were hired, reflecting a 3 percent increase over 2013. Consistent with the aim of improving support to economists, 56 research assistants were hired, representing one-third of all support contractuals.

In 2014, six appointees from three countries were enrolled in the Externally Financed Appointee hiring program (EFA). The EFA was designed to provide up to 15 member country public sector officials with two years of IMF work experience. Costs are financed by member countries through a multidonor trust fund.

Diversity and inclusion

The IMF strives to ensure that the staff is diverse in terms of geographic region, gender, and educational background, but challenges remain. Of the IMF's 188 member countries, 147 were represented by staff as of end-April 2015. Web Tables 3.1–3.3 show the distribution of the IMF's staff by geographic region, gender, and country type.

Hiring of nationals from underrepresented regions stood at 43 percent of all external hiring at the professional level for 2014. More than half of the 2014 EP intake were from underrepresented regions. The share of women in the EP remained at 36 percent, and at 25 percent of mid-career economist hires.

During the year, several measures were introduced to improve the inclusiveness of the work environment. A new cross-cultural competence assessment was added to the training curriculum and a group mentoring program targeting professional staff from underrepresented regions was introduced.

The 2014 Diversity and Inclusion report revised regional and gender benchmarks for 2020. The benchmarks focus on areas where progress is most needed: professional staff from sub-Saharan Africa, the Middle East and Central Asia, and East Asia, and female managers. In view of significant progress and a strong pipeline of staff from transition economies, benchmarks for these countries were discontinued. Further integration of diversity and inclusion into human resources policies and strong accountability toward the new 2020 benchmarks are planned for 2015.

Management structure and salaries

In 2014, a deputy managing director position was assigned the role of Chief Administrative Officer (CAO) for the first time, to improve focus on internal operational and administrative management.

Finances and Organization

IMF management remuneration is reviewed periodically by the Executive Board; the Managing Director's salary is approved by the Board of Governors. Annual adjustments are made on the basis of the Washington, D.C., consumer price index. Reflecting the responsibilities of each management position, as of July 1, 2014, the salary structure for management was as follows:

Managing Director:	$492,690
First Deputy Managing Director:	$428,410
Deputy Managing Directors:	$408,020

Management changes

On January 14, 2015, former Deputy Managing Director Naoyuki Shinohara notified IMF Managing Director Christine Lagarde of his intention to leave the IMF to return to Japan at the end of this term. His last day at the Fund was February 28, 2015.

On March 18, 2014, Deputy Managing Director Nemat "Minouche" Shafik informed Ms. Lagarde of her intention to leave the Fund to assume the position of Deputy Governor at the Bank of England responsible for Markets and Banking starting August 1, 2014.

Carla Grasso assumed office as Deputy Managing Director and Chief Administrative Officer of the IMF on February 2, 2015. Ms. Grasso is a dual national of Brazil and Italy. Before coming to the IMF, she worked for 14 years, at Vale S.A., one of the world's largest mining companies, serving as vice president for human resources and corporate services from 2001 to 2011. Prior to that, Ms. Grasso served as secretary of the Brazilian Supplementary Social Security Office from 1994 to 1997, and also held several positions as advisor and coordinator in the Ministries of Social Security, Finance, and Planning, as well as in the Office of the President of Brazil.

Mitsuhiro Furusawa assumed office as Deputy Managing Director of the IMF on March 2, 2015. Immediately before coming to the Fund, he served as Special Advisor to Japanese Prime Minister Shinzo Abe and special advisor to the Minister of Finance. Among his recent ministry postings, Mr. Furusawa served as vice minister of finance for international affairs (2013–14), director-general of the Financial Bureau (2012–13), and senior deputy director-general of the International Bureau (2009–10). His overseas postings for the Japanese government included IMF Executive Director (2010–12), minister (Finance) at the Embassy of Japan in the United States (2007–09), and counselor (Finance) at the Embassy of Japan in France (1997–99).

Selection of new IMFC Chair

The members of the International Monetary and Financial Committee (IMFC), the IMF's policy advisory committee, selected Agustín Carstens, governor of Banco de México, as chairman of the committee for a term of three years, effective March 23, 2015. Mr. Carstens succeeded Tharman Shanmugaratnam, Singapore's deputy prime minister and minister for finance, whose term ended March 22, 2015.

Mr. Carstens had been the governor of the Banco de México since January 2010. He served as Mexico's finance minister from December 2006 until December 2009, and chaired the IMF and World Bank Joint Development Committee from March 2007 to October 2009. From August 2003 to October 2006, Mr. Carstens served as Deputy Managing Director of the IMF, and was an Executive Director on the IMF Board in 1999–2000. Mr. Carstens was Mexico's deputy minister of finance from 2000 to 2003, and held a variety of posts in the Banco de México in a career spanning more than 20 years.

The IMFC, comprising finance ministers and central bank governors, is the primary advisory body of the IMF Board of Governors and deliberates on the principal policy issues facing the IMF. The committee has 24 members, reflecting the composition of the IMF Executive Board. Each member country that appoints, and each group of countries that elects, an Executive Director also appoints a member of the committee. The IMFC normally meets twice a year—in the spring and at the time of the IMF–World Bank Annual Meetings in the fall.

Independent Evaluation Office

The IEO was established in 2001 to conduct independent and objective evaluations of IMF policies and activities. Under its terms of reference, the IEO is fully independent from IMF management and operates at arm's length from the Board of Executive Directors. Its mission is to enhance the learning culture within the IMF, strengthen the IMF's external credibility, and support institutional governance and oversight.

Board reviews of IEO reports

In November 2014 the IEO released a report, "IMF Response to the Financial and Economic Crisis." The report assessed the IMF's actions to help contain the 2008 global financial crisis and navigate the global recovery, assist individual economies to cope with the impact, and identify and warn about future risks. It found that the IMF played an important role in the global response to the crisis, that the policy advice provided by staff was flexible and adaptable, and that IMF-supported programs reflected many lessons from past crises; with a reformed lending toolkit, supported by a resource mobilization effort that quadrupled the IMF's resources, the IMF helped members cope with the crisis fallout.

However, the report said that the agreed doubling of quotas has not become effective, leaving the IMF dependent on borrowing arrangements for more than two-thirds of its total credit capacity. It also said that the IMF's record in surveillance was mixed, and although the IMF's calls for global fiscal stimulus in 2008–09 were timely and influential, its endorsement in 2010–11 of a shift to consolidation in some of the largest advanced economies was premature.

The IMF Executive Board and management broadly supported most of the IEO report recommendations. These included ensuring that the IMF has sufficient resources to contribute to future crisis resolution, better structuring engagements with other organizations, and further integrating and consolidating risk and vulnerability analyses.

In July 2014, the IEO released a report, "Recurring Issues from a Decade of Evaluation: Lessons for the IMF." The report focused on the five most common issues that the IEO had identified in its past evaluations: organizational silos, attention to risks and uncertainty, country and institutional context, evenhandedness, and Executive Board guidance and oversight. It found that the IMF's Executive Board and management had taken actions to address the issues in all five areas, but that challenges remained and were likely to persist, as the recurring issues were to varying degrees inherent to the nature of the IMF. Executive Directors and management broadly supported the report's recommendations and emphasized that efforts to address these issues should continue in order to enhance the IMF's effectiveness and credibility.

IEO revisits of past evaluations

The IEO issued two reports in FY2015 revisiting past IEO evaluations. The initial impetus for this series came from inquiries from Executive Directors and member country authorities on the status of issues raised in past evaluations. The 2013 external evaluation of the IEO also found a strong case for revisiting some of these issues.

The evaluation updates are brief stocktaking exercises, more modest in scope than full IEO evaluations, but broader in coverage than the Periodic Monitoring Reports (PMRs) prepared by IMF staff. The updates summarize the original IEO evaluation, describe relevant developments that have taken place since the evaluation (including implementation of the IEO's recommendations), and identify outstanding issues and any new ones related to the evaluation topic that merit continued attention.

The two revisits issued in FY2015 covered three past evaluations. One looked back at the IEO "Report on the Poverty Reduction Strategy Papers (PRSPs) and the Poverty Reduction and Growth Facility (PRGF)" (2004) and "The IMF and Aid to Sub-Saharan Africa" (2007); the other updated the main issues of the 2005 evaluation of "The IMF's Approach to Capital Account Liberalization." The original reports and revisits are available on the IEO website.

IEO Work Program

In FY2015, the IEO launched a new evaluation, "The IMF and the Euro Area Crisis." The IEO is also working to conclude "Learning from Experience: An IEO Assessment of Self-Evaluation Systems" and an evaluation of "Statistics for Global Economic and Financial Stability: The Role of the IMF." The IEO issued a note on "Possible Topics for Evaluation over the Medium Term" in January 2015 and consulted with Executive Directors and other stakeholders on potential future evaluation topics on this basis.

Implementation of Board-endorsed recommendations

The sixth PMR on the status of implementation plans in response to Board-endorsed IEO recommendations was approved by the Executive Board in August 2014. This was the first PMR prepared by the Office of Internal Audit and Inspection under the procedure recommended by the external evaluators of the IEO and approved by the Board

in February 2013. It reviewed the status of Management Implementation Plans (MIPs) for four IEO evaluations issued during 2011–13 and provided an update on progress on relevant issues related to previous MIPs agreed upon since 2007.

In considering the PMR, the IMF's Executive Board Evaluation Committee noted that it represented an improvement over previous reports but that more could be done to sharpen the focus on whether implementation measures proposed by management have been effective in achieving the high-level objectives of the Board-endorsed recommendations. No new MIPs were issued by the IMF in FY2015.

OUTREACH AND ENGAGEMENT WITH EXTERNAL STAKEHOLDERS

The objectives of IMF outreach are twofold: first, to listen to external voices to better understand their concerns and perspectives, with the aim of improving the relevance and quality of IMF policy advice; and second, to strengthen the outside world's understanding of IMF objectives and operations. Among the specific groups with which the IMF engages in its outreach activities are civil society organizations and youth leaders, trade and labor unions, parliamentarians, academics, think tanks, and the media. Tools such as social media, videos, and podcasts have formed an increasing part of the IMF's outreach strategy in recent years.

The IMF's Communications Department has primary responsibility for conducting the IMF's outreach activities and its engagement with external stakeholders. As the institution's policies have evolved—for instance, in its increased focus on promoting poverty reduction in low-income developing countries through a participatory approach and its emphasis on transparency and good governance—outreach and communication have become an integral part of IMF country work as well.

Box 3.3: Outreach to new policy influencers

The global financial crisis and its aftermath underlined the importance of reaching out to a broad range of stakeholders, including civil society organizations (CSOs), youth, labor organizations, and parliamentarians, to explain and seek feedback on the IMF's policy advice.

In its eighth year, the IMF Civil Society Fellowship program sponsored the participation of about 40 **CSOs** from developing economies in the Spring and Annual Meetings. On the margins of the meetings, the IMF, the World Bank, and CSOs organized about 100 sessions on a broad range of policy issues that included debt sustainability, inequality, climate change, and gender. More generally, the IMF also engaged with civil society in informal discussions on key policy issues, such as the IMF's response to the Ebola outbreak and sovereign debt restructuring. Civil society was also invited to provide input through public consultations on the IMF's Fiscal Transparency Code and on the integration of countries' poverty reduction strategies with Fund-supported programs in low-income developing countries.

The IMF continued to step up its engagement with **youth**—the next generation of policymakers and world leaders—through the Annual Meetings, introductory seminars for students on the IMF, university visits by IMF management, and youth events with senior staff. The First Deputy Managing Director chaired town hall discussions with university students in Chile, Mexico, and Peru, events designed to help spotlight the 2015 Annual Meetings in Peru. In the same vein, an IMF Latin American Youth Essay contest brought eight winners to the 2014 Annual Meetings, which included a youth seminar on the topic of inclusive growth and entrepreneurship.

Given the significant impact of the global crisis on jobs, the IMF continued to regularly engage with **labor organizations** on a number of levels. At headquarters, the IMF hosted the biennial, high-level meeting with the International Trade Unions Confederation, and held formal and informal discussions with labor organizations on jobs and growth, inequality, and collective bargaining.

The IMF engages with **parliamentarians**—a group that plays an important role in their countries' economic decision-making process—mainly through the Parliamentary Network on the World Bank and the International Monetary Fund, but also through targeted in-country and regional seminars on issues such as extractive industries, structural reforms, and inequality (for example, in Bangladesh and Peru). This year's Parliamentary Network Global Conference, co-hosted by the IMF and attended by about 200 members of parliament from more than 80 countries, focused on the 2015 development agenda, health care systems, gender equality, jobs and growth, and environmental challenges.

Outreach by IMF management and senior staff

As the importance of the IMF's outreach efforts has grown in the face of the global financial crisis and aftermath, the management team has played an increasingly important role in those efforts. Outreach by management and senior IMF staff provides an opportunity to articulate the institution's strategic vision and the key policy priorities for the membership at large; to marshal support for policymakers for difficult national reforms that carry both domestic and global benefits; to learn more about issues affecting key stakeholders in member countries, including nontraditional constituents, with the aim of strengthening

Finances and Organization

IMF analysis and policy advice; and to reinforce the IMF's commitment to providing needed support to members, particularly those most affected by the crisis.

The Managing Director, Deputy Managing Directors, and senior IMF staff travel extensively in all five regions, meeting with authorities and key stakeholders in member countries and taking advantage of numerous opportunities to further the IMF's outreach objectives.

Regional Office for Asia and the Pacific

As the IMF's window to Asia and the Pacific, a region whose importance in the global economy continues to grow, the Regional Office for Asia and the Pacific (OAP) monitors economic and financial developments to help bring a more regionally focused perspective to IMF surveillance. It seeks to enhance understanding of the IMF and its policies in the region and to keep the IMF informed on regional perspectives on key issues. In this capacity, OAP has continued to be engaged in bilateral surveillance in Japan and Mongolia, and increased regional surveillance with active participation by OAP staff in forums in Asia, including ASEAN+3 (the Association of Southeast Asian Nations plus China, Japan, and Korea) and APEC (Asia-Pacific Economic Cooperation).

OAP contributes to capacity development in the region through the Japan–IMF Scholarship Program for Asia, the Japan–IMF Macroeconomic Seminar for Asia, and other macroeconomic seminars. Highlights during the year included a June 2014 seminar on fiscal policy rules and fiscal councils in Asia and the Pacific and an October 2014 seminar offered jointly by Bank Indonesia and the IMF's Monetary and Capital Markets Department to regional central bankers on modernizing monetary policy frameworks in frontier economies.

The office also conducts outreach activities in both Japan and the rest of the region and engages in dialogue with Asian policymakers by organizing conferences and events on current policy issues central to the IMF's work. A conference co-organized with the Bank of Korea in November 2014 focused on macroeconomic rebalancing for sustainable growth, and a conference jointly organized in Tokyo with Hitotsubashi University in March 2015 discussed challenges related to inequality and potential policy responses, with a particular focus on the implications of fiscal redistribution.

Regional Office in Paris and Brussels

The IMF Europe Office, located in Paris and Brussels, serves as liaison to European Union institutions and member states, as well as international organizations and civil society in Europe. The office engages with institutions such as the European Commission, the European Central Bank, the European Stability Mechanism, the European Parliament, the Economic and Financial Committee, and the Eurogroup Working Group, on euro area and EU policies as well as EU–IMF country programs. It also represents the IMF at the Organisation for Economic Co-operation and Development.

More broadly, it fosters the dialogue on global economic issues with EU institutions, international organizations, and governments and civil society in Europe, and meets frequently with representatives from industry associations, unions, academia, and the financial sector. It also supports the IMF's operations in Europe, including in economic surveillance, IMF-supported programs, and technical assistance, and helps to coordinate communication and outreach activities across the region.

IMF quota reform

Quota subscriptions are a central component of the IMFs financial resources. Each member country of the IMF is assigned a quota, based broadly on its relative position in the world economy. A member country's quota determines its maximum financial commitment to the IMF and its voting power, and has a bearing on its access to IMF financing.

In 2010, the Board of Governors, the IMF's highest decision-making body, approved a package of far-reaching reforms of the IMF's quotas and governance ("2010 reforms"), which included notably the following measures:

Completion of the 14th General Review of Quotas with an unprecedented doubling of quotas and a major realignment of quota shares—a shift of more than 6 percent from overrepresented to underrepresented members and a more than 6 percent quota shift to dynamic emerging market and developing countries, while protecting the quota shares and voting power of the poorest members.

A proposed amendment to the Articles of Agreement ("Board Reform Amendment") that would facilitate a move to a more representative, all-elected Executive Board.

A request to the Executive Board to bring forward the timetable for completion of the 15th General Review of Quotas to January 2014, and request to complete a comprehensive quota formula review by January 2013.

Members committed to make best efforts to complete their domestic approval processes of these reforms by the Annual Meeting of the Board of Governors in October 2012. However, the Board Reform Amendment and the quota increases under the 14th Review have still not become effective pending the ratification of the reforms by several members, including the United States. Initiation of the work on the 15th Review has been on hold.

Against this backdrop, and as requested by the IMFC, on January 14, 2015, the Executive Board held an informal discussion on options for next steps, building on its existing work.

On January 28, the Executive Board reported to the Board of Governors on the status of the 2010 Reforms and 15th General Review of Quotas. The Executive Board's report to the Board of Governors contained also a proposed resolution, which was adopted on February 18, 2015, by the Board of Governors. The Resolution expressed deep regret that the 14th Review quota increases and the Board Reform Amendment have not become effective, and that the 15th Review has not been completed. The resolution also emphasized the importance and urgency of the 2010 reforms for the IMF's credibility, legitimacy, and effectiveness, and reiterated the commitment to their earliest possible implementation, while urging the remaining members who have not yet accepted the 14th Review quota increases and the Board Reform Amendment to do so without further delay.

The resolution also called for the completion of the 15th Review by December 15, 2015, in line with the timetable mandated under the Articles of Agreement. It also called on the Executive Board to work expeditiously and to complete its work as soon as possible on interim steps in the key areas covered by the 2010 reforms, and thus to enable the Board of Governors to reach agreement on steps that represent meaningful progress toward the objectives of the 2010 reforms by June 30, 2015. The resolution stressed that such interim steps should not in any way be seen as a substitute for the 2010 reforms, which remain the highest priority.

On March 27, 2015, the Executive board had a second informal discussion on possible interim steps, which provided a basis for IMFC and G20 discussions on this topic at the 2015 Spring Meetings.

On April 18, 2015, at its Spring Meeting, the IMFC of the IMF issued a communiqué that included the following statement:

We remain deeply disappointed with the continued delay in progressing the 2010 IMF Quota and Governance Reforms. Recognizing the importance of these reforms for the credibility, legitimacy, and effectiveness of the IMF, we reaffirm that their earliest implementation remains our highest priority. We continue to urge the United States to ratify the 2010 reforms as soon as possible. Mindful of the aims of the 2010 reforms, we call on the IMF Executive Board to pursue an interim solution that will meaningfully converge quota shares as soon as and to the extent possible to the levels agreed under the 14th Review. We will use the 14th Review as a basis for work on the 15th Review of Quotas, including a new quota formula. We reaffirm our commitment to maintaining a strong, well-resourced, and quota-based IMF.

2014 Executive Board election

Newly elected IMF Executive Directors began their two-year term in November 2014, following an election for the 19 currently elected seats. As a result, eight new Executive Directors and a number of new Alternate Executive Directors joined the Board and will serve a two-year term until October 31, 2016.

For the first time since 1970, all eligible members participated in the election (the five members that appoint Executive Directors—France, Germany, Japan, the United Kingdom, and the United States—are not eligible to participate). At present all IMF member countries are represented on the Executive Board for the first time in more than four decades.

To guide the election process, the Board established a committee whose task was to recommend rules for the conduct of the election, including the conduct of the election under the pending Seventh Amendment of the Articles of Agreement, in the event that the amendment was ratified during the election process. The committee followed the work of the 2012 election committee, which had recommended new voting limits for multi-country constituencies reflecting a balance between the formation of constituencies by member countries and a desirable balance in the voting power at the Executive Board. The Executive Board and the Board of Governors subsequently approved the committee's recommendations.

The next regular election of Executive Directors will be conducted in October 2016.

Nauru application for membership

On May 9, 2014, the IMF announced that the Government of the Republic of Nauru had filed an application for membership in the IMF. Under the IMF's procedures, the application will be considered by the IMF's Executive Board, which will then submit a recommendation to the Board of Governors of the IMF in the form of a Membership Resolution. These recommendations cover the amount of quota in the IMF, the form of payment of the subscription, and other customary terms and conditions of membership. After the Board of Governors has adopted the Membership Resolution, the applicant country may become a member once it has taken the legal steps required under its law to enable it to sign the IMF's Articles of Agreement and to fulfill the obligations of IMF membership.

Review of the Communications Strategy

Like most modern organizations, the IMF uses communications as a strategic tool to help strengthen its effectiveness. It does so by more proactive engagement with various stakeholders to better explain Fund policies and operations, by participating in and contributing to intellectual debate on important economic issues, and by facilitating two-way learning with the IMF's global membership. This communications role was recognized in the 2011 Triennial Surveillance Review and in a 2013 assessment by the Independent Evaluation Office, which noted that the IMF is now viewed by its membership as more open, listening, and responsive.

In July 2014, the Executive Board discussed a review of the IMF's Communications Strategy. It followed the Board's establishment in 2007 of a framework guiding IMF communications, which focused on deepening understanding of IMF policies, better integrating communications in daily operations, raising the impact of communications products, and reaching different audiences through enhanced outreach.

The 2014 paper emphasized several key communications issues. The first is taking further steps to ensure clarity and consistency in communication in a world where demand for IMF services continues to rise. The second is doing more to assess the impact of IMF communications and thus better inform efforts going forward. And the third is engaging strategically and prudently with new media—including social media.

In the Executive Board discussion of the 2014 review, Directors considered that the framework guiding the communications strategy, as endorsed by the Executive Board in 2007, remains broadly appropriate. They observed that the overall strategy has allowed the IMF to communicate effectively and flexibly.

Directors encouraged continued efforts to strengthen and adapt IMF communication, with a view to deepening public understanding of the IMF's work and policy advice. They agreed that clarity and consistency are vital for effective communication and welcomed steps to differentiate more clearly official IMF policy from staff views. Directors also supported plans to conduct impact assessments to gauge the effectiveness of IMF communications and draw lessons for the IMF's communications strategy.

Directors noted that the increasing use of new technologies at the IMF—including social media—has helped strengthen communication around important events and products. They stressed that any expansion of social media activity should continue in a careful and strategic way, with adequate oversight, appropriate training, and proper resourcing.

Finances and Organization

Executive Directors and Alternates (as of April 30, 2015)

Appointed

Mark Sobel *Vacant*	United States
Mikio Kajikawa *Isao Hishikawa*	Japan
Hubert Temmeyer *Steffen Meyer*	Germany
Hervé de Villeroché *Thibault Guyon*	France
Steve Field *Chris Yeates*	United Kingdom

Elected

Menno Snel *Willy Kiekens* *Oleksandr Petryk*	Armenia, Belgium, Bosnia and Herzegovina, Bulgaria, Croatia, Cyprus, Georgia, Israel, Luxembourg, former Yugoslav Republic of Macedonia, Moldova, Montenegro, Netherlands, Romania, Ukraine
Fernando Jiménez Latorre *Carlos Hurtado López* *María Angélica Arbeláez*	Colombia, Costa Rica, El Salvador, Guatemala, Honduras, Mexico, Spain, República Bolivariana de Venezuela
Carlo Cottarelli *Thanos Catsambas*	Albania, Greece, Italy, Malta, Portugal, San Marino
Wimboh Santoso *Pornvipa Tangcharoenmonkong*	Brunei Darussalam, Cambodia, Republic of Fiji, Indonesia, Lao P.D.R., Malaysia, Myanmar, Nepal, Philippines, Singapore, Thailand, Tonga, Vietnam
JIN Zhongxia *SUN Ping*	China
Barry Sterland *KwangHae Choi* *Vicki Plater*	Australia, Kiribati, Korea, Marshall Islands, Micronesia, Mongolia, New Zealand, Palau, Papua New Guinea, Samoa, Seychelles, Solomon Islands, Tuvalu, Uzbekistan, Vanuatu
Serge Dupont *Michael McGrath*	Antigua and Barbuda, The Bahamas, Barbados, Belize, Canada, Dominica, Grenada, Ireland, Jamaica, St. Kitts and Nevis, St. Lucia, St. Vincent and the Grenadines

Audun Groenn *Pernilla Meyersson*	Denmark, Estonia, Finland, Iceland, Latvia, Lithuania, Norway, Sweden
Chileshe Mpundu Kapwepwe *Maxwell M. Mkwezalamba*	Angola, Botswana, Burundi, Eritrea, Ethiopia, The Gambia, Kenya, Lesotho, Liberia, Malawi, Mozambique, Namibia, Nigeria, Sierra Leone, Somalia, South Africa, Republic of South Sudan, Sudan, Swaziland, Tanzania, Uganda, Zambia, Zimbabwe
Hazem Beblawi *Sami Geadah*	Bahrain, Egypt, Iraq, Jordan, Kuwait, Lebanon, Libya, Maldives, Oman, Qatar, Syrian Arab Republic, United Arab Emirates, Republic of Yemen
Ibrahim Halil Çanakci *Christian Just* *Szilárd Benk*	Austria, Belarus, Czech Republic, Hungary, Kosovo, Slovak Republic, Slovenia, Turkey
Rakesh Mohan *Kosgallana Durage Ranasinghe*	Bangladesh, Bhutan, India, Sri Lanka
Fahad I. Alshathri *Hesham Alogeel*	Saudi Arabia
Daniel Heller *Dominik Radziwill*	Azerbaijan, Kazakhstan, Kyrgyz Republic, Poland, Serbia, Switzerland, Tajikistan, Turkmenistan
Paulo Nogueira Batista, Jr. *Ivan Luís de Oliveira Lima* *Pedro Fachada*	Brazil, Cabo Verde, Dominican Republic, Ecuador, Guyana, Haiti, Nicaragua, Panama, Suriname, Timor-Leste, Trinidad and Tobago
Aleksei Mozhin *Lev Palei*	Russian Federation
Mohammad Jafar Mojarrad *Mohammed Daïri*	Islamic Republic of Afghanistan, Algeria, Ghana, Islamic Republic of Iran, Morocco, Pakistan, Tunisia
Sergio Chodos *Oscar A. Hendrick*	Argentina, Bolivia, Chile, Paraguay, Peru, Uruguay
Nguéto Tiraina Yambaye *Mamadou Woury Diallo* *Mohamed Lemine Raghani*	Benin, Burkina Faso, Cameroon, Central African Republic, Chad, Comoros, Democratic Republic of the Congo, Republic of Congo, Côte d'Ivoire, Djibouti, Equatorial Guinea, Gabon, Guinea, Guinea-Bissau, Madagascar, Mali, Mauritania, Mauritius, Niger, Rwanda, São Tomé and Príncipe, Senegal, Togo

Senior Officers (as of April 30, 2015)

AREA DEPARTMENTS

Antoinette Monsio Sayeh	Director, African Department
Chang Yong Rhee	Director, Asia and Pacific Department
Poul Thomsen	Director, European Department
Masood Ahmed	Director, Middle East and Central Asia Department
Alejandro Werner	Director, Western Hemisphere Department

FUNCTIONAL DEPARTMENTS

Gerard T. Rice	Director, Communications Department
Andrew J. Tweedie	Director, Finance Department
Vitor Gaspar	Director, Fiscal Affairs Department
Sharmini A. Coorey	Director, Institute for Capacity Development
Sean Hagan	General Counsel and Director, Legal Department
José Viñals	Financial Counsellor and Director, Monetary and Capital Markets Department
Olivier J. Blanchard	Economic Counsellor and Director, Research Department
Louis Marc Ducharme	Director, Statistics Department
Siddharth Tiwari	Director, Strategy, Policy, and Review Department

INFORMATION AND LIAISON

Odd Per Brekk	Director, Regional Office for Asia and the Pacific
Axel Bertuch-Samuels	Special Representative to the United Nations
Jeffrey Franks	Director, Offices in Europe/Senior Resident Representative to the European Union

SUPPORT SERVICES

Mark W. Plant	Director, Human Resources Department
Jianhai Lin	Secretary of the Fund, Secretary's Department
Frank Harnischfeger	Director, Technology and General Services Department
Susan Swart	Chief Information Officer and Associate Director, Technology and General Services Department

OFFICES

Daniel A. Citrin	Director, Office of Budget and Planning
Clare Brady	Director, Office of Internal Audit and Inspection
Moises Schwartz	Director, Independent Evaluation Office

World Economic Outlook

950,000 downloads in FY2015

+2.2M pageviews

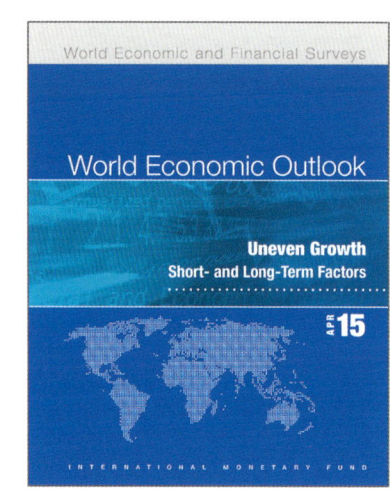

Global Financial Stability Report

142,700 downloads in FY2015

+362,000 pageviews

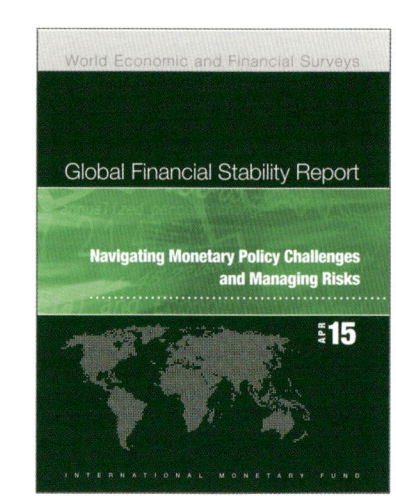

Fiscal Monitor

46,000 downloads in FY2015

+108,000 pageviews

Finance & Development

2.1M pageviews in FY2015

+121,000 downloads

Part 4 Looking Back/Looking Ahead

The IMF has built
strong followings on
a variety of platforms
in recent years,
making social media
an integral part of
the IMF's broader
communications work.

(numbers are for May 1, 2014–
April 30, 2015)

imf.org average monthly views FY2015

5.3M

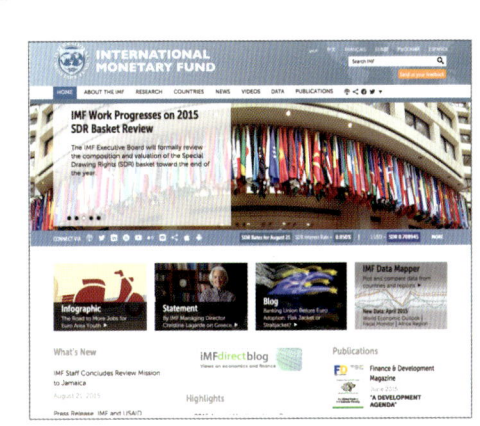

Weibo followers

5.9M

weibo

In addition to the Chinese
microblogging service
Weibo, Managing Director
Christine Lagarde has
112,000 followers on
Facebook and 275,000
followers on Twitter.

iMFdirect (blog) views FY2015

707,000

Looking Back

This year has been crucial for reshaping the world's development agenda. We also marked two important anniversaries—the 70th anniversary of the founding of the Bretton Woods institutions and 25 years since the fall of the Berlin Wall. This section looks at key events and trends shaping different parts of the world and the IMF's work to support the membership in those areas, including activities leading up to the IMF–World Bank Annual Meetings in Peru.

The Road to Lima: The 2015 IMF Annual Meetings

Latin America

Latin America demonstrated remarkable vitality in the first part of the 21st century, experiencing strong growth and an economic renewal that gave new opportunities to millions of people. But the region now is facing serious challenges as growth slows. One crucial challenge is to put in place policies that ensure continued progress with inclusive growth in the context of a regional slowdown and changing global landscape.

This combination of progress and challenge will provide the setting for the October 2015 IMF–World Bank Annual Meetings in Lima, Peru. The meetings will highlight Latin America's achievements over the past decade—particularly those of Peru, a country with its own success story to tell.

The Annual Meetings will be the first held in Latin America since 1967 in Rio de Janeiro, and only the second since 1952 in Mexico City. So for the IMF, Lima will represent an important stage in its relationship with the region. Some 13,000 people are expected to attend the meetings.

Slower growth for Latin America

The April 2015 *Regional Economic Outlook* (REO) for the Western Hemisphere projected that growth in Latin America and the Caribbean would decline for the fifth consecutive year, partly reflecting global developments but also the recent commodity price declines.

Stops on the Road to Lima

December 2014
Chile

Conference in Santiago on growth and prosperity in Latin America, followed by April 2015 regional outlook launch.

May 2015
Colombia

"Latin America: Challenges in a Rapidly Changing Global Environment," a conference in Bogota

May
Brazil

Visit of IMF Managing Director to Brasilia and Rio de Janeiro

June
United States

High-level IMF Conference on Latin America "Rising Challenges to Growth and Stability in a Shifting Global Environment" in Washington, D.C.

Growth has varied across the region, with South America and commodity exporters affected more than economies with closer ties to the United States or those that have a stronger growth potential. The REO highlighted a key priority for governments—raising investment, productivity, and potential growth. It identified improvements in business environments, infrastructure, and education as key to fostering more diversified, resilient, and inclusive economies. Another priority is to safeguard stability given the weaker growth and vulnerabilities among banks and corporations.

At a December 2014 high-level conference on "Challenges for Securing Growth and Shared Prosperity in Latin America," held in Santiago, Chile, speakers highlighted the progress in achieving inclusive growth: the proportion of people living in poverty was 2.5 times greater than those in the middle class only a decade ago, whereas now they are about the same. Continued progress will be more difficult because of slow growth and weaker prospects.

Adjusting to a challenging global environment

The Santiago conference was an important stop on an agenda of events addressing the issues facing Latin America in the months leading up to the Peru Annual Meetings. This agenda—called the "Road to Lima"—is intended to broaden public understanding of the challenges to achieving sustained growth, increased employment, and continued reductions in poverty and inequality. The Road to Lima also is intended to address the need to adjust to the challenging global economic environment. ■

Promoting Growth in Latin America and the Caribbean

Last year, the IMF held **two high-level conferences in Chile and Jamaica** that focused on strategies to raise potential output and ensure sustainable growth. Over the past 15 years, most countries in Latin America and the Caribbean have become stronger, with significant advances in reducing poverty and inequality. Growth has, however, disappointed in recent years and created doubts about the continuation of economic and social gains. The two conferences discussed options to raise potential output, improve economic opportunities, lower energy costs, improve business environments, and expand financial inclusion. With demands of a growing middle class rising rapidly,

---

June
Peru
IMF–World Bank Conference on Financial Inclusion, in Lima

July
El Salvador
13th IMF Central America Conference, in San Salvador

September
St. Kitts & Nevis
Fifth IMF Caribbean Conference, in Frigate Bay

September
Peru
Conference on "Managing Macroeconomic Success and Challenges," in Lima

(Growth, continued)

experts also took a closer look at priorities in public spending and, in Latin America, the need for widening the tax base.

Key findings of the two events were:

■ In the Caribbean, many countries are extremely dependent on imported oil for the generation of electricity and transportation. Efficiency gains can be achieved by closer cooperation between private and public sectors on generation and distribution of electricity and development of renewable energy sources. Governments, however, need to reform the regulatory framework to encourage private sector participation and also find new ways to address social inequalities without distorting pricing.

■ Rules that are clear and consistent will help attract private investment. The array of tax incentives offered in many Caribbean countries has made the tax system increasingly complex and has eroded tax bases. Countries should reassess their taxation strategies to better meet competing goals of supporting growth and funding public services.

■ In both the Caribbean and Latin America, broad access to financial services promotes growth and greater income equality. Both public and private sector involvement is needed to improve access. There is, however, a premium on safeguarding financial stability as instability has tremendous consequences for the poorest segments of the population.

■ Finally, many economies in Latin America face resource constraints and a growing middle class that is frustrated with the lack of access to public services and economic opportunity. Participants in Chile discussed the need for deeper structural reforms to strengthen the availability and quality of public services, and improve educational outcomes.

> Achieving better outcomes requires more funding, which could be collected by broadening tax bases and bringing high-income groups into public systems of taxation and benefits.

> Work will also be needed to upgrade infrastructure and strengthen regional cooperation in traditional and less conventional areas like labor, security, energy, the environment, and competition.

A more comprehensive, strategic approach would help expand the provision of public services in emerging middle-income countries and raise potential output, thereby providing the foundation to permanently reduce poverty. ■

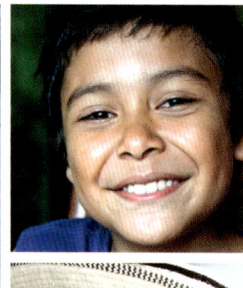

orange box

Harnessing Africa's Demographic Dividend

Africa

Over the next 20 years, sub-Saharan Africa will become the main source of new entrants into the global workforce as infant mortality and fertility rates decline in the region.

By 2035, the number of sub-Saharan Africans joining the working-age population (ages 15–64) will exceed that from the rest of the world combined.

This is a trend with significant ramifications for both sub-Saharan Africa and the global economy.

This transition was part of a centerpiece analysis of the looming changes in sub-Saharan Africa's labor force published in the April 2015 *Regional Economic Outlook* (REO) for sub-Saharan Africa. The study also describes a potential "demographic dividend" for sub-Saharan Africa, the magnitude of which will depend on how fast fertility rates decline and how strong the accompanying policies are. The region has been the second-fastest-growing in the world in recent years and has the potential to accrue economic benefits. The world economy also stands to benefit if sub-Saharan Africa's labor force is integrated into global supply chains in an era of declining working-age populations elsewhere.

Policy challenge: creating jobs

However, the policy challenge is immense: sub-Saharan Africa needs to create high-productivity jobs at an extremely rapid rate for an extended period of time to absorb the growing labor force—about 18 million new jobs per year until 2035. While sub-Saharan Africa's economic performance over the past 15 years—spurred, in part, by strong policies—gives reason for optimism that it can meet this challenge, a faltering performance could have dire consequences.

The REO analysis points to the need for policies that encourage a gradual transition of labor to formal employment in nonagricultural jobs from the informal sector, which currently accounts for about 90 percent of the 400 million jobs in low-income sub-Saharan African countries. Investments in human capital—including health

Pan-African Banks: Opportunities and Challenges for Cross-Border Oversight

(Dividend, continued)

care and education — are critical in the early phases to accelerate the transition. While the region has made significant progress improving access to primary education, there is a need to improve access to secondary and tertiary schools, and to improve the overall quality of education.

Reform priorities in sub-Saharan Africa

The policy challenges to boost employment reflect the full range of sub-Saharan Africa's reform priorities, including promoting private sector development, with emphasis on household enterprises; increasing agricultural productivity; and investing in infrastructure. Policies that

facilitate the development of labor-intensive sectors that can compete globally are also necessary, as are policies that promote labor market flexibility. Furthering financial sector development to effectively channel savings into investment also can increase employment and growth.

Higher trade openness would also aid job creation, allowing sub-Saharan Africa to benefit from technology transfers and integration into global value chains. Expanding intra-regional trade and regional markets could boost incentives for domestic production, especially in labor-intensive manufacturing, and attract higher levels of investment. ■

As sub-Saharan Africa has emerged as the world's second-fastest-growing region in recent years, economic integration has become an increasingly important driver of growth.

While trade and investment often receive the most attention, another key trend has been the emergence of pan-African banks.

The IMF African and Monetary and Capital Markets Departments cooperated during 2014 on a major research project that offered

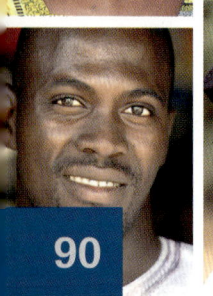
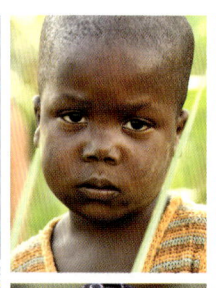

an in-depth look at the expansion of pan-African banking and the opportunities and challenges it represents. The research was presented to the Executive Board and later issued as a departmental paper. It also was summarized in the June 2014 issue of *Finance & Development*.

The pan-African financial institutions, which once largely did business in their home markets, now are creating cross-border networks and overtaking the European and U.S. banks that traditionally have dominated African banking. Along with spurring integration, they are giving impetus to financial deepening and inclusion, contributing to improved competition and innovation.

Pan-African banks originate mainly from the largest economies of Africa, such as Morocco, Nigeria, and South Africa, or from important countries within a region such as Kenya in the East African community. But an important pan-African institution, Ecobank, is headquartered in Togo; it was founded in the mid-1980s with support from the 15-nation Economic Community of West African States. Although Ecobank is not the largest of the pan-African banks in asset size, it surpasses them all in terms of the geographical reach of its network.

The rapid expansion of pan-African banks poses oversight challenges that, if unaddressed, could potentially increase systemic risks.

These banking groups represent increased demands on home country regulators and supervisors to ensure that supervision of the banking groups based in their jurisdictions is done on a consolidated basis. Supervisory capacity is already constrained and under-resourced in most of Africa. The banking networks increase the importance of transparency and disclosure, good governance, strong prudential oversight, and a legal and regulatory framework that supports effective and comprehensive supervision and the need to prepare for crisis management. Progress is being made in most areas, but efforts to extend oversight to bank holding companies is needed in some cases.

Cooperation on cross-border supervision has started, but enhanced collaboration is critical.

Regional currency unions, such as the West African Monetary Union, face particular challenges on the interface of responsibilities between regional and national authorities. Pursuing the reform agenda expeditiously will require extensive technical assistance. The IMF is prepared to continue to provide assistance in its areas of responsibility and, if helpful, to liaise with other providers to help ensure a comprehensive program to safeguard financial stability. ■

China's Rebalancing Act

Asia

The 2014–15 slowdown in China—part of a broader trend in emerging markets—was felt throughout the global economy. The slower growth was part of a rebalancing effort undertaken by the Chinese government, and this shift became a focus of attention worldwide and an element of IMF risk assessment.

Analysis and policy advice across IMF members took the trend into account, particularly through the range of surveillance activities. This was fully reflected in the work of the Executive Board, whose discussions and public statements showed a keen awareness of China's new direction.

China's rapid growth—its economy is now the world's largest in terms of purchasing power parity—has been a key driver of the world economy in recent years, particularly since the global financial crisis. Much of the current slowdown—growth declined to 7.4 percent in 2014 from 7.7 the year before and 10.2 percent in 2011—followed a generation of rapid expansion and reflected waning dividends from past reforms. But high levels of investment and credit growth created vulnerabilities.

A comprehensive blueprint of reforms announced at a high-level meeting of the Chinese Communist Party in 2013 heralded a shift in priorities toward higher levels of consumption, inclusive growth, and sustainable environmental policies.

IMF policy advice

The reform agenda is broadly consistent with past IMF policy advice, including recommendations of the Executive Board. In its assessment of China's 2014 Article IV consultation, the Board welcomed the reforms and said that the challenge "is to shift gears, reduce the vulnerabilities that have built

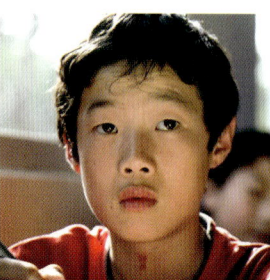

up, and transition to a more sustainable growth path."

The external implications of China's slowdown were discussed in the April 2015 *World Economic Outlook* and *Global Financial Stability Report*, and were at the core of the 2014 Spillover Report, especially its discussion of intraregional spillovers. *Regional Economic Outlooks* also took China's impact into account.

Article IV consultations of some other countries also have given considerable attention to the ramifications of China's slower growth—in terms of both reduced trade and financial linkages. Risk Assessment Matrices in staff reports for countries across Asia included specific mention of the potential impact of the slowdown.

Executive Board Assessments of several Article IV reports discussed the Chinese slowdown in the context of other countries.

Impact on commodities markets

Commodities markets also have felt the effects of China's slowdown.

> Prices have fallen for many commodities, although this also reflects weaker global demand and new sources of supply.

It was not just oil, which fell more than 50 percent at one point in the past year. For example, sub-Saharan Africa faced sharp falls in the price of natural gas (45 percent), iron ore (34 percent), cotton (23 percent), copper (15 percent), and platinum (17 percent).

Despite the short-term impact globally, China's leaders are committed to an economic path built around a more sustainable growth model. A comprehensive blueprint of reforms announced at a high-level meeting of the Chinese Communist Party in 2013 heralded a shift in priorities toward a more balanced and sustainable growth model, which would also be more inclusive and environment-friendly. ■

Islamic Finance and the IMF

Middle East and Central Asia

Although still a small share of global financial markets, Islamic finance is growing rapidly. The banking segment of the market is increasing its presence in many IMF member countries, and it is becoming systemically important in some Asian and Middle East economies. Meanwhile, global issuance of *Sukuk*—the Islamic equivalent of bonds—is expanding to encompass a wide reach of issuers and investors.

Islamic finance—the subject of a Staff Discussion Note (SDN) issued in April 2015—has the potential to make important contributions in at least three areas. First, it promises to foster greater financial inclusion, especially of large, underserved Muslim populations. Second, its emphasis on asset-backed financing and risk-sharing means that it could support small and medium-sized enterprises, as well as infrastructure investment. Finally, its risk-sharing features and prohibition of speculation suggest that Islamic finance may, in principle, pose less systemic risk than conventional finance.

Regulation and supervision

The IMF long has taken an interest in the implications of Islamic finance for macroeconomic and financial stability, engaging member countries in the context of policy advice and capacity development, particularly in the areas of regulation and supervision, and development of domestic *Sukuk* markets. The IMF also played a key role in the establishment of the Islamic Financial Services Board, an international standard-setting organization that promotes and enhances the soundness and stability of the Islamic financial services industry by issuing global prudential standards and guiding principles for the industry.

The IMF took several steps in 2014–15 to broaden its understanding of Islamic finance and to foster wider understanding. In October 2014, an interdepartmental Working Group held its first meeting with an External Advisory Group that was established to help identify policy challenges facing the Islamic finance industry and to facilitate coordination with specialized and regional institutions, in terms of knowledge sharing, capacity development, and outreach.

Assessing Concentration Risk of Banks in the Gulf

Kuwait workshop

In February 2015, the IMF hosted a regional workshop in Kuwait on "Risk-Based Supervision in Institutions Offering Islamic Services." The workshop was attended by senior officials from banking supervision departments in Arab League countries and was organized by the IMF Middle East Center for Economics and Finance and the Middle East Regional Technical Assistance Center. The workshop provided guidance and training in the methodologies and approaches for implementing risk-based supervision in institutions offering Islamic financial services.

Several challenges need to be addressed if Islamic finance is to reach its potential. As outlined in the SDN, standards have been developed, but regulatory and supervisory frameworks in many jurisdictions do not yet cater to the unique risks of the industry. Regulators do not always have the capacity (or willingness) to ensure Shari'ah compliance, which undermines consistency of approaches within and across borders. A specific regulatory challenge relates to profit-sharing investment accounts at Islamic banks, which need to be treated in a manner consistent with financial stability. Moreover, although Islamic banks appear to be well-capitalized, the implementation of the Basel III Accord will present challenges. Finally, safety nets and resolution frameworks remain underdeveloped. ■

Important regional work takes place at the IMF outside of the context of the Article IV consultation process. One example was the staff paper on "Assessing Concentration Risks in GCC Banks," presented to the October 2014 Annual Meeting of Ministers of Finance and Central Bank Governors of the Gulf Cooperation Council (GCC).

The paper, prepared by staff from the Middle East and Central Asia Department and the Monetary and Capital Markets Department, addressed concentration risks—those involved in having too much money lent out to certain categories of borrowers—in the credit portfolios of banks in Bahrain, Kuwait, Oman, Qatar, Saudi Arabia, and the United Arab Emirates.

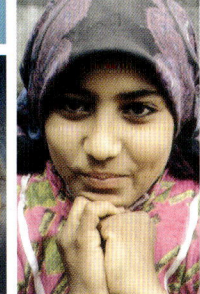
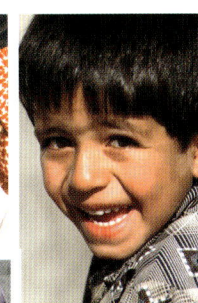

(Banks, continued)

Well capitalized, but struggling to diversify credit portfolios

The paper found that banks in the GCC countries are generally well capitalized. However, because of the structure of their countries' economies—with non-oil sectors dependent on developments in the oil sector—they struggle to diversify their credit portfolios and are consequently exposed to concentration risks that require a greater amount of scrutiny.

The analysis in the paper used credit risk modeling techniques to estimate the capital buffers required in light of the highlighted risks. The results suggest that the capital held by banks in the region is generally adequate to compensate for the concentration risks they face. Nonetheless, the paper recommended that a primary goal should be to ensure that existing strong capital buffers are maintained and that supervisors strengthen their capacity to monitor the buildup of concentration risk in banks' portfolios.

How GCC banks can be strengthened

The paper also outlined areas for which bank regulation, supervision, and information disclosure in the GCC could be strengthened. Among the recommendations:

■ Stress test exercises should be calibrated to fully capture the existing and evolving nature of interconnections and exposure concentration. Greater legal powers are required for regulators to collate information on the ultimate beneficial owners to better supervise banks' risks derived from interconnectedness.

■ To better monitor banks' risks, GCC central banks should limit their exposures to a single borrower or closely related group of borrowers to a prudent maximum, in accordance with the new Basel guidelines, and also introduce aggregate limits on large exposures.

■ Increased availability of data and further disclosures are needed for a better assessment of risks.

■ This approach to financial sector analysis could be repeated across the IMF membership, with staff employing analytical tools to address the unique circumstances of banks, other financial institutions, and government bodies to give greater focus to financial stability. ■

Looking Back on 25 Years of Historic Change in Europe

Eastern and Central Europe

Europe marked an important anniversary in 2014: 25 years since the fall of the Berlin Wall and the beginning of a historic transformation in eastern and central Europe. The reintegration of the former communist countries into the global economy—and their entry into the IMF—in most cases brought major improvements in living standards.

The IMF European Department marked the anniversary with a Special Report, "25 Years of Transition: Post-Communist Europe and the IMF," issued in October 2014. The paper summarized the stages of transition and looked at the challenges of the coming years.

The task of building market-oriented economies was difficult and protracted.

Liberalization of trade and prices came quickly, but institutional reforms often faced opposition from vested interests. The results of transition were uneven due to important differences in policy implementation. All countries suffered high inflation and major recessions as prices were freed and old economic linkages broke down.

By contrast, the early and mid-2000s saw uniformly strong growth. With macro–economic stability established and key market-based frameworks largely in place, the region experienced large capital inflows. This was supported by a benign global environment and increasing confidence in rapid convergence with western Europe—especially for the countries that joined the European Union (EU) during this period.

The increased participation of foreign banks—either directly or through subsidiaries and branches—in lending activity in central and eastern European countries brought much-needed credibility and technical know-how, and facilitated financing in the region—sometimes to excess, contributing to a rise in internal imbalances. The resulting vulnerabilities were exposed when the global and euro area crises struck at the end of the decade, hitting the transition economies hard.

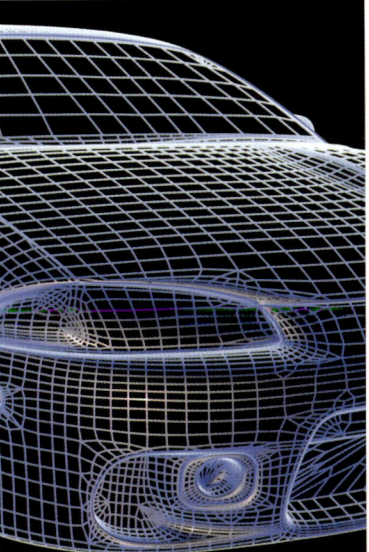

(25 Years, continued)

In the wake of these crises, countries embarked on significant fiscal consolidation, although some continue to struggle to restore competitiveness and fiscal sustainability against the backdrop of a tepid global recovery and lingering structural weaknesses. Recent analysis shows the effect of widening disparities within the region: the more advanced countries, such as the Baltics and some central European countries, now have more in common with western European economies than they do with some former communist countries. But even in better-performing economies, the pace of convergence toward EU levels of per capita income has slowed substantially. Moreover, reform momentum has generally decelerated over the years, with a risk of reversals emerging in a few countries.

To revitalize the convergence process and improve the resilience of the transition economies, a stronger commitment to market-based policies is needed. Two broad priorities stand out. First, there is a need for renewed focus on macroeconomic and financial stability in some countries. This could involve reining in persistent deficits and increasing debt, and addressing rising levels of bad loans in the banking system. Second, the pace and depth of structural reforms should be increased in areas such as the business and investment climate, access to credit, public expenditure prioritization and tax administration, and labor markets. ■

Box 4.1: European New Member States Policy Forum

As Europe marked the 25th anniversary of the fall of the Berlin Wall, another important milestone was passed: the 10th anniversary of the accession to the European Union (EU) of the first group of countries from central and eastern Europe. To mark that event, the IMF held the first New Member States Policy Forum as a platform to discuss policy issues of common interest.

The forum brought together high-level representatives of six countries that are EU members, but not yet in the euro area—Bulgaria, Croatia, the Czech Republic, Hungary, Poland, and Romania. They were joined by the European Central Bank and the European Commission. The report on the forum—part of a series of IMF Cluster Consultations—was discussed with the IMF Executive Board in an informal session.

The forum report focused on four themes: euro adoption, opting into the banking union before euro adoption, the EU fiscal framework and pension reform, and making the most of the EU single market and EU Services Directive.

Baltic Cluster Report

One innovation growing out of the 2011 Triennial Surveillance Review has been the introduction of "cluster reports" to assess logical groupings of economies in an integrated fashion.

These assessments, which complement Article IV consultations with each member that makes up the clusters, are intended to strengthen the IMF's work on interconnectedness—filling the gap between the assessments in Article IV consultations with members and multilateral surveillance of global economic trends.

The cluster reports assess spillovers across a group of interconnected countries by examining the risks from common shocks and highlighting shared policy challenges and, where relevant, the potential gains from policy coordination.

One of the pilots conducted during 2014 assessed the Baltic countries—the Republic of Estonia, the Republic of Latvia, and the Republic of Lithuania—in their trade and financial linkages to the Nordic countries. They also face common challenges.

In its assessment of the report, the Executive Board noted that while there is no articulated "Baltic Model," all three countries have made impressive strides in advancing income convergence with western Europe over the past two decades. Their policy approach has been based on generally prudent macroeconomic policies, small governments, and a relatively favorable investment climate.

Directors underscored that the "creditless recoveries" in the Baltics could become increasingly difficult to sustain.

They commended the strong economic recovery from the global financial crisis, but noted that it had been accompanied by contracting credit to the private sector. While not an unusual pattern in a boom-bust cycle, continued anemic credit could constrain investment and growth. ■

Looking Ahead

Financing Sustainable Development

A Crucial Year

Since the adoption of the United Nations Millennium Development Goals in 2000, the majority of developing economies have made important progress in terms of achieving strong growth and reducing poverty. But progress has been uneven, with outcomes weakest in fragile and conflict-affected states. The challenge now is to build on the strong results of the past 15 years, with a focus on tackling obstacles to sustainable growth and inclusion, most notably in countries that have fallen behind.

The international community is being called upon this year to commit to a shared vision of development goals through 2030 and beyond, and an action plan to make this vision possible. Achievement of these Sustainable Development Goals (SDGs)—which encompass economic, social, and environmental themes—will require a partnership among developed and developing economies, and international institutions. Most important, it will be essential to ensure that the right policies are in place and that sufficient private and public resources are mobilized to achieve the SDGs.

The IMF, with its global membership and mandate to operate at both bilateral and multilateral levels, is uniquely positioned to contribute to and help implement this compact. The Managing Director outlined the IMF's goals to the 2015 Spring Meeting of the International Monetary and Financial Committee in a document titled "Financing Sustainable Development: Key Policy Issues and the Role of the IMF." The paper was discussed with the IMF Executive Board in an informal session in April, prior to the International Monetary and Financial Committee meeting.

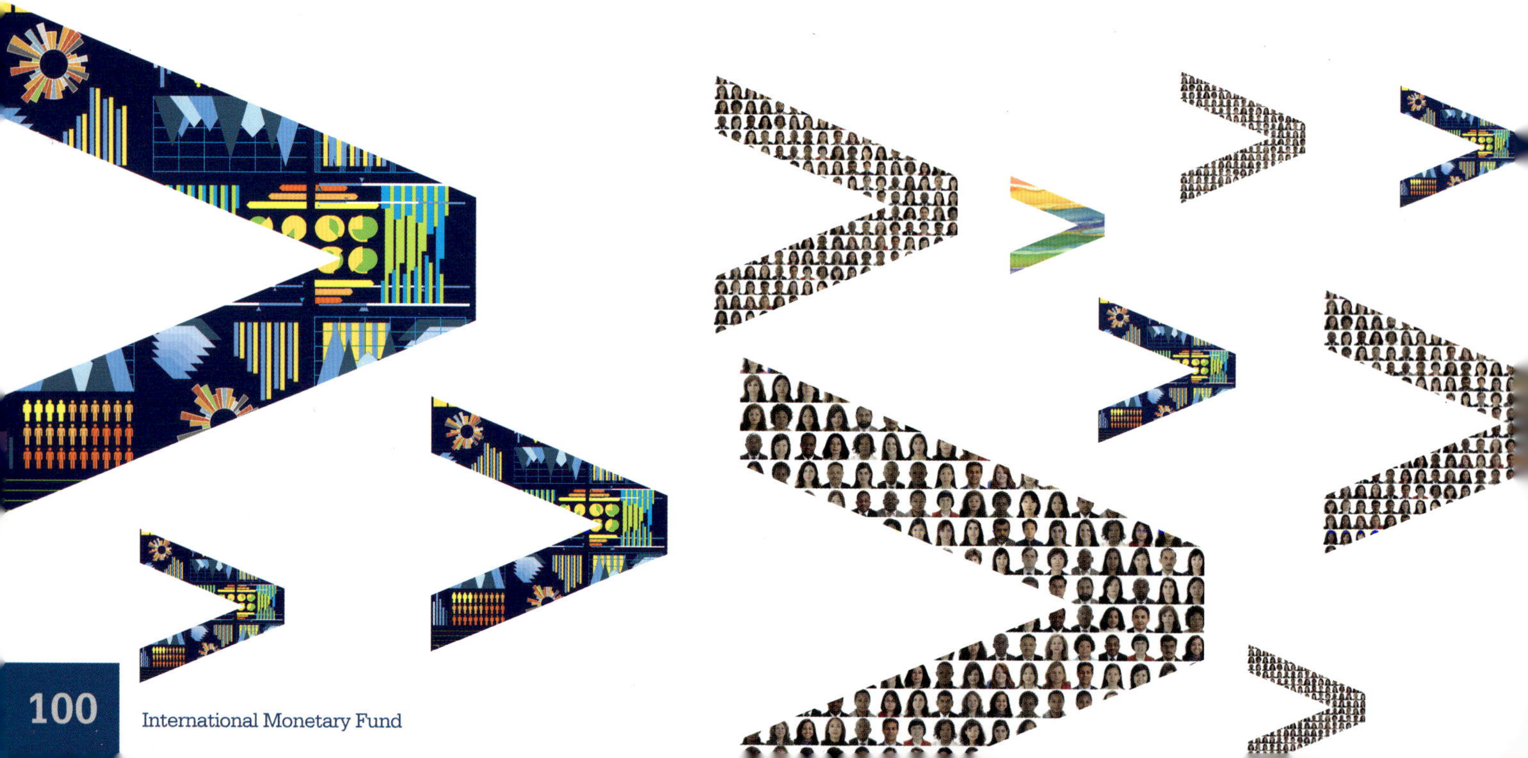

The IMF's work for the 2015 Development Agenda is focused around the agenda of three major United Nations conferences during the year:

Financing for Development (Addis Ababa in July), which will develop a shared view on the policies needed to generate the resources to achieve the SDGs

UN Summit on the SDGs (New York City in September), where the SDGs will be formally adopted

UN Climate Change Conference (Paris in December), to reach a global agreement on national targets for reduction of carbon emissions

As deliverables for this crucial development agenda, the IMF is considering the following areas of action, as outlined in the Managing Director's statement to the IMFC:

Seeking options to boost access to IMF resources provided to developing countries, thus better positioning them to handle balance-of-payments needs as they pursue growth

Expanding diagnostic and capacity-building support for countries seeking to scale up investment to tackle infrastructure gaps

Sharpening the focus of operational work on equity, inclusion, gender, and climate issues, drawing on ongoing analysis and work of other institutions

Increasing the focus on and provision of resources to work on fragile and conflict-affected states

Selectively expanding capacity-building efforts in the areas of revenue mobilization, energy taxation, and financial market development. ■

Fiscal Work in Progress

Important work in the area of fiscal policy was undertaken during FY2015 that led to Executive Board consideration of policy papers in FY2016. Two papers in particular— prepared by the Fiscal Affairs Department—were the focus of Board discussions:

Fiscal policy and long-term growth: This topic is a core theme of the IMF's Global Policy Agenda (see Part 1), which focuses on strategies to lift economic growth across the IMF membership in the wake of the 2008 global financial crisis. A paper prepared in FY2015 identifies the main channels through which fiscal policy can influence medium- to long-term growth. It distills practical lessons for policymakers by drawing on the IMF's extensive technical assistance on fiscal reforms, a vast literature, and a multipronged analytical approach.

Making public investment more efficient: The paper builds on previous analytical work on public investment issues, including in the October 2014 *World Economic Outlook*, and examines how countries can improve the efficiency of public investment and increase the effects of public investment on growth. Key findings of the paper include: (1) the economic impact of public investment critically depends on its efficiency, and there are large inefficiencies in public investment processes; (2) the economic dividends from closing the public investment "efficiency gap" are substantial; and (3) strengthening specific key institutions that shape the planning, allocation, and implementation of public investment could close most of the efficiency gap, but reform priorities vary across countries. ■

Notes

PART 1—OVERVIEW

Executive Board Calendar: http://www.imf.org/external/np/sec/bc/eng/index.aspx

The Managing Director's Global Policy Agenda:
- October 2014: http://www.imf.org/external/np/pp/eng/2014/100314.pdf
- April 2015: http://www.imf.org/external/np/pp/eng/2015/041315.pdf

Triennial Surveillance Review: http://www.imf.org/external/np/spr/triennial/2014/index.htm

Action Plan for Strengthening Surveillance: http://www.imf.org/external/pp/longres.aspx?id=4924

World Economic Outlook:
- October 2014: http://www.imf.org/external/pubs/ft/weo/2014/02/
- April 2015: http://www.imf.org/external/pubs/ft/weo/2015/01/

Regional Economic Reports: http://www.imf.org/external/pubs/ft/reo/reorepts.aspx

Global Financial Stability Report: http://www.imf.org/external/pubs/ft/gfsr/index.htm
- April 2015: http://www.imf.org/External/Pubs/FT/GFSR/2015/01/index.htm

Fiscal Monitor: http://www.imf.org/external/ns/cs.aspx?id=262
- April 2015: http://www.imf.org/external/pubs/ft/fm/2015/01/fmindex.htm

"Seven Questions about the Recent Oil Price Slump," *iMFdirect* blog: http://blog-imfdirect.imf.org/2014/12/22/seven-questions-about-the-recent-oil-price-slump/

IMF Response to the Ebola Crisis: http://www.imf.org/external/np/fad/ebola/index.htm

IMF Establishes a Catastrophe Containment and Relief Trust to Enhance Support for Eligible Low Income Countries Hit by Public Health Disasters, Press Release No. 15/53: http://www.imf.org/external/np/sec/pr/2015/pr1553.htm

Proposal to Enhance Fund Support for Low-Income Countries Hit by Public Health Disasters—Decisions: http://www.imf.org/external/np/pp/eng/2015/013015.pdf

Ukraine—Request for Extended Arrangement under the Extended Fund Facility and Cancellation of Stand-By Arrangement—Staff Report; Press Release; and Statement by the Executive Director for Ukraine: http://www.imf.org/external/pubs/ft/scr/2015/cr1569.pdf

IMF Completes Fifth Review under Extended Fund Facility Arrangement for Greece and Approves €3.41 Billion Disbursement, Press Release No. 14/254: http://www.imf.org/external/np/sec/pr/2014/pr14254.htm

"Inequality and Unsustainable Growth: Two Sides of the Same Coin?": http://www.imf.org/external/pubs/ft/sdn/2011/sdn1108.pdf

"Redistribution, Inequality, and Growth": http://www.imf.org/external/pubs/ft/sdn/2014/sdn1402.pdf

"Income Inequality and Fiscal Policy": http://www.imf.org/external/pubs/ft/sdn/2012/sdn1208.pdf

"Fiscal Policy and Income Inequality": http://www.imf.org/external/np/pp/eng/2014/012314.pdf

"Jobs and Growth: Analytical and Operational Considerations for the IMF": http://www.imf.org/external/np/pp/eng/2013/031413.pdf

Triennial Surveillance Review: http://www.imf.org/external/np/spr/triennial/2014/index.htm

Regional Economic Outlook: Sub-Saharan Africa—Fostering Durable and Inclusive Growth, April 2014: http://www.imf.org/external/pubs/ft/reo/2014/afr/eng/sreo0414.htm

Africa Rising Conference, Maputo, Mozambique: http://africa-rising.org/

Building the Future—Jobs, Growth, and Fairness in the Arab World, Amman, Jordan: http://www.imf.org/external/np/seminars/eng/2014/act/index.htm

"The Economic Power of Women's Empowerment": http://www.imf.org/external/np/speeches/2014/091214.htm

"Can Women Save Japan?": http://www.imf.org/external/pubs/ft/wp/2012/wp12248.pdf

"Fair Play: More Equal Laws Boost Female Labor Force Participation": http://www.imf.org/external/pubs/ft/sdn/2015/sdn1502.pdf

IMFx—Free online courses from the International Monetary Fund: https://www.edx.org/school/imfx

Financial Programming and Policies, Part 1: Macroeconomic Accounts and Analysis: https://www.edx.org/course/financial-programming-policies-part-1-imfx-fpp-1x-0

French version: https://www.edx.org/course/programmation-et-politiques-financieres-imfx-ppf-1x

Debt Sustainability Analysis: https://www.edx.org/course/debt-sustainability-analysis-imfx-dsax

Energy Subsidy Reform: https://www.edx.org/course/energy-subsidy-reform-imfx-esrx-0

Energy Subsidy Reform: Lessons and Implications: http://www.imfbookstore.org/ProdDetails.asp?ID=ESRLIEA&PG=1&Type=BL

IMF eLibrary online data portal: http://data.imf.org/?sk=7CB6619C-CF87-48DC-9443-2973E161ABEB

PART 2—WHAT WE DO: "THE BIG THREE"

Economic Surveillance

"2014 Triennial Surveillance Review—Stakeholders' Perspectives on IMF Surveillance": http://www.imf.org/external/np/pp/eng/2014/073014a.pdf

"2014 Triennial Surveillance Review—Review of IMF Surveillance Products": http://www.imf.org/external/np/pp/eng/2014/073014b.pdf

"2014 Triennial Surveillance Review—Analytical Background Studies": http://www.imf.org/external/np/spr/triennial/2014/index.htm

"2014 Triennial Surveillance Review—External Study—Report on Interviews": http://www.imf.org/external/np/pp/eng/2014/073014c.pdf

"2014 Triennial Surveillance Review—Report of the External Advisory Group": http://www.imf.org/external/np/pp/eng/2014/073014j.pdf

IMF Executive Board Reviews Surveillance: Supporting Sustainable Growth in a Post-Crisis Interconnected World, Press Release No. 14/454: http://www.imf.org/external/np/sec/pr/2014/pr14454.htm

"2014 Triennial Surveillance Review—Managing Director's Action Plan for Strengthening Surveillance": http://www.imf.org/external/np/pp/eng/2014/112114.pdf

"Staff Guidance Note on Macroprudential Policy": http://www.imf.org/external/np/pp/eng/2014/110614.pdf

"Key Aspects of Macroprudential Policy": http://www.imf.org/external/np/pp/eng/2013/061013b.pdf

"Review of the Financial Sector Assessment Program: Further Adaptation to the Post Crisis Era": http://www.imf.org/external/np/pp/eng/2014/081814.pdf

IMF Executive Board Concludes Review of the Financial Sector Assessment Program, Press Release No. 14/447: http://www.imf.org/external/np/sec/pr/2014/pr14447.htm

"Third Pilot External Sector Report": http://www.imf.org/external/np/pp/eng/2014/062614.pdf

"IMF Multilateral Policy Issues Report—2014 Spillover Report": http://www.imf.org/external/np/pp/eng/2014/062514.pdf

"Macroeconomic Developments in Low-Income Developing Countries": http://www.imf.org/external/np/pp/eng/2014/091814.pdf

Global Housing Watch: http://www.imf.org/external/pubs/ft/survey/so/2014/NEW061114A.htm

"Housing Bubbles: An Ounce of Prevention Is Worth a Pound of Cure," *iMFdirect* blog: http://blog-imfdirect.imf.org/2015/01/07/housing-bubbles-an-ounce-of-prevention-is-worth-a-pound-of-cure/

IIMB-IMF Conference on Housing Markets, Financial Stability, and Growth: http://www.imf.org/external/np/seminars/eng/2014/housing/

Conference on Housing Markets and the Macroeconomy: http://www.bundesbank.de/Redaktion/EN/Termine/Research_centre/2014/2014_06_05_eltville.html

"Review of the Role of Trade in the Work of the Fund:" http://www.imf.org/cxtcrnal/np/pp/cng/2015/020215.pdf

IMF Executive Board Discusses Implementation Plan Following IEO Evaluation of IMF Involvement in International Trade Policy Issues, Public Information Notice (PIN) No. 10/35: http://www.imf.org/external/np/sec/pn/2010/pn1035.htm

Implementation Plan in Response to Board-Endorsed Recommendations Arising from the IEO Evaluation of IMF Involvement in International Trade Policy Issues: http://www.imf.org/external/np/pp/eng/2009/111209.pdf

IMF Involvement in International Trade Policy Issues: http://www.ieo-imf.org/ieo/pages/CompletedEvaluation109.aspx

IMF Executive Board Reviews the Role of Trade in the Fund's Work, Press Release No. 15/132: http://www.imf.org/external/np/sec/pr/2015/pr15132.htm

"From Banking to Sovereign Stress: Implications for Public Debt": http://www.imf.org/external/np/pp/eng/2014/122214.pdf

"Cross-Border Bank Resolution: Recent Developments": http://www.imf.org/external/np/pp/eng/2014/060214.pdf

"Sovereign Debt Restructuring—Recent Developments and Implications for the IMF's Legal and Policy Framework": http://www.imf.org/external/np/pp/eng/2013/042613.pdf

"The IMF's Lending Framework and Sovereign Debt—Preliminary Considerations": http://www.imf.org/external/np/pp/eng/2014/052214.pdf

IMF Executive Board Discusses the Fund's Lending Framework and Sovereign Debt, Press Release No. 14/294: http://www.imf.org/external/np/sec/pr/2014/pr14294.htm

"Strengthening the Contractual Framework to Address Collective Action Problems in Sovereign Debt Restructuring": http://www.imf.org/external/np/pp/eng/2014/090214.pdf

IMF Executive Board Discusses Strengthening the Contractual Framework in Sovereign Debt Restructuring, Press Release No. 14/459: http://www.imf.org/external/np/sec/pr/2014/pr14459.htm

"Spillovers in International Corporate Taxation": http://www.imf.org/external/np/pp/eng/2014/050914.pdf

"Assessing Reserve Adequacy": http://www.imf.org/external/np/pp/eng/2011/021411b.pdf

"Assessing Reserve Adequacy—Further Considerations": http://www.imf.org/external/np/pp/eng/2013/111313d.pdf

"Assessing Reserve Adequacy—Specific Proposals": http://www.imf.org/external/np/pp/eng/2014/121914.pdf

IMF Executive Board Discusses Reserve Adequacy Assessment, Press Release No. 15/176: http://www.imf.org/external/np/sec/pr/2015/pr15176.htm

International Reserves—IMF Concerns and Country Perspectives: http://www.ieo-imf.org/ieo/files/completedevaluations/IR_Main_Report.pdf

"Update on the Fiscal Transparency Initiative": http://www.imf.org/external/np/pp/eng/2014/061614.pdf

Manual on Fiscal Transparency: https://www.imf.org/external/np/fad/trans/manual.htm

Guide on Resource Revenue Transparency: http://www.imf.org/external/np/fad/trans/guide.htm

"Macroeconomic Issues In Small States and Implications for Fund Engagement": IMF Executive Board Concludes Macroeconomic Issues in Small States and Implications for Fund Engagement, Public Information Notice (PIN) No. 13/39: http://www.imf.org/external/np/sec/pn/2013/pn1339.htm

"Staff Guidance Note on the IMF's Engagement with Small Developing States": http://www.imf.org/external/np/pp/eng/2014/032414.pdf

IMF Pledges Continued Commitment to Partner with Small Island Developing States in Their Pursuit of Sustainable Economic Development, Press Release No. 14/412: http://www.imf.org/external/np/sec/pn/2013/pn1339.htm

Data Standards and Codes: http://www.imf.org/external/data.htm

Lending

IMF Executive Board Approves US$154 Million Stand-By Arrangement for Georgia, Press Release No. 14/377: http://www.imf.org/external/np/sec/pr/2014/pr14377.htm

IMF Executive Board Approves US$113.2 Million Stand-By Arrangement and US$75.4 Million Stand-By Credit Facility for Honduras, Press Release No. 14/545: http://www.imf.org/external/np/sec/pr/2014/pr14545.htm

IMF Executive Board Approves US$497.1 Million Stand-By Arrangement and US$191.2 Million Stand-By Credit Facility for Kenya, Press Release No. 15/29: http://www.imf.org/external/np/sec/pr/2015/pr1529.htm

IMF Executive Board Approves €1.2 Billion Stand-By Arrangement for Serbia, Press Release No. 15/67: http://www.imf.org/external/np/sec/pr/2015/pr1567.htm

IMF Executive Board Approves US$6.2 Billion Arrangement for Morocco under the Precautionary Liquidity Line, Press Release No. 12/287: http://www.imf.org/external/np/sec/pr/2012/pr12287.htm

IMF Executive Board Approves New Two-Year US$70 Billion Flexible Credit Line Arrangement with Mexico, Press Release No. 14/543: http://www.imf.org/external/np/sec/pr/2014/pr14543.htm

IMF Executive Board Approves New Two-Year US$23 Billion Flexible Credit Line Arrangement for the Republic of Poland, Press Release No. 15/05: http://www.imf.org/external/np/sec/pr/2015/pr1505.htm

IMF Executive Board Approves US$17.6 Million Extended Fund Facility Arrangement for Seychelles, Press Release No. 14/262: http://www.imf.org/external/np/sec/pr/2014/pr14262.htm

IMF Executive Board Approves 4-Year US$17.5 Billion Extended Fund Facility for Ukraine, US$5 Billion for Immediate Disbursement, Press Release No. 15/107: http://www.imf.org/external/np/sec/pr/2015/pr15107.htm

IMF Executive Board Approves US$130 Million in Immediate Assistance to Guinea, Liberia, and Sierra Leone in Response to the Ebola Outbreak, Press Release No. 14/441: http://www.imf.org/external/np/sec/pr/2014/pr14441.htm

IMF Establishes a Catastrophe Containment and Relief Trust to Enhance Support for Eligible Low-Income Countries Hit by Public Health Disasters, Press Release No. 15/53: http://www.imf.org/external/np/sec/pr/2015/pr1553.htm

IMF Executive Board Approves US$114.63 Million in Financing and Debt Relief for Sierra Leone, Press Release No. 15/86: http://www.imf.org/external/np/sec/pr/2015/pr1586.htm

IMF Executive Board Approves US$45.6 Million Disbursement under the Rapid Credit Facility and US$36.5 Million in Debt Relief under the Catastrophe Containment and Relief Trust for Liberia, Press Release No. 15/69: http://www.imf.org/external/np/sec/pr/2015/pr1569.htm

IMF Executive Board Approves US$29.8 Million in Debt Relief under the Catastrophe Containment and Relief Trust for Guinea, Press Release No. 15/137: http://www.imf.org/external/np/sec/pr/2015/pr15137.htm

IMF Executive Board Approves New US$122.4 Million ECF Arrangement for Chad, Press Release No. 14/381: http://www.imf.org/external/np/sec/pr/2014/pr14381.htm

IMF Approves US$918 Million ECF Arrangement to Help Ghana Boost Growth, Jobs, and Stability, Press Release No. 15/159: http://www.imf.org/external/np/sec/pr/2015/pr15159.htm

IMF Executive Board Approves 3-Year US$21.7 Million Extended Credit Facility Arrangement for Grenada and Concludes 2014 Article IV Consultation, Press Release No.14/310: http://www.imf.org/external/np/sec/pr/2014/pr14310.htm

IMF Executive Board Approves US$92.4 Million Extended Credit Facility to Support the Kyrgyz Republic, Press Release No. 15/165: http://www.imf.org/external/np/sec/pr/2015/pr15165.htm

IMF Executive Board Approves a 3-Year, US$552.9 Million Extended Credit Facility Arrangement with Yemen, Press Release No. 14/408: http://www.imf.org/external/np/sec/pr/2014/pr14408.htm

IMF Executive Board Completes Sixth Review under Burundi's ECF Arrangement, Augments Access and Approves US$6.9 Million Disbursement, Press Release No. 15/134: http://www.imf.org/external/np/sec/pr/2015/pr15134.htm

IMF Executive Board Completes Sixth Review under the ECF Arrangement for Côte d'Ivoire, Approves US$94.7 Million Disbursement, and Augments Access and Extends the Arrangement, Press Release No. 14/554: http://www.imf.org/external/np/sec/pr/2014/pr14554.htm

IMF Executive Board Completes Fifth Review under ECF Arrangement for Guinea, Extends Arrangement, and Approves US$63.6 Million Augmentation, Press Release No. 15/49: http://www.imf.org/external/np/sec/pr/2015/pr1549.htm

IMF Executive Board Approves US$7.63 Million Disbursement under the Rapid Credit Facility for the Central African Republic, Press Release No. 15/129: http://www.imf.org/external/np/sec/pr/2015/pr15129.htm

IMF Executive Board Approves US$12.9 Million Disbursement under the Rapid Credit Facility for the Central African Republic, Press Release No. 14/226: http://www.imf.org/external/np/sec/pr/2014/pr14226.htm

IMF Executive Board Approves US$10.8 Million Disbursement under the Rapid Credit Facility for The Gambia, Press Release No. 15/155: http://www.imf.org/external/np/sec/pr/2015/pr15155.htm

IMF Executive Board Approves US$5.24 Million Disbursement under the Rapid Credit Facility for Guinea-Bissau, Press Release No. 14/495: http://www.imf.org/external/np/sec/pr/2014/pr14495.htm

IMF Executive Board Approves US$47.1 Million Disbursement under the Rapid Credit Facility for Madagascar, Press Release No. 14/287: http://www.imf.org/external/np/sec/pr/2014/pr14287.htm

IMF Executive Board Approves US$6.4 Million Disbursement under the Rapid Credit Facility And the Rapid Financing Instrument for St. Vincent and the Grenadines, Press Release No. 14/383: http://www.imf.org/external/np/sec/pr/2014/pr14383.htm

IMF Executive Board Completes Sixth and Seventh Reviews under the SBA for Bosnia and Herzegovina, Approves €95.7 Million Augmentation of the SBA and €191.4 Million Disbursement, Press Release No. 14/320: http://www.imf.org/external/np/sec/pr/2014/pr14320.htm

IMF Executive Board Discusses Reform of the Policy on Public Debt Limits in Fund-Supported Programs, Press Release No. 14/591: http://www.imf.org/external/np/sec/pr/2014/pr14591.htm

"Reform of the Policy on Public Debt Limits in Fund-Supported Programs": http://www.imf.org/external/np/pp/eng/2014/111414.pdf

IMF Executive Board Approves Extension of Interest Waiver for Low-Income Countries through End-2016, Press Release No. 14/602: http://www.imf.org/external/np/sec/pr/2014/pr14602.htm

IMF Executive Board Approves Three-Year Policy Support Instrument for Tanzania, Press Release No. 14/350: http://www.imf.org/external/np/sec/pr/2014/pr14350.htm

Capacity Development

"IMF Policies and Practices on Capacity Development": http://www.imf.org/external/np/pp/eng/2014/082614.pdf

IMF Launches Somalia Trust Fund for Capacity Development, Press Release No. 15/102: http://www.imf.org/external/np/sec/pr/2015/pr15102.htm

PART 3—FINANCES, ORGANIZATION, AND ACCOUNTABILITY

IMF Executive Board Approves FY2015–FY2017 Medium-Term Budget, Press Release No. 14/201: http://www.imf.org/external/np/sec/pr/2014/pr14201.htm

IMF Executive Board Adopts New Rule for Basic Rate of Charge on IMF's GRA Lending, Press Release No. 11/485: http://www.imf.org/external/np/sec/pr/2011/pr11485.htm

IMF Executive Board Modifies Rule for Setting SDR Interest Rate, Press Release No. 14/484: http://www.imf.org/external/np/sec/pr/2014/pr14484.htm

IMF Executive Board Approves One-Year Extension of the 2012 Borrowing Agreements, Press Release 14/417: http://www.imf.org/external/np/sec/pr/2014/pr14417.htm

IMF Executive Board Discusses 2014 Report on Diversity and Inclusion, Press Release No. 14/556: http://www.imf.org/external/np/sec/pr/2014/pr14556.htm

"Review of the Fund's Income Position for FY 2014 and FY 2015–2016": http://www.imf.org/external/np/pp/eng/2014/040714b.pdf

IMF Executive Board Reviews Fund's Income Position and Sets Margin for Lending Rate for Financial Years 2015–16, Press Release No. 14/231: http://www.imf.org/external/np/sec/pr/2014/pr14231.htm

Factsheet—Protecting IMF Resources: Safeguards Assessments of Central Banks: http://www.imf.org/external/np/exr/facts/safe.htm

Deputy Managing Director Naoyuki Shinohara to Leave IMF, Press Release No. 15/03: http://www.imf.org/external/np/sec/pr/2015/pr1503.htm

IMF Deputy Managing Director Nemat Shafik Announces Her Departure, Press Release No. 14/106: http://www.imf.org/external/np/sec/pr/2014/pr14106.htm

IMF Managing Director Christine Lagarde Proposes Appointment of Carla Grasso as Deputy Managing Director and Chief Administrative Officer, Press Release No. 15/04: http://www.imf.org/external/np/sec/pr/2015/pr1504.htm

IMF Managing Director Christine Lagarde Proposes Appointment of Mitsuhiro Furusawa as Deputy Managing Director, Press Release No. 15/33: http://www.imf.org/external/np/sec/pr/2015/pr1533.htm

IMFC Selects Agustín Carstens as New Chairman, Press Release No. 15/65: http://www.imf.org/external/np/sec/pr/2015/pr1565.htm

IMF Response to the Financial and Economic Crisis: http://www.ieo-imf.org/ieo/pages/CompletedEvaluation227.aspx

IMF Management and Staff Welcome Independent Evaluation Office's Report on the IMF Response to the Financial and Economic Crisis, Press Release No. 14/494: http://www.imf.org/external/np/sec/pr/2014/pr14494.htm

Recurring Issues from a Decade of Evaluation: Lessons for the IMF: http://www.ieo-imf.org/ieo/pages/CompletedEvaluation214.aspx

IMF Independent Evaluation Office: http://www.ieo-imf.org/ieo/pages/ieohome.aspx

IMF Executive Board Reports to the Board of Governors on the 2010 Reforms and Fifteenth General Review of Quotas, Press Release No. 14/22: http://www.imf.org/external/np/sec/pr/2014/pr1422.htm

Communiqué of the Thirty-First Meeting of the IMFC: http://www.imf.org/external/np/cm/2015/041815.htm

Nauru Applies for IMF Membership, Press Release No. 14/216: http://www.imf.org/external/np/sec/pr/2014/pr14216.htm

"2011 Triennial Surveillance Review": http://www.imf.org/external/np/spr/triennial/2011/

"Review of the IMF's Communications Strategy": http://www.imf.org/external/np/pp/eng/2014/063014.pdf

IMF Executive Board Discusses the IMF's Communication Strategy, Public Information Notice (PIN) No. 07/74: http://www.imf.org/external/np/sec/pn/2007/pn0774.htm

PART 4—LOOKING BACK/LOOKING AHEAD

Looking Back

Regional Economic Outlook: Sub-Saharan Africa—Navigating Headwinds, April 2015: http://www.imf.org/external/pubs/ft/reo/2015/afr/eng/index.htm

"Pan-African Banks: Opportunities and Challenges for Cross-Border Oversight": http://www.imf.org/external/pubs/ft/dp/2015/afr1503.pdf

"IMF Country Report No. 14/235—People's Republic of China": http://www.imf.org/external/pubs/ft/scr/2014/cr14235.pdf

Regional Economic Outlook Special Report—"25 Years of Transition: Post-Communist Europe and the IMF": http://www.imf.org/external/pubs/ft/reo/2014/eur/eng/pdf/erei_sr_102414.pdf

"Central and Eastern Europe: New Member States (NMS) Policy Forum, 2014; Staff Report on Cluster Consultations—Common Policy Frameworks and Challenges": http://www.imf.org/external/pubs/ft/scr/2015/cr1597.pdf

Baltic Cluster Report: 2014 Cluster Consultation—Staff Report; Press Release; and Statement by the Executive Director for the Baltic Countries: http://www.imf.org/external/pubs/ft/scr/2014/cr14116.pdf

IMF Executive Board Discusses Baltic Cluster Report on the Republics of Estonia, Latvia, and Lithuania, Press Release No. 14/203: http://www.imf.org/external/np/sec/pr/2014/pr14203.htm

Regional Economic Outlook—Western Hemisphere: Northern Spring, Southern Chills, April 2015: http://www.imf.org/external/pubs/ft/reo/2015/whd/eng/pdf/wreo0415.pdf

"Santiago Conference—Latin American Conference Discusses Ideas to Promote Growth," *IMF Survey:* http://www.imf.org/external/pubs/ft/survey/so/2014/NEW121214A.htm

"Islamic Finance: Opportunities, Challenges, and Policy Options": http://www.imf.org/external/pubs/ft/sdn/2015/sdn1505.pdf

IMF External Advisory Group on Islamic Finance: http://www.imf.org/external/themes/islamicfinance/eagmembers.htm

IMF's Middle East Center for Economics and Finance (CEF) and the Middle East Regional Technical Assistance Center (METAC) conclude Workshop on Risk-Based Supervision in Institutions Offering Islamic Financial Services, Press Release No. 15/36: http://www.imf.org/external/np/sec/pr/2015/pr1536.htm

"Assessing Concentration Risks in GCC Banks": http://www.imf.org/external/np/pp/eng/2014/102514.pdf

Looking Ahead

Financing Sustainable Development—Key Policy Issues and the Role of the IMF: http://www.imf.org/external/np/pp/eng/2015/041515.pdf

Managing Director's Global Policy Agenda: http://www.imf.org/external/ns/cs.aspx?id=318

Acronyms and Abbreviations

APEC	Asia-Pacific Economic Cooperation		IEO	Independent Evaluation Office
BEPS	Base Erosion and Profit Shifting		IFRS	International Financial Reporting Standards
CCRT	Catastrophe Containment and Relief Trust		IMFC	International Monetary and Financial Committee
DGI	Data Gaps Initiative		LIDC	low-income developing country
EAC	External Audit Committee		MDRI	Multilateral Debt Relief Initiative
EFF	Extended Fund Facility		MOOC	massive open online course
EU	European Union		OECD	Organisation for Economic Co-operation and Development
EWE	Early Warning Exercise			
FCL	Flexible Credit Line		OIA	Office of Internal Audit and Inspection
FM	*Fiscal Monitor*		OPEC	Organization of Petroleum Exporting Countries
FMCG	G20 Finance Ministers and Central Bank Governors			
			PLL	Precautionary and Liquidity Line
FSAP	Financial Sector Assessment Program		PRGT	Poverty Reduction and Growth Trust
FSB	Financial Stability Board		PSI	Policy Support Instrument
FY	financial year		RCF	Rapid Credit Facility
G20	Group of Twenty		REO	*Regional Economic Outlook*
GDDS	General Data Dissemination System		RFI	Rapid Financing Instrument
GDP	gross domestic product		RTAC	Regional Technical Assistance Center
GFSR	*Global Financial Stability Report*		SBA	Stand-By Arrangement
GPA	Global Policy Agenda		SDDS	Special Data Dissemination Standard
GRA	General Resources Account		SDR	Special Drawing Right
HIPC	Heavily Indebted Poor Countries		TSR	Triennial Surveillance Review
ICD	Institute for Capacity Development		WEO	*World Economic Outlook*

Letter of Transmittal to the Board of Governors

July 31, 2015

Dear Mr. Chairman:

I have the honor to present to the Board of Governors the Annual Report of the Executive Board for the financial year ended April 30, 2015, in accordance with Article XII, Section 7(a) of the Articles of Agreement of the International Monetary Fund and Section 10 of the IMF's By-Laws. In accordance with Section 20 of the By-Laws, the administrative and capital budgets of the IMF approved by the Executive Board for the financial year ending April 30, 2016, are presented in Chapter 3. The audited financial statements for the year ended April 30, 2015, of the General Department, the SDR Department, and the accounts administered by the IMF, together with reports of the external audit firm thereon, are presented in Appendix VI, which appears on the CD-ROM version of the Report, as well as at www.imf.org/external/pubs/ft/ar/2015/eng. The external audit and financial reporting processes were overseen by the External Audit Committee, comprising Mr. Ramos (Chair), Mr. Loeto, and Ms. Barth, as required under Section 20(c) of the Fund's By-Laws.

Yours very truly,

Christine Lagarde
Managing Director and Chairman of the Executive Board

Commemorating IMF's 70th Anniversary

During 2014 the IMF marked the 70th anniversary of its founding at the Bretton Woods Conference. The institution looked back during the year, but the focus was also forward looking: How can the Fund best support the closely interconnected global economy of the 21st century? And how will it adapt to change going forward?

At the time of the IMF's founding in 1944, the world faced extraordinarily difficult choices. Depression had produced a world war that was still months away from ending. The challenges of rebuilding a new international order were daunting.

Over the succeeding decades, the IMF helped rebuild Europe. It assisted new nations when colonial empires retreated, and as the Soviet Union collapsed. The Fund helped Latin America and Asia to navigate crises, and worked closely with the new emerging market economies that came into their own with the new millennium. Since 2008, the IMF has worked closely with all its members to overcome the most recent global financial crisis.

During the year the IMF devoted the quarterly publication *Finance & Development* to the Bretton Woods anniversary in its September 2014 issue titled "Past Forward: The Future of Global Economics." It also published a booklet on the anniversary by former IMF historian James M. Boughton titled *The IMF and the Force of History: Events that Have Shaped the Global Institution.*

Three events during the year highlighted the milestones of the past and the challenges of the present and future. The first was a July 2014 in-house celebration of the founding for members of the Executive Board, IMF staff, and retirees. The second was an Executive Board Retreat in September where Directors had an opportunity to discuss their views on "The Battle for Bretton Woods."

The third event was Managing Director Christine Lagarde's keynote speech to the 2014 Annual Meetings in October on "The IMF at 70: Making the Right Choices—Yesterday, Today, and Tomorrow." In the speech, Ms. Lagarde used the anniversary to look ahead to the new challenges facing the IMF:

Seventy years after Bretton Woods, the international community stands at another fork in the road. The tried-and-true modes of cooperation seem to be fraying around the edges. The sustainability of the global economic engine itself is increasingly being questioned.

Can it really deliver the jobs, the incomes, the better living standards that people aspire to?

There are three key collective choices to be made:

First, how do we achieve the growth and jobs needed to advance prosperity and ensure social harmony? I would call this the choice between acceleration and stagnation.

Second, how do we make this interconnected world a more inclusive, safer place for all of us to thrive? This is the choice between stability and fragility.

Third, how do we strengthen cooperation and multilateralism, instead of isolationism and insularity? This is the choice between solidarity and seclusion.

Our future hinges on our choices.